The Great Ideas of Philosophy, 2nd Edition

Daniel N. Robinson, Ph.D.

THE
GREAT
COURSES®

PUBLISHED BY:

THE GREAT COURSES
Corporate Headquarters
4840 Westfields Boulevard, Suite 500
Chantilly, Virginia 20151-2299
Phone: 1-800-832-2412
Fax: 703-378-3819
www.thegreatcourses.com

Daniel N. Robinson, Ph.D.

Philosophy Faculty, Oxford University,
Distinguished Professor, Emeritus,
Georgetown University

P rofessor Daniel Robinson is Distinguished Professor, Emeritus, Georgetown University, where he taught from 1971 to 2001. He is a member of the philosophy faculty of Oxford University and former Adjunct Professor of Psychology at Columbia University. Although his doctorate was earned in neuropsychology (1965, City University of New York), his scholarly books and articles have established him as an authority in the history and philosophy of psychology, history of ideas, philosophy of mind, and kindred subjects.

Dr. Robinson's books include *The Enlightened Machine: An Analytical Introduction to Neuropsychology* (Columbia, 1980), *Psychology and Law* (Oxford, 1980), *Philosophy of Psychology* (Columbia, 1985), *Aristotle's Psychology* (1989), *An Intellectual History of Psychology* (3rd edition, Wisconsin, 1995), and *Wild Beasts and Idle Humours: The Insanity Defense from Antiquity to the Present* (Harvard, 1996). He has served as principal consultant to PBS for the award-winning series *The Brain* and the subsequent nine-part series *The Mind*. He is past president of two divisions of the American Psychological Association: the Division of the History of Psychology and the Division of Theoretical and Philosophical Psychology. Dr. Robinson also serves on the Board of Scholars of Princeton's James Madison Program in American Ideals and Institutions, is a member of the American Philosophical Association, and is a Fellow of the American Psychological Association. ■

Table of Contents

Table of Contents

Table of Contents

The Great Ideas of Philosophy, 2ⁿᵈ Edition

Scope:

This course of 60 lectures is intended to introduce the student to main currents and issues in philosophical thought from the founding of the subject in ancient Greece to more contemporary studies. The lectures are organized around three abiding problems: the problem of knowledge (epistemology and metaphysics), the problem of conduct (ethics and moral philosophy), and the problem of governance (political science and law). Each of these has by now evolved into a specialized subject treated rigorously in professional texts and journals. But even in these more technical projections, the problems remain largely as they were when the schools of Plato and Aristotle dealt with them and imposed on them the features they still retain.

More than a series of lectures on the great philosophers, this course is designed to acquaint the student with broader cultural and historical conditions that favored or opposed a given philosophical perspective. Attention is paid to the influence that scientific developments had on the very conception of philosophy and on the scientific rejection of "metaphysics" that took place when the "two cultures" began to take separate paths.

Needless to say, the vast terrain that philosophy seeks to cover extends far beyond what can be explored in 60 lectures—or in 200 lectures! Entire areas of active scholarship have been ignored. But still other areas have been more carefully examined than is customary in an introductory course: philosophy of law, philosophy and aesthetics, evolutionary and psychoanalytic theory. The hope and expectation is that, informed by these lectures, the interested student will press on, will fashion a fuller curriculum of study, and will return to these lectures for the more general framework within which the specialized knowledge ultimately must find a place. ■

Hume and the Pursuit of Happiness
Lecture 31

> What we discover in Hume is an argument to the effect that our knowledge inevitably reflects our constitution, and that includes certain habitual tendencies of the mind.

David Hume is a central figure of the Scottish Enlightenment, a period roughly between 1700 and 1850, of great and flourishing art and scholarship and science in Scotland, particularly in Edinburgh. As with many of his contemporaries, Hume was widely read in Stoic philosophy and conducted himself in many ways according to Stoic teaching. Though Hume is routinely cast in histories of philosophy as the "Great Skeptic," he actually set out in his philosophy to defeat skepticism, to put knowledge on a firm foundation.

He has in mind not causing trouble but creating clarity by replacing what he takes to be the utter speculation of previous writers with something different. In the acknowledgment page of *Treatise of Human Nature*, Hume notes the important contributions of a number of British thinkers who had already taken steps toward establishing a scientific and naturalistic perspective on human understanding:

- Francis Hutcheson, in the tradition called *British sentimentalists*, defended a theory of the moral sense, innately planted and inclining human beings to act for the greatest happiness for the greatest numbers.

- Bernard Mandeville argues that public virtue arises from the private vice of those who seek nothing more than personal gain.

- Lord Shaftesbury's *An Inquiry Concerning Virtue or Merit* (1699) offered an explanation of moral conduct based on the notion of natural dispositions and affections.

From these writers, Hume adopts the concept that men are equipped by nature with certain sentiments that are the grounding of our values, for example, benevolence.

An empiricist, Hume was influenced by Bacon, Berkeley, and Locke. Developing Locke's program, Hume argues that the mind is formed out of sensory experience, that this is where everything begins. The external world impresses itself on the organs of sense. By the revival of earlier perceptions, the mind is capable of the act of reflection. But while the external physical world is capable of exciting the senses, the contents of the mind are just copies of what is occurring at the level of sensation. This yields a theory of knowledge as always mediated. We never have an immediate knowledge of the external world, only the mediated knowledge that comes by way of this intermediary—the perceptual or sensory capabilities of a creature of the sort we are. A century before Charles Darwin, Hume offers a quasi-Darwinian worldview, proposing that the creatures of nature survive by having the kind of constitution that renders survival more likely.

Though Hume is routinely cast in histories of philosophy as the "Great Skeptic," he actually set out in his philosophy to defeat skepticism, to put knowledge on a firm foundation.

Hume is famous for raising questions about the concept of causation and how we arrive at the concept of causation. He is known for developing core principles of association to account for how the mind comes to work on the evidence gleaned by the senses.Examples include, all other things being equal, A becomes associated with B when A and B have been present frequently in experience. Repetition becomes one of the principles. All other things being equal, when A and B occur together frequently, A and B become more strongly associated. Causation, then, is simply what the mind assigns to constantly conjoined experiences.

Hume also writes, however, that the concept of causation is not a recording of something observed in the external world. Rather, it's a habitual mental process; the determinants of the concept of causality are inherent in our mental operations themselves. The categories of moral right and wrong, likewise, are reflections of human dispositions and sentiments. Certain characteristics we have in our very biological constitutions, along with experience, determine what we will come to call right and wrong.

Hume has tied the concept of causation to certain habitual modes of thought. He contends that passion must rule reason. The reasoning for this is Darwinian: Our survival depends on our ability to avoid pain and seek pleasure. Reason becomes the deliberative means of securing what the appetites and passions of life require. We are all children of Hume. We understand that functions of government are to be understood in chiefly utilitarian terms. We understand that the world as we know it is the creation of our own mental machinery. A further concept of Hume's is the *problem of induction*, which states that the future is under no obligation to mimic the past. Any inference we might make about what will happen in the future based on past experience has no rational warrants. ∎

Suggested Reading

Hume, D. "An Enquiry Concerning Human Understanding," in *Essential Works of David Hume*, R. Cohen, ed. Oxford University Press, 1999.

Questions to Consider

1. Conclude whether you regard all regularly occurring pairs of events as causally related.

2. Explain what makes a "complex" idea more complex than a "simple" idea and give examples of both.

Hume and the Pursuit of Happiness
Lecture 31—Transcript

The year 1776 has particular significance to citizens of the United States. It also has particular significance to students of philosophy. It's the year David Hume died, and some might think that the latter event may be even more memorable, for Hume is surely one of the most—if not *the* most—influential philosophers to have written in the English language. He's a central figure in that extraordinary achievement referred to as the Scottish Enlightenment, that period roughly between 1700 and 1850, in which Scottish schools of medicine and law had pride of place, when the architecture of Robert Adam and James Playfair; the philosophies of Francis Hutcheson, David Hume, Adam Smith, Thomas Reid, and Dugald Stewart; the medical accomplishments of William Hunter, Robert Whytt, Charles Bell, and William Cullen; the paintings of Raeburn; the poetry of Burns—need I go on? This was a period of great flourishing in art, scholarship, and science in Scotland, in Edinburgh particularly, which itself was regarded by residents to be "the Athens of the North."

Now, Hume may have given some attention to the study of law initially. His maternal grandfather, Sir David Falconer, was, after all, president of the College of Justice, but as Hume tells us in his autobiography, the ruling passion of his life was literature, and that of his mind philosophy, such that he "found an insurmountable aversion to every thing but the pursuit of philosophy." Even as his family believed that he was studying the major works of law, says Hume, "Cicero and Virgil were the authors which I was secretly devouring."

Hume's five-volume history of England was published between 1752 and 1764, and would ultimately make him financially comfortable. It is still a worthy source, all the better for the exceptional literary style of its author. He was a correspondent with some of the major intellectual figures of the time. He housed the troubled Rousseau for a period of time. He'd make his way to the salons of France. His *Treatise of Human Nature* was conceived and developed during a three-year hiatus in Paris, that is, between 1734 and 1737, only, as he says, to "fall dead-born," as he said, when published in 1739. It remains, however, among the most influential treatises of the past two centuries in philosophy.

There would be another several years in Paris later in his life as Secretary to the Ambassador to Paris, and on this tour he was a veritable celebrity of the salons. He was a great conversationalist, somewhat corpulent, as it happens, and as the women of the salon were finding his conversation irresistible, the rather svelte and perhaps envious Frenchmen were sometimes overheard to whisper: "And the word was made flesh." Well, Hume was a man of great generosity of spirit, a skeptic who would give philosophy a good name for being advanced by so good a man.

Now, as with so many of his contemporaries, Hume was well and widely read in Stoic philosophy. He conducted himself, in many ways, according to Stoic teaching. The famous hours surrounding his own death give us a David Hume who is noble, fully in control of himself, and sensitive to the feelings of those around him.

The full three-volume *Treatise of Human Nature* appeared in 1739, and, as noted by Hume, attracted little attention. The work of a man not quite 30 years old, it could not compete for attention with treatises advanced by a handful of truly remarkable Scottish philosophers. Hume himself would later regard it as a somewhat immature work, but it was in fact profound in its implications. He would later refine his philosophy, make it more widely accessible, and publish it in 1751 as *An Enquiry Concerning the Principles of Morals*. His philosophical fame rests chiefly on this work and on the *Treatise of Human Nature* of 1739.

Now, Hume is routinely cast in histories of philosophy as the "great skeptic." He's similarly and often angrily charged with that by his contemporaries. He seems to be an enemy of the faith. He seems to be somebody turning over all of the tables on which our most confident epistemology depends, but Hume himself set out in his philosophy, actually, to defeat skepticism, to put knowledge on a firm foundation. He has in mind not causing trouble, but creating clarity by replacing what he takes to be utter speculation dominant in previous writers with something different—namely, the right understanding of human nature. This is made unmistakably clear in the full title of the *Treatise of Human Nature* of 1739. Here's the full title: *A Treatise of Human Nature: Being An Attempt to Introduce the Experimental Method of Reasoning into Moral Subjects.*

How, then, does he earn the reputation that he has as a skeptic? What is it that he develops that makes him so controversial a figure?

In the "Acknowledgement" page of the *Treatise* of 1739, Hume notes the important contributions of "my Lord Shaftesbury and Bernard Mandeville, and Dr. Hutcheson." Now, who are these people? Well, there's a long and, indeed, uninterrupted tradition in British philosophy sometimes referred to collectively, now, as the *British sentimentalist* moral philosophers, and Francis Hutcheson is one of its early proponents, but one might also trace it to Calvin's *Institutes*, especially on the matter of God-given natural instincts.

It is useful here, then, to begin with Francis Hutcheson, 1694 to 1746, because he was the major opponent of a number of principles that Hume would come to defend. Hutcheson was the leading philosopher at Glasgow, Adam Smith being one of his students. He was among the first professors to lecture in English, and his lectures on moral philosophy drew the best and the brightest of a very good enrollment.

Against Hobbes's nearly morose perspective on a human nature, impelled by hedonistic drives and seeking little more than security against a violent death, Hutcheson defended a theory of the moral sense, something innately planted and inclining human beings to act, as he says, for "the greatest happiness for the greatest numbers."

Now, against Bernard Mandeville's *Fable of the Bees*, which was published in 1714, and which shows how public virtue arises from private vice of those who seek nothing more than personal gain, Hutcheson counters with this:

> We are led by our moral Sense of Virtue to judge thus: that in equal degrees of Happiness, expected to proceed from the Action, the Virtue is in proportion to the Number of Persons to whom the Happiness shall extend.

Inquiry into the Origins of our Ideas of Beauty and Virtue is the work in which that passage appears; so, for all the differences obtaining between Hutcheson and Hume, there is this similarity, and it is fundamental: the grounding of morality is human sentiment. That is to say, the moral dimensions of life are not marked out by the productions of abstract rationality; they're marked out by the actual constitutive nature of our being. We are equipped by a providential God—or what Hume rather neutrally refers to as "the very constitution of our nature"—equipped in such a way as to have certain core sentiments that establish what we value—the sentiment of benevolence, for example.

Thus, what the early part of the British sentimentalist tradition seeks to establish is a kind of naturalized moral theory, not something abstract or transcendental, a gift of the schoolmen, but something very earthy. The moral domain, the domain of values—that which makes anything really count to us—is inextricably bound up with the kinds of beings we are.

A person of deep religious conviction will understand this to be the gift of a providential God, who has fitted us out with just what we need by way of a moral temper to do God's bidding in the world, but if that isn't your view, if your religious position is not the foundation for your metaphysics, then indeed you simply take this as a fact of nature—that by the very constitution of our nature, we have certain inclinations and not others.

Now, in acknowledging Mandeville and Shaftesbury right at the beginning of the *Treatise*, Hume is identifying himself as someone who is going to strive for an entirely naturalistic account of human nature, something we'll find a grounding for in epistemology and morality. That's going to be the grounding in our own nature. Hutcheson's religious account is beyond the resources that Hume requires for his own *Treatise*, but Hume and Hutcheson will nonetheless establish the basis on which Adam Smith's own moral and economic philosophies will come to depend. There's a tradition here, and Hume is a central part of it.

Now, in Hume's work, the result of this perspective is the view that you simply cannot extricate the particularities of human nature from the claims we make about morality. There will always be the stamp of our perceptual mechanisms, our sentiments, our passions on any production of ours, including the most vaunted productions of philosophy. Philosophy isn't outside the human condition; it's an expression of the human condition, and you can't get out of that bind at all.

An empiricist, Hume is influenced by Bacon, Locke, and Berkeley. Now, the last of these provided the most compelling argument for the proposition that we cannot find a point or place external to perception from which to establish our epistemic claims. Hume, however, will not be caught up in the Berkeleyan dilemma about whether or not anything exists outside the realm of what is perceived.

Rather, developing Locke's program, Hume argues that the mind is formed out of sensory experience, that this is where everything begins. It begins at the level of perception. The external world impresses itself on the organs of sense, and out of those sensory impressions, we have either our current sensations, as we actually see what's going on, or recollections of them. By the revival of earlier perceptions, the mind is capable of the act of reflection. This is reflecting on things that have previously happened, but I say, these impressions then constitute the basis upon which the mind makes representations of the external world. So, what Hume is arguing is that there is some external physical world capable of exciting the senses, but that the contents of the mind are just copies, or simulacra come of what is occurring at the level of sensation.

What we have, then, is a theory of knowledge as always mediated. We never have an immediate knowledge of the external world, only the mediated knowledge that comes by way of this intermediary—namely, the perceptual or sensory capabilities of a creature that happens to be of the sort we are. You understand then, that what is being said is you cannot know the external world as, in itself, it really is. You know the external world by way of perceptual mediation.

Now, one might see in this skepticism, except that I think it's fair to say that Hume, operating out of a naturalistic tradition, is not promoting skepticism.

Now, all this is a century before Charles Darwin, but the 18th century is already hosting an essentially Darwinian view on any number of issues. Consider Adam Smith's economic theory, which allows the maximum degree of freedom as the means by which to increase the wealth of nations. Actually, Darwin may well have been moved by his reading of Adam Smith, moved toward his own thinking about natural selection.

Hume's, then, is already a quasi-Darwinian worldview. He is quite comfortable with the proposition that the creatures of nature survive in virtue of having the kind of constitution that renders survival more likely, and so, although our knowledge is mediated, this is not to lead to an abject skepticism about our knowledge of the external world. It's simply this. I want to use this phrase: It's to "psychologize" metaphysics. It's to take the traditional problems of ontology and epistemology, the problem of knowledge itself, moral philosophy, to make these problems into problems to be understood in terms of the peculiarities of human psychology, and more generally, even the psychology of the animal kingdom. Thus, Hume's is not an abject philosophical skepticism, but the naturalization of epistemology and morals.

Now, what we discover in Hume is an argument to the effect that our knowledge inevitably reflects our constitution, and that includes certain habitual tendencies of the mind. That is, the mind does have certain operating principles, and therefore, all of our knowledge claims are going to be, as it were, infected by, colored by, shaped by, the foundational operating principles of mind as such. One of the great triumphs of rationalism is the discovery that every effect has an antecedent cause. Now, Hume is going to acknowledge that this is how rationalists have been arguing from a time going back to Plato. This is something we know by rational analysis. Nothing shall come of nothing. It's the very bedrock of religious faith, where God is the cause of all things, and it is the foundation of all of the sciences, which are devoted to unearthing—what? The causes of things.

Now, what is Hume going to do with this core rational principle? Hume is famous for raising questions about the concept of causation, how we ever arrive at the concept of causation. What I want to make a distinction between here, sometimes lost in secondary literature, is this: I think it's an error in reading Hume, occasioned to some extent by the various ways Hume defends and illustrates the problem, to think that he's dubious about causes. I don't think that there's any evidence that Hume is skeptical about there being causes. Hume is concerned about establishing the basis upon which we can have the concept of causation—that is, the basis upon which we could ever know about causes, which is a question rather different from whether events in the external world are caused. On the issue of causation, Hume is concerned to discover the reference of causal attributions, and this turns out to be certain habitual modes of operation of the human mind— so let me pause here to say again: What Hume is doing is psychologizing traditional problems in metaphysics. The reference of causal terms is going to turn out to be something about something taking place, some habit of the human mind.

Thus, starting with Locke's rather diffuse use of the notion of association, Hume develops the very laws of association. He's famous for developing core principles of association to account for how the mind comes to work on the evidence gleaned by the senses. Well, all other things being equal, A becomes associated with B when A and B have been present frequently in experience. That is, repetition is one of the principles of association.

Now, all other things being equal, when A and B occur together frequently, A and B become more strongly associated. Any time two events, says Hume, have been "constantly conjoined in experience, any one of them in the future will excite the idea of the other." All other things being equal, events that occur together closely in space and time are more fully and firmly associated, here being the principle of contiguity. Events that share a greater resemblance are more firmly associated, and when events are temporally and physically contiguous, they are more strongly associated. So, all other things being equal, when the pattern of occurrences is such that one event reliably precedes, and the other event reliably follows, the association is very strong—grounded as it is in cause and effect. Causation, then, is simply what the mind assigns to constantly conjoined experiences. Any time A and B are constantly conjoined, and A reliably precedes B, it is by virtue of a veritable habit of thought. It is one of the operating principles of mind as such that A is regarded as the cause of B.

At this point in his writings, Hume pauses to say almost parenthetically, though it's a phrase that would excite the energies of many of his critics, "that anything may be the cause of anything."

What does Hume mean by that strange claim? Look, he doesn't elaborate on that particular point, but it's quite clear what his meaning is. Suppose we had been constituted in such a way that we would sample the external world— let's say the senses worked in such a way, or the brain worked in such a way, that we would sample the external world—we would see the external world for a second, then we would go off the air, let's say, for four seconds, and we'd come back on the air for a second, and then we'd go off the air for four seconds.

Can you imagine what our notions of causality would be in that circumstance, where maybe in one second you see a pitcher in a baseball game winding up to deliver a pitch, and then you're off the air, and four seconds later, nine people are running around? You would inevitably be led to the conclusion that whenever Smith winds up, nine people are made to run around. The point Hume wants to make is that the concept of causation is not a recording of something observed in the external world. It is, instead, a habitual mental process. The determinants of the concept of causality are inherent in our mental operations themselves. He has "psychologized" the concept of causality.

In one famous illustration, he says: "I see before me a table on which there are billiard balls, and one ball moves, and it strikes the other, and the second one moves." He says: "I must own I cannot see some third term betwixt them."

"I cannot see some third term betwixt them." I see ball one move. There's a term I see. Ball two moves. There's a term, but I don't see causality, so where is the causality? Causality is in that habit of mind that renders causal any reliable anteceding and succeeding event, any constantly conjoined pair of events, or multiplicity of events—so you might say that although Hume is not skeptical about causation, he reduces the human understanding of causation to a pattern of reliable experiences such that we will invent, as it were, causations wherever these spatial, temporal contiguities and cause-effect properties are in the mind, where those terms are satisfied.

Now, suppose we walk the highways and byways of the world, and we confront some poor fallen figure. Let me make this as graphic as possible; this is the age of making things graphic, isn't it? Well, we find some poor fallen victim in a pool of blood, his pockets emptied. He's sprawled out on the pavement, and there is no sign of life at all. The question that arises is whether some moral wrong has been perpetrated.

We want to get at the ultimate grounding of morality. Well, again, if you use the billiard table example, all you see out there are various objects in space with certain colorations and the like. Now, what then is the moral content of what has taken place? It can't be anything out there. That is, if the same spectacle were looked at by a goose, there would not be some moral judgment brought to bear on it.

There are certain events, spectacles, sights, or occurrences that excite in us feelings, says Hume, of revulsion, and it is in virtue of exciting such feelings that the event in question comes to be judged as morally wrong. The categories of moral right and wrong are reflections of human dispositions and sentiments. Certain characteristics we have in virtue of our very constitution— our very biological constitution—and history of experience and learning and instruction, finally determine what we will come to call "right" and "wrong." To this extent, then, one might say: "Well, is Hume relativizing morality?"

That's a large question fit for Hume scholarship, and one that takes much greater time than we could possibly devote to it now. It's not so much a relativizing, however, as, again, I say, a "psychologizing" of morality. Hume is satisfied that we are sufficiently similar in our basic constitute of principles that he would not be greatly surprised if certain core moral precepts showed up everywhere and anywhere, although the beneficiary of—I mean, he is the beneficiary of Cook's voyages, so many 18th-century writers, Hume is aware of the great variety of cultural values among different tribal communities. He knows that even though we may be biologically constituted in very similar ways, the value judgments we reach do depend—to some extent, they are relative—to the culture, tribe, and context in which we have membership.

Hume, on the level of morality now, is again "psychologizing" it and tying it to the very constitutive principles of our nature, and so the question is: "Well, given the constitution of our nature, what's the whole point of things?" Well, of course, the whole point of our biology and our survival is the maximization of pleasure and the minimization of pain. You might think Hobbes is whispering in the background.

Morality then, and politics itself, should be looked at as social constructions designed by creatures of a certain kind who, as best they can come, are trying to maximize something. Hume has a word for what it is we are trying to maximize. He's among the first ever to use it in this sense. What we're trying to maximize is *utility*. He is among the first—even earlier than Bentham—to use this term as it will come to be used in the philosophy of utilitarianism.

Again, is Hume skeptical about morality? Well, he would reject all forms of moral realism, no doubt, but he is not skeptical about morality. Rather, he seeks to show how our constitutive nature brings about moral judgments. The moral world is not "out there" waiting to be discovered, but within the human frame and shaped by the needs and peculiarities of a certain kind of creature.

Well, let's look so far at what Hume has done now. He has taken the concept of causation and tied it to certain habitual modes of thought. The concept of morality is now bound up with what the behaviorists might call a conditioning history and certain basic sentimental predispositions.

As for reason, Hume contends that in reality it is passion that must rule—and reason that most follow—and I think we do have to pause over that to redeem Hume from his more energetic critics.

What's the sense in which passion should rule reason? Well, the sense is a Darwinian sense. You're in a dark forest, and you hear some growling, roaring sound, and out of the corner of your eye some large striped thing seems to be looming large. Now, you could sit there and with all of the arts and sciences of logic start doing an essential analysis of the *a priori* and *a posteriori* probabilities associated with entities like that actually turning out to be hungry tigers—or you could, in a manner of speaking, run like the wind.

Well, you run rather than reason because you are fitted out by nature to respond to threats against your very survival, to do what it takes to avoid pain and secure pleasure. The baby does not suck at the breast because it has read books on nutrition but because it derives nourishment through an activity that is pleasurable.

Now, this is the sense in which passion should rule reason. What we have to set out to do—well, what we have to maximize, what bears centrally on our interests as beings of the sort that we are is to behave in such a way as to maximize utilities. This is at the level of emotional, and appetitive, and passionate processes that the needs of the body, the needs of life, are most insistently recording themselves. Reason then becomes the deliberative means of securing what the appetites and passions require.

Now, the extent that this does not sound controversial, it's because we are all, reluctantly or otherwise, children of Hume's. We certainly believe that the essential functions of government are to be understood chiefly in utilitarian terms. We understand that the world as we know it is a creation of our own mental machinery. We can't get outside the box—that is, the box that includes all possible thoughts we might have. Thus, about God being the cause of all things—well, this is really a kind of *mythos* or belief system based on the very principles that ground all causal concepts.

One cannot by reason or by experience go from the facts of the external world back to an intelligent agent who has brought it about. Belief of this sort is another habitual feature of the human mind. Throughout life, constantly conjoined events are viewed as causally related. Now, one comes into a world that seems to be all set up in advance. By inference, by induction, one assumes that an unseen antecedent is responsible, and this is what leads to faith in a providential divinity. There will be more than one Presbyterian minister in Aberdeen, and Glasgow, and Edinburgh wondering whether anybody should be reading this sort of thing.

There is another aspect of Hume's philosophy that should be considered, namely his famous *problem of induction*. Hume declares that the future is under no obligation to mimic the past, and therefore, any inference made about what will happen in future based on past experience has no rational warrants. Ah, well. There's a problem of induction that we cannot solve. Causality is in the mind. Morality is somewhere in the pit of the stomach. Belief in God is a habitual mode of thought.

Hume was quite a controversial fellow, and you can see why he remains one of the most influential writers in all of philosophy.

Thomas Reid and the Scottish School
Lecture 32

> Conjectures and theories are the creatures of men, and will always be
> found unlike the creatures of God. If we would know the works of God,
> we must consult themselves with attention and humility, without daring
> to add any thing of ours to what they declare. A just interpretation of
> nature is the only sound and orthodox philosophy. Whatever we add of
> our own is apocryphal, and of no authority.—Thomas Reid

Thomas Reid (1710–1796) has come down to us as the "Father of
Common Sense Philosophy." Until quite recently, Reid was largely
ignored, and only in the last 10 years has he been restored to a
position of philosophical eminence. Reid's contemporaries considered him
an exceptional person. He studied for the ministry and held a position in
the church at New Machar for a period of years before teaching at his alma
mater, Marischal College, University of Aberdeen. Even before publication
of his *An Inquiry into the Human Mind*, Reid was called to Glasgow to
take the position recently relinquished by Adam Smith. At Aberdeen, he
founded what came to be called the Wise Club, which met every fortnight,
engaged all the major philosophical issues, wrote papers, and planned longer
treatises. A number of the club's productions turned out to be important
philosophically. In his *Inquiry*, Reid anticipated by a half century Reimann's
non-Euclidian geometry.

Reid also was a master of the science of optics. On his mother's side, he
was related to the famous Cambridge University Gregory family, known for
work in optics and mathematics. Reid, too, wrote but did not publish original
work in mathematics and astronomy. His writings were widely respected
in the United States where, in the years leading to and just following the
founding, Scottish thought was profoundly influential.

By *common sense*, Reid always referred to what was universally and
pragmatically represented in nature, including human nature, as part of the
"constitution" of the being in question, whether caterpillar or man. The
principle of common sense, for Reid, does not mean the wisdom of the

crowd. It doesn't mean the prevailing opinions, the settled ethos of a given community. Rather, it is that which we are under an obligation to accept in all of the ordinary affairs of life. Reid illustrates the point with the "lowly caterpillar" that will crawl across a thousand leaves until it finds the one that's right for its diet.

At the core of Hume's epistemology is the theory that all our knowledge is mediated. Hume, thus, continues a long, almost uninterrupted philosophical tradition that says the eternal world comes to be represented in some way via mediation by the senses, a view with which Reid disagrees. These philosophers conclude that, because all our knowledge is filtered through our senses, we can never know the real world except by way of these representations. What results are "ideas" about the external world, but there is no way of determining the adequacy of such ideas as actual records or copies of the world. If this were so, then skepticism is entirely appropriate.

Reid rejects this so-called "copy theory." More to the point, however, his analysis of the problem in this manner is intended to convey an experimental approach of the Baconian-Newtonian variety. There is no evidence to support the view that the "impressions" made on the sense organs are what the mind becomes aware of. Not even philosophers are aware of their sensory impressions. There is, therefore, no evidence that the ideas or knowledge we have should be thought of as some sort of "copy" of these impressions. Reid's experiments demonstrate to him that the image of a right triangle projected on the spherical retina of the eye is itself curved; what we *see*, however, is not a curved triangle but the triangle as it is actually configured. *We see what is there*! In fact, what happens is that physiological activity presents to the mind a system of natural signs; by a means Reid confesses he does not understand, the mind can decode these signs and move from the sign to the thing signified. There is a fit between our biology and the external world such that we are able to live in it.

The Humean conception of causation is at the very core of Hume's skepticism. It is flawed in the same way, according to Reid. Constant conjunction of two things cannot be the grounding of our belief that one causes the other.

The actual source of this concept is our own *active powers*. We know from infancy that we are able to bring things about; from this, we are led to the inference that events external to us are similarly produced by other powers.

In the same way, the ethical theory according to which morality is an essentially passion- or emotion-based set of self-interested actions is not the result of systematic inquiry and is defeated by such an inquiry. Even the hedonist must calculate long-range consequences. Immediate sensations of pleasure and pain cannot account for our ability to swallow a nasty medicine for eventual benefit. Rationality is a necessary presupposition even on the Humean account. Philosophical principles ought to be able to account for evidence gathered in the real world. The long human record of altruism is not adequately explained by the Humean theory of it. There must, in fact, be first principles of morals within us guiding our daily behavior, just as the caterpillar is guided to find the right leaf among thousands.

At the core of Hume's epistemology is the theory that all our knowledge is mediated.

Hume on personal identity argues that the continuity of identity is based on the same principles that preserve the continuity of a parade formation of soldiers: As one or another marcher drops out, another takes his place, so that the "bundle of perceptions" is held together. This is based on Hume's theory of causation as "constant conjunction." Because Reid considers this theory to be flawed, he does not believe it will work here either. Hume says, "When I observe myself, I see nothing but a bundle of perceptions." And who, then, is doing the observing? For there to be treason, there must be a traitor; for there to be a "bundle of perceptions," there must be a percipient.

Reid saw Locke's theory (upon which Hume's was based) as hopeless from the outset: Remembering the loss of the Battle of Waterloo does not make one Napoleon! A man remembers himself to have once been a boy and knows that he is today a brave young officer; an aged general remembers that he was once a brave young officer but no longer remembers he was a boy. Thus, A = B and B = C, but A does not equal C!

Against the "idea" theory and its resulting skepticism, Reid offered a naturalistic, "common sense" alternative, according to which the creatures of nature, including human beings, are fitted out with what is needed for survival, for shared actions, and for valid knowledge of the external world. He insisted that Hume and Locke before him were not always faithful to the observational methods of Bacon and Newton, nor to their means of testing competing accounts. ■

Suggested Reading

Barker, S., and Beauchamp, T., eds. *Thomas Reid: Critical Interpretations.* (*Philosophical Monographs*), vol. 3., 1976.

Reid, T. *An Inquiry into the Human Mind.* Timothy Duggan, ed. Penn State University Press, 1997.

Questions to Consider

1. Explain whether an innate principle of common sense should enjoy instant validity over a competing claim raised by philosophers.

2. Explain how one might distinguish between that which is widely shared (though only a custom) and the Reidian principle of common sense.

Thomas Reid and the Scottish School
Lecture 32—Transcript

Who was that doughty Scotsman Thomas Reid, who has come down to us known as the "Father of Common Sense Philosophy"? Who is this thinker who, until relatively recently, was largely ignored by philosophers, only in the last years to be restored not only to respectability but, indeed, to a well-earned position of philosophical eminence?

Well, if the maxim "publish or perish" had been operative during Reid's time, it is doubtful that he ever would have had an academic position. He was born in 1710, but his first publication of major consequence came out in 1764. What might today's deans and colleagues say of a 53-year-old philosopher yet to have a book to his name?

Fortunately for him, and for philosophy, the Scottish Enlightenment had different standards. Indeed by these standards, many of today's more celebrated professors might have had a better fate had they published much less, or even nothing at all.

Reid was known to be an exceptional person by all of his contemporaries. He did study for the ministry; he held a position in the church at New Machar for a period of years, and then he settled down to teach at his alma mater, Marischal College, University of Aberdeen. It wouldn't be long, and even before publication of his *An Inquiry into the Human Mind*, that he would be called to Glasgow to take the position recently relinquished by Adam Smith. The Scottish academic world knew his formidable powers long before the reading public would come to sample them.

At Aberdeen, he was the founder of what came to be called the Wise Club, which met every fortnight, engaged all the major philosophical issues, wrote papers, planned longer treatises, and otherwise improved each other. A number of the productions of the Wise Club turned out to be important philosophically, but none that equaled Reid's *Inquiry* of 1764.

I might note that it is in this work, in the section titled "The Geometry of Visibles," that Reid anticipated by a half century the non-Euclidean geometry of Riemann. Reid was a master of the science of optics. On his mother's side, he's a Gregory of the famous Cambridge University family, famous in optics and mathematics. Reid, too, wrote but did not publish original work in mathematics and astronomy. His writings were widely respected in the United States, where in the years leading to and just following the founding, Scottish thought was profoundly influential. His closest friend and student, Dugald Stewart, was judged by Thomas Jefferson to be one of the two greatest metaphysicians of the age—the other being Destutt Comte de Tracy in France. John Adams regarded Reid's work in philosophy of mind to be superior to that of Locke and even to Aristotle.

Jefferson would also write to a nephew that if the nephew would understand what the constitutional convention is all about, he might read that part of Thomas Reid's *Inquiry* on natural language. I will return to this.

The native Scot, James Wilson, one of the signers of the Declaration of Independence, a member of the Constitutional Convention of 1787, and later Associate Justice of the first U.S. Supreme Court, was greatly influenced by Reid's *Inquiry*. He even cites the work in his opinion in *Chisholm v. Georgia, 1793*, the first major jurisdictional dispute that the Supreme Court would settle. Reid's French translator, Victor Cousin, would become an important figure in French education, and he would see to it that a Reidian "common sense" philosophy would guide French education, an influence that was still evident a century later.

He was a man of extraordinary breadth and of winning character. He was a reserved and not self-promoting fellow at all. I very much agree with the Brown University philosopher Roderick Chisholm, that if you're looking for a 300-page work in philosophy absolutely luminous and clear, analytically precise, and in the English language—you probably have no other place to look than Thomas Reid's *An Inquiry into the Human Mind*.

I discuss him here as the most successful and systematic of Hume's contemporary critics. There's a story, too long to tell in its fullness, about Reid writing to Hume to read the *Inquiry* before Reid sent it to printers, just out of fairness. They had a friend in common, Hugh Blair, who passed the manuscript on to Hume, who promptly returned it, noting that clerics should devote themselves to bothering each other and should leave philosophy to philosophers.

Fortunately, Blair persisted and Hume did read the work carefully, and carefully enough to realize he was in the presence of a first-rate mind. Indeed, a decade later, preparing what was to be the final edition of his own work, Hume informs his publisher that in his revisions and additions he has answered Dr. Reid "and that silly Beattie." Well, James Beattie, as I have mentioned, was the one who had the right position on the question of slavery. His own critique of Hume's philosophy, however, was far less respectful than Reid's, and indeed, was less discerning as well.

Well, Hume wrote a glowing letter to Reid, complaining that the only part he found obscure was "the Geometry of Visibles." This is revealing, for it is just that section of Reid's *Inquiry* that challenges the very linchpin of mediational theories of perception. I'll try to cover a bit of this in today's lecture.

Reid writes back to Hume in response to his kind letter, and I think in Reid's reply one grasps the reasonableness and civility of Enlightenment sensibilities. Here are two philosophical disputants who really are at cross-purposes in the most fundamental ways, and what does Reid write back to Hume? He writes back and says that:

> Your company would, although we are all good Christians, be more acceptable than that of St. Athanasius. If you write no more in morals, politicks, or metaphysicks, I am afraid we shall be at a loss for Subjects.

Here is the smile of reason radiating over whole realms of thought.

Now, what about the *Inquiry* itself and the major claims that Hume had been making? First, Reid acknowledges what Hume himself says about causation and our knowledge of the external world. Hume tells us in his *Treatise* that once he has left the privacy of his study, he thinks the way the ordinary persons think. He quite understands common confusions here because they are his own confusions. It was only in the solitude of his philosophical reflections that he was able to produce his philosophy, and Reid finds in this the source of Hume's confusions.

First, he gently chides Hume for embracing a philosophy that is like a hobbyhorse, which a man when he is ill can keep at home with him and ride to his contentment, but should he bring it into the marketplace, his friends will quickly impanel a jury and confiscate his estates. Reid's "common sense" philosophy puts a certain requirement on a philosopher, namely the willingness to live according to the terms of his own philosophy.

Reid says that the only complete skeptic that philosophy has ever turned up is Pyrrho of Elea, who was so doubtful about the reality of threatening and dangerous things that his friends used to have to walk around the city with him lest he march into flames or fall into rivers, but Reid says even Pyrrho of Elea is said to have chased his cook down the street with a frying pan in his hand for the awful meal he had served some of Pyrrho's guests—so even Pyrrho knew where to draw the line at Pyrrhonism.

Now, Reid, here, is just being playful. He continues in the vein when he considers Descartes's famous *Cogito, ergo sum*. He says: "Here, we have a philosopher unwilling to accept his own existence until he can come up with a very good rational argument for it," and how fortunate for Descartes—and for all of philosophy—that he did, for had that argument failed, Descartes's situation and that of philosophy would have been absolutely deplorable. Reid says that a man who disbelieves his own existence is no more fit to be reasoned with than one who thinks he's made of glass.

Now, I say, this is Reid at his most playful, trying to get something quite clear in his readers' and in fellow philosophers' minds—namely, that in any significant conflict between the dictates of common sense, which I will define in a moment, and the productions of the philosophical imagination, it is philosophical theorizing that finally must yield.

Now, what does Reid mean by a principle of *common sense*? He doesn't mean the wisdom of the crowd. He doesn't mean prevailing opinions or the settled ethos of a given community. He says by a principle of common sense—a term he wished he had a substitute for—he means that which we have nothing less than an obligation to take for granted in all of the ordinary affairs of life, and it illustrates the point with the "lowly caterpillar" that will crawl across a thousand leaves until it finds the one that's right for its diet. That's how a principle of common sense operates. One cannot begin the day, engage the business of life, except on a certain set of core principles—these being undeliberated. They're not matters of opinion or belief. They are the necessary preconditions for thought and action.

At the core of Hume's epistemology is the theory that all of our knowledge is mediated, that we can never get out from behind that prism through which reality must be projected for us to know anything about it. Hume is in good company here. Reid notes the long, almost uninterrupted philosophical tradition that includes some of the most improbable soul mates, so to speak. It includes Aristotle and his theory of the phantasms; it includes Locke, of course, and most of the Scholastics before Locke. It is central to Bishop Berkeley's philosophy. Now, the theory to which they all subscribe is a mediational theory of knowledge. The external world comes to be represented in some way via mediation by the senses. It cannot be directly known. Considering this theory, Reid says that if this is true, he will lay his hands across his lips and become a skeptic.

Reid dubs this theory the "ideal" theory. We might want to call it more easily the "idea" theory, the theory according to which the contents of consciousness are the result of copies made of something at the level of the sense organs—so that we never know the external world directly, but only by way of ideas of the external world, copies. Now, whatever the senses report is what the mind has to deal with. The mind somehow constructs podiums, and persons, and stars, and sweet tastes out of something at the sensory level, but we can never know the relationship, however, between what the senses have done to all this data and the external world itself.

Reid is as much troubled by the method philosophers have employed in reaching so worrisome a conclusion as he is by the conclusion itself. If philosophers had used the methods of Bacon and Newton, experimental methods, instead of sitting back and speculating idly in an armchair—if they actually subjected views of this kind to the sort of experimental analysis that we now know to be the right mode of inquiry, strikingly different conclusions would have been reached. The Geometry of Visibles illustrates such an experimental approach, here more in the manner of a thought experiment—though one that surely could be conducted in a laboratory. The example is a subtle one, and it eluded no less a genius than Hume—so let me try to craft a simplified summary of the argument.

Imagine that the eye is positioned at the center of an indefinitely large sphere on the surface of which you might project anything that you liked. Well, anything you do project on the surface of the sphere will, of course, be spherically projected. It will map onto the spherical shape of the object that receives the projection. If you were to take a right-angle triangle and thus projected it, it would follow the curvature of the sphere. Reid here is reminding readers of how the external world impresses itself on the visual organ. Now, as the bottom of the eye is itself curved, any projection of light from the external world is going to take on that curvature, except in the very small region of the retina known as the fovea. If the area is so small, there will be very little discrepancy between a curved triangle and a rectilinear one.

Now, suppose you draw a right-angle triangle on a piece of paper. Well, here's a core question. What is it you *see*? Do you see the curvilinear projection that would take place optically, or do you see the triangle as that tangible triangle itself—that is, as a rectilinear triangle? You see it as a rectilinear triangle; it has none of the spherical properties that you would expect if the mind were simply making a "copy" of whatever is taking place at the bottom of the eye.

Now, Reid notes that when the external world impinges on the sense organs, it sets up an activity. That physiological activity constitutes a kind of sign system, what Reid calls a "natural sign." The external world creates natural consequences in our sensory biology. The mind, Reid says, by a way we do not understand, is somehow able to go from these signs, from these physiological signals, and come to the things signified. The essential mission of science in general is to work out the rules by which natural signs are connected with things signified. As Reid says in his chapter on touch, here praising Bacon for his insights, Reid says:

> The first class of natural signs comprehends those whose connection
> with the thing signified is established by nature, but discovered

only by experience. The great Lord Verulam [he's talking about Bacon] had a perfect comprehension of this when he called it an *interpretation of nature*. What is all we know of mechanics, astronomy and optics, but connections established by nature and discovered by experience or observation...

The method of Bacon, do you see?

Now, in the matter of vision, Reid came too early to know the detail of processes giving rise to our perception of objects in the external world. The first response to light, as we know, is biochemical. That is, there are changes in the pigment chemistry of the retinal receptors, and as a result of these biochemical changes, patterns of electrical activity are set up in the optic nerve fibers, and these signals are then sent back into the brain—so that the whole process is played out at the level of neuro-electric processing, but no one sees neuro-electric events; rather, we see stars and persons and carpets and bull dogs. In other words, we somehow are able to extract from the "natural" signs—the biochemical and physiological responses to stimulation—the objects they signify. How that comes about Reid does not pretend to know, referring it to that "mint of nature so productive of all sorts of marvels."

In a letter to Hume, Reid clarifies further the concept of "natural signs." He writes:

> This Connexion which Nature hath established betwixt our Sensations and the conception and belief of external Objects, I express two ways: Either by saying that the Sensations suggest the objects by a natural principle of the Mind, or by saying that the Sensations are natural Signs of the Objects. These Expressions signify one and the same thing...I do not pretend by them to account for this Connexion, but onely to affirm it.

Just as the caterpillar knows what leaf to eat, in all other transactions there is a fitness and aptness between the constitutive principles of our biology and the demands the external world places on us. This is not an accidental arrangement. If, in fact, all we knew were those chimeras, or whatever it is the mind is possessed of when it goes about making copies of whatever is in the sense organs, we couldn't get from "A" to "B." We would have to be doubtful about there even being an external world. If I adopt the philosophy of Bishop Berkeley, what is the result, asks Reid? I step into a dirty kennel. I bang my head against a signpost, and after a thousand such experiences, I come to the conclusion that there really is an external material world, and I'm located in it, and I'd better remain mindful of the fact.

Reid therefore rejects the so-called "copy theory," according to which the mind somehow makes copies of what the senses report. Indeed, the only sense modality in which such a theory is even intelligible is vision, and the Geometry of Visibles shows that it fails there. If the "ideal theory" doesn't work in vision, it surely will not work anywhere else. More to the point, however, Reid's analysis of the problem in this manner is intended to convey an experimental approach of the Baconian-Newtonian variety in opposition to the errant theorizing to which philosophers are especially prone, he believes.

I should note here that in Reid's published and unpublished works there is ample evidence of his own actual experiments in visual perception, and he encourages others to do likewise, using arguments and demonstrations that in many respects anticipate the field of experimental psychology, and the experimental psychology of perception.

Now what about the concept of causation, Hume's "constant conjunction" as the basis upon which we make causal ascriptions? Reid rejects this out of hand. No two events have been as constantly conjoined as day and night, says Reid, and yet no one regards day as the cause of night or night as the cause of day. There are any number of constantly conjoined events that we know are mere correlations. You know more than that. One need not repeat an action to discover himself to be its cause. Very often, we sort of habitually attribute causation, where if we knew better and thought more clearly about it, we'd withhold such ascriptions, but the concept of "causation" set forth by Hume, Reid believes, is entirely unsatisfactory.

Reid considers the process from the percipient's perspective, and concludes that no set of observations of events taking place in the external world could possibly lead to a concept like "A causes B." There would just be repetitive sequences.

On Reid's understanding, the concept of causation actually is an inference we make based on our own immediate knowledge of ourselves as having agentic or active power; that is, from the knowledge of ourselves as having an active power to do or to forebear from doing something, knowing that, we then attribute comparable powers to events in the external world. Our knowledge of our own active power, says Reid, must begin very early in life. Consider only the point at which an infant knows the difference between sucking his own thumb and having something else in his mouth, the point at which one recognizes that one is able to bring things about. I can darken the world simply by closing my eyes, you see.

Now since we recognize ourselves as having the power to bring about such things, the inference we make when we see things being brought about in the external world is that there must be some kindred kind of power bringing these events about also.

We see, then, that Reid actually turns the tables on Hume. Reid begins with an understanding of ourselves as having active power being the basis upon which we then might make causal attributions in the external natural world, and he concludes, then, that absent these *active powers*, the concept of causation never could be formed in the first instance. So, Reid's analysis is comparably psychological—comparable to Hume's, as it were, but it is leading very much in the direction of moral autonomy as the necessary precondition for the Humean operation to take place at all. In a word, for there to be Humean modes of causal concepts, there must be Reidian active powers.

Now what about Hume's moral theory, which would have passion rule reason, and sentiment establish all moral content? Reid is satisfied that even the committed hedonist can't possibly defend that position. Take the committed hedonist setting out to do nothing but maximize pleasure, maximize utility. Reid is not accepting that any such being outside the realm of pathology has actually ever existed, but suppose you had an entity of that sort. That entity would have to have the full rational powers and resources that Hume seems to be skeptical about. People will take foul-tasting medicine in the judgment that it will have long-term salutary consequences, and this is only possible to a rational, calculating being able to anticipate long-range consequences to come—and able to commit himself to a course of action likely to produce what is good, on the whole, over the long run—so it isn't enough to say that we are pleasure-seeking, pain-avoiding organisms, as if that settled the matter. Given human history and the inclinations of human beings, and the needs and purposes that we identify, we have to be—and are—rational entities first, even at the level of rational calculations as to what is in our long-range interest.

A philosopher should look for evidence to determine whether a theoretical position is sound or not. That's Reid's emphasis. What we know about human history affords ample evidence of an essentially altruistic disposition in human beings. There is no question that the lives of saints and heroes alone make clear our capacity for bona fide self-sacrifice, not in the interest of utility, but in the interest of what Reid refers to—here in anticipation of Kant, by the way—what Reid refers to as the "first principles of morals." Just as there are preconditions for us to be knowledgeable about the world, there must be active powers for us to have the concept of causation, and there must also be a set of dispositions of an essentially moral nature. They can't come from the outside; they have to be there to match up with events in the external world. Nor can they be mere passions or emotions, because passions and emotions as such are not principled. They're simply states of sentiment or states of feeling.

Now, Reid offers not a rational theory of morality, but a psychological theory. No one would deliberate at a choice point except in the belief that he had the power to execute one or another course of action. No one would hold himself or others responsible for actions, except in the belief that others, and oneself, had the power to do otherwise. Nor would one even make plans except in the belief that these were at least within the realm of personal power to bring to fruition. The belief that our actions are in our power is, for Reid, another gift from the mint of nature, and is more basic than the rational artifices that might be used to criticize it.

Reid must also counter forms of conventionalism that would reduce moral and epistemic claims to little more than verbal customs or uncritical modes of discourse. Locke and Hume both subscribed to a conventionalist theory of meaning, firmly opposed by Reid. As Reid noted, for words to take on a conventional meaning, there must be in place some means by which to signal agreement and enter into compacts and understandings, but this itself requires a language. Now, Reid argues that for there to be an artificial language, such as the one I'm using now, it must be grounded in what initially is a natural language—a language of facial expression, intonation, posture, invitations to cooperate, signs of fear. He finds these throughout the animal kingdom, and he reasons that artificial languages are grafted onto these natural behaviors, which allow us to have a shared kind of life with each other, and indeed, with other creatures of nature.

Finally, let's consider Reid's approach to the question or the problem of personal identity. Hume's account was an improvement on Locke. Locke's theory of personal identity was reducible to a kind of storage of experiences. Reid finds this entirely weak, and it invited the happy wrath of the Scriblerians. On Locke's account, there is still some sort of observer of consciousness, knitting together experiences that provide, in the ensemble, one's identity. Hume's account actually eliminates the middleman. Personal identity just is the train of associated or bundled perceptions. It is like a parade formation. If you take the elements of memory and the elements of consciousness as entities in a parade, well, some can be replaced by others, as marching soldiers might be replaced, but the parade formation remains continuous over time. That's Hume's approach.

Now, Reid concludes that this whole approach to personal identity is actually a non-starter. Locke's theory, he says, founders. For someone to recall having done something does not make him the person who did it. If you remembered losing the Battle of Waterloo, it would not make you Napoleon! Moreover, it fails at the level of logic. If you want to say that personal identity is just a collection of memories, then consider this. Reid here borrows a page from Berkeley's *Alciphron*.

Imagine a brave officer decorated for valor in battle who recalls having been the young boy once punished for stealing fruit from the orchard. Call the brave officer "B," and call the young boy "A." Now imagine an aging general who recalls having been the brave officer decorated for battle, but has no recollection whatever of the young boy punished for stealing fruit from the orchard, and call the aging general "C." Now, on Locke's account, "A" equals "B," and "B" equals "C," but "A" doesn't equal "C"! So, the logical property of transitivity is violated, and the identity statement simply fails.

Hume's account is more subtle, but Reid has already offered a compelling critique of Hume's concept of causation, and this is at the foundation of Hume's theory of personal identity. For the parade formation to be held together, it must be by that Humean causal chain forged out of constant conjunctions. Reid has argued that this can't work and so, in any case, if it can't work, the theory of personal identity tethered to it can't work. No. For there to be treason, there must be a traitor, says Reid, and when Hume says that when he looks for himself he finds nothing but a "bundle of perceptions," Reid wants to remind Hume that it is Hume who is doing the looking.

In the introduction to his *Inquiry*, Reid summarized his position with customary clarity, putting on notice those philosophers who might prefer the comfortable cushion of subtle speculation to the hard pavement that leads to small but cumulative understanding. He put it this way—framing it as a Presbyterian cleric, but advancing a thesis whose force remains even with the theology removed:

> Conjectures and theories are the creatures of men, and will always be found unlike the creatures of God. If we would know the works of God, we must consult themselves with attention and humility, without daring to add any thing of ours to what they declare. A just interpretation of nature is the only sound and orthodox philosophy. Whatever we add of our own is apocryphal, and of no authority.

Thank you, Thomas Reid.

France and the Philosophes
Lecture 33

If nothing else, the so-called *salon philosophes* invited the intelligent parts of the world into the Long Debate. They did not reserve philosophy to the philosophers, but understood that the philosophical mind is essentially the human mind when it takes itself seriously.

What we take to be the modern worldview is less a contribution of the Renaissance than of the age of science that followed in the 17th century. But consider this pair of quotations: "My works are the issue of pure and simple experience, who is the one true mistress. These rules are sufficient to enable you to know the true from the false" (Leonardo da Vinci [1452–1519]); and "Let us console ourselves for not knowing the possible connections between a spider and the rings of Saturn, and continue to examine what is within our reach" (Voltaire [1694–1778]). Leonardo and Voltaire have much in common, though much, of course, divides them. Both are satisfied that the light of experience casts sufficient illumination for us to understand the nature of our difficulties. As vindication of his belief in experience, Voltaire had what Leonardo did not have: the inspiration and achievement of Newton.

We do not generally think of the witty and discerning minds of the Paris salons as "philosophers." Few, if any, philosophy journal articles are written now on the musings of Diderot, Holbach, Helvetius, Condorcet, Voltaire, La Mettrie, and others of their ilk. The so-called *salon philosophes* invited the intelligent parts of the world into the Long Debate. They did not reserve philosophy to the philosophers. They opened up, into the public discourse, issues that long had existed primarily at the level at abstract philosophy. But sometimes, the wit and wisdom of the *philosophes* is in danger of losing the refinement of philosophy and dropping to the level of rank propaganda.

However, the *philosophes* weren't actually out to prosecute the agenda of academic philosophy. They were out to change the world. To change the world is to change minds. The only alternative is tyrannical oppression. This aspect of the Enlightenment project is most apparent in the publication of

Diderot's *Encyclopedia*, which focused on the authority of experience, absent any dogmatic teaching or religious overtones. The outline of the massive project was given in the form of a "Tree of Human Knowledge," developed by Diderot and d'Alembert, that includes everything from working with slate to our knowledge of God.

Voltaire (1694–1778) was a powerful influence on what became this Age of Enlightenment. As with Descartes, he had been educated by the Jesuits. At 23, he is found serving nearly a year in the Bastille for derisive criticism of the government. This event was a harbinger, for within a decade, Voltaire was exiled to England for offending the chevalier de Rohan. Voltaire's reverential attitude toward Newton is part of his general judgment that British philosophy has triumphed over Cartesianism. His *Letters on the English* makes this clear and ties the achievements in Britain to the intellectually liberated climate of thought: He compares membership in the Royal Society (science and achievement) to the French Academy (birth and orthodoxy).

The Enlightenment is, at once, a critique of traditionalism and a forward-looking movement of thought and action impelled by the methods and perspective of science.

Voltaire has a splendid model for this mode of casual criticism—Michel de Montaigne, whose famous *Essais* (1575) celebrates secular knowledge, common sense, common decency, the right way to work through problems, the philosophies worth having, and the gentle ridicule of the pomposity of self-appointed authority. With Montaigne, too, there is an enlargement of the discursive community, a movement toward the democratization of knowledge. Voltaire is in the direct patrimony of Montaigne: Knowledge is not meant to vindicate belief but to help us determine which beliefs are worth having.

It is time to turn to a mind of a radically different cast, that of Jean Jacques Rousseau (1712–1778). Against the attention to science and technology, Rousseau looks to nature in the raw, unanalyzed, spared the "resolutive-compositive" methods of the tinkering classes.

Against the rationalism of the Enlightenment—its contempt for superstition and its reverence for high civilization—Rousseau draws attention to the inauthentic lives constrained and corrupted by civilization. Rousseau is the harbinger of the *Romantic rebellion* but bears the same tools of high culture and literary astuteness that are the mark of Enlightenment thought. In *Emile*, Rousseau takes the position that civilization works to the disadvantage of what is most authentic about us, that the very process of civilizing someone strips him of certain natural tendencies and sentiments.

© 2010 JupiterImages Corporation

Jean-Jacques Rousseau (1712-1778) was a Swiss-French philosopher and author whose work largely decried the harmful effects of modern civilization.

In *Du Contrat Social* (1762), Rousseau offers one of the most summoning lines in all of political philosophy: "Man is born free and everywhere he is in chains." Rousseau referred to the chained mind—the mind tied to orthodoxies that render it incapable of its own natural functions. We find in Rousseau, too, a particular form of naturalism, a concession to nature as the last word, a skepticism toward merely human contrivances and merely habitual modes of conduct.

In La Mettrie (1709–1751), naturalism tends toward materialism. *Man—A Machine*, La Mettrie's banned book of 1748, extends to its logical conclusion the materialistic drift of Descartes's own psychology. The human body is a machine that winds its own springs. It is the living image of perpetual movement. Given that all the faculties of the soul depend on the actions of the body, the soul is an "enlightened machine." La Mettrie calls on the reader to come to grips with the fact that human life is biologically organized and that this organization is shaped by external conditions.

Locke's translator in France, Etienne Condillac (1715–1780), introduces in his 1754 *Treatise of Sensation* the model of the *sentient statue*, a block of stone, shaped by its environment. As the result of an incessant interaction with a stimulating environment, the statue comes to form elementary Lockean sensations, ideas, and more complex ideas. The point, of course, is that our essence does not precede our actual existence in the world and that the kinds of beings we are serve as a record of the experiences we've had. Not long after this, Thomas Paine, in his *Common Sense*, will speak of rank and titles as "a magician's wand, which circumscribes human felicity." Again, the guide in all things is nature. Newton and Bacon instructed us in how to read the book of nature without adding our own preconceptions to the facts.

Helvetius is in the same tradition of a radical environmentalist. But Helvetius recognizes that the classes that exist in this world must have been made, because it is obvious that political forces are needed to preserve them. Given that so much energy is needed to keep this sort of social organization in place, there must be something horrifically unnatural about it. If that much work has to be done to preserve it, it must be because it opposes natural forces.

Condorcet (1743–1794), at the end of the century, offers the promise of progress. To my mind, he represents what is most defining in this age of Enlightenment. Jesuit-educated Condorcet established his originality in mathematics early, publishing a treatise on integral calculus in 1765. Four years later, he was elected to the *Academie des Sciences,* rising to the prestigious office of Secretary of the Academy in 1777. A master of the emerging field of probability theory, Condorcet may be accorded a place among those who have developed what is called *decision theory*. His 1785 treatise on the subject of majority decisions is still instructive. Condorcet supported the Revolution, served as a member of the Assembly, and drafted a plan of education for the coming Republic.

Though a son of the Revolution, he was committed to the more moderate Gerondist faction, arguing against the killing of the king and other extreme measures of the Jacobins. This landed him in prison, courtesy of Robespierre.

In 1793, Condorcet went into hiding. During this period, he composed his *Sketch for an Historical Picture of the Progress of the Human Mind.*

In 1794, Condorcet was discovered, arrested, and imprisoned; he was found dead in his cell within two days. Condorcet reflects the dominant idea of his age and does so with special brightness and poignancy. It is the idea of progress. In its Enlightenment form, it is more analytical and scientific, more political and self-conscious than the earlier Renaissance version. Whereas the classical worldview conceives of a cosmos organized by principles of harmony and proportion, the notion of progress says that what is stationary is stagnant and the future is under no obligation to mimic the past. Condorcet's *Sketch* defends the plan to liberate the human imagination and, in the process, achieve something new, untried in world history. He concludes—in the shadow of his own impending death—with the hope that a grand association of the scientifically enlightened, drawn from diverse nations, "would meet no obstacles; and it would assure among all the sciences and all the arts directed by their principles... an equilibrium of knowledge, industry, and reason necessary for the progress and the happiness of the human race."

The Enlightenment is, at once, a critique of traditionalism and a forward-looking movement of thought and action impelled by the methods and perspective of science. France would host some of the movement's most persuasive writers and thinkers, including Voltaire, Diderot, Rousseau, and Condorcet. Their revolution in thought was to be matched by political and social revolutions based on the recovery of natural rights. ■

Suggested Reading

Condorcet. *Selected Writings.* K. Baker, ed. Bobbs Merrill, 1976.

Rousseau, J. J. "The Social Contract," in *Social Contract and Discourses*, E. Barker, ed. Dent, 1993.

Voltaire. *Philosophical Letters.*

1. Conclude whether there is good evidence to support the view that it is by way of science that society's most enduring problems are to be solved.

2. Summarize whether it is obviously the case that, only through the appearance of modern science can we say that the human mind has significantly *progressed* over the state it was in at the time of, say, Socrates.

France and the Philosophes
Lecture 33—Transcript

My works are the issue of pure and simple experience, who is the one true mistress. These rules are sufficient to enable you to know the true from the false.

These are the words of Leonardo da Vinci from his book on painting. He writes at a time of witch hunts and the burning saints, the burning of vanities, in the town square, and an age that is already featuring Erasmus and Luther doing battle with each other on the question of freedom of the will. Reformation, upheaval, counter-reformation feverishly unfolding, and here is Leonardo proclaiming: "My works are the issue of pure and simple experience, who is the one true mistress."

When we move to the Age of the Enlightenment, the 18th century, we read, as if the same author were writing, "Let us console ourselves for not knowing the possible connections between a spider and the rings of Saturn, and continue to examine what is within our reach."

This is the voice of Voltaire. Now, Leonardo and Voltaire have much in common—though much, of course, divides them. Both are satisfied that the light of experience casts sufficient illumination for us to understand the nature of our difficulties and to find a way out of the labyrinth. If Theseus needed a golden string, we need the light of experience, which is provided chiefly by an unprejudiced study of nature. Voltaire, it should be noted, had the preceding "Age of Newton" offered as a vindication of his entire perspective.

Voltaire traveled to London. He wrote a series of letters on the English people, with whom the French did not compare favorably, by the way. Especially in his reflections on Newton and his comparisons of the Newtonian and Cartesian systems, Voltaire did much to chide French thought into new ways of thinking. In Letter XIV he says this:

> The famous Newton, this destroyer of the Cartesian system, died in March 1727. His countrymen honoured him in his lifetime,

and interred him as though he had been a king who had made his people happy. It was his peculiar felicity, not only to be born in a country of liberty, but in an age when all scholastic impertinences were banished from the world. Reason alone was cultivated, and mankind could only be his pupil, not his enemy.

It is such passages that cause many to question whether the Enlightenment *philosophes* who graced the salons of Paris were mere polemicists—influential in politics, but rather light in the subtler realms of thought. More harshly, is there any reason to pay close attention to what they had to say within the context of serious philosophical inquiry? After all, how many philosophy journal articles are written now on the musings of Diderot, Holbach, Helvetius, Condorcet, Voltaire, La Mettrie, and scores of others?

Now, one answer to the question is by way of considering the mission of philosophy itself. If philosophy has some purpose in human life, presumably, it should be to help us figure out the problems of an essentially civic, social, political, moral, and intellectual nature. It can't be an activity intended chiefly for its own few professional practitioners. Recall that Socrates did not publish his ideas in journals—nor did he develop an arcane, specialist language. If he had, there's a good chance he would have lived longer.

If nothing else, the so-called *salon philosophes* invited the intelligent parts of the world into the Long Debate. They did not reserve philosophy to the philosophers, but understood that the philosophical mind is essentially the human mind when it takes itself seriously. They understood further that once invited into the Long Debate, the ordinary citizen would be able to weigh the competing claims of crown and cross, of rabble and prince, and decide for themselves with a mind now fortified by philosophical discipline and objective information about the world and its various inhabitants. So, I would say that the positive side of the productions of the philosophe was one of opening up, into the public discourse, issues that long existed primarily at the level of abstract philosophy. You might want to think of it as the "democratizing" of philosophy.

Of course, for everything the gods give us, they take two things back, and for every blessing, there seems to be a pair of curses. Clearly, when the philosophical enterprise goes public, shortcuts are inevitable, and ample room is created for an unwholesome mixture of acute analysis and rhetorical manipulation. To be accessible to an ever-larger assembly, it is necessary to adopt or to possess a style that is attractive, a tone that is appealing, and a message that arrests attention. These are not inevitably the ingredients of great ideas in philosophy, or even good counsel. Sharply put, many of the philosophical musings of an 18th-century salon dropped to the level of rank propaganda, so utterly populist as to leave all of philosophy's refinements behind—but the *philosophes*, as often they tell us themselves, weren't actually out to prosecute the agenda of academic philosophy. They were out to change the world.

Now, to change the world is to change minds, for the only alternative is tyrannical oppression. It is when the ordinary person has become convinced and converted that the grip of the past, the weight of habit, can be removed. Sometimes, conversion is achieved by holding up prevailing authority to ridicule, and in this the Enlightenment savants were expert. Often, the exposure of ignorance and the remedy of instruction set one on a new course, a new way of thinking about authority itself. This aspect of the Enlightenment project is most apparent in the publication of Diderot's *Encyclopedia*.

The project of the *Encyclopedia* was, in and of itself, the utter secularization of knowledge. Obeisance is not paid to any dogmatic teaching or any religious sect. Rather, the authority of experience, of science, of common sense, is arrayed against more traditional modes of authority. Indeed, it is the traditional modes of authority that the *philosophes* singularly and collectively are challenging.

Edited jointly by Diderot and D'Alembert, it was published over a period of two decades, beginning in 1751. Its full title is *Encyclopedia, or Systematic Dictionary of the Sciences, Arts and Crafts*. The 17 volumes of text and 11 volumes of plates featured contributions from 140 experts, including some of the greatest minds of the age. To mention just a few: Diderot, Voltaire, Montesquieu, Rousseau, D'Alembert, d'Holbach. With 72,000 articles, it left the world of learning entirely open to the reading public, and served as perhaps the greatest contribution to public education since the time of

Charlemagne. The outline of the massive project was given in the form of a "Tree of Human Knowledge," developed by Diderot and D'Alembert and published in the *Encyclopedia*. It includes everything from working with slate to our knowledge of God.

Voltaire was a powerful influence on what would become this Age of Enlightenment. His dates are 1694–1778, and as with Descartes, he had been educated by the Jesuits. There's a separate story here that I don't have time to get into, but here's another project of Jesuit instruction.

Life in Paris nurtured his natural wit and literary genius, both gaining admirers and enemies. At 23, he is found serving nearly a year in the Bastille for derisive criticism of the government. Big surprise, since it's Voltaire. This was to be a harbinger, for within a decade he would be exiled in England for offending the chevalier de Rohan. He has declared himself to be not merely an Anglophile, but perhaps an Anglomaniac. He is very much taken by England and English ways.

The years of exile were 1726–1729. They made him not merely an Anglophile, but indeed, something of an Anglomaniacal admirer. His letters on the English people are unrestrained in admiration and praise for English people and English practices. The praise has as its specific target of abuse the practices and perspectives of his own native France, the preposterous nature of French institutions—at least as he sees them—and what they set out to establish, compared with what Voltaire takes to be the entirely liberated and liberating perspective of the English people.

In Letter XXIV, he contrasts fellowship in the Royal Society with membership in the French Academy, the former based on merit, the latter based largely on who you know and what kind of influence peddling you've done. The published memoirs of the French Academy offer pages of praise for its members by whom? Well, by other members, praise for the king, praise for the famous. Meanwhile, the proceedings of the Royal Society contribute to the store of useful knowledge.

Voltaire has a splendid model for this mode of casual criticism. It is Montaigne, whose famous *Essais*, published in 1575, are a veritable celebration of secular knowledge, common sense, common decency, the right way to work through problems, the philosophies worth having, and the gentle ridicule of pompities of self-appointed authority. With Montaigne, too, there is an enlargement of the discursive community, a movement toward the democratization of knowledge more fully realized in the Enlightenment. Voltaire is in the direct patrimony of Montaigne: Knowledge is wasted when used to vindicate mere belief. Rather, it should help us determine which beliefs are worth having.

A secularized body of knowledge is naturalistic and practical. The concern is going to be with what makes itself accessible to the senses, the natural world, the world that is describable in physical terms. If a thing exists, it exists in some degree. If it exists in some degree, it can be measured, and when measured, it is known.

Now, we find in the productions of this community of philosophically inclined wits—interest in the calculus, interest in precision and precision instruments, enthusiasm for all varieties of machines and machinery. Very often, precision instruments are used metaphorically to point to what constitutes knowing something thoroughly. The metaphor of the machine is taking on a certain reality in its own right. Hobbes had conjured the Commonwealth itself as a kind of knowable, complex, mechanical entity with moving parts, designed to achieve certain ends, and Enlightenment thought and literature reflect the same orientation.

Now, the wit and iconoclasm, the attention to precision and machines duly noted, it is time to turn to a mind of a radically different cast, Jean Jacques Rousseau, 1712–1778. Surrounded by a small army of clever thinkers and masterful writers, Rousseau will come to trump them all in influence and celebrity. He is somewhat on the periphery of the glittering wits, the fashionable salons. We come to see Rousseau as a tortured person— misunderstood and, toward the end of his life, patently paranoid. If there is a musical metaphor that captures the Enlightenment, Rousseau might be cast as the counterpoint within a larger harmonic context.

Against the attention to science and technology, Rousseau looks to nature in the raw, unanalyzed, spared the "resolutive-compositive" methods of the tinkering classes. Against the vaunted rationalism of the Enlightenment, its contempt for superstition and its reverence for high civilization, Rousseau draws attention to the inauthentic lives constrained and corrupted by civilization. He is the harbinger of that *Romantic rebellion*, but bearing the same tools of high culture and literary astuteness that are the mark of Enlightenment thought.

In his *Emile*, Rousseau takes the position that civilization works to the disadvantage of what is most authentic about us, that the very processes of civilizing someone is to strip him of certain natural tendencies and sentiments. It hardens and renders indifferent its beneficiaries who forfeit an independence of mind and spirit.

If this is inconsistent with the judgment of a Diderot or a D'Alembert, it is utterly compatible with their revolutionary objectives. The education Rousseau will provide for Emile is as much against traditional authority as anything found in the writing of Voltaire or Condorcet.

Rousseau launches his best-selling *Du Contrat Social*, published in 1762, with one of the most summoning lines in all of political philosophy:

> Man is born free and everywhere he is in chains. One thinks oneself the master of others, and still remains a greater slave than they. How did this come about?

"Man, born free government and everywhere in chains." Well, in what kind of chains? Rousseau was not in chains. The English people were not in chains. Nor were the French. It is the chained mind, the mind tied to orthodoxies that render it incapable of its own natural functions. So, we find in Rousseau, too, a particular form of naturalism, a concession to nature as the last word, a suspicion, a skepticism toward merely human contrivances, merely habitual modes of conduct.

Momentous prose moves thought in one way; polemical prose in another way, but often not in an opposite way. Rousseau appeals to readers in the language of justice and rights, noble sentiments, authenticity. There is, however, another level of appeal available to one who is convinced that prevailing beliefs are grossly in error; it is the journalistic level, the late-breaking news or major stories that seem to have been neglected.

All, I turn now to Julienne Offray de la Mettrie, author of *L'Homme Machine, Man—A Machine*, published in 1748. We've heard Rousseau's affecting lines at the beginning of his *Social Contract*. Here is the way La Mettrie begins his treatise. Try this, now. Wait for it:

> It is not enough for a wise man to study nature and truth; he should dare state truth for the benefit of the few who are willing and able to think. As for the rest, who as voluntarily slaves of prejudice, they can no more attain truth than a frog can fly.

That's another level at which the crowd might be appealed to. La Mettrie had written one book that got him in trouble with the authorities because he was a young physician, and young physicians were only supposed to write treatises on the accomplishments of older physicians.

Having been reprimanded for his brashness in this regard, La Mettrie then undertook to publish *Man, a Machine*, and the scandal surrounding the appearance of that work was sufficiently intense to find its author running off to the protective custody of a Prussia now overruled, and ruled by and the tolerant tyrant, Frederick, the friend of Voltaire.

All, La Mettrie has enjoyed a very appreciative press in the last 10 or 15 years as the "brain sciences" vie for funds and popular allegiance. It is praise that must come from those who either never read that book, or assume that the people who were listening to their praise of La Mettrie would never get around to reading it themselves. It is, in fact, a thin polemic. How shall I capture it for you? This passage is especially representative, "The human body is a machine which winds its own springs. It is the living image of perpetual motion." Elsewhere he writes, "Man is so complicated a machine that it is impossible to get a clear idea of the machine beforehand, and hence impossible to define it."

At one point, he notes that motility is inherent in biological systems. You don't have to presuppose the existence of some spiritual source of motivation or movement. You don't need something external to the forces of nature to account for significant movement. It's sort of built into the thing, and what's the proof of this? Well, he gets the proof of this from a military officer, who notes that over the evening fire, if you take the heart out of a chicken and throw it in boiling water, it jumps up. Now, this is not what we would refer to as a successful employment of the methods of Bacon and Newton.

What *Man, a Machine* is, I say, is a polemic. It's a polemic that includes this intentionally insolent passage, "Since all of the faculties of the soul depend, as they do, on the proper organization of the body, and more specifically of the brain, the soul is surely an enlightened machine."

Now, that is an attention-getter. The soul, this most precious and transcendent of entities, this entity that most closely approximates the image of God within his creation, is an enlightened machine, an essentially mechanical contrivance. This is how learning, and perception, and motivation, and emotion and thought are to be understood. They are to be understood in terms of the basic mechanical properties of matter in motion, the body being a species of matter in motion. The thesis puts on notice all rationalist, or transcendentalist, or idealistic philosophies trying to make more out of man than a machine, even if an enlightened one.

Now, another thing that we find in this period of philosophical agility—which is different from philosophical originality, I must say—is taking some developed philosophical work, and through the use of metaphor and exegesis, enlarging its teaching. One of the earliest translators of Locke into French was Etienne Condillac. His 1746 *Essay on the Origin of the Understanding* accords to the senses nearly everything that would be required for knowledge, and his 1754 *Treatise of Sensation* introduces the model of the *sentient statue*, a block of stone, worked on by the environment, experiencing the impulsive assaults of a shaping environment, and out of these interactions, the block begins to take on the form of a recognizable being. The process continues, and through the result of an incessant interaction with a stimulating environment, the statue now comes to form elementary Lockian sensations, ideas, and then, more complex ideas.

The point, of course, is that our essence does not precede our actual existence in the world, and that the kinds of beings we are serve as a record, merely, of the experiences we've had. Here's the prince and the peasant developed yet further and metaphorically. What goes into the making of a prince is not a divine ordinance, but traditions and customs that are man-made. They're inventions, like gorgons; they are found nowhere, except in the human imagination.

Not long after this, Thomas Paine, in his *Common Sense*, will speak of rank and titles as "a magician's wand, which circumscribes human felicity." Thomas Paine observes that nowhere in the book of Genesis does one find reference to a duke, a prince, or a duchess; that as such terms are used, one doesn't know whether they refer to a person, or a horse, or a dog. Again, the guide in all things is nature. Newton and Bacon instructed us in how to read the book of nature without prejudice, without designated authorities, without adding our own preconceptions to the facts.

Helvetius is in the same tradition of a radical environmentalist. In fact, Diderot will take exception when Helvetius at one point argues that the main difference between Diderot and some derelict in the street is just that they had different environmental histories. Diderot, himself, willing to be a genial environmentalist, would not quite accept that account of his own achievements, but Helvetius recognizes in the world in which he lives that the classes that exist must have been made; they must have been manufactured, as it were, for it is quite obvious that political forces are needed to preserve them. How deliberately do the engines of society, and politics, and government preserve the status quo? If that much energy is needed to keep this sort of social organization in place, there must be something horrifically unnatural about it. That is, if that much work has to be done to preserve it, it must be because it is opposing natural forces.

Now, it is to Condorcet, 1743–1794, that I turn toward the conclusion of this lecture on the Enlightenment, for to my mind, Condorcet represents what is most defining in this age of Enlightenment, and indeed, also more subtly, the limitations that will become ever clearer.

Again, a Jesuit education is behind him. Condorcet established his originality in mathematics very early on, publishing a treatise on integral calculus in 1765. Four years later, he is elected to the *Academie des Sciences*, rising to the prestigious office of Secretary of the Academy in 1777. A master of the emerging field of probability theory, Condorcet may be accorded a place among those who have actually developed what is called *decision theory*. His 1785 treatise on the subject of majority decisions is still instructive.

Condorcet supported the Revolution. He served as a member of the Assembly. He even drafted a plan of education for the coming French Republic. Though a son of the Revolution, he was committed to the more moderate Gerondist faction, arguing against the killing of the king and other extreme measures of the Jacobins. This, needless to say, landed him in prison, courtesy of Robespierre.

At this point, Condorcet, seeing the grim handwriting on the wall, went into hiding. The year was 1793, during which time he composed his *Sketch for an Historical Picture of the Progress of the Human Mind*. However, 1794 finds him discovered, arrested again, and imprisoned, and then dead in his cell within two days.

Concorcet was the hopeful philosopher who nonetheless would find himself hiding out in the last months of his life, in the very France whose democratic and republican principles he had done so much to install and defend. His final hours are overcast by the shadows of a terror that is going to consume everything that doesn't stand behind the new orthodoxy. What is so poignant in Condorcet is that in this state of hiding, where you would think he would be so bitter, so melancholy, pessimistic toward an age that turned on him, we find him writing something hopeful, progressive, optimistic.

Condorcet reflects the dominant idea of this age, and he does so with special brightness and poignancy. It is the idea of progress. In its Enlightenment form, it is more analytical and scientific, more political and self-conscious, than earlier Renaissance versions.

Yet, for all of the classical revival elements of the 18th century, the classic revival in architecture, redolent of Athens and Rome, I say for all of that, for all of the self-consciousness that 18th-century writers and thinkers had about their kinship with the classical world, the world of Cicero, the world of the Stoics, the world of Pericles—for all that, this 18th-century idea is not quite compatible with the classical worldview.

The classical worldview conceives of a cosmos organized by principles of harmony and proportion, the golden mean. The middle course is best; everything has its place and function, hopeful that whatever is good can be preserved in its state, a search for an absolute that has as its defining feature its unchangeability. What is unharmonious in the ancient world comes close as classical world conceptions of sin; what is out of harmony, what is discordant, what is disproportionate, rebellious, revolutionary, is hubristic. It is to be shunned.

Now, if we take that to be an essential feature of classical thought, the 18th-century idea of progress couldn't be more different. The idea of progress is an idea according to which what is stationary is stagnant. The future is under no obligation to mimic the past. Condorcet's *Sketch* defends the plan to liberate the human imagination, and in the process achieve something new, something untried in world history. This is not a Hellenic ambition.

Even as he faces his own impending death, Condorcet rounds out his work by expressing a certain hopefulness for a grand association between science and society. He would hope, he says, that this:

> would meet no obstacles; and it would assure among all the sciences and all the arts directed by their principles...an equilibrium of knowledge, industry, and reason necessary for the progress and the happiness of the human race.

I recall Kenneth Clarke, that old and memorable figure in the series called *Civilization*, saying that he wasn't quite prepared to define civilization, but he knew it when he saw it, and in Condorcet, one sees it.

The Federalist Papers and the Great Experiment
Lecture 34

William Gladstone, who between 1868 and 1894 served on and off as Britain's Prime Minister, declared the Constitution of the United States to be: "the most wonderful work ever struck off at a given time by the brain and purpose of man."

Between May and September of 1787, a group of men convened in the State House in Philadelphia. They were there for the express purpose of creating a nation, but this was a purpose many reached with reluctance bordering on outright refusal. The measure that created the Constitutional Convention had been adopted the previous fall at the Annapolis Convention. Of the 55 delegates, some had formal college education, while others did not. It is clear from notes taken by James Madison that the quality of discourse reveals no difference between those with and without degrees.

The one delegate who certainly knew all along that a *nation* had to be created in Philadelphia was Alexander Hamilton. Hamilton's plan was extreme. It called for a president for life with total veto power over all legislative enactments. But Hamilton also contributed among the most incisive, informed, and prescient ideas produced by this extraordinary assembly. Rather than a meeting of wise old heads, this was more a young man's achievement or at least the achievement of a vigorous assortment, ranging from Jonathan Dayton (26) to Ben Franklin (81).

George Washington, already a national icon, presided over the meetings. Because we've mythologized Washington and because we're skeptical of our own mythologies, there is a tendency to underestimate the significance of this man in the forging of the American Republic. In examining the cultural history of America at the founding, however, Washington would be the central figure, the embodiment of what, at least on the level of rhetoric, was taken to be the animating principles of the new republic.

The document that came out of the 1787 deliberations seemed to be lacking in something. When the press publicized the drafts, much of the collective conscious was startled by the absence of a Bill of Rights. This obstacle to ratification would be removed by Madison's drafting of the amendments that still stand as the Bill of Rights. But the fate of the draft Constitution was in doubt.

The Federalist Papers—put together by Madison, Hamilton, and John Jay chiefly to win New York over to the ratification of the Constitution—are among the great contributions to political philosophy. Though not intended as such, the essays constitute a work of original practical philosophy in the tradition of Plato and Aristotle. The sheer realism of these essays, which offer the philosophical background to the Constitution, place them higher on the scale of political *science* than any other set of essays or dialogues.

When one contrasts the arguments in *The Federalist Papers* with the dominating political treatises of the time—Locke or Montesquieu or Rousseau—the obvious difference is that one set of arguments is actually the template for a national government. This is the main reason the so-called "American experiment" has been repeated often and successfully by newer sovereign states over the past two centuries.

Though the contributors to *The Federalist* did not cite well-known philosophers of their time and before, they were well read in political science and political philosophy, as well as in world history and law. The writers recognized their audience to be a various, large, and pluralistic community of a persons whose support and allegiance depended on specific arguments confronting specific criticisms. There is simply no anticipation of this in the record of political philosophy.

The three authors of *The Federalist* published 85 essays in New York newspapers between October 1787 and April 1788 under the name Publius. Alexander Hamilton planned the project and contributed the largest share, followed closely by Madison. Jay's contribution was slight in number of pages but addressed important points. James Madison, more than any other of the delegates, earns the praise for giving Americans their Constitution.

A graduate of Princeton, Madison brought to *The Federalist* not only an education steeped in the Scottish common sense philosophy but also a wealth of political experience.

Did we get a republic? What is a republic? Madison says that a political regime is a republic only when the government's power is derived entirely from the people and "administered by persons holding their offices during pleasure, for a limited period, or during good behavior." Nothing in this is new or controversial. But Madison observes that history shows the closer something comes to *that* sense of a republic, the sooner it dies. The republics that seem to make it are what he refers to as a kind of puritanical republic. John Adams was behind that view of republics. He said that only "pure religion or austere morals" will be capable of holding a republican form of government together.

> **There is a tendency to underestimate the significance of [George Washington] in the forging of the American Republic.**

With these concerns at the forefront, Madison distinguishes between pure democracies, subject to the factionalism that leads to anarchy, and the right sort of republic, in which power is delegated by the people. The nearly paralyzing tension, of course, arises from the need for a central government that is able to secure the finances and defense of the nation and the jealously guarded freedoms of the individual states.

The Bill of Rights: Was it necessary? A remarkable feature of the Convention of 1787, which drafted the Constitution, is that it specifically refused to incorporate a Bill of Rights. The omission was a deliberate act based on vitally important understandings. A self-governing people should decide what its own rights are—to list them is to limit them. The federal government should not trump the communities that compose the federation: The people of Maryland or New York have formed self-governing communities based on their own views of their rights. You have no need of federal guarantees of your rights against your local community: Its laws and principles are your own, and you need no defense against it.

The lesson taught by Montesquieu was that there are at base only three types of government: (1) A despotism rules by will, and in it, the people must cultivate reverential fear. (2) A monarchy, with rule by law in the hands of a single person, calls for the cultivation of honor. And (3) a republic depends on the cultivation of virtue. Power must be separated lest its concentration convert the republic into a tyranny. We find this in the Stoic outlook of Washington and many of the other founders—the recognition that the republic will succeed, because we have the resources to create and preserve lives of virtue and self-sacrifice. Power in this new republic (as the founders of the American Republic believed) would come to be taken by a natural aristocracy that would arise when the free exercise of virtue is permitted and encouraged.

The Federalist Papers and the grand experiment in self-governance mark a special chapter in human history, a chapter in which there would be a convergence of political, scientific, and moral energies capable of overturning the old order by which most of life was shaped. But the signal feature of the enterprise was the direct, open, respectful address to *the people*, an attempt to gain support by appealing to the common sense and mature political understanding of those who, in virtue of being fit for the rule of law, are fit to rule themselves. ■

Suggested Reading

McDonald, F. *Novus Ordo Seclorum*. University Press of Kansas, 1985.

Rossiter, C. *The Federalist Papers*. Anchor, 1963.

Questions to Consider

1. Explain whether the "checks and balances" of the Constitution have worked according to plan.

2. Conclude whether the national government is still (or ever was) formed by election of those abundant in virtue and merit.

The Federalist Papers and the Great Experiment
Lecture 34—Transcript

William Gladstone, who between 1868 and 1894 served on and off as Britain's Prime Minister, declared the Constitution of the United States to be: "the most wonderful work ever struck off at a given time by the brain and purpose of man." However, "struck off" is a misleading depiction of what was involved in completing this "most wonderful work."

Between May and September of 1787, a group of men convened in the State House in hot and humid Philadelphia. They took rented rooms, unless, as was the case for a few of them, they could make their way to their homes on weekends. They lived out of suitcases and spent most of their waking hours in tireless and often tiresome debate, made all the more difficult by the suspicions mounting among their countrymen. Their deliberations were, by their own vote, conducted in secret. The press was not invited, and, if they were there for the express purpose of creating a *nation*, this was a purpose many reached with a reluctance bordering on outright refusal. Rhode Island didn't even send delegates.

The measure that created the Convention had been adopted the previous fall at the Annapolis Convention. There, commissioners from New York, New Jersey, Pennsylvania, Delaware, and Virginia acknowledged the "important defects in the system of the Federal Government," and they proposed what they called a "Convention of Deputies from the United States" to assemble "for the special and sole purpose of…digesting a plan for supplying such defects as may be discovered to exist…"

Annapolis had set no limit on the number of deputies. In the end, the states named 55 delegates. Interestingly, 25 of them had no formal college education of any sort, including Benjamin Franklin and George Washington. The other thirty had earned degrees from Princeton—nine degrees from there, five from William and Mary, the same from Yale, a few from Columbia, and one each from Glasgow and from Oxford. It is clear from the notes so carefully taken by James Madison that the quality of discourse, however, reveals no difference between those with degrees and those with comparably sharp and sharply formed intelligence.

If there was one delegate who knew all along that it was a nation that had to be created in Philadelphia, it was Alexander Hamilton. He had a plan; he even presented it, but it was extreme—a president for life with total veto power over all legislative enactments. Hamilton, it should be noted, thought that the greatest man who ever lived was Julius Caesar, but Hamilton also contributed among the most incisive, informed, and prescient ideas produced by this extraordinary assembly, and then later, and especially, in *The Federalist Papers*.

It has sometimes been said that what took place during those four and a half months was nothing less than miraculous. In fact, Jefferson, who wasn't there and who later would find out everything you could possibly want to know about those deliberations by reading the notes taken by Madison, couldn't believe that Madison was at once a full-fledged participant every day of the meetings and at the same time could record these notes with such accuracy and completeness, dispassion, representing views contrary to his own with faithfulness and respect. Jefferson thought Madison's notes were miraculous, let alone what actually was achieved in the deliberations.

Was this a meeting of wise old heads? Well, there was only one old head in the room; it was Ben Franklin's. Actually, this was more a young man's achievement, or at least the achievement of a vigorous assortment—ranging in age from Jonathan Dayton, who was 26, to Ben Franklin, who was 81. The average age was 42, and this would have dropped, perhaps, into the high 30s if Franklin and the two next oldest had been removed.

The meetings were presided over by George Washington, who was already a national icon. He speaks rarely during the four and a half months, but his presence confers a nobility on the chamber. He occasionally reminds those assembled that these are, as it were, "in camera" sessions. There's nothing to be said to the press. The press commenting on day-to-day affairs of this deliberative body could only drive the country to fearfulness and confusion.

Well, how scrupulously was this principle adhered to? Quite scrupulously. There's one event that says much. Apparently, after one of the day's deliberations, someone of the representatives had his notes for the day fall to the ground so they were on the floor of the room, and apparently another one of the delegates, seeing them on the floor, and not knowing whose notes these were, picked them up and put them on the president's desk, on George Washington's desk. The next day, Washington holds up the notes, cautions about the need to preserve confidentiality, and it's a measure of the esteem in which Washington was held by his contemporaries that no one claimed the notes. No one wanted to go up front and say: "Sorry, George. These are mine."

We know, when Mrs. Adams will write back from the Court of St. James, what the estimation of Washington was even outside the continental United States. She tells us that with all the European dignitaries coming to the Court of St. James, the one person who, when he entered the room, was obviously the aristocrat in the group—all eyes turned to him—was Washington.

Now, because we've so mythologized Washington, and because we're skeptical of our own mythologies, there is a tendency to underestimate the significance of this man in the forging of the American Republic. We all have our historical villains and favorites. I should think that if I were ever to presume to examine the cultural history of America at the founding, Washington would be the central figure, the embodiment of what at least at the level of rhetoric was taken to be the animating principles of the new republic. His nightstand apparently not only had the Good Book on it, but also Addison's *Cato*. He very much looked forward to productions of Addison's *Cato*. During one of the winter campaigns, he actually had Addison's *Cato* staged for the troops. I don't know whether it was to provide them with a greater moral uplift, or perhaps to provide himself with it.

Washington had a temper, and was known to use languages that went well beyond the king's English, but when Stoic resolve and self-sacrifice were needed in uncommon measure, Washington was the man of the hour. It was proposed that his title, when we finally constituted ourselves, should be "His Excellency," or "King." Rejecting all this, he calmly informed his admirers that he had not made war on George III in order to become George I.

Now, the document itself that came out of the 1787 deliberations seemed to be lacking in something. When the press got hold of the drafts and alerted the people to what was contained, much of the collective conscious was startled by the absence of a Bill of Rights.

This was but one of the obstacles to ratification, and it would be removed by Madison's drafting of those first amendments to the document that still stand as the Bill of Rights, but the fate of the draft Constitution was in doubt. It wasn't clear at all that the arduous undertaking in Philadelphia would come to anything other than yet another pile of papers on how one day, there might actually be the United States.

Now, I should ask: What does all or any of this have to do with great ideas in philosophy? *The Federalist Papers*—which were put together by Madison, and Hamilton, and John Jay—designed chiefly to win New York over to the ratification of the Constitution, I submit, are one of the great contributions to political philosophy. If the work had come from a single hand—had it been presented as a philosophical treatise, I think it would have surely ranked with Aristotle's *Politics*. Some might actually have ranked it above Plato's *Republic*, if only on the grounds of its realistic and practical wisdom, but the contrary is the case, for the authors of *The Federalist* did not intend to philosophize, nor did they think their readers were especially interested in philosophy. In these respects, their efforts are closer to Aristotle's than to Plato's, but many will scruple over the mere mention of *The Federalist* in such lofty company.

Thus, such praise needs a vigorous defense, and mine begins with these facts. First, New York did ratify the Constitution, and the principled concerns—not to mention widespread fears—of the thinking classes were addressed with care and judgment. The sheer real-time of these essays locate them higher on the scale of political *science* than any other set of essays or dialogues, in my estimation.

As a second line of defense, I quote from the distinguished Cambridge historian, William Brock, who has edited a recent edition of *The Federalist Papers*. Brock says:

> Building with other men's bricks did not mean that *The Federalist*, or the Constitution it expounded, lacked originality. Written constitutions and fundamental laws have always been viewed

with suspicion, but every federal society has followed these American precedents.

When one contrasts the arguments developed by Madison and Hamilton and, to lesser extent, by John Jay, with the dominating political treatises of the time—and I mean with Locke, or Montesquieu, or Rousseau—the most obvious difference is that one set of arguments is actually the template for a national government, and as this is the main reason why the American "experiment," so-called, has been repeated with frequency and success by a score of newer sovereign states over the past two centuries, it's directly traceable to the fact that *The Federalist* accomplishes what it sets out to accomplish.

Finally, the contributors to *The Federalist* were thoroughly well read in political science and political philosophy, not to mention world history and law—so if they are not citing Plato and Aristotle, Rousseau and Locke, Montesquieu and Machiavelli, it is not because they are not aware of them; it is because they recognize their audience to be a various, large, pluralistic community of actual persons whose support and allegiance will depend on the success of specific arguments confronting specific criticisms. There is simply no anticipation of this in the record of political philosophy.

Perhaps another word or two should consider this matter of building with other men's bricks. Now, in the industry of thought, that, after all, is what the bricks are for. The informing question is just what it is one has built with the bricks provided by others. Most of the delegates to the Constitutional Convention were widely read, whether formally educated or not. Locke, Hume, Montesquieu, and others were a staple, of course, but I think it's more than interesting to note that the first American edition of Locke's political *Treatises* was 1773, and there wouldn't be another edition for 160 years.

Surely many had read Hume; I think Hamilton probably read Hume a little more than some of the others, though it would be Hume's historical work that would have been of general interest in any case, but we speak here of a reading public—not just of delegates who were well read, but a colonial world of surprisingly well read citizens.

When Edmund Burke addressed Parliament on the need for reconciliation with the colonies, he was eager to remind his colleagues of what he had been told by the major booksellers in London—namely, "They sell more books in the colonies than in England, and especially books dealing with law." It is useful to keep in mind, then, that the founders were setting out to constitute a government in the wake of a war of revolution that was still regarded by many as a treason. The founders and *The Federalist* offer the world the grounds of justification, and then the practical implementation of those very principles that were the grounds of justification.

Well, *The Federalist Papers*: Between October 1787 and April 1788, 85 letters, or essays, were published in New York newspapers under the name Publius by the three authors of *The Federalist*. By March 1788, interest in the essays was so great as to call for the separate publication of the first 36 of them under the heading *The Federalist*, by which they are known to this day. Of the authors, it was Hamilton who planned the project and contributed the largest share, followed closely by Madison. John Jay's contribution was slight in number of pages, but his contributions were important on the points he did address. As the two other delegates from New York opposed ratification, Hamilton, the ardent defender, hoped that these essays would win over New York.

Hamilton was not, as the expression goes, a "man of the people." He was chosen as a delegate to the Convention through the influence of powerful financial interests in New York, and he had, himself, proposed presidential powers in the Constitutional Convention that seemed to many nearly tyrannical.

James Madison, more than any other of the delegates, earns the praise for giving Americans their Constitution. He pulled things together. He was there first with the most that was needed at the time. He's a signal figure in the history of American politics. If I may say, it strikes me as the height of political and historical ignorance that the United States does not celebrate a Madison Day as a national holiday.

A Princeton graduate, Madison is the beneficiary of Princeton's new curriculum. Under the new leadership, the College of New Jersey is now under the intellectual, philosophical, and moral direction of Scotland's John Witherspoon, a promulgator of Scottish common sense philosophy and tutor to five who will come to be delegates to the Constitutional Convention. Witherspoon himself would be a signer of both the Declaration of Independence and the Constitution.

Madison completed his degree requirements at Princeton and then stayed an additional year to study with Witherspoon. So, the influence was considerable, and I refer here not to a set of mechanical interdependencies, but a broad, liberal Enlightenment outlook—rounded in a common sense philosophy that is naturalistic, scientific, and progressive. All this—and a wealth of actual political experience—is what Madison brings to *The Federalist Papers*.

Well, did we get a republic? What, after all, is a republic? Madison actually answers the question. He says that a political régime is a republic only when the government's power is derived entirely from the people, and he says, when it is "administered by persons holding their offices during pleasure, for a limited period, or during good behavior."

Now, nothing in this is new or controversial. That is, the leader of a nation that serves at someone else's pleasure. It's a term of service that is governed by a consideration of good behavior. You can have the head of state impeached, etc. There is a republic to the extent that government is self-government—that those who lead that form of government are chosen by the people, serve at their pleasure, and are required to uphold standards of conduct acceptable to those who are governed.

Alas, Madison observes, the lesson of history is that the closer something comes to approximating *that* sense of a republic, the sooner it dies. The republics that seem to make it are what he refers to as a kind of "puritanical" republic. John Adams was very much behind that view of republics. On his account, only "pure religion or austere morals" will be capable of holding a republican form of government together. Recall Adams's perplexity in a letter to Jefferson as he wonders in the matter of France how "20 million atheists can govern a country."

These concerns are at the forefront, and Madison, in Federalist 10, will distinguish between pure democracies subject to the very factionalism that leads to anarchy and the right sort of republics. In the latter, power is delegated it by the people—not, as it were, held and wielded by them. A republican system of this sort is, as he puts it, able to:

> Refine and enlarge public views, by passing them through the medium of a chosen body of citizens, whose wisdom may best discern the true interest of their country...

Moreover, as a further safeguard, a critical number of representatives must be elected, for the smaller the number, the greater the opportunity for cabals. In the same way, the Union of States is a better hedge against faction than individual states are. Indeed, against the counsel of the philosophers—Montesquieu in particular—such a government is not reserved to small and relatively unpopulous states, but may be ideal for large, and expansive, and expanding ones. Hamilton, in Federalist 9, actually discusses this notion of Montesquieu's, concluding that his positions, in the end, "are the novel refinements of an erroneous theory."

I want to pause here and say Hamilton, in this, is reflecting this general suspicion toward theoretical ways of solving practical problems. The nearly paralyzing tension, of course, arises from the need for a central government able to secure the finances and the defenses of the nation and the jealously guarded freedoms of the individual states. What, after all, is the difference between paying taxes to the British, and being taxed by a central government within the national boundaries, and why should citizens of the states commit their destiny to a document that lacks even a Bill of Rights? Isn't one tyranny being replaced by another?

In Federalist 12, Hamilton makes a strong case for the centralization of revenue, noting that:

> From the want of the fostering influence of commerce, that monarch can boast but slender revenues, and use, unable upon the strength of his own resources, to sustain a long and continued war.

In a word, it takes a nation to protect a nation, but why no Bill of Rights?

First, there's a strong principled position that if you set forth in a Bill of Rights such rights as the people have, you're in the preposterous position of giving government the right to determine what our natural rights are, and since, for a self-governing people, rights are what the people declare them to be, no one needs a list. Why put in a document what the government will grant? For to enumerate what the government will grant is to limit the rights.

However, another part of the story is this. The point of the Constitution was to constitute a nation and to give it a centrality, but not a centrality that will trump the interests of separate states—so the structuring is such that there are certain rights reserved to the individual states and their people, and these can't be abridged by the central government.

Now, why not a Bill of Rights that tells us the rights the individual has that cannot be abridged by his local government? Well, let me pause here to make this point a little clearer. You certainly have a very good reason to protect the individual against encroachments by a central government that might have tyrannical pretensions, but don't you also need to protect the individual against the encroachments of a tyrannical state? Why is there so little said about the limitations on the states?

This was something that had to be thought through by Madison, understanding that in the matter of not delineating the rights of states and the distinctive rights of their citizens, some explanation is called for. Well, it is best to specify the powers of the central government and then make clear that except for these, all the other powers are reserved to the states and the individual citizens. With a Bill of Rights in place, the Constitution secures for the individual citizen protection against abuses otherwise inflicted by a national government. What the national government cannot impose on the individual, the separate state governments cannot either, and, in any case, the states are just the resident citizens. A citizen of Maryland has voluntarily entered into that association. He can pick up and move somewhere else. It would be quite different than picking up and moving out of the United States.

It is in Federalist 46 that Madison makes all this explicit:

> The federal and state governments are in fact but different agents and trustees of the people, constituted with different powers, and designed for different purposes. The adversaries of the Constitution seem to have lost sight of the people altogether, and to have viewed these different establishments not only as mutual rivals and enemies, but as uncontrolled by any common superior. They must be told that the ultimate authority resides in the people alone, and that it will not depend merely on the comparative ambition or address of the different governments.

Ah, "We the people," but what sort of "people" is envisaged by Madison? Montesquieu taught that there are three essential forms of government, each of which calls for the shaping of a distinct characteristic in those governed. Under a despotism, it is necessary to cultivate in the people—according to Montesquieu—the character or disposition of fear. Under monarchies, the required disposition is that of honor, but with a republican form of government, Montesquieu says, what is called for is nothing less than the cultivation of virtue. Now, we find this in the Stoic outlook of Washington and many of the other founders, this recognition that a republic will succeed because we have the resources to create and preserve lives of virtue and self-sacrifice. A special kind of person is needed. Some of our people were referring to us as having natural kings and queens, natural aristocrats—not aristocratic by birth, but aristocratic by character.

Madison, in Federalist 63, leaves the realms of theory and speculation to the Montesquieus of the world, and he draws the reader's attention to actual history, the actual history of failed republics. He discusses Greece and Rome, the peculiarities of their senates and life appointments, the tendency of citizens to misplace their true interests under the enthusiasms of the moment. He puts the matter cogently. This is Madison, now:

> As the cool and deliberate sense of the community ought, in all governments, and actually will in all free governments, ultimately prevail over the views of its rulers, so there are particular moments in public affairs when the people, stimulated by some

irregular passion, or some illicit advantage, or misled by the artful misrepresentations of interested men, may call for measures which they themselves will afterwards be the most ready to lament and condemn.

Madison knows human nature to be protean, sometimes fickle, gullible, occasionally foolish. The right form of government cannot rid human nature of its defects, but it can control them long enough for persons to engage in what finally is the lifelong mission of self-correction.

There's something very powerful in *The Federalist Papers* as you read the separate contributions of Jay, Hamilton, and Madison, and that is the utter respect they have for the people whose allegiance they seek to cultivate. As with the *philosophes* and the secularization of knowledge, I would say what *The Federalist Papers* achieve is philosophy with a civic face. These are essays that require the citizen to take himself and his mission seriously, and to recognize that, all passion spent, self-governance is a risky business in which power without virtue is but a sure path to a life without a point.

Now, it is proper at this stage—*The Federalist Papers* having been reviewed, and the Constitution, which those *Federalist Papers* were designed to have ratified, considered on the whole a great work—to ask, in fact, whether the entities Madison had in mind are suitable for government of this kind, and still exist? Do you really have to be a certain kind of person? What sort of virtue is necessary in a republic of the sort that the Constitution brought about?

Whatever differences there were among the founders, there was one thing that united them all. This sort of experiment in self-governance presupposes an instructed population, products of a good education with a point, and the point being the development of citizens, the use of the resources of the community for the express purpose of creating that most unique of human entities, the citizen—the responsible, informed, inner-directed, virtuous person. This is quite different from one trailing degrees, having Ph.D.s, enjoying expertise, a great celebrity, being able to act in movies, etc. No, it's a matter of character, and the view was that that character is forged chiefly by observing good examples, and through education. Jefferson thought that public education was the absolute foundation of this.

The answer to the question, then, of "What kind of creature is right for self-governance?" is one that a worthy government works to create. One doesn't come out of the womb with the status of a virtuous citizen. As Aristotle taught, it's a lifelong labor. The authors of *The Federalist Papers* knew that. Most of the 55 sent to Philadelphia knew that. Alas, we all know that.

What Is Enlightenment? Kant on Freedom
Lecture 35

All of the interests of my reason, speculative as well as practical, combine in the three following questions: What can I know, what ought I to do, what can I hope?—Emmanuel Kant

In one of his more accessible essays—"What is enlightenment?" —Immanuel Kant (1724–1804) asked and answered a different question His answer was that enlightenment was synonymous with intellectual freedom, with expressing one's own authentic ideas, not echoing the thoughts of others. "Enlightenment is man's emergence from his self-incurred immaturity… For enlightenment of this kind, all that is needed is freedom. And the freedom in question is the most innocuous form of all: freedom to make public use of one's reason in all matters." Kant is, at once, the culmination of Enlightenment thought and the author of a philosophy that would set worrisome limits on the entire Enlightenment project.

Kant's *Critique of Pure Reason* credits Hume with awakening the author from his "dogmatic slumber." Hume argued convincingly that that everything we know is the product of experience. The concept of causation should be understood chiefly as a kind of habitual mode of mental operation. Morality is the domain of passions and sentiments, grounded in considerations of self-interest and utility. Kant can also be shown to have been influenced by Reid's concept of common sense. Kant's *Critique* (not a broadside or polemic against reason but an inquiry into it, into what can be known using our rational resources and what cannot) takes up these challenges.

In his "first critique" (the second is the *Critique of Practical Reason* and the third, his *Critique of Judgment*), Kant agrees with Hume in insisting that all of our knowledge arises from experience. However, he makes a fundamental distinction, saying it is a mistake to assume that because our knowledge *arises* from experience, that it is *grounded* in experience. According to Hume's theory of causal concepts, we come to regard A as the cause of B, when A and B have been constantly conjoined in experience. This is not the conclusion of an argument but merely a habit of the mind.

In Kant's terminology, cognitive or epistemic holdings that are not the result of experience are referred to as "pure." *Pure* in Kant's sense refers to what is non-empirical. A *Critique of Pure Reason* means a critical examination of the forms of rationality that could not come from experience but make up the framework within which experience is possible. There cannot be experience except by way of time and space. Thus, Kant reaches the concept of the pure (non-empirical) intuitions of time and space. Kant uses the word *intuitions* to mean a necessary precondition for something else to come about. Logically, then, this precondition must be prior to all experience—Kant's famous terminology *a priori*—or there could be no experiences.

Kant argues that there is something fundamentally lacking in Hume's account of "knowledge" and experience. Again, all knowledge may be said to arise out of experience but may not be grounded in experience. In his "Analytic of Concepts," Kant seeks to provide the framework for all knowledge. He contends that in all instances, knowledge involves a judgment, formed within a universal categorical framework that includes entities that could not possibly be gained by experience.

Kant presents four "Pure Categories of the Understanding" that could not be "given" in experience and that admit of no possible exceptions: There are categories of *quantity*: unity, plurality, and totality. There are categories of *quality*: reality, negation, and limitation. There are categories of *modality*: possibility, existence, and necessity. And there are categories of *relation*: inherence, causality, community, and correlation.

Certain categories may be given by experience, but nothing in experience "gives" *totality* or *necessity*, for example, we can know unity, and we can know plurality, but nothing in experience allows us to know *totality*. Nonetheless, we know, without counting, that there is an infinite number of integers. Likewise, nothing in the world of sensible matter can be known to be *necessarily* the case—anything could imaginably be different. Experience can only lead to inferences of greater or lesser probability. But even those inferences are intelligible only within the framework of necessity: That is, something is "probable" to the extent that it is not *necessary*.

If, however, we were beings of a different sort, would the categories be different? Do they arise out of our natures? No, they are the necessary conditions for knowledge of anything. As the pure intuitions are the necessary forms of experience, the pure categories are the necessary forms of knowledge.

Kant claims that Hume is wrong to say that no "synthetic" propositions can be known to be true *a priori*, only "analytic" ones. What is meant by these terms? An *analytic* proposition is one in which subject-term and predicate-term are essentially synonymous: All bachelors are unmarried men. The truth of analytic propositions is known *a priori*, which is to say, prior to, and independently of, experience, for what is involved here are mere truths about words. A *synthetic* proposition is a factual statement about items and events in the world: Bill is wearing shoes. In Hume's epistemology, no synthetic proposition can be known to be true except by way of experience, that is, *a posteriori*.

The Kantian rebuttal depends on the pure intuitions and pure categories.

- Every experience we shall ever have is within the intuited framework of space and time.

- All our knowledge claims will match with the categories of quantity, quality, and so on.

- Thus, every empirical statement we make will have certain properties that can be established *a priori*.

- Therefore, we *can* make synthetic statements whose truth is known *a priori*; for instance, "Every experience will take place in space and time."

Forms of knowledge, like forms of experience, are not themselves given in experience but determine the ordering, organizing, and patterning of all possible knowledge. Thus, in a manner of speaking, for Hume to be right, Kant has to be right. The Kantian *a priori* framework is required for Hume's account of causation and knowledge to work. When Kant grants that Hume was right to conclude that all knowledge comes from experience, he is recording his own modest credentials as an empiricist. He is also stating his position to be in the province of the ideal theorist, as Reid used the term.

The world known and the world knowable is the world as processed by the organs and principles of perception. What we know of the external world factually takes the form of *phenomena*. The question is: How accurately does our mental representation of reality reflect actual reality? Kant makes a distinction between phenomena and the realm beyond experience, which he refers to as *noumena*—the thing as it really is. The phenomenon is the experience it creates in a percipient. The knowable is confined to the categorical framework within which all elements of the understanding are located. Reason can step outside of this and, thus, has a certain reach superior to the understanding, but its reach is not limitless.

In his "Analytic of Concepts," Kant seeks to provide the framework for all knowledge.

There is a lot of Hume in Kant and very little Kant in Hume. But in Kant, we begin to see what a rationalist critique of a systematic and relentless empiricism looks like—it looks a lot like Kant's first critique. ∎

Suggested Reading

Kant, I. *Critique of Pure Reason*. N. K. Smith, trans. St. Martin's, 1965.

Questions to Consider

1. Given that all knowledge is shaped and determined by the pure categories and the pure intuitions and that we know only *phenomena* rather than *noumena*, explain whether Kant doesn't end up *supporting* Hume.

2. Conclude whether Kant's categories are mere descriptions of "human" ways of knowing or formal features of knowledge as such.

What Is Enlightenment? Kant on Freedom
Lecture 35—Transcript

> All of the interests of my reason, speculative as well as practical, combine in the three following questions: What can I know, what ought I to do, what can I hope?

These were the ultimate questions to which Emmanuel Kant devoted most of his adult life. He died in 1804. Twenty years earlier, he asked and answered a different question in one of his more accessible essays: "*Was ist Aufklarung?*"—"What Is Enlightenment?" and his answer was that enlightenment is synonymous with intellectual freedom, with a special form of maturity that finds one expressing his own authentic ideas, rather than echoing the thoughts of others. He put it this way:

> Enlightenment is man's emergence from his self-incurred immaturity…For enlightenment of this kind, all that is needed is freedom. And the freedom in question is the most innocuous form of all: freedom to make public use of one's reason in all matters.

The question that arises is whether the best way to understand Kantian philosophy is as something of the culmination of Enlightenment thought, or a philosophy that brings down the curtain on the Enlightenment, showing that many of its loftier aspirations are simply impossible because grounded in a certain kind of mistake. Well, let's see.

Kant wrote three major critical treatises. The so-called "first critique" is his *Critique of Pure Reason*. The second is the *Critique of Practical Reason*, and the third is what he called the *Critique of Judgment*.

The *Critique of Pure Reason: Kritik der Reinen Vernunft*. The German *kritik* is not to be understood as a mere negative appraisal, but as a close analysis intended to reveal the assets and limitations of its subject.

In his first critique, then, his *Critique of Pure Reason*, Kant is engaged in a critical examination of the nature and the limits of reason itself, an inquiry into the extent to which we can solve problems of knowledge—the problem of knowledge—in virtue of the rational resources that are available to us. Just what is the reach of reason? What are the limits imposed on reason, and, where reason leaves off, well, what else might there be to serve in its place? What else might we have any right to hope for?

Similarly, the *Critique of Practical Reason*. This is an analysis of the grounding of ethics, the principles by which choices are made among morally weighty alternatives, and the *Critique of Judgment* affords the same, but now in the context of aesthetics.

Here you have in Kant, then—if I pause just for a moment to sort of encapsulate these three colossal works—an address directly to the problem of knowledge, then, the problem of conduct, and then, the domain of aesthetics, but the domain of aesthetics in the sense of how we go about making judgments of what is right; what is apt; what is harmonious; what, in fact, instantiates universal principles; etc. These, then, are monumental works—all, by the way, extremely difficult in his language, and in at least one other, English.

Kant himself was well read, but he was not well traveled. There, he lived in Koenigsburg all his life. It is said that he never went more than 50 miles from his front door, a man of very methodical habits. It's well known that people could set their clocks to the time Kant took lunch. He did have a housemaid. There is a student whose memoir records the fact that Professor Kant could be a quite affable and genial host, and that indeed, of all things, Kant had a sense of humor. Now, I should say that evidence for Kant's humor is not abundant in his philosophical writings, but then, as the comedian says, I guess you would have had to be there.

If I could just pause one moment, I do know one Kant joke. It may be the only joke that Kant ever told. I don't know; it shows up in his anthropological writings, where he's making a distinction between emotion and passion. Now, passion is something that can rise quickly. It's an unnatural state, etc., as opposed to the rather stable feature of one's personality, and to illustrate the effect passion can have, he says: "The young man, passionately in love with the lady of his choice, sees her no imperfection whatever," and then comes Kant's only joke, at least the only one I know about. He says: "This condition of blindness generally clears up about three weeks after marriage," so that is the Kant joke. I can guarantee my audience that I shall not attempt another. He may not have, either.

The *Critique of Pure Reason* is a work that comes about, Kant says, because he has been awakened from his "dogmatic slumber" by—whom? By David Hume. Now, Bertrand Russell, writing as bombs were falling on London, would not be very kind to the Prussian Kant, declaring that having been thus awakened by Hume's writings, Kant quickly returned to a state of philosophical somnolence. Well, Kant was awakened to the benefit of all philosophy in general. Now, what is it in Hume that would awaken one from one's dogmatic slumbers, and what's the dogma to which, in our slumbers, we are more or less attached to, or controlled by?

Hume argued convincingly that everything we know is the product of experience, that such a basic concept as that on which all science and inquiry will depend, the concept of *causation*, is to be understood chiefly as a kind of habitual mode of mental operation. More, that the *moral* domain, properly understood, is the domain of passions and sentiments, grounded in considerations of self-interest and utility—so this is the stuff of which wake-up calls are made.

There is circumstantial evidence supporting the proposition that Kant was well aware of Hume's local critics, especially Reid. He mentions them dismissively in the first critique, thinking that they would counter Hume's philosophy by consulting nothing more substantial than "common sense." Now, Kant did not read English, and the translation of Reid's *Inquiry* that would have been available to him had been anonymously translated, by the way, and rendered "common sense" as *gemeine menschenverstand*, the way you might talk about a common criminal—so, if Kant wanted to have it his way, he could have regarded Hume's critics as relying on *gemeine*, "common" in the sense of very common, vulgar, the usual, you see?—mere consensus, that sort of thing, what the great generality of people happen to have as an opinion. In this, he grossly underestimated Reid, and there were academic political reasons for this, which I shan't go into.

Nonetheless, we do know that Kant knew better, and we know that in Kant's time, German scholarship was in regular contact with summaries, redactions, of major works in the English-speaking world of philosophy, and by the way, especially the world of Scottish philosophy. So the ink was not long dry on major Scottish treatises before summaries of these works would be available in German, and as it happens, Kant can be shown to have been influenced by Reid. Indeed, there are aspects of Kant's moral theory that more or less track the Reidian notion of moral first principles. This, clearly, is the subject for another occasion, and of much, much closer study than would be called for in a general lecture.

Now, getting to Hume. Well, starting with the first critique, Kant agrees with Hume in insisting that all knowledge *arises* from experience. Obviously, you can't know whether George has his shoes on unless you look and see. This isn't some sort of ratiocinative or introspective procedure for answering questions like that. Kant says it's a mistake to assume, however, that because our knowledge arises from experience, that it is *grounded* in experience.

Now, this is a distinction that is fundamental. There is a difference between something arising from something else and something being based necessarily on something else. How does Kant make the point?

Let's begin with Hume's theory of causal concepts. According to Hume, we come to regard A as the cause of B, when A and B have been constantly conjoined in experience—that is, when the associative principles of repetition and contiguity, and cause and effect, have worked their magic. At that point, the mind is so constituted that the inevitable conclusion it reaches is that A is the cause of B.

Now, it is not the conclusion of an argument. It's just a habit of the mind. We have the case of billiard balls: ball one hits ball two. One moves, and hitting ball two, two moves. Now, witnessing such conjunctions, says Hume, one cannot see "a third term betwixt them." Causation is not visible on the billiard table; rather, it is an idea formed in the mind as a result of constant conjunctions. Now, this was all rehearsed in my lecture on Hume. All right.

Kant recognizes in this account a fundamental and necessary precondition not addressed by Hume. Billiard ball one moves. Then, billiard ball two moves. That's what succession is all about. First, one event, then another event. Now, clearly, that "third term," this time is then and is also not on the billiard table. We can't look at a billiard table and see temporality. We can't see time or feel time. That is to say, there cannot be succession, and therefore, there cannot be constant conjunctions unless time is present as a categorical framework for all experience. Time, then, is one of the necessary preconditions for the temporal ordering of events in time itself, and it is not given in any empirical experience. In other words, time is not a stimulus that works on a sense organ. Time cannot be provided by experience. It's not a "something" out there that stimulates me.

In Kant's terminology, cognitive or epistemic holdings that are not the result of experience are referred to as "pure." *Pure* in Kant's sense refers to what is non-empirical—so a *Critique of Pure Reason* means a critical examination of the very forms of rationality that could not possibly be provided by experience, but, nonetheless, constitute the framework within which experience becomes possible. I shall return to this more than once in today's lecture.

Now, remaining with Hume's billiard table, we can ask: "What else is not given in experience?" If Hume refers to something as being seen before him, as in, "I see a billiard table before me," well, the question that arises is: "By what faculty or sense do we come to experience space itself?" Space as such is not "given" in experience. Objects are in space, but space is not a stimulus. It is not an object. What is it then?

It's something that must be present for there to be experience at all. All experience presupposes a spatial-temporal framework. There cannot be experience except by way of time and space. Thus does Kant reach the concept of what he calls the "pure intuitions" of time and space, "pure" in the sense of non-empirical.

Now, *intuitions* is one of those words that in both German and English can give rise to great confusion. Let's just say that what Kant is referring to is a necessary precondition for something else to come about. He refers to the pure intuitions as being *a priori*—*a priori*, prior to any and every experience. So the *a priori*, pure intuitions of time and space become the necessary preconditions for there to be experiences of just the sort required by Hume's theory. Now, remember, *a priori* here is not just a matter of "prior in time." It is that conceptually, logically, something must be for something else to take place. The concept of causation is not simply a habit of the mind, then, based upon certain common experiences. The concept of causation must be grounded in something more fundamental, and grounded in that which experience itself could not possibly convey. You get the point. "Grounded in" as distinct from "arising from."

Now, if time and space are the necessary preconditions for there to be any and all possible experience, are there any necessary preconditions for our having any understanding of the world, any understanding at all?

Now, Locke's *Essay on the Human Understanding* says: "How comes the mind to be furnished? I answer in a word—from experience," and Locke goes on to argue, as I mentioned in my lecture on Locke, that these complex ideas are formed associatively. Hume carries the notion further in the empiricist tradition.

Kant, however, insists that the scheme won't work because it fails to capture the very form of the understanding. Understanding does not take the form of a constellation of merely and haphazardly connected events that just happen to be experienced frequently. No. All of our understanding, all of our knowledge claims, all of the epistemic claims we ever make—have certain formal properties about them. That is, they all take place within a categorical framework that includes entities that could not possibly be gained through experience.

In that part of the first critique that Kant calls the "Analytic of Concepts," he seeks to provide the framework for all knowledge. He contends that in all instances, knowledge involves a judgment, and that judgments are formed within a universal categorical framework. It is in the "Metaphysical Deduction," as he calls it, that Kant presents his fourfold table of the "Pure Categories of the Understanding." Remember, again, now, "pure" means non-experiential, not given in experience, not empirical—so the "Pure

Categories of the Understanding" turn out to be those of *quantity*, *quality*, *modality*, and *relation*.

Now, let's begin by considering the category of quantity. All of our quantitative judgments have this in common. They are based either on the concept of unity, or the concept of plurality, or the concept of *totality*. One, many, all—so all quantitative judgments answer to that categorical framework. Something is either a unity, a plurality, or a totality.

Now, if all you had were fingers and toes, you'd have no trouble with quantities, let's say, up to 20. You'd have no trouble with unity, and you'd have no trouble with plurality, but there is nothing that the senses can convey about the totality or universality. Everyone knows that there's no number so large that you cannot add one to it, but nobody knows this by counting.

If I can pause for a moment and reflect on something of a joke that the cognitive psychologist Piaget years ago made. He said that the radical empiricist believes that the series of positive integers was discovered one at a time.

Now, past experience will never give one the number infinity. Infinity isn't a number, so you're probably not going to get one—you're not going to get an infinite series by counting. It's not a probability estimate, either. Rather, the understanding has this category of quantity within it that all empirical data seek a place within and an order within. It's a categorical framework that includes infinity, plurality, and totality.

Now, consider the category of modality. Something either is actually the case, or it is possibly the case, or it is necessarily the case. Now, take the modal category of necessity, and think about it for a minute. If A is greater than B, and B is greater than C, then necessarily, A is greater than C.

If all men are mortal, and Socrates is a man, necessarily, Socrates is mortal. Now, consider the certainties of logic and mathematics, generative of what we call "necessary truths." Is it not obvious that nothing in the world of sensible matter is what it is necessarily? You could not possibly get the concept of necessity from sense experience. Nothing experienced in the sensible world is of such a nature that it could not be different—so the concept of "necessarily X" can't possibly be the gift of experience. It is not an empirical, but a pure category of the understanding, do you see?

Now, it might be argued that what Kant is providing here is merely a list of descriptions that we use for our experiences, and these are somehow reflections of how the brain organizes things. That is, let me pause here to say, suppose you wanted to grant all this much to Kant, but you say: "Look, he couldn't know this, having died in 1804, and what he's really accounting for is the particular manner in which the nervous system processes inputs."

Well, although he died in 1804, Kant actually did address the possibility in the first critique—whether the best way to understand the categories of the understanding is in terms of the particular organization we have, Hume's old "constitutions" of our nature, the kinds of beings that we are, but as Kant points out, if that were the case, then the pure categories of the understanding would merely be contingent. That is to say, they would simply be contingently tied to a particular kind of cognitive being—a different brain and the categories would be entirely different, but Kant has shown through his analysis that call judgment requires a categorical framework necessarily.

His theory is not about how we go about describing and ordering things, but the necessary framework for all understanding. It wouldn't matter if you were a Martian or anything else. Quantity, quality, modality, and relation constitute the necessary epistemic framework within which there can be understanding. The pure categories determine the conditions under which there can be any understanding of the world at all. It is therefore not a matter of the peculiarities of the particular nervous system. It has to do with the nature of what can be understood, and how.

The pure categories of the understanding are not themselves generative of content. Kant is not specifying in advance how many quantitative things we can know, or whether we can ever know the difference between something being certainly true or merely highly probable. These constitute the forms of the understanding, just as the pure intuitions of time and space constitute the form of experience. What Kant is providing is the form. The form of all understanding, the form of all experience, is by way of the pure intuitions of time and space. The form of the understanding is by the pure categories of the understanding—so Kant is not specifying what experiences we're going to have done, only that if there is to be an experience, necessarily there must be the pure intuitions of time and space.

Similarly—and again, Kant is not specifying what the understanding comes to have, only that the form of all understanding is in terms of the pure categories of the understanding, and these are not empirical.

Well, back, now, to Hume and the wake-up call. Hume may be understood as claiming the following: There are two classes of things we can know about. One class involves the relations among ideas, and the other, matters of fact. Now, this division is sometimes called "Hume's fork." When we declare that "All bachelors are unmarried men," which is, by the way, necessarily true, we are expressing no more than a relation between two ideas—namely, the idea of "bachelor" and that of "unmarried man," but, of course, this is an utterly uninforming truth; it's a mere tautology. It's a truth by definition.

Now, propositions, where the meaning of the subject-term is contained in the predicate-term, as in "All bachelors are unmarried men"—what in philosophy are called "analytic" propositions—well, this simply shows relationships between ideas and analytic propositions are true, and necessarily true; their truth can be known entirely independently of experience—so that we say, they can be known to be true *a priori*.

Here's a proposition: "Bill is wearing shoes." Now, that's a different kind of proposition. There isn't anything in the subject-term, "Bill," that includes in the predicate-term, in the meaning of the predicate-term, "wearing shoes." Bill could be shoeless. He could be barefoot. He might not have feet—so this is a claim about the factual content of the world.

If you needed a brief summary to Hume's solution to the problem of knowledge, it would be Hume claiming this: Statements of the sort "Bill is wearing shoes" present facts about the world. They are "synthetic" propositions, and their truth can never be known prior to the relevant observation or experience. Hume insists, then, that no synthetic proposition can be known to be true *a priori*. That is, any factual statement about the world has as a condition of its truth a relevant observation. You cannot establish its truth prior to some relevant experience, some relevant test—so the Humean epistemology, the Humean solution, as it were, to the problem of knowledge is that there can be no synthetic proposition whose truth is knowable *a priori*.

Now, Kant's rebuttal is by way of the pure intuitions of space and time, and the categories of the understanding. The form of all experience is given by the pure intuitions of time and space, and the form of all knowledge by pure categories of the understanding. As this refers to things in the external world, including Bill wearing shoes, all empirical statements that we make will necessarily have certain properties that can be established *a priori* by way of the pure intuitions of time and space, and the pure categories of the understanding.

Now, let me pause here. What Kant is setting out to establish is that there are some synthetic propositions the proof of which can be known *a priori*— namely, that whatever experience you're about to have, it takes place within a spatial framework, and that is going to be a fact of the experience.

Now, if that is the case, then I am able to offer such synthetic propositions as this: Any event that takes place takes place in time, or has a limited duration, or has either a unity or plurality or totality. Now, these are actually going to be statements about real world events and, described this way, their truth, we might say, is known *a priori*.

The forms of knowledge, like the forms of experience, are not themselves given in experience, but they do determine the ordering, organizing, and patterning of all possible knowledge, and so, in a manner of speaking, for Hume to be right, Kant has to be right. That is, the Kantian *a priori* framework seems to be a requisite in order for Hume's account of causation and knowledge to work.

Now, when Kant grants that Hume got this much right, that all of our knowledge arises out of experience, Kant is already recording his modest credentials as an empiricist, and he is also stating his own position to be very much in the patrimony of the ideal theorist, as Reid used the term, from

Aristotle on. What we know of the external world factually takes the form of *phenomena*—phenomena meaning "objects of perception." The world known and the world knowable is the world as processed by the organs and principles of perception, but there's got to be something behind this realm of phenomena, and the question is: "How accurately, how veridically, how validly, does the mental representation of reality that we have reflect the actual reality?"

Kant here makes a distinction between the world as it is experienced, which is the world of phenomena, and what must stand behind the experience, which he calls the realm of *noumena*, that noumenal realm of things as, in themselves, they really are. It is not for us to ever be able to penetrate through the phenomena, to the noumenal level, and so, there is in this aspect of Kant's philosophy, what we can know and the validity of our knowledge claims.

There's a lot of Hume in Kant and very little Kant in Hume. But in Kant, you begin to see what a rationalist rebuttal of a systematic and relentless empiricism looks like. It looks like what Kant serves up in the first critique.

Moral Science and the Natural World
Lecture 36

"Autonomy" is a word whose Greek roots are *auto*, or self-reflexive, and *nomos*, which is law. The morally autonomous person is not one who is lawless, but one whose freedom is governed by laws he gives himself.

Hume had made a strong case for the proposition that the grounds on which we judge things to be good or bad is not some abstract external moral reality, but the manner in which the event in question affects us cellularly and physiologically. Hume's moral theory arises from his epistemology. Once the problem of knowledge is "solved" in favor of impressions and ideas, moral issues can be collapsed into questions about impressions and ideas. But "since morals, therefore, have an influence on the actions and affections, it follows that they cannot be deriv'd from reason, and that because reason alone, as we have already prov'd, can never have any such influence." "Morals excite passions, and produce or prevent actions. Reason of itself is utterly impotent in this particular. The rules of morality, therefore, are not conclusions of our reason."

The principal adversary to latter-day versions of utilitarianism is in the form of moral theories patterned after Kant's and referred to as *deontological* theories. Central to any deontological moral theory is the idea that it takes the imperative of certain moral precepts to be unconditional (that is, a given action is right or wrong under all circumstances). Deontological moral theories are explicitly opposed to utilitarian theories, to the idea that something is right because it achieves good or desirable outcomes.

Kant accepted an essentially scientific conception of human nature but rejected the proposition that the merely natural dimensions of human life exhaust the characteristics of our humanity. However, in addition to being subject to the laws of nature, human beings are also *rational* beings. What that means is that in addition to occupying the natural realm, we occupy what Kant calls the *intelligible realm*. In the intelligible realm, we account for events not by invoking physical causes but by examining reasons.

We understand the course of action taken in the intelligible realm by understanding the reasons that guide the action.

The other feature central to Kant's moral theory is autonomy of the will. If our actions were entirely determined by our physical constitutions, they would simply be reactions. Autonomy is the necessary condition for any moral ascriptions or judgments to apply to any actions.

Kant argues that we arrive at the concept of freedom via our intuitive awareness of moral law. The means by which the concept is reached is rational, not empirical. There can be no "scientific" proof of freedom. "Laws of freedom" sounds contradictory, but only because one thinks of laws in the scientific sense of strict determinism. The morally autonomous person is one whose freedom is governed by laws he gives himself.

The reasons to act in one way or another are of two sorts: hypothetical imperatives and categorical imperatives. If the choice of one alternative over another is made to attain a specific end, it is called a *hypothetical imperative*. Hypothetical imperatives are tied to a particular context and to the needs and desires of natural creatures under the press of the need to survive, to avoid pain and gain pleasure. Decisions thus grounded are non-moral, because they arise from our natures not as rational beings but merely as human beings: They are essentially reactions.

The *categorical imperative*, on the other hand, declares an action to be morally necessary in itself, without reference to any purpose. Morality begins with a rational and autonomous being in the intelligible realm, where we are called on to have reasons for action. We must find a rule or precept or principle that guides actions of a given kind and that is universal.

The categorical imperative is not tied to a particular desire or impulse or motive; rather, it asserts its own moral authority. One of the characteristics of a moral precept is that it's universalizable, not tied to a particular condition and, hence, dependent on the contingent facts of the natural world.

Moral maxims, as reasons for acting, are applicable to all situations in which generically that given kind of action might take place. The categorical imperative is not tied to a particular desire or impulse or motive; rather, it asserts its own moral authority. The authority of the imperative is contained in the maxim itself, not something that it brings about, not some contingent outcome.

John Stuart Mill believed that Kant's categorical imperative was a license to perform absolutely hideous acts. Kant's pure categories of the understanding do not supply content but the framework governing the possibility of understanding. Kant advised that we "act in such a way that the maxim of your action would, if you were able, be instituted as a universal law of nature." What troubled Mill was the prospect of, say, an arsonist invoking the categorical imperative and wishing to install as a universal law of nature the successful destruction of property by fire.

> **Deontological moral theories are explicitly opposed to utilitarian theories, to the idea that something is right because it achieves good or desirable outcomes.**

This fear can arise only from a misunderstanding of Kant's entire argument. Any ignoble end or any end whatever tied to considerations of pleasure or keen desire or emotion comes under the heading of a hypothetical imperative, not a categorical imperative. The imperative is a law the will gives to itself. There are sufficient resources within Kantian moral thought to rule out arson as a candidate universal law!

Kant offers another version of the categorical imperative: "Man is never merely a means to an end, but always an end unto himself." To use another person as a means or a tool is to deny that person the very moral autonomy on which "right" and "wrong" become possible. To do so would mean that you qualify for the same treatment. As Abraham Lincoln said, "As I would not be a slave, I would not be a master." Kant is famous for concluding from this that one must never lie. If Smith lies to Jones to get Jones to do something that Jones would not do if properly informed, Smith trumps Jones's moral autonomy, thus violating the categorical imperative.

Kant's epitaph summarizes much about him: "The starry sky above him, the moral law within him." Kant gives us moral law, not as a means to seek pleasure or avoid pain, but as a way of doing the right thing and, thus, substantiating ourselves as moral beings. ■

Suggested Reading

Kant, I. *Critique of Practical Reason*. Cambridge, 1997.

———. *Groundwork of the Metaphysic of Morals*. H. Paton, trans. Cambridge University Press, 1998.

Questions to Consider

1. A hypothetical: Only five persons can survive in the lifeboat, but there are six still alive after the ocean liner has sunk. Summarize how Kant's moral precepts would determine the course of action.

2. If you would not kill five innocent persons to save another, explain whether you would kill a thousand innocent persons to save the world.

Moral Science and the Natural World
Lecture 36—Transcript

In the previous lecture, I mentioned Kant's claim that Hume's philosophy had awakened him from his dogmatic slumbers. Now, that was at the level of epistemology, the level of knowledge, understanding, reason, but there was much more in Hume that awakened the whole world from dogmatic slumbers, particularly at the level of morality.

Hume had made a very strong case for the proposition that our moral reasonings, so to speak, are based finally on considerations of emotion, sentiment, utility—that the grounds on which we judge things to be good or bad is not some abstract external moral reality, but the manner in which the event in question affects us cellularly, physiologically. The issue of morals is taken up in Book III of his *Treatise*, and right at the outset, in Part I, Section I, he provides as a major heading—Hume, now—"Moral distinctions not deriv'd from reason." Nothing could be clearer.

Hume's moral theory arises from his epistemology. Once the problem of knowledge is "solved," as at war, in favor of impressions and ideas, which is Hume's solution, moral issues can be collapsed into questions about, what? Impressions and ideas—but treated in these terms, Hume contends, there would be little left of what we take to be the business of morals, which is to guide our actions. He makes his case with characteristic clarity that:

> Since morals, therefore, have an influence on the actions and affections, it follows that they cannot be deriv'd from reason, and that because reason alone, as we have already prov'd, can never have any such influence. Morals excite passions, and produce or prevent actions. Reason of itself is utterly impotent in this particular. The rules of morality, therefore, are not conclusions of our reason.

Again, then, what could be plainer? No reason can move a muscle or cause a gland to secrete anything. Events that arouse in us feelings of revulsion are judged to be wrong in virtue of the fact that we respond to them that way, and those events that conduce to human pleasure and happiness are, on the whole, judged to be morally right, and morally right for that reason.

Summed across all actions and possibilities, then, what we judge to be the morally acceptable course of action is the one that answers to the criterion of utility, general usefulness, pleasure.

The business of moral philosophy, then, is not to attempt to deduce moral first principles. The business of moral philosophy is to come to grips with the nature of human nature, and to recognize the obstacles, to recognize the challenges that that nature faces in a complex world, how it uses its own natural resources to frame forms of government, moral propositions, to frame moral propositions, to put together moral systems. Recall the subtitle of Hume's *Treatise*. I remind you again of the subtitle: *Being an Attempt to Introduce the Experimental Method of Reasoning into Moral Subjects*.

The grounding of morality with respect to considerations of happiness and usefulness has proven to be profoundly influential, the idea that morals match up with utility and pleasure. The roots are very deep in philosophy; they extend back to the Epicureans. Now, the principal adversary to latter-day versions of utilitarianism is in the form of moral theories patterned after Kant's and referred to as *deontological* theories. The adjective is derived from the Greek *deon*, meaning "duty." What is central to any deontological moral theory is the idea that it takes the imperative of certain moral precepts to be unconditional, such that an action of a certain kind is "right" or "wrong" under any and all circumstances, whatever the consequences. That is to say, find the right moral precept, and that moral precept is applicable in every imaginable situation—so considerations of utility, sentiment, emotion, and the like are entirely irrelevant.

Deontological moral theories are explicitly opposed to utilitarian theories, explicitly opposed to the idea that something is right because it happens to achieve good or desirable outcomes, that something is right because—as it were—in your heart, you know it's right.

Now, Kant had a lifelong interest in the sciences, and he certainly was not at war with an essentially scientific conception of human nature, but what he did reject was the proposition that the merely natural dimensions of human life exhaust the characteristics, exhaust the essence, of our humanity. Granting that human beings are, in one sense, natural objects is different from concluding that they are no more than this. Surely, if a human being is dropped from a height—my favorite example—the rate of descent will be 32 feet per second. As purely physical entities, human beings are subject to all of the causal laws of the physical world. Kant knows that.

However, human beings are also *rational* beings, and what that means for Kant is that in addition to occupying the natural realm, as all physical entities do, human beings who are rational as such occupy what Kant calls the *intelligible realm*. In the intelligible realm, we account for events not by invoking physical causes but by examining reasons. That is to say, you understand the course of action taken in the intelligible realm by understanding the reasons that have guided the action.

Now, the other feature central to Kant's moral theory is the autonomy of the will. There could be no morality at all, says Kant, except insofar as we have the freedom to act or not act as an expression of our authentic will to do so, or to forbear from doing so. If our actions were entirely determined by our physical constitution, then we could neither be praised nor blamed for the actions. Our actions, then, would simply be reactions.

The grounds on which we become subject to moral judgment, moral censure—any kind of moral judgment at all—are grounds of autonomy. There must be sufficient freedom for us to be charged with wrongdoing, or praised for doing what is regarded as virtuous or worthy. Autonomy, then, is the necessary condition for there to be moral ascriptions or judgments of any kind.

Now, Kant is quite direct in saying that the kind of freedom at issue here can't be proven empirically, but it is established in another way. In the preface to his *Critique of Practical Reason*, Kant puts the matter this way:

> Inasmuch as the reality of the concept of freedom is proved by an apodictic law of practical reason, it is the keystone of the whole system of pure reason, and all other concepts, those of God and immortality, which, as being mere ideas, now attach themselves to this concept and by it, obtain objective reality; that is to say, their

possibility is proved by the fact that freedom actually exists, for this idea is revealed by the moral law.

Now, here, let me say that this is a difficult passage in Kant, and it is a distillation of a highly detailed argument that includes as a factual premise the presence within us, which is to say our conscious awareness of a moral law. It is this, however, that grounds the concept of freedom, for were there not such a law apparent to consciousness, the concept of freedom itself would be unintelligible.

It is useful here to recall in this connection Reid's critique of Hume on the matter of causation. Reid argued that the mere phenomena of constantly paired events would never, by themselves, generate the concept of a causal sequence. It's only because of our intuitive understanding of ourselves as having the power to bring things about that we are then led to the belief that events external to our will are similarly brought about by some sort of power.

Kant's argument for freedom is similar. It is owing to our intuitive awareness of the moral law that we arrive at the concept of freedom. The means by which the concept is reached is rational, not empirical. There can be no "scientific" proof of freedom. What form do scientific proofs take? They generally take identifying the laws of causality, but how unsuited, then, would empirical methods be for identifying the laws of freedom?

Let me stop here to clarify this point. Suppose you wanted a scientific proof that there is freedom. Well, what goes into a scientific proof? What goes into a scientific proof is establishing the determinative laws that make something the way it is. Well, this is so contrary to the very idea of freedom that you would simply be using not just the wrong instrument to establish whether there is freedom or not, but you would be using one that defies the very concept of it.

However, Kant does talk about "laws of freedom," even though that sounds contradictory, but it only sounds contradictory because one thinks of laws in the scientific sense of strict determinism.

Now, "autonomy" is a word whose Greek roots are *auto*, or self-reflexive, and *nomos*, which is law. The morally autonomous person is not one who is lawless, but one whose freedom is governed by laws he gives himself. Do you see? Though not constrained by the laws of physics in this domain, the will is not anarchic. Were it lawless, Kant says, it would dissolve into an absurdity. Rather—and let me take another passage from Kant: "A free will, and a will subject to moral laws, are one and the same." This much ground covered, let's return to the utilitarian and passion-based moral theory advocated by Hume, and examine Kant's critique of it.

Now, suppose I say something like this: "It's a beastly hot day, and I've been out gardening all afternoon. The throat is parched. Well, now I see a nice, tall glass of lemonade, and I am very thirsty. If I am to slake this thirst, well, then, necessarily I must drink something, and in this case, that's the only thing available. I must consume that glass of lemonade." Thus, there is a connection there, a kind of causal connection, between eliminating the thirst and consuming the lemonade.

Now, I am operating in this circumstance under a kind of imperative. If I would slake my thirst, necessarily I must drink something. Let's say in this case, I must drink the lemonade.

Kant refers to all such cases as governed by what he calls a *hypothetical imperative*. It's a phrase you can find in Aristotle, too—a "hypothetical imperative." A hypothetical imperative decrees the following: "If you would achieve this specific outcome, necessarily you must do that." Now, Kant argues that hypothetical imperatives of this sort are invariably grounded in our natural being, where we are subject to the causal laws of science. That is to say, hypothetical imperatives are tied up with conditions of particular motives and wants, arising within us as natural entities, as physical systems.

We have the capacity to have thirst, pain, hunger; we can be overheated. These are conditions that descend on us in virtue of our being creatures of nature. In these respects, we are under some sort of coercive, even non-rational influence when acting on the basis of such motives and impulses— the coercive press of hunger, of thirst, frustration, visceral sensations, antagonism, worry, fear, intense pain.

Now, in his *Fundamental Principles of the Metaphysics of Morals*, Kant addresses these hypothetical imperatives, noting that such an imperative—and here's a passage from Kant with respect to hypothetical imperatives—"only says that the action is good for some purpose, possible or actual," and he contrasts this with what he comes to call the *categorical imperative*: "which declares an action to be objectively necessary in itself without reference to any purpose, i.e., without any other end."

Note, then, the distinction between hypothetical and categorical imperatives.

Now, noting further how the ends and aims of life change with circumstances and possibilities, Kant reduces choices in these contexts to prevailing hypothetical imperatives. Joining Aristotle as well as Hume, Kant finds an anchor-point amidst the shifting choices of a lifetime:

> There is one end which may be assumed to be actually such to all rational beings, and therefore, one purpose which they not merely may have, but which we may with certainty assume they all actually have by a natural necessity, and this is happiness.

It could have been Aristotle saying that.

The rational beings here, however, are understood to be in a state of dependency in that the goal of happiness cannot be attained merely by willing it. In order to secure such happiness as is afforded by the circumstances of life, the required virtue is prudence, and this is the disposition that will best support actions under any and all hypothetical imperatives. You see, even granting that we are moved by these conditions of the body, there is going to be a state of character that's necessary if these wants, desires, and aims are to be satisfied. Prudence is the one that Kant affirms here.

Note, then, that the Humean desires establish no more than hypothetical imperatives. They work on rational beings in their condition of natural dependency. In these instances, where we are under the general press of desires for pleasure, or to avoid pain, the keen desire to avoid what is painful, we function as natural beings dependent on the laws of natural causation.

In a word, moral philosophy need not apply here, do you see? What you do in response to someone holding a gun to your head is not in the *moral* domain, now. It's not what morality is about, because in this domain, sooner or later, the right explanation of why I'm doing what I'm doing is not going to be in terms of a rational, autonomous being choosing a course of action on a ground produced by reason itself; rather, it is going to be a course of action chosen by a natural kind of entity, essentially coercively worked on by the forces of nature, and responding to its own internal physiology, its own constitution. Actions in that context really are more akin to reactions.

What Kant is setting up here, then—if you want to see the great eminence, the shadowy figure of Hume as the target, what Kant is setting up here—look, the part of the story that you get from Hume really is outside of morality. It has to do with what creatures do under conditions of disturbance and desire.

Morality, Kant argues, doesn't begin in that domain. Morality begins with a rational and autonomous being in the intelligible realm, the realm in which we are called upon to provide reasons for action. That is to say, if I take my hand off a hot stove, no reason for that action is necessary. That's a reflex, but when we move into the intelligible realm, where reasons and justifications are called for, what we invariably must find is a rule, or precept, or principle that guides actions of a given kind. A rule or precept that guides action must apply to all situations of a particular kind. Now, one of the characteristics of a moral precept is that it's universalizable. That is, if it were not universalizable, it would be tied to a particular condition, and if it's tied to a particular condition, then, it's dependent on the merely contingent facts of the natural world, but when we consider bona fide moral canons, they are of the sort: "Do this," or "Thou shalt not kill," not: "Thou shalt not kill on Tuesdays."

Moral maxims, as reasons for acting, are applicable to all situations in which, generically, a given kind of action might take place. Now, as they are universalizable, they carry with them an imperative that is not hypothetical. It's not a case of "If I would get across the street, then," or, "If I would slake my thirst, then." Rather, these imperatives state: "Do x, or forbear from doing x." The categorical imperative is not tied to a particular desire, or impulse, or motive; rather, it asserts its own moral authority. The authority of the imperative is contained in the maxim itself, not something that it brings about, not some contingent outcome, not some consequence as such.

Now, before discussing Kant's versions of the categorical imperative, I pause to note what no less a philosopher than John Stuart Mill thought of the categorical imperative. He believed Kant's categorical imperative was a license to perform absolutely hideous acts. Well, perhaps we'd better see what troubled John Stuart Mill. If it troubled John Stuart Mill, perhaps we should at least be prepared to be troubled as well.

Recall Kant's pure categories of the understanding. These do not supply content. Rather, they supply the overall framework governing the possibility of understanding. The categories of quantity, quality, relation, and modality don't supply the understanding with specific content; that's the business of experience—so, too, with the pure intuitions of time and space. As intuitions, these do not supply a "this" or a "that." Well, similarly, the categorical imperative does not supply moral content. Rather, it expresses the form of the moral law.

Well, what is the categorical imperative, then, this imperative accessible only to a creature that is rational as such? You are not a moral being because you are a human being. Any number of human beings can have no moral standing at all. Infants are not moral beings, on Kant's account. The profoundly retarded, I should think, on Kant's account would not qualify as moral beings. A really serious defect of the nervous system might strip one of one's autonomy and rational powers and thus remove one from the domain of moral beings. What constitutes an entity as a moral being is rationality itself, which it inheres in human beings, rendering us fit for moral judgment; this happens to be the way things are, but we aren't fit for moral judgment in virtue of the fact that we are human beings. It's in virtue of the fact that we are rational beings.

Now, consider the successful insanity defense. The conclusion of law is that the perpetrator lacked sufficient rational power to frame means/ends relationships, or to comport his behavior according to the requirements of law. The defendant, we would say, is not a member of that community found to be fit for the rule of law. Well, so, too, with human beings lacking autonomy of the will: Whatever else might be said, at least on Kant's account, they could not qualify as moral beings.

What, then, are versions of the categorical imperative? The categorical imperative is summarized this way by Kant—this is perhaps his most famous expression: "Act in such a way that the maxim of your action would, if you were able, be instituted as a universal law of nature." Again, so act that the maxim of your action, not the physical details of the behavior, but the maxim of the action, the principle that that action instantiates, would be, if you could make it happen, instituted as a universal law of nature. You would make this principle dispositive everywhere and for all time, if you could. Act in such a way, so act, so comport yourself, that the principle on which that action is based, if you could make it so, would guide all action everywhere and at all times.

Now, you see what troubled Mill was the prospect of, let's say, an arsonist invoking the categorical imperative, and wishing to install as a universal law of nature the successful destruction of property by fire.

Well, all respect to Mill—and it's a great bit of respect that's due to Mill, to be sure, but this fear can only arise from a rather daring—I should say systematic—misunderstanding of Kant's entire argument. First, any ignoble end, or, for that matter, any end whatever tied to considerations of pleasure, or keen desire, or emotion would come under the heading of a hypothetical, not a categorical, imperative. Second, the imperative is a law that the will gives to itself. There are sufficient resources within Kantian moral thought to rule out arson as a candidate universal law!

I think Mill was probably on to this, but Mill, by the way, is so opposed to intuitionism in all forms that he's going to have to be opposed to a kind of moral intuitionism.

Now, Kant offers another version of the categorical imperative: "Man is never merely a means to an end, but always an end unto himself."

Man is never merely a means to an end. Now, what is Kant getting at with this? Suppose I intentionally use another as an instrument of my purpose? If I intentionally set out to use another as an instrument of my purpose, then I am formally denying that person the standing of a morally autonomous being, which means I am prepared to suspend the presumption of moral autonomy, and that means I am prepared to suspend precisely what is necessary for there to be morality at all. Moreover, if I am prepared to install that precept as a universal law, I do so with the understanding that I, too, now qualify for such a treatment. Let's recall Abraham Lincoln's famous statement: "As I would not be a slave, I would not be a master."

Do you see? The point that Lincoln is making is so coextensive with the argument that Kant has developed that the very institution of slavery establishes as a permissible maxim the use of another human being as an instrument. Well, who's to say in what direction that master/slave operation is going to work, do you see? Whatever principle would ground the right to use another person as a tool, grounds the right to use other persons as tools.

"Man is an end unto himself." Kant is famous for concluding from this that one must never lie.

Never, ever lie? Never, ever, ever lie? Not even a little white lie? Not just sort of making each other feel a little better?

Well, we know Kant never married, and presumably he was not called upon to judge the fall fashions, but consider the nature of the lie, and I want to say maybe consider the nature of the lie, big or small. If Smith lies to Jones in order to have Jones do something that Jones, if properly informed, would never do, then Smith is using Jones as a tool. He's using him as an instrument of Smith's own purpose. That is, he is trumping Jones's own moral autonomy and thus violating the categorical imperative, but what if the SS is at the door, demanding to be told where the Jews are hiding?

Now, what does Kant say? What does a Kantian say? It's a vexing question, and I think the right answer—at least if you are a Kantian—is that a Kantian says nothing at all.

Now, it is easy to make Kant into a kind of stick figure, Prussian, late 18th century, awfully formal, awfully abstract, utterly rationalistic. Life is richer than that. It's more robust and, inevitably, far more confusing than any system like Kant's is going to allow, but this is too easy, especially when alternative theories place the highest value on practical consequences. An illustration might help.

Let's turn, instead, to one of the stock problems in ethics these days—let's say bioethics. An ocean liner has sunk. There is a lifeboat. The lifeboat can support five people. Six actually made it through. Which one do we pitch overboard?

Well, Mother Theresa says: "Let me jump in." You can work these scenarios out for yourself, and you begin to see what happens. The minute you adopt consequence as the basis upon which you are going to treat people, and indeed, the basis upon which you might be prepared to end their lives, there has to be something firmer than just a delineation of consequences.

Kant's epitaph summarizes so much about Kant: "The starry sky above him, the moral law within him." Kant, the starry sky above him, the moral law within him, and on Kant's account, within us all—not as a way of gaining pleasure, not as a way of easing pain, but as a way of doing the right thing and, thus, substantiating ourselves as moral beings. Quite a contribution.

Phrenology—A Science of the Mind
Lecture 37

Gall's career was centered on three of the most important historical events in European history: the French Revolution, and the rise and fall of Napoleon.

Even as Hume, the *philosophes*, Kant, and other major philosophers of the Enlightenment were changing the map of thought, the scientific imagination of the period was scarcely at rest. Pierre Gassendi, who helped to revive Epicurean philosophy and the ontology of Democratus and the atomists, argued that, ultimately, everything is reducible to an atomic particulate form. Newton's physics is corpuscularian, and his methods, as well as Galileo's, sanctioned a reductionistic approach to complex problems. Locke's philosophy of mind is corpuscular—reduce mind to its elementary sensations, then figure out the principles by which it is built into more complex ensembles.

Despite the claims of his mind/body dualism, Descartes's psychology is radically biological. Descartes eventually finds a super-rational, abstract, theorem-generating part of the mind that saves the whole system from vulgar materialism. Except for the uniquely rational powers conferred on human beings by Descartes's philosophy, the rest of his philosophical psychology is entirely biological. Descartes establishes a solid philosophical foundation for a materialistic approach to issues of mind and mental life. La Mettrie's *Man, A Machine* becomes almost a rallying cry for those who think that scientific understanding of the brain is the key to solving the problems of knowledge, conduct, and governance.

By the end of the 18th century, commitment to this precept was increasing in scientific and medical circles. The Swiss naturalist Joseph Lavater developed the theory of physiognomy, which correlated human facial characteristics with various social types, such as artists, geniuses, and criminals.

Franz Joseph Gall (1758–1828) developed a similar scientific theory meant to explain the complexities of human personality. Born in Baden, Germany,

Gall studied medicine at Strassburg and the University of Vienna. Gall formed the theory in his youth that a close relationship obtained between large eyes and a large memory and, more generally, that one might be able to judge all sorts of talents by examining physical features. By 1791, in his early 30s, Gall committed himself to his first full-blown theory—cranioscopy, which held that careful examination of the cranial formations allows a doctor to assess a patient's underlying mental and moral faculties. Concerned that Gall's theory—now dubbed *phrenology*—led to a materialistic, atheistic account of human moral and mental powers, the clergy successfully had government sanctions imposed on Gall in 1802. Gall abandoned Austria and made his way as a lecturer in various German university towns, settling finally in Paris in 1807. Over the next years, Gall would answer charges of atheism, fail to be elected to the French Academy of Sciences, and otherwise spread his celebrity with multivolume treatises on the functions of the brain.

Though phrenology proved a waste, Gall's larger achievement was to rescue philosophy of mind from speculative philosophy and locate it in the sciences.

Though his system would be mocked as "bumpology" and later appear as a kind of charlatanism or parlor game, Gall was, in fact, one of the great neuroanatomists of his time and established his theory with compelling evidence. He examined changes in brain mass of human fetuses spontaneously aborted during various periods of gestation, thus laying the foundations for human developmental neuroanatomy. He made similar observations of the non-human species, thus carrying further the specialty of comparative neuroanatomy. He made studies of the cranial features of living celebrities, criminals, mental defectives, and insane patients and of their brains after they had died.

On the basis of a substantial database, he offered what he called "four incontestable truths": (1) Every mental and moral faculty of the mind is associated with a specific "organ"—a functional unit or what today might be called a *module*—in the brain. (2) The degree of a faculty that a person possesses is associated with the relative mass of brain connected to that faculty. (3) The mental and moral faculties are innate—by *moral*, Gall means the temperamental and dispositional. And (4) the conformation of the adult skull provides at least a good first approximation to the dominant or deficient moral and intellectual faculties of the underlying brain, thus, of the person.

It would be but a matter of a few years before physiologists begin to test Gall's theory directly, putting France at the center of the field that would become psychobiology or physiological psychology. The technique of choice—practiced by Francois Magendie and Xavier Bichat, among others— was to surgically destroy selective regions of the brains of unanesthetized animals and observe among the survivors whatever deficits were produced by destruction of areas of the brain.

In the early 1840s, Pierre Flourens performed such research and published his findings, along with a careful critique, in his *Phrenology Examined*. Flourens discovered that the areas of the brain Gall had linked with certain functions were not identified with those functions. But Flourens's work did show evidence of just the sort of localized function that was at the center of Gall's theory. Gall had put on the map of scientific thought a problem that continues to animate current cognitive and brain research—localization of function.

Though phrenology proved a waste, Gall's larger achievement was to rescue philosophy of mind from speculative philosophy and locate it in the sciences. He played an important part in the emergence of psychology as an independent experimental discipline. The speculative approach of Locke or Hume was now complemented, if not replaced, by clinical and experimental inquiries into the relationship between psychic and physical processes. From a few suggestive studies to what arose as a veritable movement, the "brain sciences" would take on profound philosophical importance. If Gall is not the father of that movement, he is surely one of it most influential modern tutors. ∎

Suggested Reading

Borst, C. V., ed. *Mind/Brain Identity Theory.* New York, 1970.

Churchland, P. *Neurophilosophy.* Cambridge, 1986.

Robinson, D. *The Enlightened Machine.* New York, 1980.

Questions to Consider

1. If salient aspects of human mental and emotional life are conditional on particular states and processes in the brain, explain why anyone should be held responsible either for knowledge or for conduct.

2. Infer what Descartes might have said about Gall's theory.

Phrenology—A Science of the Mind
Lecture 37—Transcript

As Hume, the *philosophes*, Kant, and other major philosophers of the Enlightenment were changing the map of thought, the scientific imagination of the period was scarcely at rest. Recall Descartes's contemporary critic, Pierre Gassendi, who had so much to do with reviving Epicurean philosophy and the atomic ontology of Democratus and the atomists, Gassendi arguing that the right understanding of what the constituents of the universe are is a physical and physicalistic understanding, that ultimately everything is reducible to an atomic particulate form. Newton's physics is corpuscularian, and his methods, as well as those of Galileo, will sanction a reductionist approach to complex problems. Then, too, Locke's philosophy of mind is corpuscular. Reduce the mind. Reduce it to its elementary sensations, and then figure out the principles by which it is built into ever more complex ensembles.

For all the claims about Descartes's mind/body dualism, his psychology is really quite radically biological. Oh, yes, in the 11th hour, he finds an aspect of the mind or soul—a super-rational sort of abstract, theorem-generating kind of a mind that saves the whole system from vulgar materialism. Some have even argued that with Galileo called before the Inquisition in 1633, perhaps Descartes eschewed a quite public avowal of the very materialism that is fairly explicit in his posthumously published work.

I don't think that is the right explanation, by the way. Descartes's position is not a failure of nerve. I think he is quite sincere in his dualism. Still, except for those uniquely rational powers that he confers on human beings, the rest of his philosophical psychology is entirely biological.

Thus, Descartes, too, establishes a solid philosophical foundation for a materialistic approach to issues of mind and mental life, and as for La Mettrie's *Man, a Machine*, it becomes almost a rallying cry for those who are going to try to advance the materialist agenda of philosophy, those who think that philosophical speculation is fine for the salons and the coffee shops, but to discover the nature of human nature and everything that goes with that—the problem of knowledge, the problem of conduct, the problem of governance—one must understand the subject to be a scientific one, finally based on, what? The brain.

Now, let me pause on this just long enough to say that whatever one's position on this might be, perhaps we can all agree that if you are going to settle on an organ to do this kind of work—and the choices are kidneys, spleen, lungs, and so forth—the brain is surely the right organ.

By the end of the 18th century, commitment to this precept was increasing within scientific and medical circles. Before considering Franz Joseph Gall and phrenology, I might mention other contemporary attempts at scientific theories intended to explain the complexities of the human personality.

There was, for example, Lavater, the Swiss naturalist, the father of a theory we call "physiognomy." Thus, by a careful examination of human facial characteristics and by correlating these facial types with various social types—such as geniuses, artists, and criminals—it should be possible to develop a science of human types with pretty good predictive power One should be able to unearth the inside of psychic life from the outside—through observations of the face, the cephalic index, the shape of the nose, etc., the intraocular distance.

Now, this was not the first attempt of its kind. In fact, Theophrastus, who took over Aristotle's Lyceum after Aristotle's death, had also developed a physiognomy for various personality types, and some of his sketches have been preserved in later copies.

There is an amusing application of physiognomy that appears in Darwin's account of his application for the position of naturalist on the *HMS Beagle*. He was interviewed by the estimable captain of that craft, Captain Fitzroy, himself, by the way, a most interesting figure. Fitzroy wrote quite an interesting account of the same voyage that Darwin famously wrote about, and their two accounts are profitably read in tandem.

Well, Darwin tells us that throughout the interview, Fitzroy kept looking at Darwin's nose. Darwin finally did get the position of naturalist. The *Beagle* didn't have separate quarters for a naturalist, so Darwin and Fitzroy were sharing the captain's quarters, and they did become very good friends. Apparently, one night over conversation, Fitzroy disclosed the fact that Darwin nearly did not get appointment as ship's naturalist, because, according to the captain, Darwin did not have the nose of a naturalist. Well, as you might have guessed, Fitzroy was a Lavaterian. Darwin concludes his account by saying that—happily for Darwin—the captain was prepared to accept, at least in this case, the possibility that Darwin's nose had lied.

Now, what we have here is not some freakish sort of outlying mode of thought. The Enlightenment ethos is one of confidence—I'm inclined to say a kind of naïve confidence—that no problem is so complex as to be beyond the reaches of the methods of science. As these methods are observational and systematic, it should always be possible, at least in principle, to reduce any degree of complexity to system, to general theories. Then, these generate ever more general integrations. Naturalists, biologists, physicians of the period are engaged in the same sort of enterprise, and none is better prepared academically or scientifically than the star of our show over the next few minutes, anyway—Franz Joseph Gall, the father of phrenology.

Gall's dates are 1758 to 1828. He was born in Baden, Germany, and he studied medicine first at Strasbourg and then in 1781 at the University of Vienna; at the time, it was certainly the leading medical school on the Continent, and surely on a par with Edinburgh.

Vienna had a medical faculty from the time of the University of Vienna's founding in 1365, and, by the time of Gall's education, had some of the most famous names in the medical science of the age. Van Swieten, for example, who had been the star pupil of the great Boerhaave at Leyden was one of the senior medical faculty members. In Vienna, van Swieten would be Court Physician to Maria Theresa, the empress favoring him with a baronetcy. All this is to say that Gall's promise was sufficient to earn him a place at Vienna—a tough place to get into—and that his education there was as good as medicine could provide late in the 18th century.

We aren't, therefore, dealing with some outlying, freakishly thinking person. This was a mainstream—I'm inclined to say, "gifted" but conventional— student of medicine, going to one of the best places to get prepared.

Even as a youngster, however, Gall had his own independent ideas about science. He formed a theory in his youth that a close relationship obtained between large eyes and a large memory and, more generally, that one might be able to judge all sorts of talents by examining physical features.

By 1791, in his early 30s, Gall was ever more decisive in his theorizing, now committing himself to what would be his first full blown theory, that of *cranioscopy*. By the careful examination of the cranial formations, a doctor should be able to assess underlying mental and moral powers or "faculties."

Well, Gall's career was centered on three of the most important historical events in European history: the French Revolution, and the rise and fall of Napoleon. The domains of religion, politics, and science—never totally distinct and independent—were now more mutually influential than under normal conditions. Gall's theories, as they unfolded, could not please any of these factions.

As his popular lectures spread the theory of the now dubbed *phrenology*, churchmen in Vienna took notice. Concerned that such a theory finally must lead to materialistic and deterministic, atheistic accounts of human moral and mental powers, the clergy successfully had government sanctions imposed on Gall.

This was in 1802, and within a few years, Gall is found abandoning Austria and making his way as a lecturer in various German university towns. By 1807, we find he has settled in Paris. Over the next years, he would come to have to answer charges of atheism. He would fail at his attempt to be elected to the French Academy of Sciences, and otherwise would spread his celebrity with multivolume treatises on the functions of the brain, as well as quite popular lectures on what William James years later would come to call the science of "bumpology." Well, James's estimation aside, Gall himself had numerous admirers and celebrated patients, the latter including Stendahl, St. Simon, and even Metternich, one of the ablest statesmen of the 19th century.

Now, I should point out that a doctor may have very famous patients not because he's a great doctor. There might be something peculiar in the famous patients themselves. Why do you go to a phrenologist? Well, perhaps because traditional medical approaches have not succeeded.

In any case, for all the criticism—and phrenology had many critics—it gained many adherents, including such unlikely a pair as Goethe and Thomas Edison. The first journal devoted to the "science" of phrenology appeared in 1823, based in Edinburgh, Gall's efforts now stoutly defended and promulgated by his collaborator, Johann Spurzheim, who began as Gall's dissectionist, and ended as his most influential disciple, later parting with the master over theoretical differences.

Well, in time, there would be more than 30 journals devoted to the subject of phrenology. There were phrenology heads in the offices of some of the leading medical figures of the day. This was a "science" that really took on the status of a movement for a period of time, and, I say, it's very easy, retrospectively, to think of the whole thing as a kind of charlatanism perpetrated by some eccentric, but nothing could be further from the truth.

Gall showed great promise as a medical student, and that promise was redeemed by the research that Gall actually undertook. It was Franz Joseph Gall who got hold of fetuses spontaneously aborted during different stages of gestational development, and he carefully drew and sketched the development of the nervous system during these periods. I should be inclined to say that he is a pioneer in human developmental neuroanatomy, perhaps the pioneer, at least for his time. It was also Gall who differentiated between the brain's gray and white matter. This required very, very careful dissections, very great skill. The anatomical studies were painstaking as he set out to develop the functional anatomy of the brain.

Of course, Gall's focus was chiefly on the cerebral cortex, which shows the most readily visible aspects of the brain. Physically, it's the dominant part of the human brain and, of course, it's the easiest one to get to if you just simply peel back the cranium. Gall was doing that. He was one of the pioneers in what today we call comparative anatomy, because of his careful examinations of the structural nuances one finds, going from species to species, in the matter of neuroanatomy, recognizing the differences in the conformations and the relative contribution of the cerebral cortex to the nervous systems of the various animals, of creatures different from ourselves. This was a serious, research-oriented medical person with the best medical training you could get at the time.

Gall was interested in the characteristics of the brains of exceptional people, exceptional in both directions—the profoundly retarded, the violent, the assaultive criminal, those executed for the most ghoulish of crimes, those who had served distinguished careers as political leaders, as leaders in the field of music, in the arts—he did everything he can to get hold of their post mortem brains and see what was different about them. You know, there are little pieces of Einstein's brain making the rounds. This is not something that began and ended with Gall. I'm sure there are people, fairly confident, that if you want to know how those two great theoretical papers from physics came from the same person in so short a period of time, the best way to answer is to look at a little piece of Einstein's brain. Good luck.

On the basis of his anatomical studies, he was prepared to propound what he rather immodestly referred to as "the four incontestable truths of phrenology." Now, "phrenology" was just the name he gave it from the Greek *phrenesis*, or *phren*, for mind, a science of the mind, a mental science, a scientific psychology. This was circa 1800. We've got somebody who was trying to develop a scientific psychology.

Now, what are these incontestable truths? First, every mental and moral faculty of the mind—every intellectual, emotional, and dispositional feature of mental life is associated, since Gall, with a specific "organ" in the brain. Gall had identified 27 basic "faculties" of the mind, and the theory would call for each of these to be associated with a specific "organ" of the brain. Later, Spurzheim would add another 10. Note the tendency of the brain sciences to become "inflationary" as matters become more complicated. We simply invent more faculties to do the job. However, ignore the peculiar phrase: "organ of the brain." What Gall has in mind is a functional unit, or what today might be called a *module*. His is a modular theory of mind.

The second incontestable truth is that the amount of that faculty that a person possesses is associated with the relative mass of brain connected to that faculty. Gall is not contending that larger heads are better heads—though he could not have pleased Napoleon in his observation that Napoleon's head-size was not proportioned to his ambitions. However, the point is more subtle: For a given brain mass, it is the fraction of that brain that's devoted to a given faculty that affects the extent to which that faculty predominates.

Now, the third incontestable truth of phrenology is that the mental and moral faculties are innate, and I think one answer to the question why many of the *philosophes* tended to hold Gall at arm's length was this rather inegalitarian aspect of phrenology, the idea that major differences between and among persons at the level of mental and moral qualities are innately determined and, by the way, locked into nothing less than the permanent structure of the brain.

Let me offer several qualifications here. First, in Gall's multivolume treatise in which these ideas are presented and defended, he is quite clear in acknowledging the profound influence of the environment, of learning and experience, of social life, on how a person develops. He is not fatalistic in contending that the faculties are innate. Instead, he is noting that for environments to have any influence, they have to have an influence on *something*, and that something is genetically given. All brains are not going to be precisely the same at the outset, and some are going to be far richer in potentialities, which nonetheless may never be realized, far richer than other brains are, which though quite diminished in their potentialities, may be nurtured in such a way as to compensate for native limitations. This is similar to Socrates's position when the ancient philosopher takes lines from Hesiod and speaks of "men of gold, men of silver, men of brass, and men of iron." This is an old idea.

The Enlightenment has generally satisfied itself that under the right set of social arrangements, the differences between and among us become negligible, and that what accentuates the differences among us are those artificial forms of governments—class systems, caste systems, other pretensions and the like—so I do say that Gall's position on this third "truth" is out of step with the prevailing optimism of the Enlightenment.

What about the fourth incontestable truth? Well, this gets a bit Byzantine. When we are infants, the bony covering of the brain is quite soft. The covering—the caldarium—is soft during fetal development and early infancy, and is thus somewhat elastic. It will stretch to accommodate the growth of the tissue it is covering.

Now, add to this the proposition that a given brain is genetically predisposed to have certain areas much more developed ultimately than other areas; that is, that there is a disposition within the given brain for certain parts to become much more elaborate than other parts. This is the innate nativistic feature of the theory. All right, so here's little Billy and little Jane— they are developing, and let's suppose that in both of them the faculty of "destructiveness" is going to become particularly pronounced. Gall had written on murderers, cruel tyrants, acts of senseless torture, the sadism of Nero. As he said in one of his works: "Who now will dare to maintain that there is not in man an innate propensity which leads him to the destruction of his own species?"

Well, the phrenology chart shows this "destructiveness" faculty to be an area that more or less is wrapping around the top of each ear. Now, if Billy and Jane are predisposed to destructiveness—let's say more so than others—this part is now going to start elaborating itself during early development, so that it's going to start pushing out against the calvarium near the apex of the ears.

But suppose some other faculty—say the faculty of causality, which is located high on the forehead, close to the midline—is going to be present in much less potency. Here, then, we have Billy and Jane with strong tendencies toward destructiveness, but with innately diminished capacity for the comprehension of causality. This would be an odd couple, by the way. Their brains develop accordingly, pushing out against the ear area, but being somewhat stunted in the forehead. The process goes on throughout the development of their nervous systems, before and after birth, until the sutures close and the cranium becomes harder and relatively inelastic. Well, of course, by that time, their skulls will reveal in their conformations, providing evidence of the cerebral growth that has occurred until things got too hard.

Gall's critics early on made much of the difference between cranial bumps and crannies and what you would find in the underlying cerebral cortex. That is, the cranial confirmations do not perfectly match the conformations of the brain's surface itself, that being criticism against Gall. Guess what? It was Gall himself who did most of the systematic studies of the degree of relatedness between the conformations of the skull and the conformations of the cortex underneath the skull. He knows the relationship is not perfect, but said that it was good enough for general purposes. Accordingly, after systematic observations and correlational studies, it should be possible to palpate the cranial surface and discover in the anatomy of the brain the underlying moral, temperamental, emotional, and intellectual potentials characteristic of a given individual.

Off we go. We've got a theory, we've got some data, we've got a world diverse in its makeup, and we are ready to explain the diversity.

The four incontestable truths of phrenology, indeed. It would be but a matter of a few years before physiologists begin to test this theory directly, thereby putting France at the very center of the field that would become psychobiology, or physiological psychology. The technique of choice was to take animals, non-human animals—may I say unanesthetized, non-human animals—cut their skulls open and surgically destroy selective regions of the brain, sew the animals back up, and observe among those animals that survived the deficits that had been produced by destruction of areas of the brain. The names that stand high on the list here, in my own view, I would have to say, to some extent high on the list of villainy, would be François Magendie and Xavier Bichat, and most significant of all, the earliest critic of Gall and the one who was the first to develop this technique, Pierre Flourens. Now, I might mention that with some of these, in the case of one of these luminaries, he actually lost the affection of his wife and daughter for the kind of research conducted on these animals, these unanesthetized animals. There are instances of students being amused by having live animals pinned against a waxed board as their brains were exposed and surgically destroyed.

This is not the occasion to launch a defense of animal rights, etc., but it would be neglectful to let this sort of research pass without comment. After all, our characters are shaped by our activities, by what we do and what we support. That is, we make ourselves into the sorts of beings we are in virtue of the manner in which we conduct our lives. Now, the seemingly noble motto that would permit anything and everything for the sake of knowledge can be a license for villainy. One has to wonder the extent to which one really does transform one's character when one is prepared to bring insufferable pain and suffering to bear on innocent beings to test a theory, even one judged to be as important as Gall thought his theory was.

In the early 1840s, Flourens performed this research and published his findings, along with a careful critique, in a work he titled *Phrenology Examined* and dedicated to the memory of Descartes. A second edition appeared in 1844, and two years later, an English language edition. In the preface, Flourens tells the reader that the 17th century recovered from the philosophy of Descartes; the 18th, from that of Locke, and that the question now was whether the 19th would recover from that of Gall. In other words, Gall, he thought, had a very, very stultifying effect on thought in the sciences. The criticism that followed led many to conclude that the death knell of phrenology had been sounded, and sounded by Flourens.

Flourens, however, paradoxically discovered that the areas of the brain Gall had identified with certain specific functions were not identified with those functions, and he thought that this was a telling, devastating critique of Gall. But what he ended up publishing was evidence of just the sort of localized function that was at the center of Gall's theory, increasingly showing a quite reliable relationship between specific areas of the brain and specific functions. It didn't redeem phrenology. There was no specific "seat of the understanding" found or eliminated, but it did do this: Gall had put on the map of scientific thought a problem that continues to animate what we call today the "cognitive and brain sciences," and that is the problem of localization of function. Where in the nervous system is one or another psychological, or moral, or emotional, motivational, perceptual function determined, controlled, operated?

The search continues to this day. With brain-imaging techniques and other non-invasive methods, one is in a position to get very good answers to questions like this without pestering cats and dogs. Indeed, one of the most reliable sources of information in this area—and Gall was not ignorant of this—is the neurology clinic itself.

Gall's larger achievement—a matter of record even as the record of phrenology proved to be largely a waste—was to rescue philosophy of mind from speculative philosophy and locate it within the sciences. It would be permissible to say that he played an important part in the emergence of psychology as an independent experimental discipline. The speculative approach of Locke or Hume was now complemented, if not replaced, by clinical, experimental inquiries into the relationship between psychic and physical processes. From a few suggestive studies to what arose as a veritable movement, the "brain sciences" would take on profound philosophical importance. If Gall is not the father of that movement, he is surely one of the most influential modern tutors.

Phrenology itself had great staying power. Learned essays and texts were still published and respectfully discussed as late as the 1930s. In the second half of the 19th century, any number of books by medical specialists took the science quite seriously, largely ignoring Flourens and others who really didn't understand the matter.

One title indicates how popular this was. James Carson, *Fundamental Principles of Phrenology*, providing the only principles he thought capable of being reconciled with the immateriality and immortality of the soul, in 1868.

Well, we don't see titles like that anymore. Now, we see the cover of *Time Magazine*, indicating that we have located, through a functional MRI, the place in the brain that makes moral decisions. Some silly ideas die hard.

The Idea of Freedom
Lecture 38

> **There's something else in Kant. His moral theory ... places us as rational beings in that "intelligible realm" that is outside the causal order of the natural sciences. Accordingly, human nature as a rational nature cannot be adequately understood in terms of causation in the scientific sense, but only through the rational apparatus of the introspecting, thoughtful being who discovers at once that he is a morally free being.**

Romanticism is one of the perennial achievements of the human imagination and, in its philosophically developed expression, one of the significant productions of the 19th century. If Romanticism is a reaction to and rejection of the Enlightenment, its origins are clearly traced to the Enlightenment itself. The principle agenda of the Enlightenment is to challenge traditional authority through the tools and resources of a scientific worldview. Thus, the Enlightenment sets itself up against what is taken to be artificial contrivances—the overly analytical Scholastic philosophies, the authority of Scripture or revelation, the invented powers of rank and title, and slothful acceptance of tradition and the alleged wisdom of bygone times. If Descartes is one of the fathers of the modern worldview, let us recall that he helps to set the stage for the Enlightenment by rendering doubt the beginning of all knowledge.

With Rousseau, we get what might be regarded as the beginning of a veritable religion of nature. His writings show what was immanent in the ethos of the Enlightenment from the first: namely, a religion of nature that cannot be fully described with the artificial instrument of language.

Kant inserted this insuperable barrier between the world of phenomena and the noumenal reality behind that world. Kant's philosophy at once entices us to get to the bottom of things, to see what's behind the screen, and to understand at the outset that the formalisms that guide and edit perception are of little avail. But if perception in this rule-governed sense will not disclose the real nature of things, and if science is based primarily on observation, and if we know that observation reveals merely phenomenal, not noumenal, reality, then science has built-in limitations.

We now begin to hear deep resonances to the effect that what really defines us is our freedom, that freedom renders us unique in the entire cosmos, apart from all other things. Consider the appearance in the late 18th century of the Gothic novel, such as Mary Shelley's *Frankenstein* and Horace Walpole's *The Castle of Otranto*. What are these horror stories all about? The revelation of mysteries and half-seen, half-grasped realities. Likewise, Blake and Fuseli see the realm of fact driven by hidden and mysterious forces. In Fuseli's "Polyphemus," the blind monster suggests the realms of truth inaccessible to the eye and, therefore, inaccessible to the light of science.

The so-called *Romantic rebellion* conveys the sense of the mystery behind the reality, which somehow is uncovered through the genius of art and literature.

The so-called *Romantic rebellion* conveys the sense of the mystery behind the reality, which somehow is uncovered through the genius of art and literature.

It's not accessible to the eye until the eye is liberated from the formalisms of science, logic, and philosophy itself. Goethe (1749–1832) is one of the very souls of Romanticism. His *Farbenlehrer* (1810) is one of the most detailed analyses to that date of color vision! Goethe argues that the Newtonian theory of light explains everything except *what we see*! There is nothing in the physics of light that tells us anything about how the world appears to us. It tells us nothing about the perception of beauty.

Goethe's 10-year friendship with Friedrich Schiller was decisive in Goethe's writing of *Faust.* In Schiller's *Letters on the Aesthetic Education of Man*, freedom creates and determinism limits and kills. We are never our authentic selves so fully as when at play. The idea is that the divinity within us expresses itself most fully when we do something for the sheer intrinsic worth of the activity itself and not for anything external to it. This is Schiller's sense of the authenticity of play, his aesthetic creed.

The Faust legend depicts the limits of science and the transcendental nature of freedom. The Faust of Part 1 is the bored polymath who, knowing everything, finds nothing in knowledge that offers abiding pleasure. What it would take for Faust to pledge his soul is for Mephistopheles to create in him an experience of such a nature that he would never tire of it. "What would you sell your soul for?" is the question at the bottom of the play. What is clear is that a scientific knowledge of the world does not make us at home in it. Clear, too, are the lengths to which one goes in order to achieve the transcendent—an experience of such quality and sublimity as to command time to stop in her tracks. It is only our autonomy, our radical freedom, that allows us to enter into such "Faustian bargains"—the soul being bet on the possibility of total satisfaction.

The Faust of Part 2, created by Goethe years later, is one for whom the transcendentally joyous experience is the *freedom of others*: the spectacle of a free people, engaged in the art of life. The question in Part 2 is how this whole Faustian bargain is going to work out. Complete freedom is the authenticity that comes from what we have freely chosen to do. The German philosopher Johann Fichte, one of Kant's young contemporaries, asked: How do we know when we are free? He answers: when we meet opposition. Having gone through the range of possibilities that only the devil can present, Faust has an utterly novel experience—the transcendent joy of having his lands given over to all the people who have toiled on them. Romantic freedom is ultimately selfless, the absorption into a totality, freely giving up private freedom for the sake of others. Thus, Faust is redeemed in the end of the story.

The idea of freedom, central to Kant's moral philosophy and celebrated by Goethe, Schiller, and their kindred "Romantic idealists," is an informing chapter in the long debate. What the aesthetes concluded was that science in the wake of Newton had become mechanical, reductive, indifferent to the human condition, and depreciating of the human condition when it does consider it. What they would put in its place is the truth of nature against the fabrications of the natural philosopher, a generous recognition of the creative power of genius, and the transcendent sources of beauty and wonder. The attribute of wonder is central to our humanity in the Romantic view. Any philosopher who would explain the world mechanically has not seen the world. ∎

Suggested Reading

Bate. W. *From Classic to Romantic*. Harvard University Press, 1946

Clark, K. *The Romantic Rebellion*. J. Murray, 1973.

Questions to Consider

1. Explain whether the problem of the received sciences is that they are too narrow or that they are simply unable in principle to inform us on matters of deepest concern.

2. Conclude whether an "authentic" life is possible—or even desirable—in light of the "freedom of play" that Schiller takes to be its essence.

The Idea of Freedom
Lecture 38—Transcript

Alfred Tennyson, in his *In Memoriam*, writes: "I trust I have not wasted breath; I think we are not wholly brain."

Romanticism is one of the perennial achievements of the human imagination and, in its philosophically developed expression, one of the significant productions of the 19th century. Its residuals are very much with us, and if it is a reaction to—and even a rejection of—the Enlightenment, its origins are clearly traced to the Enlightenment itself. Let me quickly rehearse the larger aims of the Enlightenment, and then consider the Romantic reaction to it.

The principle agenda of the Enlightenment is to challenge traditional authority through the tools and resources of a scientific worldview. In rejecting superstition—or at least what they took to be superstition—in all its forms, and in reserving to experience alone the final authority on what can be known, the leaders of Enlightenment thought placed nature itself at the center of philosophical concern. "Nature" here includes human nature in its various social, political, and personal projections, "nature" as in the essential nature of law, government, belief; "nature" as in the nature of the world and the cosmos.

Thus, the Enlightenment sets itself up against what it takes to be all artificial contrivances, the overly analytical, Scholastic philosophies; the authority of Scripture or Revelation; the merely invented powers of rank and title; the slothful acceptance of tradition, and the alleged wisdom of bygone times. If Descartes is one of the fathers of the modern worldview, let us recall that he helps to set the stage for the Enlightenment by rendering doubt about the beginning of all knowledge. Well, of course, in all of this, there were ancient Greek anticipations.

With Rousseau, we get what might be regarded as the beginning of a veritable religion of nature, the abundance of nature, the sheer beauty and power of nature, natural man being something that has a majesty about itself that's covered over, and concealed, and distorted by the awkward and artificial impositions of what we are pleased to call "civilization"—such that with these impositions, we cease to live an authentically human life. This is what Tom Paine is getting at when he talks about rank and titles "circumscribing human felicity."

Under attack in Paris for his *Social Contract*, Rousseau retreated into himself on the island of St. Pierre in 1765, later composing *Les Reveries du Promeneur Solitaire*, his *Recollections of the Solitary Prominade*.

Now, in these reflections, we find Rousseau arrested by the sound of the ocean waves, which—here are lines that are quintessential Rousseau:

> Held my senses still, drove out of my mind all other kinds of agitation…What is it that one is enjoying in such a situation? Nothing external; nothing but oneself and one's own existence. As long as this state lasts, one is self-sufficient, like a god.

All of that coming from the waves of the ocean. Later, Rousseau commits himself to a disinterested surrender to sensation alone, thus merging with fields of flowers, with streams and woods and "enamelled meadows." This transcendent peace is fragile, for, as Rousseau goes on to say: "As soon as one wishes to only be an author or professor, all this sweet charm vanishes."

I might say that willing to be a professor doesn't necessarily eliminate all sweet charm, but the challenge is there.

Now, what these passages show is something that was immanent in the ethos of the Enlightenment from the first: namely, a religion of nature that cannot be fully described with the artificial instrument of language. Had not Kant inserted this insuperable barrier between the world of phenomena and the noumenal reality behind that world? To accept this is not to reject sensual experience, though; it is to liberate perception itself from its professorial mission.

Kant wouldn't be quite pleased with our drawing out those implications, but his philosophy at once entices us to get to the bottom of things, to see what's behind the screen, as it were, and to understand at the outset that the formalisms that guide and edit perception are of little avail. But if perception in this rule-governed sense will not disclose the real nature of things, and if science is but systematic observation, then one conclusion that jumps out at us is that science is just another obstacle to the truth of things. Again, if science is based primarily on observation, and if we know that observation reveals merely phenomenal, not noumenal, reality, then science has built-in limitations.

What happens, then, is we begin to think there may be a text behind the text. Behind the scene, behind the appearances and the measurements, there must be something really true waiting to be found, and if we can't find it with the eye or the ear or the anatomical blowpipe, well, how do we find it? Romanticism is, as it were, science grown shame-faced.

There's something else in Kant. His moral theory establishes—it places us as rational beings in that "intelligible realm" that is outside the causal order of the natural sciences. Accordingly, human nature as a rational nature cannot be adequately understood in terms of causation in the scientific sense, but only through the rational apparatus of the introspecting, thoughtful being who discovers at once that he is a morally free being. Rousseau's "Man is born free and is everywhere in chains" is one version of the story; Kant's moral autonomy and the liberation of the will from the constraints of causation is another. With Kant, the laws of freedom are what operate in the intelligible realm.

We now begin to read a literature; we now begin to hear deep resonances to the effect that what really defines us is our freedom, that what renders us unique in the entire cosmos, apart from all other things, is our freedom. It is the free play of ideas that finally is at the bottom of genius itself. Alas, the way to get behind the world of mere appearances to the world of reality is through that freedom expressed by the exceptional person who actually can come to see things, and when he sees things the way they really are, he sees that there's much more mystery than can be scientifically observed and recorded. You see the movement of thought, here.

Consider the appearance in the late 18th century of the Gothic novel: Two that come to mind are Mary Shelley's *Frankenstein* and Horace Walpole's *The Castle of Otranto*. In the latter work, Walpole writes a preface as if he is merely in possession of an English translation of a work appearing in Italian in the 16th century, telling of events that occurred centuries earlier. Walpole then inserts a maiden's sonnet, which begs that the marvels to be reported be guarded against—what? "Reason's peevish blame."

Mary Shelley's classic is a tale of power-mongering at the expense of nature itself, something of a gloss on the Industrial Revolution, but more a searching examination of the promise and then the peril of attempts to reduce nature to something merely assembled. Victor Frankenstein will make his creature, will stand as a god of creation himself, and will not scruple over the moralist's philosophical niceties. He leaves these to his poet friend, so deeply concerned about all this. You see science and poetry now in a kind of adversarial relationship, with the scientist taking a kind of high-minded "Well, I can leave that to the poet." How telling, then, when the poet Henry Clerval is killed by the monster, and remember what the monster says to Dr. Frankenstein: "You are my creator, but I am your master."

Pause here, and think about what is going on. It is the poet whose moral sensibilities are the one thing that could save us from tragedy. That is precisely what the scientifically created monster kills, and the scientifically created monster is a creation now coming to master the creator.

What are these horror stories all about? Think only of the paintings of Henry Fuseli, for example. Think of Blake's work. What are these productions expressing? What's the monster all about? What are we prepared to make of Fuseli's "Nightmare" and his "Polyphemus"? The latter presents this giant half-man, half- beast. He's sort of sitting there sulking. Odysseus having driven a stake through the one eye, Polyphemus, the Cyclops, doesn't quite know what's going on. For Fuseli, it was the mystery and fantasy in the works of Shakespeare that allow us to enter a dream world closer to reality than the mere and shifting items seen under the sobering light of day.

Well, in all, Romanticism conveys this sense of the mystery behind the reality and the mystery that somehow gets uncovered through the genius of art and literature. It's not something accessible to the eye, as such, until the eye is liberated from the formalisms of science, logic, and, yes, philosophy itself. This is what is behind the phrase often used by scholars—the so-called

Romantic rebellion against the line-and-angle precision and pretensions to knowledge of the scientific community, the mixed bounty of an Industrial Revolution that began as a servant and now stands as a master of the human condition.

With whom do we want to date these developments? Is there a birthday for this line of thought? Of course, grand movements of thought do not lend themselves to birthdates, but certainly one of the very souls of the movement we call Romanticism is Goethe, who was surely viewed this way by his contemporaries.

His dates are 1749 to 1832. A lawyer's son, Goethe would play many parts in his long life: painter, statesman, botanist, poet, playwright. He is a towering literary figure, so much so that one of his major works is often overlooked. I refer to his *Farbenlehrer*, published in 1810. It weighed in at 1400 pages and presented what was to that time one of the most detailed analyses to that date ever devoted to, of all things, color vision.

Now, what is Goethe doing writing a book on color? He tells us straightaway that he is:

> The only person in this century who has the right insight into the difficult science of colors; that is what I am proud of, and that is what gives me the feeling that I have outstripped many.

You see, then, Goethe regards this as one of the premier productions of his life. In point of fact, he believes he has outstripped Newton. The work itself, indeed, is a sustained critique of the Newtonian theory of light. It is a broadside against Newton's physics of light, the corpuscular theory, the entire approach to understanding color as an experience. You see—the burden of Goethe's book is to establish that Newton has told us everything about light, except *what we see*! There is nothing in the physics of it all that tells us anything about how the world actually comes to appear to us, and the meanings that we will come to extract from it. It tells us nothing about that most central of visual experiences, the perception of beauty.

Goethe, then, once stood back and in this work, I mean, he doesn't—it's not just this work obviously, it's in his great literary works, Goethe's stepping back and saying: "Wait a minute—if this is the culmination of scientific thought on a subject, science must be woefully limited as an enterprise. If this is the most we're ever going to get out of what we all agreed to be the greatest scientific achievement of the modern age, Newton, well, we're not even on page two, yet."

We want to know about light for one central reason, because the visible world is a world that moves and summons us. It's the world that presents us with the emblems and icons of possible lives. None of this is existing at a corpuscular level.

Moreover, if the visual system is stimulated alternately with light and dark, color experiences can be generated that way. Thus, we don't need the Newtonian physics of color in order to generate color out of black and white, and, of course, the implication of this is quite clear. We have creative resources within us. We are not entirely dependant on the physics of the external world, even for the richest experiences that we might have. Perception can defy physics. It has organizing and inventive powers of its own; it's not merely a passive process—so that what defines human nature is not going to be the mechanical causation examined in the realm of physics. It's going to be something deeper.

Goethe's 10-year friendship with Friedrich Schiller was decisive in Goethe's writing of *Faust*. Schiller, you know, is the author of that *An die Freude*, the *Ode to Joy* that Beethoven incorporated so magnificently into the choral movement of the *Ninth Symphony*. There is time here to consider just one of Schiller's influential works. I refer to his *Letters on the Aesthetic Education of Man*. A core precept in Romanticism, of course, is that the dimension of human life that counts most is the aesthetic dimension, and in his *Letters on the Aesthetic Education of Man*, Schiller states boldly that: "Man is never so authentically himself as when at play."

Man is never so authentically man. We are never our authentic selves so fully as when at play, and you say to yourself: "What could he be getting at here?"

Schiller, as with all the Romantics, was deeply read in the classics. Recall Aristotle on the matter of life on the Isle of the Blessed—where, almost like a god, one engages in contemplative activity for its own sake, not for any purpose beyond itself, but for the sheer eudaimonic form of life that is lived when one is engaged in contemplation of the right kind, though the idea being that the divinity within us expresses itself most fully when what we are doing, we are doing for the sheer intrinsic worth of the activity itself, and not for anything external to it.

This is Schiller's sense of the authenticity of play. It is his aesthetic creed. Now, play is not effortless. People consume far more energy when at play, usually, than when they are at work. We take play seriously. Find a person who has a passion for a hobby. Find a person who sculpts, or paints, or tries to write poetry, or sails, or plays chess. Such persons would give up life's essentials for these consuming passions, and "passions" is the operative word. Romanticism is about passion—not lust, but authentic commitment, and commitment, by its nature, is not the gift of reason, but of feeling, and what is the characteristic of play? It's what we do when we are free, what we do to be free. It is freedom that allows play, and it is in play that we discover our authentic selves. I think too many students who have heard versions of this lecture have drawn from it the implication that "goofing off" is a mode of authenticity, but one has to digest these propositions very carefully.

In any case, here is Romanticism speaking in a voice that, if anything, the modern citizen hears more clearly than perhaps even the 19th century heard it. I'm not sure the 19th century was quite as given to play as we are, though I'm not at all sure that the forms of play we've developed for ourselves retain that liberating and authentic quality of play that Schiller had in mind. In important respects, to "professionalize" an activity is to transform play into business. There may still be commitment, there may still be even the obsession, but one wonders if the aesthetic of the activity has been lost in the metamorphosis.

Let me return now to the more famous Goethe—not the author of a thick book on color, but the genius who wrote the *Faust*. In Goethe's hand, the Faust legend is in two parts, written years apart. The optimistic Goethe is the Faust in Part 2, saved by attending angels at the moment when the devil has claimed his soul. But let me go back to what the Faust story is a story about. It may well be based on the life of one Johann Fausten, who flourished at about 1480 as a magician and master of alchemy and the darker sciences and arts. Almost all of you surely will know about it. Faust is a gentleman-scholar, a donnish man who knows much, really everything. He's a fellow who has read a lot. He's got glass tubes and Bunsen burners, astrological maps and flowcharts. He is studious. He has a great library; he might just has well have rooms at All Souls, Oxford—and, he is bored to tears. Life has lost its meaning. He knows everything. Nothing means anything. There he is.

As the legend of Johann Fausten himself is usually told, his Christian upbringing finds him a master of Scripture, but also a searcher after truth. He becomes an original thinker, an alchemist, but one who longs to commune with the devil in order to possess supernatural knowledge and power. This the devil grants, on condition that the devil's service be confined to a period of 24 years and that, at the end of that time, Fausten—having renounced his religion—the devil may now possess his soul.

In Goethe's version, there is a wager of sorts between God and Satan. Faust has replaced his religious devotion with devotion to, what? Science and rationality, but God believes he can be redeemed and will renounce Satan and his ways. The devil chides God for giving man reason by which he has become "more brutish than any brute," and Faust, as all this is going on, laments the fact that all his studies have not given him access to the real truths of things.

You've now got the picture of this titanically filled head with an empty heart, looking for some meaning, trying to get something out of this earthly life beyond what is earthly. Mephistopheles shows up, all tricked out and smiling, ready for service. Faust makes it quite clear he's prepared; he's prepared to play the game; he's a sophisticated man, a man of the world. He knows that there are no free lunches in Weimar.

Well, what it would take for Faust to pledge his soul is for Mephistopheles to create in him an experience of such a nature that he would command time itself to stand still—an experience of such a nature that he would never tire of it. Think of it. Bored stiff. What is one looking for? One is looking for things that one doesn't habituate to, and become bored with—so: "Create in me an experience of such a nature that I would have time stand still." It means: "Create an experience that I would never tire of."

The Faust saga, then, includes love, power, romance, passion. These are all things that people aspire to. Faust goes through one dilemma after another. This fellow is on an ocean of turmoil and possibilities, and it is quite a bargain that he entered into, that Faustian bargain. "What would you sell your soul for?" is the question at the bottom of the play, do you see? What is it that you would sell your soul for? What's your price? Are you a calculating person? Are you caught up in something other than the categorical imperative, do you see? Here you are—you're free, and part of what it means to be free, of course, is that you can engage in transactions of this sort.

Goethe worked on this story on and off over a period of decades, beginning in 1773. The finale, Part 2, did not appear until just after Goethe's death in 1832. Faust by now has been the beneficiary of the good and the bad of his own choosing by the way, and so the question in Part 2 is how this whole Faustian bargain is going to work out. Having gone through the range of possibilities that only the devil can present—and with the terms of the agreement now about to be finally fulfilled—Faust is found looking out over a field that his workers have been toiling on. Then, he has an utterly novel experience—the transcendent joy of having his lands given over to all the people. At this point, he begins to be engulfed by blindness, and at this point, he sees more clearly the prospect of men and women working a land that is their own, and for themselves. What does Faust say with this spectacle?

> This is the highest wisdom that I own—the best that mankind ever knew…Wisdom's last verdict goes to say:
>
> He only earns freedom and existence
>
> Who must reconquer them each day.

Stop with this, now. Here's a man who has gone through everything, and what he cherishes most is the spectacle—the reality—of freedom, and to have it, it must be reconquered every day. The celebration here, the experience one can have that one would never want to end, doesn't happen to be something at the bottom of a bottle. In fact, it isn't anything that happens to you, do you see? It is the externalization of the ideal of liberty, the ideal of freedom—freedom for its own sake as the creative, ultimate, moral force of the universe. God make the world freely and gave it as a gift, knowing that it was good.

One of Kant's young contemporaries was Johann Fichte. More will be said about him in another lecture. He had written several very important works, one titled: *The Way Toward a Blessed Life*, and another titled: *Characteristics of the Age*. Fichte is taken by Rousseau's claim that "Man is born free, but he is everywhere in chains." Fichte then raises the interesting question: Born free? How would you know it? As fish will never discover water, how can one "know" freedom if it is nothing less than a condition of one's birth?

Now, on Fichte's understanding, the very idea of freedom only comes about as an aspect of consciousness when it is opposed. We see a bit of this in the position that Faust is taking at the end. It's their freedom that is something he relishes. It is, in the trite phrase we now use, "the gift of giving." There is finally this moment of selflessness. It is the externalization of desire, it is rendering universal as a universal law of nature something that he himself will not experience, or doesn't think he'll experience.

Now, having had that glorious moment where he's seen something that would have him arrest time itself, stop time in its tracks, Faust must now submit to the agreement. But as his spirit descends and falls toward that depth from which no soul returns, his soul is suddenly borne up by the angels. Faust is redeemed.

There's an interesting parallel, I think, between the way *Faust* ends and Fichte's view that in the selfless life, in de-individuating ourselves, in giving up the merely personal, private exercise of freedom and externalizing all of the possibilities of freedom for the benefit of the many, we end up at once with a life that is thoroughly authentic. At the same time, it is no longer in fact a personal life—but now a life that possibly can find itself absorbed into an eternal and immutable cosmic scheme defined by its very nature.

Well, what about psychological materialism and phrenological charts? Might Faust's problems not have found a readier solution in contemporary pharmacology? I should tell you that Carlyle was a particularly influential figure in the 19th century, a critic and stern Scotsman. One of the leaders of thought in the French materialist tradition was Pierre Cabanis, and we are going to see a reflection on Cabanis on the part of Carlyle.

After the Revolution, Cabanis was made head of the hospital system in Paris. He was an influential and, indeed, very capable advocate of the brain sciences. He wrote a series of essays on the relationship between the psychological and physical dimensions of human life, concluding that the surest way of understanding human nature is through neurology.

Cabanis would have quite a following and, indeed, was worthy of one. His writings to this day read very well, but when Carlyle looked at the claims of Cabanis, who would have poetry grounded in the viscera, he said: "There he stands, with his anatomical blowpipes and dissecting needles, going through a world of wonder unwondering." The Romanticists want us to go through a world of wonder, wondering.

The Hegelians and History
Lecture 39

The systematic development of truth in scientific form can alone be the true shape in which truth exists. To help to bring philosophy nearer to the form of science—that goal where it can lay aside the name of love of knowledge and be actual knowledge—that is what I have set before me.—Georg Wilhelm Friedrich Hegel

It is difficult to fully discuss Hegel's thought within the scope of a 30-minute lecture. However, Hegel, a product of both the German Enlightenment and Romantic thought, accepted the essential Romantic critique of science as one-sided, narrow, and largely incapable of explaining the natural world. Hegel's early education featured the classics and was preparatory for theological studies, which in time, proved boring to him. At Teubingen's Stift Theological Seminary, Hegel was judged to be of "middling industry and knowledge." There, he roomed with two young men who would distinguish themselves in future years, the poet Holderlin, whose two-volume *Hyperion* is a classic in German literature, and Schelling, who will be associated with Hegel in years to come and figure importantly in what came to be known as German Idealism. The academic world of Germany and of Teubingen, especially, was in turmoil as a result of the French Revolution and the ideas surrounding it. Hegel is among that intellectual elite aware of the debts to the past but aware, as well, of the changing conditions of the world.

Hegel shares with his immediate predecessors, and with Romanticism at large, the judgment that science, as traditionally understood as "perfected" in the age of Newton, is a narrow, one-sided, misleading affair. If science stays at the level of mechanistic explanation and the particularization of the complex into some reduced non-reality, then it will be capable of explaining very little. Science will, in fact, become merely an exercise in the vindication of its own flawed methods. The subject of truth itself is what has real being, in the sense of nothing being added or modified by peculiar or merely conventional modes of analysis. Descartes's own revolution was never lost on Hegel. As understood by Hegel, Descartes's achievement was to recognize that knowledge in all its forms is but "the unity of thought and being."

Though he admires Newton, Hegel regards Newton's work as making it possible for Locke's philosophy to become nearly official. The commitment to perceptual modes of knowledge and the shunning of deeper metaphysical considerations are products of this mode of thinking. If the world is defined as merely the action of corpuscles, the laws governing corpuscles will be all that will be studied; everything else will be ignored. And the discovered causal laws could, in fact, be entirely different without raising any surprise or concern. If instead of $F = ma$, the relationship had been $F = 5m + 3.2a$, it would be no occasion for debate. Thus, the scientist gives us no complete comprehension of the natural world. Through these mere summaries of correlations and cause-effect sequences, he never arrives at what the rest of us call "reality." Nothing in the Newtonian achievement explains just *why* the laws are as they are. Why is everything the way it is and not some different way instead?

To include Hegel within the tradition of Romanticism or German Romantic Idealism requires that we turn to Johann Fichte. Indeed, the famous "Hegelian" triad of thesis, antithesis, and synthesis is actually Fichte's contribution and was rarely employed by Hegel himself. Fichte recognized a fundamental conflict in Kant's epistemology: If there is a conceptual or logical barrier between reality as it is and reality as it is perceived, philosophy must commit to either bypass mind in every possible way or to accept that it is mind that is the worthy object of attention. Fichte argues that the ultimate reality is that of idea, the starting point of philosophy then being the transcendental ego. According to Hegel, we ought to be looking not merely for those causal connections revealed in scientific laws but for the reason behind the laws, because reality is rational.

> **In the synthesis, or final stage, man passes the stage of freedom for its own sake and comes to know freedom as an instrumentality to be used for the good of all.**

To understand an event is finally to identify the reason behind it, and reasons are not "causes" by another name. Causes can be final or merely efficient, but they carry no sense of necessity with them; they are merely contingent facts of the world. But knowing the *reason* for an event is to understand that the event had to take the form it did.

Hegel applies this to human history itself. There is a distinct evolutionary perspective in Romanticism. There must be a reason for human development: from basic survival to human communities to literacy and rationality, each stage higher than the previous one. Romanticism perceives an evolutionary struggle—*Sturm und Drang*—that produces new and better things not predictable in a mechanistic view. Human history is the result of something trying to work itself out or realize itself through this great evolutionary struggle. It is out of the struggle itself that something gets resolved. And it is in the resolution that we find life lived at a higher plane. There is reason in human history. Hegel gave several names to this something, most commonly "the Absolute" but also "soul" or "spirit"—*Geist*. In Hegel's day, the Absolute expresses itself in the *state*, declared by Hegel to be "the march of God in the world." So-called "Hegelians of the right" would defend the claims of the state against any and every claim from the mere individuals who live in it.

Hegel finds that the state, as the ethical aspect of the Absolute, takes precedence over Kant's "good will" of the individual. Kant claimed that good will was the only pure good in the universe: the will to bring about, if we could, that which we would bring about in our most rational moments. For Hegel, this dependence on the will of the moral agent leaves room for arbitrary and even wicked conduct. The claims of conscience have a moral superiority over mere convention but cannot be substituted without peril for the commands of the just state. Hegel prefers the formulations of the brilliant young philosopher Fichte: The greatest freedom of the will consists in surrendering freedom for the sake of the whole.

What really exists does so in virtue of an essentially dialectical process. Reality is the synthetic outcome of affirming and negating forces. Fichte is important philosophically as the architect for the Hegelian ontological logic that features the famous dialectical triad of *thesis*, *antithesis*, and *synthesis*—the progress through conflict, reality arising from opposing tendencies.

Fichte's description of the dialectical realization of human freedom is an example: Man is born free (thesis). But he cannot know this until his freedom is first opposed and constrained by others (antithesis). In the synthesis, or final stage, man passes the stage of freedom for its own sake and comes to know freedom as an instrumentality to be used for the good of all.

The dialectical ontology defended by Fichte enters Hegel's metaphysics at every point.

Romanticism brings the recognition that with the sublime comes a dialectic of terror and conflict and conflagration, that progress is won at a price, that history is organic. Nothing stays in place. And reality is always more than what we see. ■

Suggested Reading

Findlay, *Hegel: A Reexamination*. London, 1958.

Stace, W. *The Philosophy of Hegel*. Dover, 1955.

Questions to Consider

1. Compare Hegel's thinking of the state as "the march of God in the world" and Hitler's development of "the maximum State."

2. Infer whether Hegel read Kant's categorical imperative correctly. Conclude whether the good will is really that which causes moral mischief and evil in the world.

The Hegelians and History
Lecture 39—Transcript

I think anyone who sets out to develop Hegel's thought within the ambit of a 30-minute lecture really deserves all he gets—suits for libel, perhaps even actions by surviving members of the Hegel clan, if there are any. Sometimes when students ask for a quite sharp distinction between the classical and the Romantic worldviews, I've said half-seriously to recall that Aristotle's will calls for him to be buried next to his wife, and Hegel's will calls for him to be buried next to Fichte.

Now, I'm not quite sure that conveys all of the distinctions I'd want to make between classicism and Romanticism, but it certainly is an introduction to some of the distinctions that I would offer in this lecture.

Hegel was born in 1770 to a middle-class family in Stuttgart. His early education featured the classics and was preparatory for theological studies that, in time, proved boring to him. His record at Teubingen's Stift Theological Seminary was unremarkable, his record indicating that he was judged to be of "middling industry and knowledge." He roomed with two young men who would distinguish themselves in future years: the poet Holderlin, whose two-volume *Hyperion* is a classic in German literature—and Schelling, who will be associated with Hegel in years to come and who figured importantly in what came to be known as German Idealism.

The academic world of Germany and of Teubingen, especially, was in turmoil as a result of the French Revolution and the ideas surrounding it and arising from it. Hegel in 1792 is ranked by his fellow students as one of the great defenders of freedom. It is a period of reform, of rejection of the past, and Hegel is among that intellectual elite aware of the debts to the past, but aware as well of the changing conditions of the world, a political world the Greeks could not have anticipated and that conventional science could not even address, as Hegel saw things.

Now, there is so much that is elusive in Hegel that it is best to let him state what he takes to be his mission. The briefest expression of this is provided in the preface he wrote for his monumental *Phenomenology of Mind*. Here's the quote:

> The systematic development of truth in scientific form can alone be the true shape in which truth exists. To help to bring philosophy nearer to the form of science—that goal where it can lay aside the name of love of knowledge and be actual knowledge—that is what I have set before me.

A noble ambition. What Hegel shares with his immediate predecessors and, indeed, with Romanticism at large, is the judgment that science, as traditionally understood as "perfected" in the age of Newton, is a quite narrow, one-sided, misleading affair—that if science is going to stay at the level of mechanistic explanation, and the particularization of the complex into some reduced non-reality, then what science will be capable of explaining is very little, indeed. It's just going to be an exercise in the vindication of its own flawed methods.

The subject of truth itself is what has real being, and "real" in the sense of nothing being added or modified by peculiar or merely conventional modes of analysis. The possession of such truth is in the form, Hegel says, of a concept—in German: *ein begriff*. Writing again in his preface, he says:

> Scientific knowledge, *Erkennen*, demands that one give himself to the life of the object or, to say the same thing in different words, that one have before oneself and express in speech the inner necessity of this object.

Descartes's own revolution was never lost on Hegel. In his *Lectures on the History of Philosophy*, Hegel declared Descartes to be the thinker who revived, after a thousand years of neglect, the very foundations on which philosophy is based. As understood by Hegel, the achievement of Descartes was to recognize that knowledge in all of its forms is but "the unity of thought and being." His starting point is universal doubt, says Hegel, and thus serves as "an absolute beginning." Thus, Descartes—and here again are the words of Hegel on Descartes—"makes the abolition of all determinations the first condition of philosophy."

Accordingly, thought as such is not merely an aspect of philosophy, but is its foundational subject. It is in this respect that Hegel's *Phenomenology of Mind* is the foundational science.

In his *Lectures on the History of Philosophy*, Hegel turns to Newton admiringly, but with what is finally a devastating criticism. He regards Newton's work as making it possible for Locke's philosophy to become nearly official. The commitment to perceptual modes of knowledge and the shunning of deeper metaphysical considerations are products of this mode of thinking. What, then, of Newtonian science and the enterprises that would mimic it? Here is Hegel's judgment. Referring to Newton, he says:

> 'Physics, beware of metaphysics' was his maxim, which signifies, Science, beware of thought; and all the physical sciences, even to the present day, have, following in his wake, faithfully observed this precept, inasmuch as they have not entered upon an investigation of their conceptions, or thought about thought. Physics can, however, effect nothing without thought. Regarding matters as he did, Newton derived his conclusions from his experiences; and in physics and the theory of color vision, he made bad observations and drew worse conclusions.

Well, this is quite a judgment. One wonders how we ever got to the moon, but there is a deeper lesson in the judgment, even if the Newtonian science proved itself to be adequate in many ways. The deeper lesson is that a thoughtless application of thought itself may confuse us into believing we have witnessed reality as such, when in fact we've merely recovered the product of a method. If you assume that the ultimate reality is corpuscular, you will then develop a set of methods designed to deal with, what? Corpuscles, and guess what you'll discover if you do that? Well, corpuscles, of course, and what will you conclude? "Ah, I said that the whole thing was corpuscular, and now I've proved it." Against this, Hegel will contend that the true is the whole, and that there are no "parts" of truth.

The other ingredient that Hegel finds sorely wanting in science is explanation. Ironically, science doesn't actually explain anything, he insists. Now suppose we take one of the classic laws of physics: *F=ma*. To impart acceleration to an object, a force must be applied that is proportional to the mass of the object: Force equals mass times acceleration.

Suppose, though, we had a high school student, or a youngster who had not been taught anything in physics at all, and we went to the blackboard, and instead of writing $F=ma$, we wrote $F=5m + 3.2a$. Would the student protest? No. He would keep taking notes. In fact, none of the laws of physics makes any more sense than some radically different form of the law. The laws of physics simply describe what is. It turns out that if you make accurate and repeated measurements, the equation $F=ma$ is the one that keeps coming up. The world could have been constituted in such a way that F would have equaled something other than ma.

Now what Hegel is getting at, when he says that the scientific laws produced by mechanistic science don't really explain things, these laws don't tell us *why* things are the way they are. What is the point of all of this precision and lawfulness? There's got to be a story behind this, and it surely isn't revealed by the equation. The scientific community might sit back in a rather arrogant way and say: "Well, look, that's the way it is," but the question returns: "Why is it that way, and not some other way?"

To include Hegel within the tradition of Romanticism or German Romantic Idealism requires that we turn again to Johann Fichte, whose *Science of Knowledge* was published in 1797. Fichte is a pivotal figure in the history of philosophy. Indeed, that famous "Hegelian" triad of *thesis, antithesis,* and *synthesis* is actually Fichte's contribution and was rarely employed by Hegel himself.

At this point, all that needs to be said of Fichte is that he recognized in Kant's epistemology a fundamental conflict: If there is some sort of conceptual or logical barrier between the reality as it is and reality as it is perceived—between the noumenal and the phenomenal—a choice must be made by philosophy. Either there must be a commitment to bypass mind, as such, in every possible way or to accept that it is mind, as such, that is the worthy object of attention. Fichte's argument is that the ultimate reality is that of idea, the starting point of philosophy then being the transcendental ego. Against the Kantian thesis that the mind cannot know anything except under the forms of appearance and never as the entity is in itself, Fichte will counter that the mind knows itself noumenally, and not as appearance. We might say at this point: "Enter Hegel." What we ought to be looking for is not merely those causal connections revealed in scientific laws. Rather, we should be looking for the reason behind the laws, for reality is rational.

There is a profound difference between explanations based on causes and explanations based on reasons, and it is useful here to summarize the differences. Aristotle had argued that genuinely scientific knowledge, *episteme*, requires a complete causal account, but went on to note that a complete causal account must include the "that for the sake of which," the end, or purpose, or *telos* for the sake of which the other causal modalities operated. It is the final cause, then, the "that for the sake of which," that is the reason why the event or object came about.

One way to illustrate this is within the context of adjudication. Suppose we have someone brought before the bar of justice for having mortally wounded another. Smith is charged with shooting Jones. Now, the answer to the question: "Why did Jones die?" can take a variety of forms. We might say with the poets: "Dust thou art; to dust returneth." We might turn to page one of the Logic textbook and read: "All men are mortal. Jones is a man. Necessarily, Jones is mortal," and now we have proof of it, but, of course, what the court will say—what a jury will say—is that this syllogism is true indifferently across all human beings. This doesn't identify just what it was that brought about Jones's death.

We might next hear from the expert pathologist who tells us that the offending bullet severed the basilar artery, or something like that; the brain was denied blood supply, and so forth, and Jones died. Here, then, is an account in terms of the "efficient cause." Then, all of a sudden, Smith stands up in frustration and says: "I shot him. He was carrying on with my wife, and I killed him." Now the jury will breathe a sigh of relief. Those in attendance will breathe a sigh of relief—so will the judge. There is now an answer to the question. The event was brought about because there actually was a reason behind it. This explanation is entirely different from those based on biology, or mortality, or poetry. In a nutshell, Hegel's thesis is that there is no sufficient concept without a comprehension of the *reason* for the object, establishing that inner necessity that accounts fully for its reality.

Hegel applies this to human history itself. There is a distinct evolutionary perspective in Romanticism. Romanticism contains nothing if not the idea of struggle, the idea of struggle that produces newer, and different, and ultimately better, more developed forms through the *Sturm und Drang*.

A word about this *Sturm und Drang*, this "storm and stress," that is at the heart of Romanticism. The phrase appears in the title of a 1776 play by von Klinger, but its essence had already been revealed in Goethe's 1774 *The Sorrows of Young Werther*, a tragic tale of young and unrequited love leading to suicide. The story produced a small epidemic of suicide attempts. At the center of the idea is the problem of life itself, accommodating to the storms and stresses of existence. It is at its worst in youth, when all vital energy seeks to express itself, when the authentic and creative thought bursts forth as genius, but always is the struggle, and each victory is followed by yet another struggle.

History is the *Sturm und Drang* writ large, and what does it reveal? Suppose we were to conduct an anthropological study of human communities over the full course of human life on earth. Well, we find in the earliest tiny tribal enclaves attempts to scrape a living out of the rocky soil. Often, members are found running fast from predators. Others wait in hiding for something edible. This is a very limited sort of life, but out of the struggles in that life will evolve an ever more resourceful kind of humanity; and out of that will evolve a more settled human community; and out of that might evolve certain social forms and practices; and out of that will evolve, particularly with literacy, a more defined and abstract level of the rule of law, etc., etc.

Now, Hegel would ask: "Are we to assume that this is just some sort of accidental set of occurrences? Instead, doesn't this patently point to a plan or a scheme of some kind?" These are not developments that take place in a haphazard way. They are progressive developments of an evolutionary nature. It's out of the struggle itself that something gets resolved, and it is in the resolution that we find life lived at a higher plane. There is reason in human history, says Hegel. In fact, one of Hegel's most accessible works is the essay titled *Reason in History*. In that work, which is the collection of Hegel's lectures on philosophy of history, the conclusion reached is that "history" is a creation by reason guiding the affairs of the world. Through its own self-sufficiency, reason is unconstrained by any merely physical or causal law. It is the source of its own laws—you can hear of Kant, here—which it then realizes through human history.

This is not a reworking of Aristotle, though the Aristotelian dimensions of this are not difficult to discern. Hegel makes rather more of it. Aristotle did say that if the art of shipbuilding were in the wood, we would have ships by nature. With Hegel, the idea is enlarged. Nor will we get the progressive refinement and rationality of human life, except as a result of something that realizes itself thereby. There is something that is working itself through human history, and Hegel is satisfied that that something is ontologically real—that, indeed, in the absence of that ontologically real something, you could not have such an evolutionary and progressive course. Hegel refers to it with more than one term, typically as "the Absolute." Of course, that's with a capital "A." Sometimes he refers to it as the "Absolute Idea." In his *Science of Logic* he defines it this way:

> The absolute Idea (is) the identity of the theoretical and the practical idea…the rational Notion that in its reality meets only with itself. All else is error, confusion, opinion, endeavor, caprice and transitoriness; the absolute Idea alone is 'being,' imperishable, life, self-knowing, truth, and is all truth.

William James, that great phrasemaker—James will say at one point that when the Hegelians refer to the "Absolute Idea," they sound like they're going up in a balloon. Well, James's philosophy is quintessentially pragmatic, and as I will show in later lectures, quintessentially American and, of course, must be at war with this Hegelian kind of thinking, but the Romantic Idealism of the German intellectual world is committed to a quite brave rejection of a mechanistic science that never could get around to addressing reality as in fact we find it.

Now, the Absolute, in this Hegelian sense, expresses itself in a variety of ways, and in Hegel's time, he is satisfied that the fullest expression of it is in the ordered *state* itself. In fact, in a passage that I should say is in the wake of two world wars that are taking place in our own century, shall I say that this is a phrase that has a kind of chilling property to it. Don't blame Hegel for what a later history engages in, but when Hegel reflects on the state, when he sees in the state, the *au courant* expression of the "Absolute" in human history and says of the state that it is "the march of God in the world," well, now.

You might be thinking: "Goodness gracious, is this the sort of state hegemony that the Nazis were claiming for themselves, the march of God in the world?" Is this not what they claimed for the state—the duty to realize the rational plan for the world and to create a regime that would last for a millennium?

More than one scholar has pointed out that one can derive any number of bad things by way of what are sometimes called "the Hegelians of the right." The Hegelians of the right will be the ones who in Marx's day believed— and thereafter believed—that the power of the state should be obeyed, that fidelity to the laws of the state is the first obligation of citizenship, and the Hegelians of the left—some arriving as Marxists—will find in the same works of Hegel an understanding of freedom that requires the dissolution of the state and the installation of rule by the proletarian class. Hegel might have been clearer, thereby saving us from two world wars and a long cold one.

Much of Romantic Idealism, however, was devoted to moral issues of the sort generated by these various conceptions of authority and responsibility to it, for these morals arise directly from freedom and from the free play of concepts. Kant, recall, had insisted that there is only one morally good thing in the universe. The only thing that is unequivocally good in the entire cosmos is the "good will," and Kant had grounded morality ultimately in what we would be disposed to bring about if we could bring about anything that we could, in our most rational moments.

Hegel is not satisfied with this. He believes that it leaves room for what is arbitrary, even for what is wicked. He grants to conscience a certain moral authority, but this is incomplete, for the individual himself is incomplete. Rather, one's identity is shaped and sustained through political and social associations. Thus does social ethics reach far more closely to an ideal than would the merely individuated nature of values—so the emphasis now is going to be not on the freedom of the individual, but on the duties of the individual. Where the state itself reflects the general will—this a key notion in Rousseau's theory of the social contract—there is a complete duty to the state. In his *Philosophy of Right*, Hegel leaves little doubt as to his position:

> The state is the realization of the ethical idea. The true State is the ethical whole and the realization of freedom. The State is the march of God through the world. The State is an organism. The State is the world which the spirit has made for itself.

To trace this collectivization of consciousness in Hegel's political philosophy, Fichte again becomes an authoritative voice. In his *History of Philosophy*, Hegel says of Fichte that, "with Fichtean philosophy, a revolution took place in Germany."

Recall three critiques: *The Critique of Pure Reason*, *The Critique of Practical Reason*, and *The Critique of Judgment*. Those were Kant's. Then, anonymously, Fichte—whose dates are 1762 to 1814—published a work entitled *An Attempt at a Critique of All Revelation* in 1792, when he was just 30 years old. It was not only Kantian in tone and character cycle, it struck many as being Kantian in its philosophical power and insight, and, indeed, many people began to attribute it to Kant himself—so Kant had to write publicly that this fine treatise was not his, but was written by this young philosopher, Fichte.

Well, of course, if at that time in Germany you want to become a household name, just be thought of as someone whose work is of such a nature that you might have thought Kant was the author.

Fichte was a well-known champion of liberal movements. Early on he published, again anonymously, a controversial essay titled "Reclamation of the Freedom of Thought from the Princes of Europe, Who Have Oppressed It Until Now." At the age of 31, he was appointed to the Chair of Philosophy at the prestigious University of Jena, later becoming the rector of the new University of Berlin in 1811; this at a time when Napoleon's troops were occupying all of Prussia, and when, indeed, German-speaking people were tripping over themselves to affect the manner of the French, even to learn French, to adopt French modes of dress, etc. Fichte then delivered a lecture that ultimately cast him, by post-World War II lights, as the wrong sort of chap. He delivered an address, a lecture to the German people in 1807, his *Reden an die deutsche Nation*. This address did much to excite German nationalism and to preserve German cultural forms in the face of formidable challenges.

Fichte is important philosophically as the architect for that logic, that kind of Hegelian ontological logic that features that famous dialectical triad of thesis, antithesis, synthesis, progress through conflict—reality arising from opposing tendencies.

Freedom itself—the idea of freedom—arises from just such a dialectic of conflict. Man may be born free, but one could not know this until the first occasion on which *that* freedom is resisted and oppressed by another. It is in attempts to constrain your freedom that the world presents you with the possibility now of being conscious of your freedom—so that it is through the dialectic of a free being facing oppressive and coercive forces that the idea of freedom dawns, thereupon directing us as moral beings.

Freedom is not the last word. In his *Characteristics of the Age*, Fichte traces the stages of moral development of the entire human race, culminating in our self-conscious awareness of our freedom. However, we then have become so in awe of this freedom that we exercise it for its own sake. Freedom now has no purpose beyond its almost arrogant, hubristic exercise, by Fichte's account. Thus intoxicated, mankind enters what Fichte calls "the stage of perfected sinfulness." What he means by "perfected sinfulness" is acting for the sheer sake of expressing freedom against any and all grounds of constraint, opposition, or coercion.

Fichte insists that this is a stage that must evolve into something higher, where freedom is understood instrumentally. It's to become the means by which to produce what is finally good in the world, and for all. Only when one abandons individuality—which is materiality itself—can there be an eternal life; as an individual entity, you're a material particulate entity, and it is in abandoning that and surrendering oneself to the good of the whole that the possibility of a life that transcends mere materiality becomes possible.

The dialectical ontology defended by Fichte then enters Hegel's metaphysics at every point. It is by way of the dialectic that any "this" arises from all that is not "this." Take a pair of spectacles, and you might say: "Well, this is a particular thing." In traditional logic, you'd distinguish between particulars and universals, but how do you get a particular thing? The only way that these could be a pair of spectacles is by not being everything else. The only way there can be a "this" is in virtue of its not being everything else—so that each particulate is, in its own right, a universal. Now, this puts Hegel into the idea that there may be particulars that, in their very nature, instantiate cosmically important universals. There are three domains in which this happens, on Hegel's account: the domain of philosophy, the logical domain that I just described, in which the ontological possibility of the individual is only in virtue of the universal, to which it stands in dialectical relation. There is artistic genius who produces, in the singular, particular work, the instantiation of the universally beautiful, and so, it is in the domain of aesthetics as well; in the domain of philosophy and in the domain of aesthetics, the dialectic operates in such a way that individual instantiates give rise to the universals themselves.

It is finally in religion that Hegel was persuaded that the religion that succeeds most fully is Christianity—and this, chiefly, because of the ethics instantiated by the individual man, Jesus, who is universalized as the Christ. You can see the effect Hegelian philosophy and physics would have on Christian philosophy and the philosophy of religion at large; Hegelian influences are abroad in the world today and powerfully influential.

The Aesthetic Movement—Genius

Lecture 40

One of Oscar Wilde's more devastating epigrams declared that "the birth of America was the death of art." That's a punishing phrase. This sort of criticism is old hat, of course, and, at least in the matter of painting, has been utterly overtaken by the world of art in the 20th century. What Wilde was pointing to, however, is the conflict between the ideal and the practical, between the world of spirit and the world of things.

By the middle of the 19th century, a divorce had taken place between philosophers—especially aestheticists in the tradition of Hegel—and scientists. The great physicist and physiologist Hermann von Helmholtz put it this way during a lecture at Heidelberg (Nov. 22, 1862):

> [Hegel's] system of nature seemed, at least to natural philosophers, absolutely crazy....Hegel...launched out with particular vehemence and acrimony against the natural philosophers, and especially against Isaac Newton. The philosophers accused the scientific men of narrowness; the scientific men retorted that the philosophers were insane.

The rift between aesthetes and men of science was not complete by 1862, but it was certainly on the way to becoming so. The Romantic movement held that a mechanistic science was incapable of seeing anything clearly and truthfully. We are much more likely to find an underlying, fundamental noumenal reality in the great productions of art. This division all took place in the Aesthetic movement, from the middle to the end of the 19th century.

The Aesthetic movement did not have the 19th century to itself; it nourishes and is nourished by other movements. The 19th century was the great age of reform, of the effort to relieve the masses of people from traditional patterns of oppression. The roots of this great effort lay both in the Enlightenment and in the Romantic "rebellion" against it. Many reforms were on the inspiration of the Earl of Shaftesbury and other leaders of what were regarded as radical groups, including John Stuart Mill's father, James Mill. Many of the changes advocated and philosophically bolstered during the Enlightenment materialized in the success of the American experiment and the Constitution of the United States.

However, the American institution of slavery doesn't quite go along with this. Antislavery rhetoric is among the finest productions of the entire history of humanitarian discourse. The antislavery movements in the United States were launched by some of the best minds in the country. In the Romantic tradition, there is a growing sense that our sentiments of benevolence are our noblest sentiments. If, in fact, the defining feature of human nature is its moral freedom, nothing can be worse than to institutionalize that which denies the very exercise of moral autonomy. The great promise of the Enlightenment was that social problems—traditional modes of oppression and narrow-mindedness—could be conquered with scientific solutions.

There was already within Romanticism a recognition that science's understanding of nature is incomplete. Additionally, Romanticism recognized that we become more aware of our essential nature through the arts. Through an understanding of that nature, we also become more aware of the kind of world we should try to bring about.

A particularly convenient way to illustrate the tension and competing perspectives between the Romantic and Aesthetic movements can be found in a speech by Thomas Henry Huxley given at the founding of the University of Birmingham and a reply to that speech by Matthew Arnold, one of the saints of the Aesthetic movement. Huxley raises a question that continues to animate discussions of higher education: Should a youngster making his way in the world study natural science or "two dead languages"? The answer he gave was obvious. Greek and Latin might be proper if one intended to review books; the rest of the world was the domain of science. Huxley characterizes Matthew Arnold as a "Levite of culture" carrying with him a hieratic and remote past into an age overtaken by scientific advances.

Arnold replied by asking how human nature is to be understood. Can it be understood simply by digging into its remote biological past? He quotes

Darwin's statement that our ancestor must have been a hairy quadruped, with pointed ears and a tail, "arboreal in nature." Assume it to be so, says Arnold: There was yet something in that quadruped that "inclined him to Greek." There must have been, because Greek is what he became!

Consider what we achieve when we look inside ourselves and know that we are not complete, when we are driven to perfect ourselves in works of art and in the words of Aeschylus and Sophocles. The whole point of classical study, like the whole point of the Aesthetic movement, is not to prepare for the life of a book reviewer but to prepare for the life of a rational being. The whole point of culture, Arnold says, "is to make a rational being ever more rational" and to achieve what Arnold famously refers to as "sweetness and light." But this is the age of atomic and thermonuclear weaponry, and the National Football League, and vicious stock transactions on Wall Street. What are we to make of "sweetness and light?"

Antislavery rhetoric is among the finest productions of the entire history of humanitarian discourse.

Ruskin's *The Stones of Venice* inspired the Victorian age to rediscover the power of the Gothic. In his "Seven Lamps of Architecture," Ruskin included the "Lamp of Obedience": In an age (such as his own) that is without originality or creative force, the best thing to do is to copy the work of a better age.

Ruskin contrasted the free play of form and invention in the Gothic with late-Renaissance symmetrical and geometrical design, which he denounced as the "servile ornamentation of the Ninevite." Renaissance decoration might have been produced by a stamping machine of his own century: It reduces the craftsman to the status of machine. The Gothic is the *free* expression of those who have not been reduced to machinery.

One critic of America—Matthew Arnold—wrote two lengthy essays on culture in America. One was published before he had ever visited the United States; the second, after a tour of the States in which he was wined and dined at the White House and otherwise lionized as the ultimate arbiter of "high culture."

In his *Last Words on America*, Arnold rehearsed a judgment made earlier by Sir Lepel Griffin in print. He concludes that America has largely solved the political problem, the problem of poverty, and the social problem, but not the human problem. What Griffin is getting at is this: America is vast, rich, and getting bigger all the time. The problem is that it is not interesting. What makes a nation interesting is its capacity to inspire awe, which it does chiefly through the creation of beauty. And until America makes itself awe-inspiring by an attachment to beauty, it will remain uninteresting. For this reason, the gentle spirit will not find a home there.

The aesthetes of the 19th century were not simply proclaiming the value of art but its creative power. They insisted that our very character is formed by our practices and perceptions, that as these become more mechanical and tied to vulgarizing features of the world, we are transformed into something less than we were. Art, on the other hand, is the supreme instance of Schiller's insight that "men are never so free as when they are at play": Art is the free play of the spirit bringing into being what could not have been predicted in advance. ■

Suggested Reading

Arnold, M. *Culture and Anarchy*. Yale University Press, 1994.

Ruskin, J. *The Stones of Venice*, vol. 1. Smith, Eldeer & Co., 1853.

Questions to Consider

1. Explain whether the "freedom" of the Gothic and the diminished freedom of the high Renaissance is obvious to you.

2. If architecture has a moral side, explain what contemporary architectural genres teach and affirm.

The Aesthetic Movement—Genius
Lecture 40—Transcript

In November of 1862, one of the great scientists of the 19th century, Hermann von Helmholtz, was one of the important figures in the conservation laws in physics—conservation of momentum, conservation of mass, etc. Helmholtz gave a lecture at Heidelberg, and one of the issues that he was trying to clarify was why it was that as of 1862, the leading people in science not only had very little to do with philosophy, but were quite visibly shunning philosophers. The question before the house was: "How do you account for a divorce between those who a century earlier were living in the same house, doing the same work?" The natural philosopher was the natural scientist, and vice versa, and here we are in 1862, and you hardly can get a conversation going between members of those two domains.

Let me read a passage from Helmholtz, where he answers that question, how this all came about. Helmholtz says—he refers here to Hegel's philosophy, Hegel's system— Helmholtz says that:

> Hegel's system of nature seemed, at least to natural philosophers, absolutely crazy. Hegel launched out with particular vehemence and acrimony against the natural philosopher, and especially against Isaac Newton. The philosophers accused the scientific men of narrowness; the scientific men retorted that the philosophers were insane.

Well, the rift between the aesthetes and the men of science was not complete by 1862, but it was certainly on the way to becoming complete. The Romantic movement had made clear, at least to its own disciples, that a mechanistic science was incapable of seeing anything clearly, and anything truthfully, and that, indeed, if you're looking for some underlying, fundamental noumenal reality, you're never going to get it through some reductive scientific scheme based on microscopes, anatomical blow pipes, astronomical tables, etc. You're much more likely to find it in the great productions of art, which is to say, in that manifestation of the absolute that expresses itself through the progressive refinement, and beautification, and deep sensibilities of a rational and, indeed, spiritual creature.

The world bequeathed by the Romantics is a gift of genius, and this is all taking place within a movement that comes down to us as the Aesthetic movement, an original set of ideas. We find it from the middle to the end of the 19th century. The main contributors to the movement include Walter Pater; Matthew Arnold; Anthony Trollope; John Ruskin; later in the century, and wonderfully, Oscar Wilde.

Now the Aesthetic movement does not have the 19th century to itself. It is joined by other movements. It's nourished by them, and it nourishes these other movements. One of the salient political facts of the 19th century is that it is a century of reform. It is a genuinely humanitarian century, a century whose major ethicists at the level of public discourse are setting out to remove obstacles to progress, to save people from traditional patterns of oppression. It's a century that is particularly concerned with those in society who are least able to care for themselves—those who have suffered the heaviest burdens of discrimination.

Now, many of the reforms were on the inspiration of the Earl of Shaftesbury and other leaders of what at the time were regarded as radical groups. John Stuart Mill's father, James Mill, was one such radical. "Radical" meant someone committed to a radical reshaping of society along lines that were argued for and advocated and philosophically bolstered during the Enlightenment, and that materialized in the success of the so-called American experiment and the Constitution of the United States.

Have I failed to notice a little something in 19th-century America that doesn't quite go along with this? Ah, yes—the institution of slavery. Of course, the antislavery rhetoric is among the finest productions of the entire history of humanitarian discourse. The antislavery movements in the United States were launched by some of the best minds in the country—Benjamin Rush, for example, who was a signer of the Declaration of Independence, medically educated at Edinburgh, and a famous physician, quite well-known for the reform of sanitariums, hospitals. Benjamin Rush co-founds the first antislavery movement in America with Pemberton, and Benjamin Rush writes passionately about how the crimes we commit against each other, the horrific conduct that we behave in toward each other, is matched by things we do to defenseless creatures, to animals. He's making a kind of

145

animal rights speech—indeed, it *is* an animal rights speech—that if you can harden yourself in such a way as to cause pain and suffering to any creature capable of experiencing it, what is going to discipline you when it comes to exploiting fellow human beings?

Well, I say, there's this growing sense that our sentiments of benevolence are our noblest sentiments—that, in fact, if the defining feature of human nature is its moral freedom, nothing can be worse—there can be no graver sin—than to institutionalize that which denies the very exercise of moral autonomy by others; so, we have an antislavery movement.

I want to say that utterly Romantic views of the causes of the Civil War have been successfully defeated by historians, and no one any longer says with a straight face that the only reason there was a Civil War is because right-minded people wanted to put an end to the institution of slavery, but there's a tendency for the pendulum to go too far in one direction when we use our critical scholarly faculties. There is no question but that the moral impulses behind the Civil War included, centrally, the grave recognition of the sin of slavery as a denial of the very condition on which we would identify ourselves as human beings.

When Abraham Lincoln argued more than once that if slavery isn't wrong, nothing can be wrong, he was essentially taking a page from Kant's moral philosophy.

The great promise of the Enlightenment was that social problems would admit of scientific solutions, and, of course, the great hope of the reform movements was that now, in a scientifically knowledgeable period, with the right methods and the right perspective, with traditional modes of oppression and narrow-mindedness and the like put on notice, or indeed through revolutions, when necessary, we actually could solve problems, and the trick here was to keep our nose to the scientific grindstone, to keep our shoulder to the scientific wheel.

Now, there had to be a reaction to this, because, in fact, as I made clear in the previous lecture, there was already within Romanticism a recognition that science's understanding of nature is incomplete. It's too narrow. Yes, indeed, the Hegelians might have sounded crazy to men of science, but the Hegelians were already onto something when they insisted that science provides descriptions, provides correlations, and that it provides correct—but rather empty—equations. What it doesn't give is the reason for things, and, of course, until we understand the reason behind things, we've understood them not at all. We've understood them so superficially that the understanding is distorted.

Now, added to this aspect of Romanticism is the recognition that it is through art—through beauty, poetry, a commitment to these needs of the soul—that we become ever more aware of our essential nature, and through an understanding of that nature, ever more aware of the kind of world we should be trying to bring about. So, the Aesthetic movement, as part of the Romantic movement, is to supply something widely perceived as having been neglected by science, or beyond the reach of scientific methods and perspectives.

There are any number of ways of illustrating the tension, of illustrating the competing perspectives between the Romantic and Aesthetic movements. I find a particularly convenient way to be the review of a speech that Thomas Henry Huxley gave at the founding of what today would be called the University of Birmingham and, then, a reply to that speech that would be published by one of the saints of the Aesthetic movement, Matthew Arnold. The Scientific College of Birmingham was made possible by a gift of 180,000 pounds from Josiah Mason, a carpet weaver's son who had become quite wealthy. Josiah's industry earned him a fortune, much of it donated to charitable organizations, and for this service, he was knighted in 1872.

The Scientific College of Birmingham opened on October 1, 1880, with Huxley as the featured speaker. It was within the terms of this gift, however, that classics not be taught. Josiah Mason wanted to make a statement, and the choice of Huxley for the Founder's Day address could only amplify and give authority to that statement: "No classics taught here."

Huxley is a great writer, a solid thinker, and a passionate man—a man who can turn a phrase into almost anything he wants it to be and make it do any work that he wants it to do. Well, Huxley gives this wonderful address on

"Science and Culture," the place of science in education, and he raises a question that continues to animate discussions of higher education.

Consider a student, he said, setting out on a path in life in which he would hope to have some real, practical, worthwhile effects on the world. There are two distinct curriculums of study available. One, says Huxley, featuring a pair of dead languages, perhaps of some use to a future reviewer of books, and one devoted to the laws and principles and methods of scientific discovery. Well, Huxley asks, is there anyone who has any doubt about what course should be chosen by that youngster?

The critic Huxley knows he is facing is Matthew Arnold, the great advocate of culture in Victorian England. Thus do we find Huxley referring to Arnold by name. First he speaks of the toffy set of classics dons. He says this about them:

> They hold that the man who has learned Latin and Greek, however little, is educated; while he who is versed in other branches of knowledge, however deeply, is a more or less respectable specialist, not admissible into the cultured caste. The stamp of the educated man, the University degree, is not for him.

Then, he gets to Matthew Arnold and he says this:

> I am too well acquainted with the generous catholicity of spirit, the true sympathy with scientific thought, which pervades the writings of our chief apostle of culture, to identify him with these opinions; and yet, one may cull from one and another of those epistles to the Philistines, which so much delight all who do not answer to that name, sentences which lend them some support.

For all of Arnold's "catholicity of spirit," then, he, too, belongs to the club of non-Philistines, thanks to what? Well, his classical learning. Then, Huxley reads a passage from Arnold's works, where culture is defined:

Mr. Arnold tells us that the meaning of culture is "to know the best that has been thought and said in the world." It is the criticism of life contained in literature.

Arnold and Huxley were friends, and there was a certain amount of tweaking that went on, and the Victorian prose writers bring the essay to the level of an art for the express purpose of tweaking one another. You can't read much in Arnold, Walter Pater, John Ruskin, McCauley, John Stewart Mill, Thomas Henry Huxley, without recognizing the use of the English language in a way now deader than Latin.

Referred to in a public address, Matthew Arnold now has reason to reply in an essay frequently anthologized and titled "Literature and Science." Having been pegged as one of the "Levites of culture," Arnold begins his reply first by acknowledging that the world of Plato does indeed seem strange nowadays. Here's a quote from Arnold's essay:

> Practical people talk with a smile of Plato and of his absolute ideas; and it is impossible to deny that Plato's ideas do often seem unpractical and impracticable, and especially when one views them in connection with the life of a great work-a-day world like the United States. The necessary staple of the life of such a world Plato regards with disdain; handicraft and trade and the working professions he regards with disdain (and) bring about a natural weakness in the principle of excellence in a man, so that he cannot govern the ignoble growths in him, but nurses them.

Turning to the challenge laid down by Huxley, Arnold confesses to his lack of qualifications to debate the point:

> I wish to proceed with the utmost caution and diffidence. The smallness of my own acquaintance with the disciplines of natural science is ever before my mind, and I am fearful of doing these disciplines an injustice. The ability and pugnacity of the partisans of natural science make them formidable persons to contradict.

Nonetheless, Arnold is prepared to defend the proposition that a nation's greatest interests may not be secured by a scientific knowledge. Long an inspector of schools for the crown, Arnold has had ample exposure to what youngsters have been learning. So he passes on this vignette. You'll want to follow this closely:

> I once mentioned in a school-report, how a young man in one of our English training colleges having to paraphrase the passage in Macbeth beginning, "Can'st thou not minister to a mind diseased?" turned this line into, "Can you not wait upon the lunatic?" And I remarked what a curious state of things it would be, if every pupil of our national schools knew, let us say, that the moon is two thousand one hundred and sixty miles in diameter, and thought at the same time that a good paraphrase for, "Can'st thou not minister to a mind diseased?" was, "Can you not wait upon the lunatic?" If one is driven to choose, I think I would rather have a young person ignorant about the moon's diameter, but aware that, "Can you not wait upon the lunatic?" is bad, and that a young person whose education had been such as to manage things the other way be far better off.

Then, though, Arnold will rely on one of the greatest of scientists, Charles Darwin, to supply his own want of knowledge. He will focus on a passage found in Darwin's *Descent of Man*, where Darwin tells us that our ancestor, the ancestor of ourselves, was "a hairy quadruped furnished with a tail and pointed ears, probably arboreal in his habits."

Granting this much, Arnold concludes that:

> This good fellow carried hidden in his nature, apparently, something destined to develop into a necessity for humane letters. Nay, more; we seem finally to be even led to the further conclusion that our hairy ancestor carried in his nature, also, a necessity for Greek.

Now, we want to understand the profundity of that retort. This is not just Arnold being Arnoldian. This is Arnold saying something about an understanding human nature. Here are your options. You can do a very careful biological inquiry into the remote ancestry of the human species. If you keep going back far enough, you'll go back to eggs and spermatozoa, and before that, you'll go back to genes and DNA. If you keep going back on a particular theory, you come to some sort of slimy primitive soup with all sorts of gook around it and immersed in it, and if favoring conditions are right—humidity, etc., sparks of lightning, or whatever it takes—maybe some of this stuff actually will come together and forming a living thing. It might have all the attributes of a bacterium or something, but if you keep it going long enough, good things might happen. That's one way of understanding the nature of human nature—the scientific, reductive way. You start with the primitive soup, and if conditions are favorable and it goes on long enough, good things happen.

The way of culture, however, is entirely different. Now we are summoned to examine the achievements of humanity under favoring conditions. Take a look at what it creates when it takes itself most seriously and recognizes within itself a need, a virtual addiction, an addiction based on the proposition that I am not complete ever, and that the point of life is the perfecting of life, and I begin to perfect the life through examples. Culture provides the examples in the form of statesmen and statues, the Acropolis, poetry, drama, the deep dark mystery of things as conveyed by Euripides, Sophocles, and Aeschylus. There must be something in us inclining us to Greek.

This isn't a matter of sending boys and girls to school to learn the aorist voice in ancient Greek or a thousand lines of Homer. It's not the mastery of "two dead languages." In fact, you don't have to learn those dead languages at all. Moreover, rightly considered, those languages aren't dead, and they're not dying. They are the wellspring of the ideas and values that have now been expressed in a variety of languages. The whole point of classical study, Arnold would insist, like the whole point of the Aesthetic movement, is not to prepare for the life of a book reviewer, but to prepare for the life of a rational being. The whole point of culture, Arnold says, "is to make a rational being ever more rational" and to achieve what Arnold famously refers to as "sweetness and light."

Now many have found in that very phrase something so precious actually as to be rather prissy. "Sweetness and light." I mean, we do take our age in measures that are rather Herculean, and if so, where is "sweetness and light" figuring in? This is the age of atomic and thermonuclear weaponry, and the National Football League, and vicious stock transactions on Wall Street. What are we to make of this Arnoldian "sweetness and light"?

One of Arnold's friends, Frederick Harrison—a well known liberal of the time—is quoted in one of his political speeches as saying that the reason that the world's attention is focused on England (this was Harrison) and what makes England great, Harrison said, was coal. Well, you know that this is precisely the sort of claim that Arnold is going to have a field day with. It's coal, and you find Arnold in another essay stepping back and saying:

> If I understand this right, it would be as follows: that if this nation had never produced Shakespeare, and Johnson, Marlowe, and Milton—if it had never produced John Locke, Isaac Newton, and Robert Boyle—if it had never had any accomplishment of this sort to show for itself—but if it really had a lot of coal, then, in fact [Arnold was arguing] its standing in the pantheon of nations would be high and untouched. Whereas, it could have all these people, but if it didn't have any coal to speak of, there wouldn't be much point in paying attention to it.

Coal, actually, is the basis upon which people like Josiah Mason can make big gifts to support a curriculum that forbids the teaching of Latin and Greek—but again, Arnold, speaking for the Aesthetic movement, says: "No, no. It's not coal. It's not even the warm house. That will never do. The utilitarian calculus includes everything except what we're finally prepared to die for," or less dramatically, "what we are fully prepared to live for." So, that's going to be a central feature of it—and, of course, the idea of freedom remains alive and well in this Aesthetic movement.

Another leader of the Aesthetic movement was John Ruskin. His three-volume *Stones of Venice* had much to do, in architecture and art, with the revival of the Gothic form and the appreciation of the Gothic. Ruskin also wrote a collection of essays, which later in life he says he wished he hadn't written—but I don't think he really wished he hadn't written them. These were titled "The Seven Lamps of Architecture." One of the lamps is the

"Lamp of Obedience," where Ruskin raises the question of what an age is to do just in case it is found destitute of artistic energy and genius. What should it do? Well, for goodness sake, make pastiches. Make copies. It is better to offer a convincing Acropolis than to enlarge the McDonald's arches, for example.

In *The Stones of Venice*, Ruskin urges us to see in the Gothic—the so-called "Gothic," which is a derisive term—something long missing in later architecture. If you compare the High Renaissance architecture—you know, the High Renaissance design patterns, these inexhaustible little curlicues and rosettes—they repeat themselves up and down the page. Book pages are marked out with these things. The buildings have them. Ruskin sees in this the reduction of workmen to the status of tools. The precise, perfectly repeated pattern is at the cost of moral freedom and human dignity. The decorations themselves reflect what Ruskin calls the "servile ornamentation of the Ninevite."

When you turn from that to the Gothic, something entirely different is conveyed—this freedom in the very imperfection of the thing. You actually see expressed the personality of the craftsman, and it's expressed in the variety and diversity, the imprecision. The whole enterprise has a great, summoning harmony about it, but each particular is done by someone who is laboring freely in behalf of what he takes to be a noble enterprise. The noble enterprise might just be celebrity for his guild, but there's a personal element in this. Ruskin then, in his celebrations of the Gothic, is recovering the idea that we are never so authentically ourselves as when at play, and that one of the greatest productions of play is art itself. The authentication of human nature is found in its aesthetic enterprises—not in its mechanical, routine, servile undertakings.

One of Oscar Wilde's more devastating epigrams declared that "the birth of America was the death of art." That's a punishing phrase. This sort of criticism is old hat, of course, and, at least in the matter of painting, has been utterly overtaken by the world of art in the 20th century. What Wilde was pointing to, however, is the conflict between the ideal and the practical, between the world of spirit and the world of things.

A more discerning critic of America—and we now would use this good and great name to represent nearly all that passes for progress in today's world—was, again, Matthew Arnold. He wrote two lengthy essays on culture in America. One was published before he had ever visited the United States; the second, following a tour of the States in which he was wined and dined at the White House and otherwise lionized as the ultimate arbiter of "high culture."

In his *Last Words on America*, he rehearsed a judgment made earlier by Sir Lepel Griffin in print. He was an officer for the crown in India, and he had toured the United States, and he wrote an article in which he complained that of all the countries in the world the country in which a gentlemen would least want to live, next to Russia, would be the United States. Arnold attempts to understand this appraisal. Griffin comes, he says, from just that class of people you'd consult to determine where gentlemen would like to live, so what is it that Lepel Griffin is missing here?

Arnold does a very interesting analysis, not a Tocquevillian analysis. He even mentions Tocqueville and says: "I'm not a systematic thinker; you turn to Tocqueville for that." But he does perform a quite interesting service to us when he says: "Look, no people ever had political institutions that better matched themselves than the United States. The political problem is solved. It's the right form of politics for people like that. Can't improve it." He doesn't see much poverty here. He doesn't think poverty amounts to much here, because this is the country where you can turn that around overnight. To a very considerable extent, he thinks the social problem has also been solved here, at least during his visit.

At least it's not going to be plagued by class wars, but, he says, we've not solved the human problem, and what Sir Lepel Griffin is getting at is this—he says that Americans don't listen to the critics. It is already the most powerful country in the world. It can protect itself. It's vast. It's rich. It's getting bigger all the time. The problem is this. The problem with America, Arnold says, is not one of power, wealth, or politics. The problem is: "It's not interesting," and he says the reason it's not interesting is this: "What makes a nation interesting is its capacity to inspire awe, which it does chiefly through the creation of beauty. And until America makes itself awe-inspiring by an attachment to beauty, it will remain uninteresting, and therefore, the gentle spirit will not find a home there."

America can stand up to criticism sharper than this, needless to say, but the world at large will always be seen by the aesthete in terms and measures that the ruler and the butcher's scale miss entirely. It is a great idea in philosophy to urge a fundamental connection between truth and beauty. Socrates suggested the connection, and the aesthetes raised it to a religion. It probably is a religion perilously worshipped, but it is surely one to which we should accord great respect and find in it a rather dangerous criticism of what seems to be almost a passion for vulgarity.

Nietzsche at the Twilight
Lecture 41

> **Nietzsche was ... a writer of great power and a thinker of dark, suggestive, and daring ideas, a radical with a style and ingenuity capable of making the most developed philosophical systems and arguments seem jejune.**

There are two ways to contribute originally to the study of philosophy. One well known way is through rigorous analysis, built on the foundation of logic. Another way is by the use of aphorisms, by use of penetrating personal reflection. In modern times, no one enjoys the status of wielding this kind of influence more than Friedrich Nietzsche. Nietzsche, born in a rural region of Germany in 1844, would require care either within institutions or in the home of his mother or sister from 1888 until his death in 1900.

Despite his troubled life, however, Nietzsche was a writer of great power and a thinker of dark, suggestive, and daring ideas. His ideas run far afield of Matthew Arnold's "sweetness and light." Nonetheless, there was a common bond between Arnold and Nietzsche: Their arguments are addressed to the public at large, not to the "schoolroom." Arnold's "something in us that inclines us to Greek" leaves aside the question: Which Greek? Apollo and reason are but one face of the classical world—the other face is Dionysian and ecstatic.

Schopenhauer's *The World as Will and Representation* (1819) greatly influenced Nietzsche. The first and irrefutable fact that Schopenhauer presents is that "the world is my idea...No truth is more absolutely certain than that all that exists for knowledge and, therefore, this whole world, is only object in relation to subject—in a word, idea." This is the subjectification of knowledge that was to be a starting point for Nietzsche. As for the interests and aims, Schopenhauer held that the primary, basic aim is self-preservation. In time, however, Schopenhauer's philosophy would wear thin for Nietzsche. The will to live was radically transformed into the will to power. If, indeed, progress is won by destruction, then progress may be less the aim than the consequence of this motive—a side of the Greek that we don't see when we fix our gaze on Apollo.

In his first notable work, *The Birth of Tragedy and the Spirit of Music* (1872), Nietzsche contrasted the Apollonian and the Dionysian, these two faces of the Greek world—the two "art deities" of the Greek world. Greek tragedy aims to resolve the conflict or relax the tension between these two art deities by giving the Dionysian element the means by which to give the fullest expression of pent-up emotions, passions, dread, and madness but all framed within the Apollonian framework of story, plot, coherence. Nietzsche said it was the fault of Socrates and the Greek academic philosophers to give too much to the Apollonian at the expense of the Dionysian. Terrified by pessimism: This is all-prevailing in Nietzsche's thought as he looks at the world around him.

Nietzsche was an admirer and one-time friend of Wagner, whose operatic characterization of the natural though godlike man surely shaped Nietzsche's conception of that *Oberman* who would come to replace the weak and degraded contemporary man. Both Nietzsche and Wagner were influenced by Schopenhauer. Both were drawn to the world of the classical Greeks. Both sought to restore to art what was lost to convention and reasonableness.

It is a maxim in Nietzsche's philosophy that suffering, mistrust, self-loathing, and rejection of all comforting superstitions are the staples of a defensible conception of life.

Wagner's operas were northern myth, rather than Apollonian, and they abandoned Christianity for the secular and cultural. Nietzsche broke with Wagner over Wagner's vulgar anti-Semitism and Wagner's last opera, *Parsifal*, with its open recovery of the Christian mythos.

Society must tame the destructive Dionysian passions and the uncontrolled will to power by taming persons. Nietzsche understands that much of what we do during our conscious daily lives is actually a sublimation of the very basic instinctual impulses that we refuse to face. He is the first to use the term *sublimation* in a way that it will come to figure in Freud's psychoanalytic theory.

The man capable of living an authentic life in the face of society's bribes and corruptions embodies the *Oberman*. Nietzsche surely does not regard himself as the *Oberman*. His candidate is Goethe, whom Nietzsche believed lived his life authentically, faithful to his vocation.

The Enlightenment and even the Darwinian picture is one of *progress*: constant improvement and refinement. But this is not what the record of human history reveals. Even less does it reveal that divine progression in which the "absolute" realizes itself. What history reveals are cycles of brutality interrupted by seasons of creative energy. Every act of creation is a destruction, as every lived moment is a movement closer to death.

The Judeo-Christian teaching, with its emphasis on guilt, redemption, sacrifice, and turning the other cheek, is what keeps us from feeling this summons to creation and destruction. The teaching of Jesus (an ineffectual, unworldly innocent) weakens those who believe it; it makes them more servile and tractable. Christian teaching is devoid of the impulse to power.

It is a maxim in Nietzsche's philosophy that suffering, mistrust, self-loathing, and rejection of all comforting superstitions are the staples of a defensible conception of life. Suffering has to be almost a goal. The lived life must be defeated once we recognize that our lives have been inauthentic, our natures corrupt and corrupting. We will suffer, knowing there is no light at the end of the tunnel, but our suffering confers a certain kind of dignity that makes us worthy of ourselves. Not long before his death at the age of 56, Nietzsche caused a stir by collapsing in a public street in Turin, Italy. He had been embracing and comforting a cart horse that had just been abused by the coachman. Perhaps he had seen in its condition all that human beings deny in their own natures and, in their denial, inflict suffering on innocent beings. ∎

Suggested Reading

Hollingdale, R. *Nietzsche: The Man and His Philosophy*. Louisiana State University Press, 1965.

Kaufmann, W. *The Portable Nietzsche*. Viking Press, 1961.

1. Identify in what senses Nietzsche might be classified as both "classical" and "Romantic."

2. Summarize how Aristotle might have judged a theory of authenticity based on the need for self-assertion and the will to power.

Nietzsche at the Twilight
Lecture 41—Transcript

There are two quite different ways of influencing the world of philosophical thought, two very different ways of contributing originally to the literature, to the animating spirit of philosophy. One is a very well known way. It shows up in philosophy journals; it is taught in schools of philosophy, in departments of philosophy. It is often rigorously analytical. It is built on a foundation of logic. It is richly indebted to Plato and Aristotle. It takes off from there, etc. Much of what is covered in these 60 lectures is fortified and fleshed out by that school and mode of philosophizing.

There's another way, and that way is by aphorisms, by way of a kind of wise, personal, penetrating reflection on the meaning of all the things that philosophy deals with. Sometimes, the influence of those operating out of that tradition is so pervasive, so extensive, that you can't identify the source of the influence. It seems to be broadly atmospheric. I would say in modern times, no one enjoys the status of that kind of influence, that kind of influential status, equaling that of Nietzsche, about whose ideas my remarks in this lecture are concerned.

Well, if the objective of philosophy is the discovery of truth, and its mission is the search for it, then what is it that we can say about the author of such aphorisms as this one?

> What are man's truths, ultimately? Merely his irrefutable errors.

That from Nietzsche's *The Gay Science*.

> Erroneous articles of faith include the following: that there are things, substances, bodies; that a thing is what it appears to be; that our will is free; that what is good for me is also good in itself.

That also from *The Gay Science*. Try this one:

My concept of the philosopher is worlds removed from any concept that would include even a Kant, not to speak of 'academic ruminants' and other professors of philosophy.

We all know what an "academic ruminant" is. It is a cud-chewing, cow-like creature who simply keeps his jaws moving with little by way of nourishment arising from there, academic ruminant, so that he won't even include Kant, let alone academic ruminants.

Now, Friedrich Nietzsche was born in a rural region of Germany in 1844. He died in 1900 under the care of his sister, Elisabeth, who had come home from Paraguay, where she had devoted her energies to the founding of an anti-Semitic colony. You begin to see that this was a rather mixed family background. She was good enough to come home and take care of her brother and abandon the colony for anti-Semites that she was laboring to produce in Paraguay.

From 1888 until his death, Nietzsche would require care either within institutions or in the home of his mother or his sister's rented villa. His was a troubled life, made all the worse by a syphilitic infection that may well have resulted, ultimately, in utter madness.

He was, however, a writer of great power and a thinker of dark, suggestive, and daring ideas, a radical with a style and ingenuity capable of making the most developed philosophical systems and arguments seem jejune. Is there a greater distance to be found between his ideas and those of Matthew Arnold, of "sweetness and light," the Matthew Arnold whose idea of culture is just the best things said and done by the human race?

As far apart as was their thought, there is this common bond between Arnold and Nietzsche: Their arguments are addressed to the many and not to the "schoolroom." The second half of the 19th century witnesses a proliferation of public forums—magazines, pamphlets, newspapers, public lectures, adult education centers—hosting the best minds of the age, now seeking to instruct and, yes, covert the new and growing middle class. The democratization of knowledge is richly underway, a takeoff from the encyclopedia long before the Internet, and it is shaping the sensibilities of entire nations. How unsurprising, then, that a technical college in Birmingham will have Thomas Huxley give the Founders Day address and, in that address, feature the battle between the classical learning of the aristocrat and the practical, classless knowledge of the scientist.

This age of reform—with its ethics of liberation, its war on discrimination and class oppression—ranks high on the list of the world's political achievements, and we mustn't ever forget that, but a price does get paid for this. You very often find the unleashing of forces that all of those now transformed institutions and now abandoned social practices had once brought under control. There are not many periods in intellectual history in which a Nietzsche would gain a publisher, let alone a readership, and the second half of the 19th century just is one of those periods.

He is a luminary, but "luminary" is somehow an odd word to use in a brief lecture on Nietzsche, whose world is anything but "sweetness and light." It is a world of light and dark. It is a world of opposing polarities and opposing tendencies. Is there something in us, as Arnold insisted, that inclines us to Greek—but which of the Greeks? Nietzsche was a gifted philologist schooled in ancient Greek and a devoted student of the Greek tragedies, which he prized for their courageous acceptance of the reality of human life.

Which Greeks, indeed? The gods? The philosophers? The everyday citizen? Are we equally inclined—if we are inclined to Greek—are we inclined to Apollo, Eros, Thanatos, Medea, Clytemnestra, Agamemnon, Alcibiades? Are we inclined to the Greeks given to us by Euripides, Sophocles, and Aeschylus? Are we inclined to Aristotle or Plato? Attempts to anchor humanity to a fixed star—moral, or aesthetic, or political—illustrate what Nietzsche judged to be the source of philosophy's failures:

> All philosophers have the common failing of starting out from man as he is now and thinking they can reach their goal through an analysis of him. They involuntarily think of man as an *aeterna veritas*, as something that remains constant in the midst of all flux, as a sure measure of things. Everything the philosopher has declared about man is, however, at bottom, no more than a testimony as to

> the man of a very limited period of time. Lack of historical sense is
> the family failing of all philosophers.

That from *Human, All Too Human*. You see what he says. This essentialism,
do you see —"Man is essentially X, Y, and Z" —simply ignores the fact that
a given person is a product of the conditions under which one finds him.
Nietzsche was satisfied that the religious superstitions of a race disclose their
self-perceptions, giving the gods exaggerated versions of what they take to
be their own powers and passions.

How did the ancient Greek world understand Eros? Is it this wonderful,
life-giving force that gives us spankingly new seven-pound babies—the
world is their oyster, and the future is theirs? Eros is at once a creative and a
powerfully destructive force. It's behind rape and pillage. It's behind victory
and conquest. It's behind what Nietzsche will call the *will to power*.

Over his productive years, Nietzsche would form two radically different
estimations of the philosopher Schopenhauer, whose *The World as Will and
Representation* (published in 1819) had great influence. Nietzsche's initial
estimation was of Schopenhauer as philosopher and teacher—a man facing
reality and bringing its truthful challenge to the attention of those who would
prefer to ignore or deny it. The first and irrefutable fact that Schopenhauer
presents is that:

> The world is my idea. No truth is more absolutely certain than that
> all that exists for knowledge, and, therefore, this whole world, is
> only object in relation to subject; in a word, idea.

That's Schopenhauer.

Here, then, is just that subjectification of knowledge that was to be a starting
point for Nietzsche. There is no external truth reached by some sort of
objective method with, as it were, the observer's own interests and aims
held constant. As for the interests and aims, it was Schopenhauer, again, who
wrote with candor that the primary, basic aim is self-preservation, the will
to live. It is the primary human drive, directing all the life-saving and life-
generating impulses. Moreover, it is embodied. The body is the immediate

object of the will, and it is the awareness of one's will that renders the actions of a person intelligible to himself.

In time, Schopenhauer's philosophy would wear thin in the increasingly cynical and passionate thoughts of Nietzsche. The will to live was radically transformed into the will to power, with Eros now not merely an engine of survival but one of conquest. We are destroyers, and, if indeed progress is won by destruction, then progress may be far less the aim than the consequence of a motive that at base may be a motive of willfulness, and destruction, and darkness—a side of the Greek world too often overlooked, a side of the Greek world that we don't see when we fix our gaze on Apollo.

It was Nietzsche who, in *The Birth of Tragedy and the Spirit of Music*, contrasted the Apollonian and the Dionysian, these two faces of the Greek world—as Nietzsche says, the two "art deities" of the Greek world. The Dionysiac sects, which by the way very often were populated chiefly by women, had as their goal a liberation from the strictures of the ancient Greek world, a liberation from the strictures of life within the *polis*. Celebrants surrendered themselves, seeking to be possessed by the gods, for the purpose of liberation and to experience transcendence. Indeed, there is a word in the Greek for rendering oneself accessible in this way, and what is the word? *Enthousiasmos*. "Enthusiasm" in the original acceptation is not simply being quite excited by something; it's in fact being possessed by something, and to be possessed by something you have to abandon yourself. You have to step outside yourself. You must stand outside yourself. It has to be a total out-of-body sort of thing, to leave room for the movement in of the god.

To be sure, the Greeks had a word for that, too: *ekstasis*. "Ecstasy" is not simply being in a swoon; it is being removed from oneself. It's a kind of death. One must die to be born again. All this, however, proceeds within a group of kindred spirits, each facilitating the experiences of the other—each contributing to something of a mass hysteria. This is the best we can tell about some of these ancient Greek mystery religions.

The merging or "marriage" of the Apollonian and the Dionysian is treated by Nietzsche in *The Birth of Tragedy and the Spirit of Music*, which was published in 1872. It is the achievement of Greek tragedy to resolve the conflict or relax the tension between these two art deities by giving the Dionysian element the means by which to give the fullest expression of pent-up emotions, passion, dread, and madness—but all this framed within the Apollonian framework of story, plot, and coherence. What a remarkable integration Nietzsche is achieving here.

He said that it was the fault of Socrates and the Greek academic philosophers to give too much to the Apollonian at the expense of the Dionysian. In his preface to *The Birth of Tragedy*, he makes this explicit:

> Socratic ethics, dialectics, the temperance and cheerfulness of the pure scholar; couldn't these be viewed as symptoms of decline, fatigue, distemper? Might it be that the "inquiring mind" was simply the human mind terrified by pessimism and trying to escape from it, a clever bulwark erected against the truth?

Terrified by pessimism: This is all-prevailing in Nietzsche's thought as he looks at the world around him. There cannot be many people who have felt the presence of the world as directly, as heavily, as abidingly, as Nietzsche did.

He had been an ardent admirer of Wagner in his youth, eager and proud later to enter into a friendship that inevitably collapsed under the weight of both of their ideologies and egos. Both of them had been influenced by the philosophy of Schopenhauer. Both were drawn to the world of classical Greece. Both were seeking to restore to art what was lost in its concessions to convention and reasonableness. It is interesting to consider his comments on Wagner's *Parsifal,* at once deeply disturbing to Nietzsche for its open recovery of the Christian mythos, but also so deeply moving that Nietzsche would say that hearing it, hearing *Parsifal*, "one lays Protestantism aside as a misunderstanding."

The genius in the work, says Nietzsche, is the "alliance of beauty and sickness. It casts a shadow over Wagner's earlier art, which now seems too bright, too healthy, health, brightness having the effect of a shadow."

Again, the urgency of the Dionysiac no longer tamed by the Apollonian confers a truthfulness on *Parsifal* not present in Wagner's triumphant Germanic epics. Thus, although it was Wagner's courageous adoption of Germanic legend and law over the submissive rationality of Christianity that first attracted Nietzsche, still he finds in *Parsifal* an authenticity that cannot be denied.

He visited Wagner in his home, and they struck up a relationship that lasted for a time. Wagner, of course, was obsessionally anti-Semitic. It is one of the sad chapters in the history of the biography of great artists that Wagner could never get past his anti-Semitism. In fact, it had so pernicious an effect on his thought that one must conclude it is at the bottom of those aspects of his music that seem to be merely vulgar. A mere glimpse of this pathological contempt is all time will bear, and I take it from one of his letters to Franz Liszt:

> I felt a long-repressed hatred for this Jewry, and this hatred is as necessary to my nature as gall is to blood.

However, Wagner's own characterization of the truly natural if godlike man surely was behind Nietzsche's conception of that *Oberman* who would come to replace the weak and degraded contemporary man. The "Sigfried" of Norse mythology is a dragon slayer, a prince who gains the treasure of the Nibelungs by killing those who guard it. He wins the love of Brunhilde, daughter of Odin and fearless leader of the Valkyries, Norse goddesses who had the power to choose which great heroes would be killed in battle, the Valkyries. I note this chiefly to call attention to Nietzsche's attraction to power, imagery, and lusty unconventionalism.

Nietzsche surely is the first of the great "depth psychologists" of modern times. He is actually committed to probing the depths of the unconscious. Freud acknowledges as much later. He understands that at the level of our conscious daily lives, so much of what we do is actually a sublimation of the very basic instinctual impulses that we refuse to face. Nietzsche is the first to use the term *sublimation* in a way that it will come to figure in Freud's own psychoanalytic theory.

166

Now, in reading Nietzsche, one confronts soon enough the famous *Oberman*. This is one who will "overcome man," overcome those committed to a life of comfort, staying out of trouble, keeping their noses clean—a society of essentially servile, mechanically living people whose lives are empty, pointless sets of distractions. It is Zarathustra now who speaks:

> I teach you the Oberman. Man is something that shall be overcome… What is the ape to man? A laughingstock or a painful embarrassment, and man shall be just that for the Oberman. Once the sin against God was the greatest sin; by God died. To sin against the Earth is now the most dreadful thing…What is the greatest experience you can have? It is the hour of the great contempt. The hour when your happiness, reason and virtue, too, arouse your disgust.

Nietzsche surely does not regard himself as the *Oberman*. He certainly doesn't regard Wagner as the *Oberman*. His candidate is, perhaps, Goethe, and what he finds in Goethe is a life lived at the aesthetic level—life authentically lived faithful to one's vocation.

Oberman here has to refer to something rather more penetrating than a mere anti-conventionalist. It's Goethe's integrity, not his manners. It's not in the surface Goethe; it's in the interior Goethe that Nietzsche finds a spirit capable of rising above the welter of mere conventionality, mere opinion, the stock beliefs and phrases of a narcotized, self-hypnotized population that will do anything to keep itself out of trouble. This is political correctness written large.

Nietzsche, the nihilist, the cynic, so often portrayed as either melancholic or angry, a tiresome scold, but one must love in an ultimate way to be so painfully concerned about the number of persons, the large majority of people, who have yet to enter what he at least takes to be as an authentic form of life. We see this in his reflections on all that we might be inclined to regard as progress. The cheerful prospect of evolutionary forces that prune, and improve, and lead inexorably toward progress and perfection is but another myth that Nietzsche exposes.

These very evolutionary pressures have as their central mechanism destruction. Creation is always at the expense of something else. Every creative act has to destroy. In human affairs, the penchant for destructiveness may give rise to what, at the superficial level, looks like progress, thus concealing the prime impulse itself, which is the will to power and its impulse to destruction. How does power express itself? Typically, destructively.

How did we ever come to see reality as the setting for rationality and "sweetness and light"? How did we ever fail to notice what most deeply moves us? Now, when Nietzsche assays what we are pleased to call "Western civilization," he finds the body of Judeo-Christian religious beliefs, and he declares them to be religions of servitude. Declaring himself to be the anti-Christ, he presents a scandalous depiction of Jesus as a character very much akin to Dostoevsky's *Idiot*. This is someone who is so utterly innocent and naïve—referring to Jesus, now—so utterly devoid of the impulse to power that in fact he goes through life as an almost unbelievably good person, but he's not emblematic of anything. His salient characteristic is that what is authentic in him is almost childlike. That is the salient characteristic unless he becomes little children; it might be a gloss on his own life. The lesson of the life of Christ, what Christianity has taught—which is turn the other cheek, born in sin, love thy neighbor, take care of the needy—Nietzsche says this is just the rehearsal, a religious rehearsal designed to keep people in their place, to set a limit on their progress, to set a limit on their expression of their feelings. It is a religion of guilt. It's a religion of servitude. Nietzsche believed that Jews are even worse at this. The Jews are spending all of their time under thick clouds of guilt and sin. They've got a God that punishes them. They've got to enter into compacts and covenants with him. "If we do this, will you do that for us?"

Now, it is a maxim in Nietzsche's philosophy that suffering, mistrust, self-loathing, the rejection of all comforting superstitions, are the staples of a defensible conception of life. The process of actual suffering has to be almost a goal. One has to go through a kind of striving and suffering that includes, he says, "self-loathing, the torture of mistrust, and the misery of him who is overcome."

This is what has to take place within the lived life. It is a life that first has to be defeated. One has to recognize that one has been so in the thrall of an inauthentic theater piece, scripted by others—one has not yet begun to live the life of man.

The first time you recognize what you are willing to give your life in return for—these tawdry little baubles of a distracted world—the suburban house, the children with perfect teeth—self-loathing is the inevitable consequence. Once you begin to recognize that the human relationships on which you've placed such a high premium—the so-called loving relationships and faithful friendships—have been based on little more than habit, and sloth, and mutual exploitation, you are finally overcome, and it is in the depths of suffering that you finally look for a palliative, and the palliative has to be in the form of rejecting everything that had given substance to an inauthentic life. It has to be the death of that life. Once you come to grips with what is in the unconscious that has the real claim on your life, and how long you have repressed it and sublimated it in ways that are treasonous to it—it's only at that point that you begin to see some light at the end of the tunnel. Now you begin to see that you are in a tunnel, and you're going to stay in that tunnel, and you're going to make the best of it.

To know oneself is to know a divided nature, a corrupt and corrupting nature in which the best thing that can be said about it is that it might suffer with a certain kind of dignity; so through the dignity of the struggle one makes oneself worthy of—what? Well, of oneself.

Nietzsche died at 56. His health was uneven for years. In 1889, he caused a crowd to assemble when he collapsed in a public street in Turin, Italy. Before he collapsed, he had run over and put his arms around a horse. He was hugging, caressing, and kissing a horse that had been mistreated by a coachman, and he must have found in the suffering of that innocent animal just the sort of authentic experience that human nature sets out to deny itself, and, in denying itself, that it inflicts suffering on another and on the innocent. The picture I have of Nietzsche is the picture of Nietzsche caressing an innocent who has been the subject of abuse, and that picture forgives almost all the rest.

The Liberal Tradition—J. S. Mill
Lecture 42

Mill's essay *On Liberty* is probably one of the most widely assigned in the university curriculum in political science. It is the *locus classicus* for arguments that oppose any and all forms of state paternalism, moral paternalism. It stands as a ringing defense of the right of the individual person to fashion a form of life for himself, freed from the despotism of fashion and of tyrants.

Along with David Hume, John Stuart Mill (1806–1873) might be properly regarded as the most influential of philosophical scholars in the English language. He laid the foundations for what we would take to be the scientific psychology of the 20th century. His essay *On Liberty* is the *locus classicus* for arguments that oppose state and moral paternalism.

Mill's *System of Logic* stands as a "bible" for experimental science. His defense of utilitarianism remains perhaps the clearest and most supple. He has placed his mark on the widest range of issues in science, politics, and ethics.

Mill's autobiography thoroughly outlines his life. Mill was home-schooled, with a grounding in Latin and Greek classics, economic philosophies, world history, logic, and mathematics. His father insulated him from other boys and from influences that might infect his thinking with vulgar or mundane habits. Thanks to the patronage of the Stuart family, Mill received instruction at Edinburgh. Though educated for the clergy, Mill was a strident atheist and proceeded to make do as an occasional writer for profit and as an employee of the East India Company. In that post, he composed the authoritative *History of India*.

Early influences on Mill included Bentham, Coleridge and the French writer Auguste Comte (1798–1857), one of the fathers of a version of what is called *positivism*. Distinctions are in order, however, when that term is used. Comte's use of the term *positivism* is perhaps most divergent from the sense now employed by philosophers. Comte's thesis is that human thought, as it must address pressing problems, passes through distinct stages: the theological, the metaphysical, and the positive.

The first of these stages he regards as the age of superstition, with belief in occult and personal but supernatural agents directing the affairs of the cosmos. This gives way, in the second stage, to what appears to be a demystified set of beliefs. In fact, however, the mind sees—instead of supernatural beings—entities that may be invoked to "explain" things. Inevitably, this all must give way to the third stage, in which the mind applies itself to the study of natural laws. In the final state, we're all supposed to be Humeans! This is key, because Mill's philosophy is so closely mapped onto

> **Mill goes so far as to define matter itself as but "the permanent possibilities of sensation."**

Hume's that his affinity for Comte was predictable, if not entirely long-lived. Note that the term *positivism* is also used in connection with a certain philosophy of law, as in *legal positivism*, the subject of a later lecture.

A third sense of *positivism* gets closer to Comte's use of the term and to what Mill works to develop in his philosophy of science. Its most cogent defense comes from Ernst Mach, a great figure in physics at the University of Vienna late in the 19th century. His *An Analysis of Sensation* is part of his larger project of ridding science of all metaphysical speculation. In a word, you can tell you're engaged in a scientific enterprise to the extent that you are *not* engaged in metaphysical speculations.

John Stuart Mill should be understood as promoting a philosophy of science compatible with Mach's and with the general positivistic view of science. Science is what takes place in the domain of experience. It is an empirical enterprise. Mill goes so far as to define matter itself as but "the permanent possibilities of sensation," meaning that the material world is a permanent possibility of sensation. Reality exists insofar as it is the subject of experience. He rejects rationalist arguments of philosophy, saying that the introspective method employed is faulty. By reflecting on what we recall from our early years, we fail to come up with any experience that might have conveyed an idea and incorrectly conclude that our current awareness is "intuition." Mill places in opposition to this what he calls the *psychological method*. He argues that we learn things in the present by being presented with what it is to be learned, being rehearsed through repeated presentations, and forming the necessary associations. Mill is very much the echo of Hume in this argument.

With Mill, the problem of knowledge solves itself in that well-known empiricistic way, fortified by methods of experimental inquiry. In Mill's treatise on inductive logic, he actually sets forth a methodology for experimental science. According to the *principles of concomitance*, A is the cause of B whenever, in presenting A, you can bring B about. The *method of agreement* would have the experimenter record all factors present whenever B occurs. The *method of difference* is comparable; now we look to see if there is an event whose presence is always the case when B occurs, but whose absence is matched by the absence of B. There are other "methods" and various refinements of each. In the end, a manipulability hypothesis grounds the entire approach: A is the cause of B when—taking B to be an empirical feature of the world—A can be used to manipulate that feature of the world.

In the matter of ethics—the problem of conduct, as we've called it— Mill says the right test ethically is not whether something holds up in logic but whether it holds up in life. He thinks that, with some significant modifications, Bentham got it right. We do what we do chiefly as creatures of nature, constituted in such a way as to maximize our pleasures and minimize our pains.

What Mill concludes is that the most significant sources of human activity are grounded in considerations of utility. The ultimate test of a course of action is whether it is useful, whether it serves some fundamental human purpose. But Mill does not want to be misunderstood in affirming utilitarianism as the standard by which we judge the ethical content of actions. He rebukes those who see utilitarianism as a caricature of the Epicurean: "Eat, drink, and be merry, for tomorrow you shall die." Mill's thesis is that when people set out to assign utilities to courses of action, what they include is what makes life more meaningful, more developed, more purposive, and more under rational control. The ultimate pain is a life that is not authentically one's own, and what is profoundly useful is a meaningful and fully lived life. In this same connection, Mill argues that we develop a sense of duty, which is the chief motive impelling us to promote the general welfare.

Mill's position on freedom is also utilitarian. If the wildest, most pernicious and degrading view is false, we can discover its falsity only by exposing it to criticism. If, instead, what seems to be patently false, reckless, and destructive turns out to be true, it's a truth we would deny ourselves were it to be silenced by the censor. John Stuart Mill presents the liberal position on freedom of inquiry, freedom of expression, the free marketplace of ideas. It has become almost a mantra in modern times, but Mill sees in this freedom the surest engine of progress. No one's ideas, by virtue of personal authority, take precedence over anyone else's. Precedence is won by being earned, and it is earned in the arena of utility, usefulness, what finally works in the public interest, for the general good.

Liberty extends to a liberty of conscience, because anyone may be wrong and certainly may be wrong at the level of basic moral precepts. Everyone has a right, in virtue of his or her own autonomy and dignity, to frame a form of life that makes sense to that person. There are limits on this, however; liberty must be used in such a way as not to limit the liberty of others. ■

Suggested Reading

Mill, J. S. *Autobiography.* Penguin, 1989.

———. *On Liberty*. Prentice Hall, 1996.

Questions to Consider

1. Explain how one determines what is "useful."

2. Conclude what might be Mill's recipe for cases in which what Smith takes to be useful, Jones takes to be painful—and where Smith and Jones are whole nations?

The Liberal Tradition—J. S. Mill
Lecture 42—Transcript

I should think that after David Hume, perhaps even before David Hume, John Stuart Mill might be properly regarded as the most influential philosophical scholar writing in the English language, and his influence extends over a wide range. He certainly laid the foundations for what we would take to be the "scientific" psychology of the 20th century. He wasn't alone in this, but in developing arguments in defense of inductive science, inductive experimental science—indeed in developing a systematic, associationistic psychology in its own right—John Stuart Mill would be cited by more than one of the authorities in the 20th century history of psychology as a source of philosophical inspiration and philosophical justification for a scientific psychology.

His essay *On Liberty* is probably one of the most widely assigned in the university curriculum in political science. It is the *locus classicus* for arguments that oppose any and all forms of state paternalism, moral paternalism. It stands as a ringing defense of the right of the individual person to fashion a form of life for himself, freed from the despotism of fashion and of tyrants. His *System of Logic* stands as something of a "bible" for experimental science. His defense of utilitarianism remains perhaps the clearest and most supple. In all, he has placed his mark on a very wide range of issues in science, politics, and ethics, and if his constructive proposals remain subject to serious reservations, his critiques of alternative formulations resulted in refinements and in significant reformulations. To all of this, we can add his genius as a prose writer, which he has in common with at least a dozen of his Victorian contemporaries.

Mill's life, stretching from 1806 to 1873, is well told in his own autobiography. He was a prodigious learner in youth. His father, James Mill, saw to it that his schooling would take place on his father's knee. This was home schooling, by the way, with the benefit of advice from no less than Jeremy Bentham. I would say what was perhaps the most ambitious program of home schooling on record, James Mill paced his son through the Latin and Greek classics, the economic philosophies of Adam Smith and David Ricardo, world history, logic and mathematics. A man of tireless industry himself, not to mention settled opinions, James Mill insulated the boy from other boys and all other influences that might infect his thinking with vulgar or mundane habits. James Mill revered Milton. Oddly, he had disdain for Shakespeare and a controlled hostility toward all religions, but with special contempt reserved for Christianity and any God "who would make a Hell."

The father was poor in youth and would have been desperate in early adulthood had it not been for the patronage of the Stuart family—this being the reason for John being named John Stuart Mill. Thanks to their support, James Mill received instruction at Edinburgh, his philosophical interests piqued by the lectures of Dugald Stuart. Though educated for the clergy, James Mill, his strident atheism in hand, proceeded to make do as an occasional writer for profit and as an employee of the East India Company. Now, as in that post and through persistent study and high native intelligence, he composed what, as of that time, was the authoritative *History of India*, the result of which was the first economic security he had known.

His conduct toward John Stuart Mill was that of eager tutor, patient taskmaster. He made such a point of understating John's abilities that Mill came to regard himself as a rather indifferent student, perhaps even somewhat backward. He also placed such great stress on material that would render the mind strong as to leave the heart in a state of neglect, this leading, Mill tells us, to a severe depression that lifted only as Mill himself turned to the Lake Poets.

He would come to write an essay on two men who, apart from his father, had the greatest influence on him, Bentham and Coleridge. It is a most informing essay at several levels, for to some extent, it is autobiographical as well as an insightful appraisal of two distinct and highly articulated personalities, as well as an appreciation of the perils of keeping the head too far from the heart as we develop. The genius of Coleridge is illuminated by the deficiencies of Bentham, says Mill, though the greatness of both will be acknowledged in this essay. Here is part of what he says about Jeremy Bentham:

> He lived from childhood to the age of eighty-five in boyish health. He knew no dejection, no heaviness of heart. He never felt life a sore and weary burthen. Self-consciousness, that daemon of the

men of genius of our time never was awakened in him. How much of human nature slumbered in him he knew not. No one, probably, who ever attempted to give a rule to all human conduct, set out with a more limited conception either of the agencies by which human conduct is, or of those by which it should be, influenced.

Another of the early influences on Mill was the French writer Auguste Comte, whose dates are 1798–1857, an interesting but deeply troubled French *savant* whose depression and suicidal attempts found him institutionalized. As of 1838, he resolved never to read again, this in the interest of what he called his "cerebral hygiene." His correspondence soon would be habitually signed by "the founder of universal religion, great priest of humanity." For all this, his *A Course of Positive Philosophy* won many adherents. Among them, Harriet Martineau ranks high, for her condensed translation of 1853 would bring Comte's *Positive Philosophy* to the wider audience of the English-speaking, English-reading world.

Auguste Comte is one of the fathers of a version of what is called *positivism*, but distinctions are in order when that term is employed. Let me begin with Comte, however, whose use of the term is perhaps most divergent from the sense of the term as now employed by philosophers.

Comte's thesis is that human thought, as it must address pressing problems, passes through distinct stages, which he dubbed the theological, the metaphysical, and the positive. The first of these stages finds the mind, as he says: "seeking the essential nature of beings, the origin and purpose of all effects; in short, absolute knowledge."

Auguste Comte regards this as the age of superstition, with belief in occult and personal but supernatural agents directing the affairs of the cosmos. This gives way, in the second stage, to what appears to be a demystified set of beliefs. In fact, however, this second, metaphysical stage, says Comte, "is only a modification of the first; the mind supposes, instead of supernatural beings, abstract forces, veritable entities," and it pleases itself to believe that by invoking such entities it has actually explained things.

Inevitably, this all must give way to the third and final stage, in which "the mind has given over the vain search after absolute notions, and applies itself to the study of their laws; that is, their invariable relations of succession and resemblance."

Alas, in the final state, we're all supposed to be Humeans! This is key, for John Stuart Mill's own philosophy is so closely mapped onto Hume's that his affinity for a theorist such as Auguste Comte was entirely predictable, if not entirely long-lived.

The Comtean bequest is a philosophy of science first made canonical by Francis Bacon and now enjoying the fruits of the age of Newton and what followed. It is a conservative, systematic approach to phenomena, science settling for the measurement and recording of reliably conjoined events—all this entering into the record of how the world works. There is no need to hunt for causes. It is sufficient to acknowledge that all phenomena are subject to invariable laws. To discover these is to be able to predict the course of events and exercise some control over them. Now, what about social phenomena? These are no exception. Auguste Comte is quite clear on the point:

> The positive philosophy offers the only solid basis for that social reorganization that must succeed the critical condition in which the most civilized nations are now living.

Here is one of the modern fathers of social science.

I should note at this point that the term *positivism* is also used in connection with a certain philosophy of law, as in *legal positivism*, a point I will get to in one of the final lectures of this series. There is also a third sense of *positivism*, which gets rather closer to Auguste Comte's use of the term and to what John Stuart Mill works to develop in his more refined philosophy of science. However, its most cogent defense comes less from Mill than from Ernst Mach late in the 19th century. This is less a digression than something complementary to Mill's programming.

Ernst Mach was one of the great figures in physics at the University of Vienna. His treatise, *An Analysis of Sensation*, is part of his larger project of ridding science of all metaphysical speculation. In a word, you can tell you're engaged in a scientific enterprise piously to the extent that you are *not* engaged in metaphysical speculations. By the 1930s, Mach's influence had been absorbed fully by a group that came to be known as the "Vienna Circle," who produced a positivistic program for science and philosophy—*positivism* as the term now would be employed. The group dubbed their early convergence *"Verein Ernst Mach,"* acknowledging their intellectual debts.

Well, that's a bit of a necessary digression. I would say that John Stuart Mill should be understood as promoting a philosophy of science compatible with Mach's, and with the general positivistic view of science. Science is what takes place in the domain of experience. It is an empirical enterprise. Mill goes so far as to define matter itself as, "the permanent possibilities of sensation." That is, all we mean by a material world is that which in principle, either directly or through some kind of aid, becomes an object of experience. It's a permanent possibility of sensation. Reality exists insofar as it is at least potentially the subject of experience.

Who is the enemy, then? The enemy, so to speak, is any and every form of intuitionism, a priorism—Kant's version or any other—innate ideas, substances, essences, occult forces. Mill is opposed to nothing more explicitly than to intuitionist theories of knowledge, the idea that there is some non-empirical level at which we know things. He is as opposed to Reid's principles of common sense as to Kant's pure categories. He regards intuitionism as the great intellectual support of false doctrines and bad institutions.

What of Meno's servant who seems to comprehend the Pythagorean theorem without benefit of experience or instruction, though? What of the fact that we know there is no number so large that one cannot be added to it? What of Leibniz's *nisi intellectus ipse*—that intellect or mind that must be there and integrating experience, for experience to amount to anything?

Mill rejects these ageless arguments of the rationalist schools of philosophy on the grounds of their adopting a faulty method. The method of inquiry employed by them he calls the *introspective method*. Reflecting on what we recall from our early years, we fail to come up with any experience that might have conveyed an idea, and we quickly conclude that our current awareness of it is the gift of "intuition."

Mill places in opposition to this what he calls the *psychological method*. Rather than memory and introspection standing as the final arbiter of the sources of knowledge, we should study the principles at work when we set about now to learn things. You learn things now by being presented with whatever it is to be learned, being rehearsed through repeated presentations, forming the associations by frequent repetition—so John Mill is very much echoing here Hume in all of this. It is through the laws of association that we come to learn. This can be shown by experiment. Since we can establish right now and today that associative principles and experience are all that has to be taken into account to account for new knowledge, why assume that anything else was involved in learning things through experiences of which we have no current recollection?

Let us demonstrate experimentally how to bring something about in the here and now. Isn't that to be the method chosen for explaining? Why assume that it was known intuitively, when we can show that all learning in your present consciousness, in your adult life, is by way of association and experience?

You see what the scheme is here. The scheme is this: If you sit back, introspecting in the philosopher's armchair, you can say that you now know some things that, as far as your memory tells you, you never learned in school, you never learned from anybody else. You know it certainly to be the case, and, therefore, it must be intuitively known. Mill says: "Wrong method. The right method is the psychological method."

See what it takes to learn something now. Why assume that the manner in which you thought you knew intuitively came about in any other way than the way things now come about?

Well, if we've come this far with Mill, the problem of knowledge solves itself in that well-known empiricistic way, now fortified by the methods of experimental inquiry. In Mill's treatise on inductive logic, he actually sets forth a methodology for experimental science, to determine what is causally efficacious in a particular context.

Thus, according to the *principles of concomitance*—here is part of Mill's methodology for science, the principles of concomitance. A is the cause of B whenever, in presenting A, you can bring B about. The *method of agreement* would have the experimenter record all factors present whenever B occurs. The *method of difference* is a comparable method; now we look to see if there is an event whose presence is always the case when B occurs, but whose absence is matched by the absence of B. There are yet others of "Mill's methods" and various refinements of each. In the end, a manipulability hypothesis grounds the entire approach: A is the cause of B when—taking B to be an empirical feature of the world—A can be used to manipulate that feature of the world. That is Mill's sense of a causal relationship. A is causally related to B in the sense that A can be used causally to manipulate B.

Now, in the matter of ethics—what we have called the problem of conduct—Mill is content to consult the historical record. History is a laboratory of sorts, and human behavior is a guide as to which variables, so to speak, powerfully incline our conduct. Mill judges the record of history to be clear on the question of what moves us. He thinks that, with some significant modifications, Bentham got it right. What we do we do chiefly as creatures of nature, constituted in such a way as to maximize our pleasures and minimize our pains. What Mill concludes is that the most significant sources of human activity are grounded in considerations of—here comes Hume's word—utility; of course, it is also Bentham's word. The ultimate test of a course of action is whether it is useful, whether it serves some fundamental human purpose. The justification for it is not in terms of an abstract moral theory. The justification is found in practice. The right test ethically is not whether something holds up in logic but whether it holds up in life.

Mill makes this clear in the first chapter of his *Utilitarianism*, where he distinguishes between the "intuitive" and the "inductive" schools of moral philosophy. Again, you will see a rejection of intuitionism. Kant, of course, is the quintessential spokesman for the intuitionist school. Mill defends the second, which is really the school of experience, generating regularities and providing a means by which to develop the laws of a social science, what he calls *ethology*. In this same work, he offers a most economical statement of the chief ethical canon of utilitarianism. Here is Mill, one of its fathers, telling you what it is:

> Actions are right in proportion as they tend to promote happiness, wrong as they tend to produce the reverse of happiness.

There it is.

Now, Mill does not want to be misunderstood in affirming utilitarianism as the standard by which we judge the ethical content of actions. In fact, the traditional complaint against the utilitarian is that he is some kind of caricature of the Epicurean—the "eat, drink, and be merry, for tomorrow you shall die" caricature of Epicureanism. He rebukes those who characterize utilitarianism that way, for in the process, they have depreciated the very nature of human nature. The very nature whose dignity they would set out to affirm is depreciated by the view that what we find pleasurable is always at a low and vulgar level.

Mill's thesis is that, in fact, when people do set out to assign utilities to courses of action, surely what they include is what makes life richer, more meaningful, more developed, purposive, more under their rational control, more elevated. Utilitarian terms are not to be reduced to caloric intake or episodic pleasures. The ultimate pain can be a kind of existential pain. Mill, after all, had his own periods of depression. The ultimate pain is a life that is not authentically one's own. What Mill found lacking in Bentham—this is a sure guide to what he recognizes as profoundly useful to a meaningful and fully, maturely lived life. His reflections on Bentham, his reflections on his own depression, should tell you what he's taking to be included in the notion of utility.

In this same connection, Mill argues that a sense of duty is developed in us over the course of a lifetime, and that this turns out to be the chief motive that impels us to promote the general welfare. It is the pleasure of this achievement, and the pain caused by our disregard of it, that stand as the imperatives to good conduct.

Utilitarianism, then, here need not be understood in prosaic terms. It can rise to great and even sublime heights, depending on how we conceive of human nature. Of course, one can complain with any form of utilitarianism that if you're pretty loose on the side of how utilities are calculated, then almost any moral theory can be rendered in utilitarian terms.

If it turns out to be that what maximizes utility is a perfectionist orientation in life, let's say. Well, in that case, Aristotle's *Ethics* would be utilitarian. Let's say that it's making sure that there is a perfect harmony in the composite nature of the soul such that reason rules, etc., the passions. Then, of course, Socrates is a utilitarian. I think for utilitarianism to be a serious player in the game of ethical theories, then, it must strive for some consistency and discipline in the identification and quantification of "utility."

An empiricist of the John Stuart Mill stripe understands that we enter the realm of the observable as *fallibilists*. We can always be wrong. We can form all sorts of fuzzy and foolish ideas, developed on the basis of incomplete data and eccentric perceptions. It's just in the nature of associational processes that we may come to regard any number of things as causally related that aren't. Remember Hume, where anything can be the cause of anything.

The whole point of experimental, systematic, and disciplined inquiry is to correct mistakes at this time, prevent and correct them. Outside the laboratory, the way we can correct mistakes is to own up to them and expose oneself to corrective influences. However, we never know where the corrective is going to come from, so how do we put ourselves in a position where self-deception becomes less likely and correction becomes more likely? By opening up the curriculum to all ideas. All ideas have an equal right to a hearing. Nothing at the level of censorship should in any way interfere with the freest and fullest expression of thought.

Mill's position on freedom is also utilitarian. If the wildest view, the most pernicious view, the most degrading view, is false, its falsity will only be discovered by exposing it to criticism. If, instead, what seems to be patently false, reckless, and destructive—for whatever reason turns out to be true— it's a truth we would have denied ourselves were we to be silenced by the censor, or if we were to be the censor.

So, in the tradition of Milton's *Areopagatica*, we find John Stuart Mill presenting the liberal position on freedom of inquiry, freedom of expression, the free marketplace of ideas. It has become almost a mantra in modern times, but Mill sees in this freedom the surest engine of progress. It's the way a fallible creature spares himself repeated error arising from persistent ignorance. Nobody's ideas by virtue of personal authority take precedence over anyone else's ideas. Precedence is won by being earned, and it is earned in the arena of utility, usefulness, what finally works in the public interest, for the general good.

Well, does it have to be a general good, because this would seem to leave room for a tyranny of the majority? Mill is quite consistent here. Liberty extends to a liberty of conscience, because anyone may be wrong, and certainly may be wrong at the level of basic moral precepts. Everyone has a right in virtue of his own autonomy and dignity to frame a form of life that makes sense to that person. There are limits on this, and the limit is this: Your actions are permitted free and full expression as long as they do not harm others. That is, liberty must be used in such a way as not to limit the liberty of others.

The staying power of Mill's defense of liberty should be understood as the result of the forces that most oppose liberty in precisely those settings that allegedly revere human freedom. The current expression " political correctness" is illustrated by such ridiculous modes of social control that we tend to ignore the truly pernicious and corrosive power it wields.

Mill worried most about the tyranny of majorities, as well he should have. Typically, a great collection of persons can impose their will on small minorities, but tyranny, recall, is actually a minority achievement—often the achievement of a single tyrant. Today's Western democracies, chastened by historical indifference to injustices perpetrated against minorities, have instituted regulations and policing functions now so intrusive, often offensive and always clumsily applied, patently ridiculous in many instances, and all for the express purpose of preventing precisely that expression of judgment, opinion, and core values that Mill thought essential to social progress.

Recall, also, the form of social control that Mill leaves intact as a means by which what strikes others as offensive might be discouraged. He assumes that society, even as it withholds coercive measures, retains the ability to embarrass, to isolate, to scold. That is, as long as one can either avoid the unpleasant or unpopular views, or can display resentment and disagreement, all parties are provided with all they need: The speaker says his piece; the audience either turns away or, if inclined, registers audible signals of disapproval. What, however, if the very signal of disapproval becomes an actionable offense? What if society is actually incapable, in any practical way, of avoiding such confrontations?

Mill was consistent in his defense of liberty. Even in the instance of a potential suicide, he reserves to the individual ultimate authority as to have his mind and his body disposed as he chooses.

Well, we have come a long way from Mill's defense of liberty and dignity, from Fichte's concern that an age of perfected thankfulness wants to express its freedom. Now, we have come to a point where the sensitivity to the needs and, indeed, the temperaments of others is such that thought must be censored, and speech must be transformed. If Mill isn't turning in his grave, he should be.

Darwin and Nature's "Purposes"
Lecture 43

As a result of the Darwinian perspective, the traditional problems of knowledge, of conduct and of governance, refer not to abstract principles, but to various modes of adaptation, to environmental pressures that work on us to adapt. With change now the dominating principle, the search for absolutes comes to seem anachronistic and naïve.

Charles Darwin revolutionized modern thought and, in the process, revolutionized much in the traditional subject matter of philosophy. His influence stretches across the humanities and the social sciences, biology and genetics, ethics and political theory. As a result of the Darwinian perspective, the traditional problems of knowledge, conduct, and governance refer not to abstract principles but to various modes of adaptation to environmental pressures. However, Darwin comes out of what is very much an Enlightenment context. The Enlightenment, after all, is a period that venerated the idea of progress through conflict and competition.

Darwin's early influences provide a picture of the context in which his own ideas formed. Darwin was born in Shrewsbury in 1809 to a physician father and to the daughter of Josiah Wedgwood. the family famous for porcelain china. He entered Edinburgh with a view toward medicine, then moved to Cambridge with a plan to study for the ministry. There, however, he befriended John Henslow, who helped turn Darwin's attention to biological subjects. Darwin took field trips with the geologist Adam Sedgwick. Encouraged by Henslow, Darwin served as Naturalist on H.M.S. *Beagle* from 1831 to 1836. At the conclusion of the long voyage, he had a mountain of notes and a thoroughly focused mind. In considering the influences on Darwin's thought, we mustn't overlook his grandfather, Erasmus Darwin (1731–1802), a physician who studied at Edinburgh and Cambridge, as well as an accomplished poet and inventor, who theorized that all varieties of living things evolved from an original type.

These influences do not lessen Darwin's originality. Although others had written about the plan and order of nature, the fitness of plants and animals to meet the challenges of the natural world, Darwin proposed the concept of design without a designer—a theological theory about ends being served by variation but not contrived by some providential super-intelligence. Darwin published *Origin of Species* in 1859. The allegedly great and hostile controversy that surrounded its appearance is largely fiction. Critical reviews were remarkably detailed and highly positive.

Eleven years later, *The Descent of Man* saw quite a different reception. There is an argumentative tone in *Descent of Man*, and of course, there is that great inductive leap according to which the particular characteristics of our humanity are to be understood as lying along the same continuum that covers all of animal life. There is no room for qualifying the radical implications of Darwinian thought. We now confront an uncompromisingly evolutionary psychology in which human nature is not separated in any way from the balance of nature.

Charles Lyell's *Principles of Geology* (1830–1833) provided a time frame compatible with the requirements of Darwin's theory. Lyell's *uniformitarian*

British naturalist, Charles Darwin (1809-1882) developed the theory of evolutionary selection.

theory (that the same geological forces that operated in the remote past were still operating and in the same fashion) meant that there was enough time in the earth's past for evolution to work. Lyell had also proposed, based on the fossil record, that older species had died out and been replaced. (Lyell, however, believed that progress was not by way of modifying existing species but by their replacement.)

Some of Darwin's critics, as late as the second half of the 19th century, insisted that he had not proceeded according to the established methods of Bacon and Newton, reaching broad generalizations without the necessary step-by-step inductive process. Even in our own time, scientists have concluded that the "natural selection" account is farfetched. A scientific theory is expected to be both *retrodictive*, in that it explains how things came to be the way they are, and *predictive*. Thus, gravitation laws not only explain why objects have fallen but also predict *that* and *how* they will fall.

Evolutionary theory, however, is non-predictive: It is impossible to tell how natural selection will work in the future. Darwin himself called his method a kind of natural history. Some also argued that the fossil record—which Darwin insisted was incomplete—was actually too good. These critics said that the record was quite complete but failed to reveal the minute progression of change and gradual appearance of new species that the theory required.

Alfred Russell Wallace, the co-discoverer of the theory and a distinguished scholar in his own right, answered these criticisms, saying that although the fossil record is complete, it is not an accurate record because of the upheavals that have taken place at the level of the strata. They provide a broken and shifted record. Were the record undisturbed, it would support the theory. Many pointed out that though farmers and breeders had been selectively breeding livestock and domestic animals for millennia, they had never been able to create a new species.

More significant for most was Darwinism's implication that nature has its own creative and renewing resources, deployed with no plan or intention. Evolutionary theory does not offer the peaceable kingdom of a providential God, but a hellish place of competition, and conflict. Herbert Spencer first used the expression "survival of the fittest" in his *Social Statics*, published eight years earlier than *Origin*. Darwin borrowed the phrase but remained aloof to the radical libertarianism and "social Darwinism" advocated by Spencer. The evolutionary principles advanced by Spencer were, unlike

Darwin's, forged into a moral imperative: Given that progress depends on the achievements of the best, these are not to be held back by accommodating the needs of the less talented.

Yet another implication of evolutionary theory is that what matters are collectives, not individuals. It is not coincidental that Darwin's cousin, Francis Galton, was writing on hereditary genius in 1869. He made the point that, in a large sample of human beings, there will be a negligibly small number of truly exceptional instances, but the entire race ultimately depends on the achievements of that small group. Galton himself was totally committed to the hereditarian view of natural variations and to the need to improve society by genetic means, even proposing cash payments for voluntary sterilization to those measuring low in estimates of intelligence.

Darwin comes out of what is very much an Enlightenment context.

If nature can prune and purify at the level of intellect, it can also select moral predispositions, if these enhance the species' adaptive potential. Ethics thus boils down to biology. There is room for altruism but only as defined biologically: It is the behavior of individuals that favors the survival of the species as a whole. This is not what moral theorists call "altruism," which depends on intentionality and consciousness. Darwin's proponent Thomas Huxley wondered whether natural selection could ever match with human moral conceptions.

Alfred Russell Wallace, the co-founder of the theory and a man deeply admired and respected by Darwin, ultimately asks whether the theory of natural selection succeeds as an explanation of human nature. He identifies three domains that are so distinctly removed from the theory as not to be assimilated by it. Purely abstract thought seems to serve no particular evolutionary end. In the domain of aesthetics, resources are squandered in the interests of what is merely beautiful, and that surely cannot serve the kinds of ends envisaged by the theory itself. In the domain of moral thought and ethics, we intentionally sacrifice our most cherished interests for the benefit of others.

The Darwinian theory, though it met opposition, was rapidly and universally successful as a description and as a method. The question may be asked, however, whether this theory can tell us finally who we are and how we should live. Yet, in our Darwinian world it seems almost no longer possible to think in terms that are non-Darwinian, let alone anti-Darwinian. ■

Suggested Reading

Darwin, C. *The Expression of the Emotions in Man and Animals*. New York, 1998 (1896).

Galton, F. *Hereditary Genius*. New York: 1978.

Young, R. *Mind, Brain and Adaptation in the Nineteenth Century*. Oxford, 1970.

Questions to Consider

1. Conclude how sound the proposition is that the defining psychological attributes of different species vary only in degree, rather than in kind.

2. Darwin regards altruism as having positive adaptive value. Explain whether this is consistent with "survival of the fittest."

Darwin and Nature's "Purposes"
Lecture 43—Transcript

In his essay, "The Influence of Darwin on Philosophy," John Dewey drew attention to the ancient concept and conception of "species" and the extent to which philosophy and science depended on the notion of the fixity of species. The principle of, to use his words:

> A uniform type of structure and function seemed to give insight into the very nature of reality itself, the conception of *eidos*, species, a fixed form and final cause, with the central principle of knowledge as well as of nature. Upon it rested the logic of science.

Charles Darwin revolutionized modern thought, and in the process he revolutionized much of the traditional subject matter of philosophy. That's what Dewey was getting at. His influence is pervasive, stretching across the humanities and the social sciences, biology and genetics, ethics and political theory. As a result of the Darwinian perspective, the traditional problems of knowledge, of conduct and of governance, refer not to abstract principles, but to various modes of adaptation, to environmental pressures that work on us to adapt. With change now the dominating principle, the search for absolutes comes to seem anachronistic and naïve.

If Darwinian thought has had this effect, it has nonetheless not come to us full-blown from the brow of Zeus. Darwin, too, comes out of a context, to some extent very much an Enlightenment context. The Enlightenment, after all, is a period that venerated the idea of progress, progress through conflict and competition. We find these precepts in any number of writings in Enlightenment philosophy, in social and political philosophy, not to mention more scientific productions of the period that actually anticipate central features of Darwinian theory. Let me quickly summarize the early influences on Darwin, just to get a clearer picture of the context in which his own ideas formed, and, as it were, struggled for dominance.

He was born in Shrewsbury in 1809 to a physician father and to the daughter of Josiah Wedgwood, the family famous for porcelain china. Darwin's schooling was unfocused and generally disappointing. It looks like early Newton again, you see.

He entered Edinburgh with a view toward medicine, finally finding both less than appealing—I mean, utterly unappealing. He moved next to Cambridge, now with a plan to study for the ministry, but, thanks to the fates, he actually established a close friendship there with John Henslow, who taught biology. Their discussions turned Darwin's attention increasingly to biological subjects, Darwin then taking advantage of the invitation to take field trips with the geologist, Adam Sedgwick. Now, through the influence and encouragement of Henslow, Darwin made application for the position of naturalist on the *HMS Beagle*, and served in that capacity from 1831 to 1836. When the voyage began, Darwin was 25, and the Captain of the *Beagle*, Robert Fitzroy, was 26.

At the conclusion of the long voyage, Darwin had a mountain of notes, and now a thoroughly focused mind. His reading was systematic. He tells us that in October of 1838 he read Thomas Malthus's *Essay on Population*:

> And being well prepared to appreciate the struggle for existence which everywhere goes on from long-continued observation of animals and plants, it at once struck me that under these circumstances, favourable variations would tend to be preserved, and unfavourable ones to be destroyed. The result of this would be a new species. Here then I had at last got hold of a theory by which to work.

Did he ever.

In considering the influences on Darwin's thought, we mustn't overlook his own grandfather, Erasmus Darwin, 1731–1802, who also studied at Edinburgh and Cambridge, and was a good enough physician to have once had a chance to serve as George III's doctor. He was also an accomplished poet and inventor, and he was highly regarded by such well-known inventors as Wedgwood, and James Watt, and Joseph Priestley. He combined his scientific and poetic talents in the book *Zoonomia*, in which, with rhyming couplets, he theorized that all varieties of living things evolved from an original type.

Such influences duly noted, however, there is no lessening of Darwin's originality, not to mention the most painstaking and systematic program of data gathering perhaps in the history of the natural sciences. Others had written about the plan and order of nature, the fitness of plants and animals to meet the challenges of the natural world, but with Darwin you do get something different. You get design without a designer. You get a teleological theory, a theory about ends being served by variation, but these are not ends contrived by some providential super-intelligence.

In this connection, it is interesting to reflect on exchanges between Darwin and the American botanist, Asa Gray, who had offered much support to Darwin's theory, indeed, judged by Darwin as the person who best understood the theory. Now, what troubled Asa Gray was just this "design without a designer," a teleological theory, but one for which the end, the Aristotelian "that for the sake of which," is mere and brute survival. Darwin's respect for Gray caused him to take these concerns seriously and reply to them respectfully. In one letter he sends to Gray, he says this:

> It has always seemed to me that for an Omnipotent & Omniscient Creator to foresee is the same as to preordain; but then when I come to think over this I get into an uncomfortable puzzle: something analogous with "necessity & Free-will" or the "Origin of evil" or other subjects quite beyond the scope of the human intellect.

In another exchange, Darwin tells Gray that given all the misery in the world, including the animal world, the suggestion that it's all part of a design by a beneficent creator is unconvincing. What sort of beneficent plan leads to the creation of "the Ichneumonidas—feeding within the living bodies of caterpillars"?

You see that the picture he's giving you is one creature living inside the body of another, and living by consuming it. This doesn't look quite like a providentially created cosmos or world.

As for the allegedly great and hostile controversy that surrounded the appearance of *Origin of Species*, it is important to separate fact from fiction. At this point, I want to talk about *Origin of Species*. The book and its author received a respectful, and even encomiastic, reception in the major literary journals of the period, the journals that would provide lengthy critical reviews of important books. *Origin of Species* was published in 1859 and was promptly reviewed in the *Dublin Review*, the *Edinburgh Review*, London's *Fortnightly Review*—critical reviews that might run 40 pages in print. These reviews were remarkably detailed and highly positive.

The publication coming closest to a journal of official Roman Catholic opinion was the *Dublin Review*, and in that review, it does refer to an aspect of the work that he describes as a "horrid genealogy," but otherwise it's an entirely respectful commentary, admiring of a scientist who's been so careful in presenting his findings, so systematic in his observations, etc.

That is the case for the *Origin of Species*. We don't want to guild the lily. We don't want Darwin as the suffering, misunderstood, sort of Dostoyevskian character. Not at all. A highly respected naturalist who has served up a highly regarded, highly praised—in some respects, worrisome—work.

Eleven years later, with *The Descent of Man*, there is quite a different reception, and, indeed, this is quite a different book, one in which the ratio of fact to assumption is smaller by orders of magnitude. Natural selection, which was the theory of choice in *Origin of Species*, is now replaced by sexual selection. There is also a quite argumentative tone in *The Descent of Man*, and, of course, there is that great inductive leap according to which the particular characteristics of our own humanity are to be understood as lying along the same continuum that covers all of animal life. Thus, what we are to understand about human nature is that it is an extension, an enlargement, perhaps some kind of an elaboration, of an animal nature that is there for all to see.

The Descent of Man is a controversial work, and I think it was intended to be. When Darwin adds to this *The Expression of the Emotions in Animals and Men*, there would be no room whatever for qualifying the radical implications of Darwinian thought. Now, we are confronting an uncompromisingly evolutionary psychology in which human nature is not separated in any way from the balance of nature.

Darwin was not flying here without a parachute. There were already important scientific developments that his theory required, particularly in the field of geology. If evolution was to account for the gradual creation of new types, far more time was required than the biblical span.

Between 1830 and 1833, Charles Lyell had produced a monumental three-volume work creating something of a revolution in its own right. Close study of the fossil record made clear that whole species had been eliminated over the course of time. Moreover, these studies indicated further that the earth was far older than anything anyone might have got from Scripture. Lyell and Hutton propounded a *uniformitarian* theory, according to which earthquakes and volcanic eruptions witnessed at the present time have occurred in much the same way over whole eons of time. Thus, the physical features of the world have, as it were, evolved slowing under various pressures. Lyell's *Principles of Geology* went through 12 editions and were praised frequently by his now good friend, Charles Darwin.

Before considering Darwin's theoretical work, it is worth taking a few minutes to comment on theory as such, and the work that theories are to accomplish. One of the characteristics of a developed scientific theory of the sort advanced by Newton or Einstein is that it not only accounts for events, but it also predicts them. That is, there is a symmetry between explanation and prediction, so that if we take the stock textbook example of dropping an object, and noting that it falls toward the center of the earth, we can explain this by the universal law of gravitation: All objects attract each other with a force directly proportional to the product of their masses inversely proportioned to the square of the distance between them. By virtue of this law, we can explain the free-fall of an object that is released from a height, but we can also predict what the object will do in the future. A scientific theory, then, is expected not only to account for what has happened—but to predict what will happen.

Now, it is worth noting that evolutionary theory has the right kind of *retrodictive* power. It explains, or proposes to explain, how variations came about, but it does not predict future forms. We have no idea what selection pressures might arise. We don't know what cataclysmic changes might take place in the world. We don't know if we're going to be hit by a meteor, or if dust clouds will eliminate giraffes. This has led some to wonder whether the theory of evolution is really cut from the same cloth as developed scientific theories.

Indeed, Darwin himself described his method as a natural history method, and people in the 19th century would have understood what he meant by that. In a certain respect, Darwinian theory is much more like a kind of historical explanation, perhaps more like an historical explanation than a scientific one, in the sense of Newtonian-type of laws, etc.

Some of Darwin's critics, as late as the second half of the 19th century, were insisting that Darwin here had not proceeded according to the established methods of Bacon and Newton. In our own time, knowing in exquisite detail the microstructure of cells and the extraordinary micro-mechanisms by which cellular functions are accomplished, well, other scientists have concluded that the "natural selection" account is simply far fetched. I shall have to leave the matter at that point and return to Darwin's own time and scientific context, but I just want to insert these points lest we think that we are following the natural history of something unfailingly true. It is an evolutionary theory with many, many strengths and some weaknesses, and the weaknesses are very telling.

Now, among the other complaints was that the fossil record—contrary to what Darwin's defenders were saying—was not incomplete. It was too complete for the good of the theory. If you take a look at the fossil strata that would have been available in Darwin's time to see what variations are taking place, you will find no evidence whatever of some sort of linear progression of features, no evidence whatever of the appearance of a new species from gradual modifications of older types. That is, if you were to think of the fossil record as a kind of motion picture of evolutionary developments, you should see the actual emergence of any species by the successful modification of earlier types. That is not what the fossil records showed.

It would be Alfred Russell Wallace, the co-discoverer of the theory and a distinguished scientist in his own right, who would put forth in his book *Darwinism*, that, indeed, although the fossil record is quite complete, it's not an accurate record because of the upheavals that have taken place at the level of the strata. They provide a broken and shifted record. Indeed, Wallace argued, had the record been undisturbed, it would support the theory in just trying to bring the listener back into the controversial period surrounding the publication of these works.

Now, yet another telling criticism was based on the history of breeding. Over a course of many centuries—and with all the possible environmental controls at one's disposal—breeders, attempting to refine any number of features, nonetheless had never produced a new species.

Darwin's era was not in possession of the science of genetics and the mechanisms by which mutations arise. Thus, Darwin and his contemporaries were not aware of the rapidity with which evolutionary changes can come about. Darwin's is a theory of gradualism, and, indeed, Lyell's geological work reinforced that view.

Evolutionary theory does not offer the peaceable kingdom of a providential God; rather, it offers a hellish place of violence, competition, and conflict. It's a bloody process that has, mindlessly, the means by which to liquidate, to make disappear, anything that can't keep up, and to promote in number and in kind those able to succeed in the struggle for existence. It's a bleak picture.

It was Herbert Spencer who first used the expression "survival of the fittest" in his *Social Statics*, which was published eight years earlier than *Origin of Species*. Darwin borrowed the phrase but remained rather aloof to the radical libertarianism and "social Darwinism" advocated by Spencer.

The evolutionary principles advanced by Spencer were, unlike Darwin's, forged into an imperative: As progress depends on the achievements of the best, these are not to be held back by accommodating the needs of the less talented.

I'm inclined at this point to say that there's something of an apologia in a theory of this kind, given the nature of commercial life in Victorian England and places very much in the model of Victorian England. The idea of survival of the fittest and progress through competition captures much of the ethos of Victorian England. Spencer's interest in Malthus's prediction should be understood in these terms: The growth of population will exceed the capacity for the production of food, the effect being the starvation of the weakest members of society, and this being the process by which society prunes itself of its least fit. Now, how macabre that all this would attract the better minds of England as Ireland's Great Famine would come to claim three million lives.

Social Darwinism is but one of the implications arising from evolutionary theory, though one that Darwin would have rejected. Yet another implication is that what matters are collectives, not individuals. I want to pause for a second here, just to underscore this.

Emphasis now shifts to the survival of genre. The individual is consequential insofar only as it breeds, and breeds true, so that you already get a perspectival toward the fate of collectives. The individual is now instrumental, but not of individual value, so to speak. The forces of nature are such as to generate wide-ranging variations. Large populations are needed for there to be a wide range of variations on which natural selection can work productively. Nature—not consciously or providentially, but mindlessly and relentlessly— will favor certain variations and punish other variations. There's only a small set within the collective that may display variations guaranteeing success. Focus now shifts to the collective for the purpose of finding the unique instances that nature will favor.

It is, then, not at all coincidental that Darwin's cousin, Francis Galton, is writing on hereditary genius in 1869, and making a point of this, that if you take a large sample of human beings, there'll be negligibly small numbers of truly exceptional instances, but that the entire race is finally going to depend on the achievements of that small group. Galton took the lead in establishing the British Eugenics Society, and he was a hero to those who founded a comparable society in the United States. Galton had tried to interest Darwin in the work of Mendel, but to little avail. However, Galton himself was totally committed to the hereditarian view of natural variations and to the need to improve society by genetic means. Remember the Socratic technique for producing guardians. Well, raise that by orders of magnitude and you begin to get Galton's perspective on these matters. He actually proposed cash payments for voluntary sterilization to those measuring low in estimates of intelligence; the amount of such payments were to be proportioned to the degree of mental deficiency.

You get the picture here. Galton's scheme was to pay certain people not to reproduce but to sterilize themselves. You pay them more and more as your estimate of their mental ability finds them less and less.

If nature can prune and purify at the level of intellect, so also can it select certain moral and ethical predispositions if these enhance the adaptive potential of the species. Ethics, then, boils down to biology. Consider altruism. Evolutionary theory makes ample room for such a "virtue," even expects it. Animals behaving in such a way as not to favor their own survival but to do things that might benefit, or aid in, or make more likely the survival of the species as a whole are behaving in a way that is quite in keeping with natural selection.

Until recently, very few moral philosophers would regard as altruistic behavior something causally brought about by natural selection. After all, someone who simply comports himself selflessly would not qualify as altruistic, for—as with all the virtues—the necessary ingredients begin with the conscious intention to serve the interests of others at one's own expense. Intentionality is everything here. You don't judge an act as altruistic in terms of its outcome, but in terms of what motivated the action in the first instance. There is much to be said against this, too, and I would not hazard a guess as to the fraction of today's philosophers who would accept sociobiological accounts of morals. I shall get to that question in one of the final lectures in the series.

Now, Darwin himself made his reservations clear in more than one essay as to whether natural selection was a principle that ever could match up with what we take to be the ethical dimensions of life, and the question is alive to this day.

The world bequeathed by Charles Darwin and his theories is an organic, evolving world. Nothing is fixed; all is in transition. This is no longer just the idea of progress. There are natural engines of change. Those engines are operating 24 hours a day, and what is it they're operating on? They're operating on each of us, each of our characteristics, internal and external, behavioral, visceral, neurological. Each of those characteristics either does or does not meet the daily moment-to-moment challenge of survival, the survival of an organism that must keep itself alive by competing for resources. How this is going to be played out over the long haul, no one knows. We do know that the laws operate, and the question of who is most fit is answered after the fact.

The theory, then, assumes that beneath rationalized accounts of our various social and moral practices, behind the superficial self-congratulatory accounts of how good we are, how altruistic we are, how decent we are, there is a subtext in the form of laws of nature that achieve ends without intention, patterns without a pattern-maker. There's something always at work behind the scenes. It brings things about that, indeed, our rationality pompously takes credit for, but what is brought about doesn't come about as a result of our rationality. It comes about as a result of certain basic core impulses and instincts that, if they were lacking, would make survival impossible.

There are no fixed values, eternal verities, one-size-fits-all moral precepts, rules of conduct, forms of law, form of social organization that is the last word. Rather, all is contingent. All is based on the moment-to-moment facts of the natural world and how these interact with what is, finally, a natural creature. There's no telling over the long haul which particular set of attributes will prove to be most serviceable. In the interest of survival, the best strategy is, as the Maoists cynically proclaimed, to "let a thousand flowers bloom."

Now, what do we want to say about this? In a previous lecture I mentioned the speech Huxley gave at Birmingham and the reply it evoked from Matthew Arnold. Defending himself against the charge of being one of those "Levites of culture," as Huxley called him, Arnold thumbed the pages of *The Descent of Man* and confronted a long-lost relative, that hairy quadruped with a pointed ear and tail.

Let me not repeat all that business about the hairy quadruped being "inclined to Greek." Instead, I should underscore what Arnold is getting at, for it remains important to this day. The question is whether a theory of the evolutionary sort is the right kind of account as to what sort of creatures we are, what kind of life we should live, and how we should be governed.

Alfred Russell Wallace, the co-founder of the theory and a man deeply admired and respected by Darwin, wrote one of the best defenses of Darwinism, but in the final chapter, he asks whether the theory of natural selection succeeds as an explanation of human nature. He identifies three domains that are so distinctly removed from the theory as not to be assimilated by it. There is first of all the domain of what might be called purely abstract thought, which seems to serve no particular evolutionary end. There is the domain of aesthetics, where resources are squandered in the interests of what is merely beautiful, and that surely cannot be serving the kinds of ends envisaged by the theory itself. Then, there is the domain of moral thought and ethics, in which we intentionally sacrifice our most cherished interests for the benefit of others. Wallace cannot see how natural selection matches up with this, or how sexual selection matches up with it either. Wallace is inclined to think that, in the aesthetic, intellectual, and moral dimensions of life, the theory just misses the point.

Well, debate goes on. E.O. Wilson has argued that natural selection shapes morals in much the way it shapes other adaptive features. In his *Sociobiology: A New Synthesis*, he urges us to consider this. That:

> A science of sociobiology, if coupled with neurophysiology, might transform the insights of ancient religions into a precise account of the evolutionary origins of ethics, and hence explain the reasons why we make certain moral choices instead of others.

I don't think this is an apt account. I do think there is something in us that inclines us to Greek. The late returns are not in.

Marxism—Dead But Not Forgotten
Lecture 44

Karl Marx wrote that "Darwin's work ... serves me as a natural scientific basis for the class-struggle in history." He went so far as to dedicate *Das Capital* to Darwin.

It is difficult to bring a balanced, neutral perspective to bear on Karl Marx (1818–1883) or Marxism. We associate much of the second half of the 20th century, politically, with his writings and teachings. We probably pay him too much credit or heap too much scorn on him. Much of what comes down to us as Marxism is by way of Mao Tse-tung, Lenin, and Stalin. In these characters, there is very little that matches the depth of Marx's own systematic writings.

Marx was quite assiduous in declaring that he was not a philosopher. He considered philosophical speculation an activity that goes on because of the undeveloped nature of societies. Marx posited that a successful scheme of social revolution would put an end to philosophy. Marx regarded himself as a social scientist making contributions chiefly to economic and social theory. He regarded his method and his mode of explanation as drawn from the sciences and specifically *not* philosophy. Nonetheless, his ideas have animated philosophical discourse almost since the time they were recorded on paper. There is no doubt that, whatever Marx thought he was doing, his principal contributions will be to that part of the history of ideas in which we find philosophy itself.

Marx was born in Prussia to a middle-class family that claimed a long line of rabbis, though his father—to preserve his successful law practice—had converted to Protestantism. Karl Marx followed in his father's footsteps, attending Bonn University's Faculty of Law, where he met and became engaged to a daughter of the aristocracy, Jenny von Westphalen. Shortly after, his studies took place at the University of Berlin, where he joined the Young Hegelians. At age 26, he was appointed editor of the *Rheinische Zeitung* and guided it quickly toward dissolution at the hands of the Prussian authorities. His movements, with faithful Jenny and a growing family, were frequent, until he settled in London. He is buried in Highgate Cemetery.

In his writings, we can feel Marx's impatience with the standard problems of philosophy. His contributions as a scientist, social or otherwise, are negligible compared with their influence. He earns less dubiously the title of non-philosopher, because he paid rather little attention to systematic philosophies and the abiding problems in philosophy.

For example, the mind-body problem is surely an abiding problem in philosophy. But when Marx briefly engaged an issue such as this, one can almost feel his impatience. Amidst the European revolutions of 1848, the idea of sitting around and asking a question like that would have struck Marx as an example of how effete thought and thinkers had become by the mid-19th century. On the mind-body problem (in *The Holy Family*), he accepts Gassendi's atomistic materialist solution, just to set the problem aside.

Marx is a materialist, but not a Democritean or mechanistic Gassendian one. His materialism is dialectic. He is a Hegelian who stands Hegel on his head: The struggle to bring forth new forms of human life does not take place on the level of the spirit or the Absolute but on the level of economics. If we were to classify Marx as a materialist, it would be what he himself referred to as a *dialectical materialist*, more in the tradition of Hegel. Dialectical materialism accounts for all change in terms of the *struggle of opposites*. It is on this basis that progress becomes possible; change comes through conflict. The class struggle is the engine of progress through history.

As a "social scientist," Marx is convinced that determinative laws operate at the level of society and throughout history. This determinative process is entirely materialistic, though not mechanistic, and works through economic forces. The Darwinian model was a source of inspiration for Marx. In proposing that it is economics that imposes change on societies and on persons, Marxism represents a reversal of the traditional way of looking at how systems and institutions come about.

Aristotle, for example, argued that the political and legal framework of society shapes the moral character of citizens, and that this—surely not anything "economic"—represented the decisive factor in social life. The Marxist version turns this around.

Every society depends on given *forces of production*. We begin with the productive resources that a tribal enclave, a small community, or an entire empire might claim for itself. This inevitably recruits the physical power of a laboring class. The laboring class becomes the instrument by which production becomes possible. In the process, things are produced more efficiently by cooperation, because the agricultural yield works to the advantage of all. In time, possession of property is taken, thus establishing class distinctions between the propertied class and the laborers. It becomes necessary for the propertied class to devise means by which to safeguard its possession; hence, this same class proceeds to write the laws and exact the punishments. For the Marxist, law is a class concept and a class tool, arising from the material interdependencies of bourgeois and proletarian classes. The reaction to unionization in the 19th century was the sort of datum that Marx could adduce in support of such a theory.

Marx was quite assiduous in declaring that he was not a philosopher.

Capitalism depends for its success on selling products for more than they cost to produce. The cost is chiefly labor; the surplus is profit, which accumulates as capital. This is Marx's *labor theory of value*. Feudalism did not follow the rules of capitalism. Social class was not a measure of ultimate personal worth; the feudal lord was not amassing capital but preserving a society that was the image of God's providence. Capitalism, however, must grow to survive. Once basic needs are met, artificial desires must be created in order to keep demand high. A *consumer society* must be created and enlarged.

Only through a revolt of the laboring class can such a system be destroyed. The owning class has the means to fend off this outcome, though not to prevent it finally. Those in control of the means of production also control and define the consciousness of the oppressed. The model for this type of control is religion, what Marx famously called "the opiate of the masses." Religion is always handed down from upper to lower classes. Class consciousness is the necessary first stage in transforming the power relations, and class struggle, the inevitable next stage. It becomes the necessary engine of revolutionary change and progress.

The first thing a worker must recognize is that he has been exploited and is being manipulated, that in fact, those who are availing themselves of his labor are not acting in his interests but in the interest of preserving a system in which they happen to be successful. Their success depends centrally on the worker's failure, namely, his failure to change anything materially about the nature of his life and social arrangements. What is needed is a revolutionary change. And that revolution cannot be bloodless, because those in power do not relinquish power. Power is taken from them. Revolutionary upheavals, then, are the only basis on which an economic and social stasis is impelled to change and, indeed, compelled to change.

In the ordinary run of things, science and technology alone radically alter the means of production. Tremendous changes in the productive resources of a society can occur because of science and technology, recasting labor in a radically different mold. Workers might now require great technical skills and education, gaining a much greater sense of themselves and their place within the productive scheme of things. This class consciousness, however, recognizes its essentiality to the entire social life. This sort of change can take place without any adjustments in the social structure at all.

Marxist theory leaves no room for revolutionary changes effected technically and scientifically. It is a "deterministic" theory, defeated by actual persons living real lives on their own terms. In practice, it fails to explain and fails to achieve what its defenders promised. But it has altered perspectives in an enduring way and remains in the background of the "constructionist" theory of personality, personal identity, and class consciousness. ∎

Suggested Reading

Lichtheim, G. *Marxism: A Critical Analysis*. Praeger, 1961.

Marx, K. *Selected Writings*. Hackett, 1994.

1. Marx obviously accepts the forceful powers of the individual, or his summons to revolution would be meaningless. Explain how "deterministic," then, are the economic forces operating on the individual.

2. Conclude whether the economic failure of all 20th-century "Marxist" states is evidence enough that the theory in part and in total is hopelessly flawed.

Marxism—Dead But Not Forgotten
Lecture 44—Transcript

I have titled this lecture "Marxism—Dead But Not Forgotten," and I think here perhaps there are echoes somewhere within me of an American boy of the 1950s assuming that, if it's Marxism, it's bad, and that's the end of it. It's very difficult to bring a balanced, entirely neutral perspective to bear on Karl Marx or Marxism. We do associate much of the second half of the 20th century, politically, with the writings and teachings of Karl Marx, and I think in this we probably either pay him much too much credit or heap far too much scorn on him. Much of what comes down to us as Marxism is by way of Mao Tse-tung, and Lenin, and Stalin, and the like, and in these characters there is very little that matches up with the depth of Marx's own systematic writings.

I'm also somewhat reluctant to talk about Karl Marx in a series of lectures titled "Great Ideas in Philosophy," chiefly because Karl Marx was quite assiduous in declaring that he was not a philosopher. Indeed, he had a certain—well, I don't want to call it contempt for philosophy, but he thought philosophy had an expiration date on it. He thought that philosophical speculation was really an activity that goes on because of the undeveloped nature of societies, because of the purely habitual modes of social organization; that, indeed, a successful scheme of social revolution would put an end to that. In fact, once society was on a footing that bore some relationship to reality, philosophical speculation would go the way of tarot cards and astrology.

Marx regarded himself as a social scientist making contributions chiefly to economic and social theory. He regarded his method and his mode of explanation as drawn from the sciences and specifically *not* philosophy. Nonetheless, his ideas have animated philosophical discourse almost since the time they were recorded on paper, and there are whole departments—in fact, until quite recently, whole departments in Central Europe and in what used to be called the Soviet Union—devoted to little more than composing glosses on one or another Marxist tract. So there is no doubt whatever but that Marx thought he was doing—his principal contributions, that is, would be to that part of the history of ideas in which we find philosophy itself, his protestations to the contrary notwithstanding.

Marx's dates are 1818–1883. He was born in Prussia to a middle-class family that claimed a long line of rabbis. To preserve his successful law practice, Marx's father had converted to Protestantism. His son, Karl, followed in his father's footsteps, matriculating in Bonn University's Faculty of Law at the age of 17. It was there that he met and became engaged to a daughter of the aristocracy, Jenny von Westphalen. Shortly after, his studies took place at the University of Berlin, where he joined the Young Hegelians, a momentous event in his intellectual development.

His radicalism made an academic career impossible, but he found a nurturing medium in journalism. At the young age of 26, he was appointed editor of the *Rheinische Zeitung*, and he would guide it quickly toward dissolution at the hands of the Prussian authorities. If you want to get a newspaper closed down at this time, Marx would be the chap you would want as your editor. The editor sought an enlargement of liberty next in France, from which, in about two years, he was expelled. There's Marx, again. His movements, with faithful Jenny and a growing family, were frequent, sometimes fitful, until he would finally settle in London. He is actually buried in Highgate Cemetery in London. You do get the picture of this fellow born to be a revolutionary and finding no home genial to his presence for very long.

Of his contributions as a scientist, social or otherwise, I would have to judge them to be negligible when compared with their influence. Little of what Marx offered would even be testable, and such predictions as he made, when at all specific, were disconfirmed with extraordinary regularity. Marx's estimation of himself as a scientist, therefore, I would have to say, is an exaggeration, or perhaps an expression of an aspiration more than an achievement.

He earns less dubiously the title of non-philosopher, if this is some sort of distinction, for he did pay rather little attention to systematic philosophies and the abiding problems in philosophy. Let's take as an example the mind-body problem, which surely is an abiding problem in philosophy. How is human nature to be understood? Is it ultimately a congeries of biological, physiological processes, the brain being centrally responsible for thought, action, and the like, or is there something of transcendence about our humanity, such that we rise above the level of mere matter?

Well, when Marx briefly engaged an issue like this, you can almost feel his impatience. Why, in the times he lives in, that anyone would pause to consider a matter of that kind simply amazes him. Amidst the European revolutions of 1848, the idea of sitting around and asking a question like that would have struck Karl Marx as an example of how effete thought and thinkers had become by the mid-19th century.

He does pause in *The Holy Family* to record his satisfaction with Gassendi's solution to the problem. Recall what Gassendi's position was. It was a thoroughgoing materialistic theory of mind, a physiological theory of mind and mental life. Note that Marx's Ph.D. dissertation, his doctoral dissertation, was on Democritus and Epicurus. The title of the dissertation was "The Difference Between the Democritean and the Epicurean Philosophy of Nature." In his draft of a new process to the dissertation, he says this about Pierre Gassendi. Gassendi:

> ...freed Epicurus from the interdict which the Fathers of the Church had placed upon him. He seeks to accommodate his Catholic conscience to his pagan knowledge and Epicurus to the Church, which certainly was wasted effort.

Again, then, you see the reaction against religion, the idea that Gassendi is trying to achieve some sort of rapprochement between a pagan materialist philosophy and the church of which he was a member. The whole project was wasted, but at least what we see in Marx is the solution to the mind-body problem; as far as he's concerned, it was already immaterialistic, so that he was, at least early on, very interested in materialistic philosophies in the stricter sense of materialism. Surely, taking on a project like that for a doctoral dissertation shows not only an interest in such questions, but an early allegiance to a particular approach to solving problems of that kind.

Perhaps it also reveals the influence of his teacher, Feuerbach, whose own war on religion and tradition was as incessant as was Marx's. Marx in 1844 would declare Feuerbach to be "the true conqueror of the old philosophy." As a leader of the Young Hegelians, Feuerbach attacked what he identified as Hegel's idealism. He agitated for a more thoroughly biological understanding of human nature, and he relentlessly assailed religion and its social influence. His *Essence of Christianity* reduces reality to man and nature, with no room left over for what he takes to be the fantastic ontology of the religious mind. It would not be too much to say, no Feuerbach, no Marx.

Both were materialists, but if we were to classify Marx as a materialist, it would be a different kind of materialist. It would be what he himself referred to as a *dialectical materialist*, more in the tradition of Hegel. Marx and Engels claim to have "stood Hegel on his head," but they were both early admirers of, and intellectual disciples of, Hegelian philosophy. The difference between a dialectical materialism and the sort I've spoken of in lectures in this series is that the latter tends to be grounded in mechanistic considerations, considerations that would be quite at home with Newtonian science, or with Galileo, or with the atomism of Democritus, or with Epicurus.

Dialectical materialism is different. It retains the materialistic ontology of philosophical materialism, but then it accounts for all change in terms of what? The *struggle of opposites*. It is on this basis that progress becomes possible; change comes through conflict. The same forces are at work within societies, where under the laws of historical materialism, human character is shaped by the material modes of production.

Hegel, recall, based reality itself on the dialectic, with the "Absolute Idea" realizing itself through history. In Hegel's philosophy, there occurs a transcendent and not a material mode of progress. It's not at the level of mere earthly materiality that progress takes place. The Absolute stands at the rational foundation of historical developments. It's therefore reason realizing itself in human history. Thus, the Hegelian scheme is a cosmic scheme based on some abstract rational or intelligent precept that does its silent work in the world. Historical processes now become emblems, as it were, or bits of evidence of what's taking place behind the scenes.

Marx and Engels dismissed the idealism, declaring Hegel to be "standing on his head," and accepting for themselves the duty to place Hegel's feet back on terra firma. One begins by abandoning that whole field of absolute egos and absolute ideas and attaching oneself to a dialectical materialism in which the events of the social and political world are brought about by factors that are, at base, not transcendent, but economic. Economic forces are not the sole determinants of social dynamics and individual behavior, but they are the dominant forces. As biological entities, people are motivated from the first by the needs of the body—not by philosophical or moral abstractions, but by the creature-needs that arise from their very materiality.

The Darwinian model was a source of inspiration here. Karl Marx wrote that: "Darwin's work...serves me as a natural scientific basis for the class-struggle in history." He went so far as to dedicate *Das Capital* to Darwin. We have no evidence to suggest that Darwin was in any way pleased by this.

In proposing that it is economics that imposes change on societies and on persons, Marxism represents a reversal of the traditional way of looking at how systems and institutions come about. Aristotle, for example, argued that the political and legal framework of society will shape the moral character of citizens, and that this—surely not anything "economic"—represented the decisive factor in social life. On an Aristotelian account, the laws and institutions of the *polis* are established to achieve certain ends. In the right *polis*, these are the ends of virtue. For Thomas Aquinas, law is, recall, an ordinance of reason promulgated by one who has the good of the community at heart, or who is responsible for the good of the community. Social organization on this understanding is again based on ends that serve the dictates of conscience. The economics of the situation would be just a surface phenomenon and not at the center of an objective of this sort.

The Marxist version turns this quite around. What you begin with are the productive resources that a tribal enclave, a small community—or, indeed, an entire empire—might claim for itself. This inevitably recruits the physical powers of a laboring class. The laboring class becomes the instrument by which production becomes possible. Now, in the process, things are produced more efficiently by cooperation, as the agricultural yield works to the advantage of all. In time, however, possession of property is taken, thus establishing class distinctions between the propertied class and the laborers who are working the property. It becomes necessary for the propertied class to devise some means by which to safeguard their possession; hence, this same class proceeds to write the laws and exact the punishments. For the Marxist, then, law is a class concept and a class tool, arising from the material interdependencies of bourgeois and proletarian classes.

With the rise of capitalism and the disappearance of feudal society, the process works in an almost mechanical way. Suppose we want to accumulate capital, which is what capitalism is all about; we want to accumulate wealth. Now, the way you accumulate wealth is by seeing to it that you can sell something for a price that exceeds the cost of producing it. Well, what this requires is that the cost of producing it, which is primarily the cost of labor, has to be kept as low as possible relative to the price that will be charged for the product in question. The difference between the cost of the labor involved in producing something and the price that is won in selling it is the profit. This is what you're trying to amass.

Now, suppose it turns out that everybody in the world can make shoes. Well, of course, if everybody in the world can make shoes, then no one has to buy shoes. If it were the case that a large number of people in the world make shoes, there would be far too many shoes for the number of feet in the world. You begin to see, then, that the price you'll be able to get for a pair of shoes drops as the supply becomes entirely disproportionate vis-à-vis the need for the item.

Within a capitalist system, then, it becomes necessary to control the means of production, to make sure that production does not significantly outstrip need. This requires an accumulation of power over the primary mode of production. What is the primary mode of production? Labor. Therefore, what you now have is the formation of sharply distinguished classes. There is a laboring class, but the laboring class now is understood to be a kind of device. It's like an assembly line; it's like a system of pulleys. Labor is something that makes things, just as machinery makes things. As with machinery, it is necessary to keep labor, as it were, "in good repair," and also make provision for replenishing the supply of it. This is precisely what wages are all about. Wages aren't paid out of some consideration of obligation or decency. Wages are instead the means by which labor is preserved. Indeed, wages become the means by which labor reproduces itself. You form a laboring class, which, in almost clone-like fashion, is kept in such a condition of life that its offspring are likely to enter the same mode of employment, engage in the same productive enterprises, and be kept at a subsistence—or slightly above subsistence—level in order for the productive resources of the society to be used to their fullest.

My, oh my.

Now, if you're at the top of the food chain, so to speak, in this enterprise, you've got to see to it that your interests are protected. Your interests are protected chiefly by law; so, there is a hand-in-glove relationship between those who are most successful at forming capital and commanding the productive resources of the community, and those who are responsible for writing and, indeed, implementing the laws. They are mutually serving; they are serving each other—serving important ends. The legislative and executive activity within such a context might just be another of the tools for the exploitation of the laboring classes.

Certainly, at this point, you understand what the Marxist interpretation, what the Marxist philosophy of law, is going to look like, and it is alive and well in many of our law schools.

The reaction to unionization in the 19th century was the sort of datum that Marx could adduce in support of his theory. The idea that the law is being used fairly to distribute resources and to compensate persons in proportion to the value of their work was routinely violated everywhere that Marx looked, everywhere in the European world.

What Marx found in feudal society was a system in which the pattern of dependencies was rather more homogeneous than what would obtain when capitalism replaced feudalism. I might mention at this point that Marx has a surprisingly—well, perhaps not surprisingly—Marx has a very positive attitude toward feudal societies—and toward the medieval world itself. It has to be replaced, but he does see in it something that is replaced by capitalism in the worst sense of being replaced.

The feudal lord is not amassing capital. He's not amassing power. He seeks instead to attain a kind of status compatible with a certain religious worldview. At least at the public and social level, then, his aim is to preserve what has been achieved. To do this, however, he recognizes not only the need for labor, but he recognizes also the very nobility of labor. He lives within a society in which class structure is not a measure of a person's worth, but a reflection rather of what the divinely intended order of the cosmos would bring about.

Now, Marx has his criticism of feudal society, not to mention of the church it served, but for all the criticism that he heaps on modern economic systems and on modern society itself, he does pause in his writings to make comparisons with a feudal mode of economy and social organization. Those comparisons are, I say, always to the advantage of the feudal society, its economics, and its mode of social organization.

On Marx's account, the movement from feudalism to capitalism is quite complex, the two existing side-by-side for periods of time. The undoing of feudal society arises from its very success, for with security and life's basics provided, there is a growing desire for new goods. As the feudal estate prospers, there is greater opportunity for trade, and this brings to the attention of the laboring class possibilities previously hidden.

Ah, again, the dialectic. Now, there are feudal guilds formed by skilled laborers who will limit production to keep prices high. Against this are the rising expectations associated with economic security—rising expectations that can be met only be manufactured goods produced in quantity at rates that the feudal craftsmen couldn't possibly match, but manufacturing requires now a division of labor and essentially the end of craftsmanship itself. The unskilled laborer replaces the craftsman, and capital formation proceeds at an accelerating clip, thanks now to cheaper labor and the concentrated ownership of the modes of production.

What does this lead to? Well, unchecked, the rich get richer, the poor get poorer, and revolution is the only remedy. Q.E.D.!

What is "capital"? According to the *labor theory of value*, in capitalism, labor produces more than what is paid for it, and the surplus, or remainder, or difference yields capital. Of course, this works only insofar as there are consumers. According to the theory, for capitalism to survive, it must continue to expand. The consumer class must be increased. I often wonder what Marx, if revived and traipsed through a contemporary shopping mall, say the Mall of America, might say. He might just smile and declare himself utterly vindicated.

The main point, however, is this: Unlike a feudal mode of production, for the progressive capitalistic mode of acquisition of wealth, the formation of capital has to grow, which means it has to create appetites for products since the basic necessities of life finally can be satisfied one time around. How many shoes do you need, after all? How much food has to be in the larder? How many shirts can you get through a week with, and so forth? How many toothbrushes? How many cars can you cram into that garage? In time, you finally have to start producing things that are utterly unrelated to any consideration of survival—so you must create a consumerism. You must create consumer ethos, and to do this, of course, you have to rely on certain characteristics of individuals that render them ever more pliable, ever more concerned with considerations of status and class. Class structure therefore becomes an integral part of a capitalist economy, because it has to do with the most basic impulse, and that is one's self-identity, one's self-image, one's sense of fellowship and worth. You know, "I am what I buy." No, "I am what I am able to buy."

Now, the model for this kind of psychology Marx draws from the history of religions. Marx famously declares religion to be "the opiate of the masses." I've sometimes said to students that, in fact, for the better part of three-quarters of a century, Marxist teaching—at least as rendered by Mao, Stalin, Lenin, and company—really functioned precisely as an opiate. Staggeringly large numbers of persons put up with a form of life that many would have revolted against, and they put up with it not merely because there were tanks on the street, but because they accepted a theory according to which that form of life was a necessary stage of some sort—some alleged evolutionary process. Now, this is a kind of self-numbing, a kind of intellectual numbing, that religion has rarely achieved, or rarely attempted to achieve.

What did Marx have in mind in condemning religion as an "opiate of the masses"? Marx was a revolutionary within a world of powerful centers committed to the status quo. The great obstacle to a revolutionary enterprise is complacency, and one source of complacency is the belief that prevailing conditions are natural, or right, or divinely ordained. If you are convinced that your current situation is but an instance in an immense sea of time, and that all the important things are going to happen after this purely meager earthly interval, well, you already have become tolerant of your situation in life. Religion redirects focus from the "here and now" to the "then and there," and the "there" is untouchable, and the "then" is unreachable, until you perform that necessary act of dying.

The opiate effect is this: You begin to take less seriously the day-to-day affairs of your life, and you begin to place the highest premium on a set of values that inevitably are promulgated by classes above your own. It's the masses who find religion to be an opiate. The upper classes—the most influential classes, the moneyed classes, the aristocratic classes—don't have particularly good records of religious credulity. This is where you find skeptical philosophers, cynics, men of the world, but the churches are just the right place to have people reassured that there is some future reward that will be theirs.

Marx therefore sees not just a convenient aid to a particular economic system, but a deliberate, motivated attempt on the part of the powers to keep the masses in place through a *mythos*, a set of rites and rituals, a set of superstitions, futuristic promises—all of it grounded in something absolutely unreal, but entirely serviceable for the purposes.

Now, you begin to change this only by recognizing that you are a victim of it. The class-consciousness becomes the necessary engine of revolutionary change and progress. The first thing you've got to recognize is that you have been exploited, that you are being manipulated—that in fact, those who are availing themselves of your labor and paying you wages are doing so not in your interests but in the interest of preserving a system in which they happen to be successful. Their success depends centrally on your failure— your failure to change anything materially about the nature of your life and social arrangements, so that what is needed, of course, is a revolutionary change. And that revolution cannot be bloodless, because the powers are not relinquishing power. Those in power do not relinquish power. Power is taken from them. Revolutionary upheavals, then, are the only basis upon which an economic and social stasis is impelled to change and, indeed, compelled to change.

In the ordinary run of things, science and technology alone radically alter the means of production. If you step back from this for a moment and forget the drama of classes in conflict and vulgar capitalists attempting to amass wealth, just step back for a moment, and consider how the world of the late Renaissance and the 17th century, the realms of science and technology, how those worlds were changed by science and technology, how the cotton gin changes things, or an automobile.

Marx provides a theory that really leaves no room at all for the revolutionary changes brought about technically and scientifically without any blood being let at all, and as far as the static status of the laboring class, consider only the Western democracies of the past century to see how mobile persons are within that framework. His is a "deterministic" theory, and this inevitably is defeated by actual persons living real lives according to terms they articulate for themselves.

The Freudian World
Lecture 45

Freud, of course, needs no introduction. He has shaped contemporary perspectives on the nature of knowledge, on our understanding of the sources of our conduct, on our sense of the very nature of the person.

Some of the great ideas in philosophy have not been contributed by philosophers. The list of contributors is long and the specialties are diverse. Sigmund Freud is on the list but less by way of medicine than through a specialty he personally did much to create. After graduating from the *Gymnasium* first in his class, Freud studied medicine at the University of Vienna when he was 17. There, he came under the influence of one of the significant scientists of that period, Ernst Brucke, who was associated with Johannes Mueller, as well as Karl Ludwig, Emil DuBois-Reymond, and Hermann von Helmholtz. Brucke and his compatriots agreed that they would accept no principle in biology that was not grounded in the basic sciences of chemistry and physics. Helmholtz delivered a groundbreaking lecture on the principle of the conservation of energy, the main points of which are that we can get no more from a physical system than the energy it begins with; there is no perpetual-motion machine; and biological systems are physical systems.

The *conservationist* principles of Helmholtz are central to Freudian theory, particularly Freud's theory of hysterical symptoms as conversion reactions; that is, that hysterical blindness, paralysis, or deafness is just the physical manifestation of something occurring at the level of psychic energy.

Far more important to Freudian theory than conservationist principles in physics was the Darwinian revolution, which Freud accepted, chapter and verse. Darwinian theory gave us, as mentioned in a previous lecture, design without a designer and design features coming about as a result of raw, brutal, daily biological conflict and collision. Survival is dependent on the constant selfish struggle to get pleasure and avoid pain. It was, thus, impossible to construct a biological psychology such as Freudian analysis without the principles of evolution.

Freud's ambitions were fairly modest to begin with. He wanted to be a research scientist in medicine and hold an academic post at Vienna. It was clear that Freud, as a Jew, was going to face a fairly low ceiling in the very Catholic city of Vienna, as far as academic prospects were concerned. For this reason, he began to practice neurology, which is what he was trained in.

In his practice, Freud would see a variety of "hysterical" symptoms—blindness, insensitivities, paralysis—that had no physical basis. *Hysteria* takes its name from the Greek word for "uterus." Pre-19th century, it was widely thought that conditions of this kind occurred only in women and generally as part of the complexities of their reproductive biology.

The primal unconscious instincts (the *id*) must be controlled through the cultivation of a moral conscience (the *superego*) derived from parental and, ultimately, from social strictures and constraints.

Freud was not the one who turned things around on that. Between 1885 and 1886, Freud studied under Charcot, who was reporting some success in treating hysterical patients with hypnosis. Freud would imaginatively develop the idea that traumas generate physical symptoms by way of unconscious processes. With six months of experience behind him, Freud returned to his practice in Vienna and, for a time, used hypnosis, giving it up chiefly because of what he took to be its "mysteriousness."

Meanwhile, Freud's friend and colleague Josef Breuer, also a practicing neurologist, reported success in one patient—the famous Anna O, who suffered from a persistent cough, a paralysis on the right side of her body, sensory disturbances, and even hallucinations—by a "talking cure." The two determined that the hysterical symptoms must be based on a blockage of some sort that is partially released by cathartic means. As a psychic disturbance, the hysteria must be the physical manifestation of events involving "psychic" energy. With Breuer, Freud reached the conclusion that hysterical symptoms were the result of a psychic mechanism: *repression*. Repression resembled a hydraulic principle: Things not able to be expressed at one level must be expressed at another.

Father of psychoanalysis, Sigmund Freud (1856-1938) in collaboration with Joseph Breuer articulated and refined the concepts of the unconscious, infantile sexuality, and repression and proposed a tripartite account of the mind's structure.

Armed with these findings and inspired by evolutionary theory, Freud focused on survival mechanisms. Our ancestry guarantees that the individual will do everything possible to promote survival, to enhance pleasure and minimize pain. That is the *pleasure principle*—that we come into the world designed in such a way as to enhance pleasurable experiences and minimize those that are in any way painful. What Freud calls the *reality principle* lies in dialectical tension to the pleasure principle. Most of the time, we conduct ourselves in a way that denies us certain pleasures so as to exist in an integral society. The primal unconscious instincts (the *id*) must be controlled through the cultivation of a moral conscience (the *superego*) derived from parental and, ultimately, from social strictures and constraints.

The self as known to the self, the person we know as "I," the person in the mirror (the *ego*), is constructed out of a process of socialization being brought to bear in opposition to impulses and drives at a level inaccessible to the actor. The ego is the synthesis, as it were, of the dialectical tension between id and superego. It is to the defense of the ego that the mechanisms of sublimation, repression, displacement, and so on are committed. The tensions generated in the conflict between the pleasure and reality principles may, to some extent be relaxed but not eliminated. The demands of society being what they are, it is necessarily the case that the life we live will not be an authentic life.

Beneath surface rationality and simplicity is the busy workshop of the unconscious, directing and forming complex intuitions, causing weird dreams and disturbing symptoms, rendering one at once fit for, and discontented with, civilization. Examples include people waking up blind or with paralyses because they harbor horrid wishes they cannot face. What kind of wishes might these be? Sexual, of course! Here is the theory of the Oedipal complex. As a boy moves toward heterosexual sexuality, the obvious target of his affections will be the source of his preexisting gratification—his mother. Socialization of sexuality requires redirecting the sexual energies to a socially acceptable target, a development that can be a profoundly traumatic experience.

Freud faced criticism by his contemporaries perhaps less for the sexual content of the theory than for the fact that it was so theoretical itself. In Freud's time, science is an essentially observational enterprise designed to generate general testable and refutable laws. What evidence is there for the unconscious at all? How can repressed elements be uncovered?

Dreams, slips of the tongue, humor, and other "psychopathologies of everyday life" reveal the symbolic disguise of basic drives toward self-gratification. Dreams disguise our forbidden desires at the same time that they reveal them—the disguise doesn't entirely work. The interpretation of dreams is "the royal road to the unconscious." ■

Suggested Reading

Freud, S. *Interpretation of Dreams*. Penguin, 2003.

Sulloway, F. *Freud: Biologist of the Mind*. Basic Books, 1979.

Questions to Consider

1. The hysterical symptoms encountered in his practice by Freud are quite rare now. And Freud scarcely considers depression, which is the now the most common psychological problem reported by those seeking therapy. Explain what this has to say about the generality of the theory.

2. Identify what is lacking in Freud's theory that prevents it from securing scientific status.

The Freudian World

Lecture 45—Transcript

The themes and issues that have guided the lectures in this series are subsumed under three broad headings that I have mentioned often: the problem of knowledge, the problem of conduct, and the problem of governance. Different figures have attached themselves to one or more of these, important contributions often coming from quarters beyond academic philosophy. Some of the great ideas in philosophy have not been contributed by philosophers. Indeed, if by "philosopher" one means a student of the subject who has earned advanced degrees in it, then very few of the great ideas have been contributed by philosophers at all. Socrates, Plato, and Aristotle come to mind immediately, but so, too, do the ancient physicians, a number of medieval theologians, several mathematicians; the list of contributors is long and the specialties are diverse. Sigmund Freud is on the list but less by way of medicine than through a specialty he personally did much to create.

Freud, of course, needs no introduction. He has shaped contemporary perspectives on the nature of knowledge, on our understanding of the sources of our conduct, on our sense of the very nature of the person. He has profoundly influenced thought across the entire spectrum—aesthetics, literary criticism, moral philosophy, and indeed, philosophy—to such an extent that one has good reason to refer to the "Freudian World."

Who is this fellow? Freud was born in 1856 in Moravia, moving with his family to Vienna four years later. He was the eldest of seven children born to his father's third wife. Graduating from Gymnasium first in his class, Freud undertook the study of medicine at the University of Vienna when he was 17. It was there that he came under the influence of one of the significant scientists of that period, Ernst Brucke, about whom Freud would later write: "He carried more weight with me than anyone else in my life."

Ernst Brucke was a professor with whom Freud actually did some original research. In light of the influence he had on Freud, Brucke is someone we should know a little bit about.

Early on in his own scientific education, Brucke became associated with one of the great figures in 19th-century physiology, Johannes Mueller. At the time he was there, there were three other young men who would become leaders of thought in German biology and science in the second half of the 19th century. They were Karl Ludwig, Emil DuBois-Reymond, and the most famous of the four, Hermann von Helmholtz. The four of them were of one mind in regarding all biological functions as based on physics and chemistry. No "vital force" or *élan vital*, no occult powers, no *vis vitae*. Brucke and DuBois went so far as to take an oath to each other to the effect that they would accept no principle in biology that was not grounded in the basic sciences of chemistry and physics. Specifically, they would accept that, "no other forces than common physical chemical ones are active within the organism." You see a heroic oath, here.

Now, I say, of the four, surely the one who achieved the greatest celebrity was Hermann von Helmholtz, and indeed, one of Helmholtz's early contributions was at the 1847 meeting of the Physical Society of Berlin, in which he gave a short, trenchant, and now classical paper titled *Die Erhaltung der Kraft; On the Conservation of Energy*. It is interesting that the first version of the essay had been submitted to the journal *Deutsche Annalen Physik*, roughly, *the German Annals of Physics*, and was rejected for being too speculative.

Helmholtz makes clear at the beginning of this essay, this brief presentation, what his remarks of the day are intending to establish. He will explain why it is that no one has been successful in attempts to make a perpetual-motion machine. What Helmholtz was establishing in that lecture, and what other *conservationist* principles by mid-19th century established is this: that within a closed system, the energy content is constant. You can vary the form it takes, but that, indeed, at the end of the day, you get no more than you started with. That's the whole conservationist perspective.

I mention this because when we get to Freud's theory of "hysterical" symptoms as conversion reactions—that the hysterical blindness, or hysterical paralysis, or hysterical deafness is just the physical manifestation of something occurring at the level of psychic energy—we see conservationist notions surfacing in Freudian theory that, indeed, Freud's repression theory of hysteria is part and parcel of a more general conservationist physics—

not only picked up at the knee of Ernst Brucke, so to speak, but obviously part of the general scientific ethos during the time of Freud's education. I do, therefore, want to say that Freud is not only ever the scientist, but he is always in touch with leading developments in the sciences.

A fine work by Frank Sulloway, titled *Freud: Biologist of the Mind*, really makes the case very well as to how close Freud was in his thinking to the best scientific thinking of the time, and how consistent he was in attempting to ground psychoanalytic theory in the more basic sciences.

Far more important than conservationist principles in physics was the Darwinian revolution, which Freud accepted, chapter and verse. Darwinian theory was the opening of a window; the whole perspective on the natural world changed. We now had, as I said in a previous lecture, design without a designer, and the design features were coming about as a result of raw, brutal, daily, biological conflict and collision. The real world was not peaceable. It was a kingdom in which the creatures take the form they do in the process of a self-serving, selfish commitment to survive. That's the bottom line. The individual organism does this through modes of self-gratification, and procreativity achieves the same for the species as a whole. This is all written in the thick book of evolutionary theory.

By the time you're a student at the University of Vienna in the 1880s, this is no longer a topic for debate. It may be hotly debated in cafés in and around Vienna, but to the scientific community, whatever was wrong in Darwin was more or less in the footnotes, not in the main points, and so Freud accepts evolutionary theory as a starting point for any general theory about human nature. That much, I think, has to be credited—put in the credit column—to Darwin's influence on the world.

Now, I say, Freud's ambitions were fairly modest to begin with. He wanted to be a research scientist in medicine and have an academic position at Vienna. Vienna was probably the most Catholic city in Europe, and the University of Vienna was surely the most Catholic university, perhaps, outside the pontifical Gregorian and a few other places, and it was fairly clear that Freud, as a Jew, was going to face a fairly low ceiling as far as academic prospects were concerned. He was already contemplating marriage and a family, and so—with some reluctance—he enters the medical practice rather than taking on a full-time academic life. He's therefore going to go off and practice neurology, which is what he was trained in.

Now, what kinds of patients will he see as a neurologist? Well, he'll see patients not unlike the patients seen today by neurologists. People come in complaining of a headache that won't go away; or there seems to be a sudden change in their visual sensitivity; or they wake up in the morning and one of their extremities, the left arm, has greatly reduced mobility; or they got out of bed and they seem to be dragging a leg behind them; or one of their pupils is dilated—that sort of thing, or they might have a region of the body completely bereft of sensation.

Now, what Freud knew, and all neurologists at the time knew, is that some of these symptoms are directly traceable to neuropathies. That is, there's actually a lesion or insult of some sort in the nervous system producing symptoms of this kind—but that some symptoms took a form that could not possibly be accounted for on the basis of anything we know about the anatomy of the nervous system.

The textbook example is so-called "glove anesthesia"—that is, the patient comes in and has lost all sensitivity in the hand, an area that would be covered by a glove. The area covered by a glove would actually not be based on anything we know about, the neuroanatomy of the arm and hand. The nerve distribution to the arm and hand cannot produce an anesthesia of the hand alone. So, here is a symptom that is not a bona fide neurological symptom, or at least not a pure neurological symptom. It's some other kind of symptom, a symptom of some other kind of condition. In Freud's time, generically these were referred to as "hysterias," and in the example I've cited, it would be called "hysterical anesthesia." To this can be added hysterical paralyses, hysterical blindness, and the like.

Hysteria takes its name from the Greek word for "uterus." Before the 19th century, it was widely thought that conditions of this kind occurred only in women and generally as part of the complexities of their reproductive biology. Now, Freud was not the one who turned things around on that. Charcot—whom I will mention in a few minutes—had a lot to do with getting rid of that, but even before Charcot, medical practitioners knew that the hysterias did hit men, and good and hard, though they already recognized the tendency of men not to show up with complaints like that, but for women to do so with regularity. Let me just say one of Freud's tasks, then, is just distinguishing between hysterical symptoms and bona fide neuropathies.

Between October 1885 and February 1886, Freud resided in Paris to study under Charcot who was reporting some success at the time in treating hysterical patients with hypnosis. The old "mesmerism," which had become a target of ridicule in large part because of Mesmer's own claims, had gradually returned to respectability in the hands of doctors seeking some form of anesthetic. This is before anesthesia, and Charcot extended the use of hypnosis, now, to diagnose and treat hysterical patients. It is known, for example, that hysterical symptoms—unlike neurological disorders—can be moved around the body by way of hypnotic suggestion. It was a keen insight on the part of Charcot to see in some of his hysterical patients a psychic response to traumatic experiences. Freud would imaginatively develop this idea that traumas generate physical symptoms by way of unconscious processes.

With six months of experience behind him, Freud returned to his practice in Vienna and, for a time, used hypnosis, giving it up chiefly, I suspect, owing to what he took to be its "mysteriousness."

Freud's friend and colleague Josef Breuer was also a graduate of the University of Vienna, practicing neurology in Vienna. The two would meet and compare notes. The patient of greatest interest to Freud was one that Breuer had been treating since about 1880, and who comes down to us as the famous Anna O. She had been caring for a tubercular father for years. At 21, she presented herself to Breuer suffering from a persistent cough, a paralysis on the right side of her body, sensory disturbances, and even hallucinations.

While in treatment, Anna O developed a total aversion to drinking. She avoided dehydration by eating fruit, but would not take in fluids directly. On one occasion, she lapsed into a state of self-hypnosis during which she reported the disgust she felt when she had seen a dog drinking from a glass. Post-hypnotically, Anna O was cured of her aversion.

Now, what Freud and Breuer concluded was that each of her symptoms was the residual of some earlier trauma, which—when purged from memory—resulted in recovery. It was Anna O herself who referred to Breuer's discovery as a "talking cure," and of the process as akin to "chimney sweeping."

Freud and Breuer proceeded to make a series of systematic observations in their patient population, satisfying themselves enough that they interpreted correctly what had taken place with Anna O. Their treatise, published in 1896, was titled *Studien uber Hysterie; Studies of Hysteria*, in which the theory is advanced that hysterical symptoms are invariably the outcome of *repression*. Psychoanalysis was born.

Years later, in his lectures on introductory psychoanalysis given at Clark University, Freud would say that Breuer deserved credit for the earliest beginnings of the discovery in his work with Anna O at a time when Freud was actually still in medical school.

As for the theory, it supposes that the patient has incorporated a traumatic event, a traumatizing thought, at an unconscious level. Certain fears and desires have been placed beyond conscious awareness, presumably because of their content. As a result of this repression, this blockage at the "psychic" level—a process is developed that converts this to a physical, hysterical symptom.

This is in a way something of a "hydraulic theory," in a manner of speaking. The normal flow is stopped up and pressure builds, released by way of other outlets. You stop things from getting expressed at one level, and they pop out somewhere else. Add to this notion those principles of conservation dominant in the physical sciences: Take a piece of paper, and set it on fire in an enclosed vial. What results is a mixture of heat, light, and ash, but the total energy in this closed system has not changed. The total energy is the same, but the form is different.

Now, granting the validity of the repression theory of hysteria—which already presupposes a quite active unconscious life—the question that naturally arises is: "What kind of thought, or wish, or desire is of such a nature that the patient's psychology would keep it out of mind at the price of lost sight, or lost sensitivity, or lost movement? This seems to be a hellish price to pay. Obviously, then, what's getting repressed must involve fairly high-stakes issues. What might these be?

Now on his own, with Breuer content to leave theorizing to others, Freud embarks on one of the more daring theoretical voyages ever. Inspired by evolutionary theory and taking human nature to be drawn from animal nature, Freud focuses on survival mechanisms. Our very ancestry guarantees that at the level of the individual, everything will be done to promote survival. Everything will be done to enhance pleasure and minimize pain, and in the process we will engage in such procreative activities as to guarantee the survival of the species as a whole—so that what you have *de novo*, now, is a creature that is self-regarding, selfish, self-protecting, hedonistic, and impelled by instinctual forces designed to gratify. That is the *pleasure principle*; that *de novo* we come into the world designed in such a way as to seek end enhance pleasurable experiences and minimize those that are in any way painful.

Pleasure is the sensation that nature endows us with, so that we do what we have to do to survive. Do you see? It works like this. Why does an infant suck at a nipple? Not because the infant has read a nutritional treatise or handbook, or knows about Krebs cycles and the like. If you hang a strain gauge on the cheek of an infant you find out it takes an awful lot of work to drain a bottle. It's really quite effortful. Hourly wages would probably have to be astronomical to keep somebody doing this—unless, of course, it created a kind of sensual pleasure. The infant sucks for reasons, Freud says, that at the bottom, the reasons are expressions of this very well developed instinctual tendency to survive, and he therefore reaches the concept of infantile sexuality, and it does what it does because it derives sensual pleasure from doing it. That precious, wonderful, little creation of love is in there, pleasing itself in one of those well-known sensual ways.

As you move through these Freudian stages of psychosexual development, you find that what shifts is the mode of gratification, but gratification remains the constant goal; it's just how one achieves sensual gratification that changes. The culmination of this—quite consistent with evolutionary theory, through the oral stage and the anal stage—is, finally, adult heterosexual sexuality.

However, why is it that adults do engage in heterosexual sexuality? Very few people do this chiefly on demographic grounds. They do not calculate the replacement ratio and notice that some number of births is needed to compensate for fatalities, etc. The behavior does not proceed from considerations of duty. Rather, the activity is a source of pleasure, and it is the pleasure that explains it. What people do for pleasure is what nature would require for success of the species—so that adult heterosexual sexuality, in virtue of the fact that it yields pleasure, serves the purposes of nature.

Now, all this is at the level of the pleasure principle, but what sort of world would we have if human beings simply labored in the service of the pleasure principle 24 hours a day? Now, some of you are going to say: "Well, I suspect it would be the world we do have." This is a separate topic, though. In point of fact, most of the time we conduct ourselves in a way that denies us certain pleasures. Indeed, we even write laws that will punish those who act solely according to the pleasure principle—which is to say that in order for there to be an integral society, the pleasure principle has to yield, and this creature, designed by nature to gratify itself, to please itself, to avoid punishment, to be selfish—this creature has to become civilized, and socialized, and acculturated. That is to say, the pleasure principle has to come face to face with what Freud calls the *reality principle*.

Yes, there is here that Hegelian dialect in yet another manifestation, as it was seen in Karl Marx's theory, the idea being that this *ego*, this self, the self that we recognize in the mirror, the sorts of people we regard ourselves as being, each of us singly—how we regard each other—well, it's a reconciliation of two quite opposing forces: The self, or the ego, arises from the opposition of two powerful principles: the pleasure principle and the reality principle.

The pleasure principle itself arises from what is most basic and instinctual in our animal nature, described by Freud as the *id*. Society gets working on us from the earliest moments to fashion a being that becomes a tolerable member of society, so society can preserve itself, and that is through the education and acculturation of the conscience—the development of a conscience. It's the world that begins each day with: "No. No. Don't do that. Behave yourself. Stop, etc." announced to a creature that is constantly saying at the unconscious level: "Now. Me. More. Right away." You see the conflict here, and out of that comes, I say, not quite a happily reconciled entity. Life is never as pleasurable as we know it could be, and indeed, we never quite measure up to the highest social expectations that have been set for us. So, out of the tension between the id and what Freud calls the *superego*, there emerges the ego, the self. The ego is that synthesis out of the thesis-antithesis sort of dialectic. This puts a new light on the problem of knowledge, the problem of conduct, the problem of government.

The first lesson to be learned is that the tensions here are to some extent relaxable but not eliminable; that, indeed, the demands of society being what they are, it is necessarily the case that the life we live will not be an authentic life. Which is to say, we will not act as our own truest and most basic impulses and instincts would have us act. We begin the compromise from the earliest possible time, and to make sure that these compromises are made, we have parents; we have institutions set up to do it.

Now, parents, of course, have us doing things and not doing things based on what parents take to be good reasons. So, parents might tell children: "Don't do this until you're married, and don't do that, and don't do this," and they might tie it into basic religious precepts, or certain ethical precepts and the like.

Of course, these very religious precepts, these very standards and social customs themselves, are the outgrowth of processes that are essentially unconscious. You do some kind of rationalizing after the fact. "Well, we tell our children that there should be no sexual intercourse until marriage, and that's because..." The "because" then offered as a justification may be taken from Scripture, or from the Baltimore Catechism, or even the Surgeon General's Annual Report, but that's not what's actually prompting the directives. That's just what occurs at the conscious, superficial level—the surface level of society.

What actually is going on here is that institutions and practices are being formed to move people toward heterosexual modes of sexual gratification within the framework of marriage for the purpose of securing the needs and interests of society itself. Whether you're dealing with a tribal community or the fashionable East Side of Manhattan—whether it's the Oxbridge crowd, or something radically different—the institutional and social arrangements are designed in such a way as to secure the interests of the society at large, and those interests are finally and basically of a biological Darwinian nature. At stake is the survival of the collective. Now, it may take on a variety of institutional, tribal, religious, customary forms, but once you read through the symbolism, you see that the same thing is going on in all these places.

Well, now, this is quite a bizarre theory when you think about it. As with evolutionary theory itself, psychoanalytic theory has this Gothic character, something we might expect from, say, Mary Shelley, or to be painted by Henry Fuseli. Beneath surface rationality and simplicity is the busy workshop of the unconscious, directing and forming complex institutions, causing weird dreams and disturbing symptoms, rendering at once fit for—and discontented with—civilization. Of course, to make matters stranger, there are people waking up blind or with paralyses because they harbor horrid wishes that they cannot face. What kind of wishes might these be that could cause such symptoms?

Take a guess—sexual, of course! This is Freud, after all—so, as Junior is moving toward heterosexual sexuality, the obvious target of his affections will be the source of his preexisting gratification. Yes, it will be Junior's mother, and so what Junior has to learn, in no uncertain terms, is that mother is off-limits. Here, then, is the theory of the Oedipal complex, in which the socialization of sexuality requires redirecting the sexual energies to a socially acceptable target. This can be a profoundly traumatic experience in the life of the developing young man.

One prominent physician asked to comment on the recent theories of Dr. Freud declared that this was not a fit subject for academic discussion, but a reason to call the police. Note, then, that Freud was castigated by his contemporaries, I think perhaps less for the sexual content of the theory, than for the fact that it was so theoretical in the first place. He was writing at a time when Ernst Mach and the whole positivist movement in science were developing its full stride. Doing science means especially not doing metaphysics. Science is an essentially observational enterprise designed to generate general testable and refutable laws, and here comes this Dr. Freud out of Vienna, talking about Oedipal complexes, totem poles, dream-censors, and all of that. Freud was destined for criticism, I should think, even with the sexual content muted, or—for that matter—removed.

What evidence is there for the unconscious at all? Freud claimed that "the royal road to the unconscious is through the interpretation of dreams," that the dream world is the world in which wishes are fulfilled. This is the closest we ever come to facing up to what our real desires and wishes are—but, in fact, if we saw them in all their reality, we'd never be able to sleep. So, there's a kind of censoring mechanism that puts into symbolic form something that you see; here's the bottom line. The bottom line is, life doesn't work. The dream doesn't quite work. The symbolism is enough to let you sleep, but because it's symbolism you're not really dealing with the reality of it all anyway—so that it's another one of these compromises.

The persistent dream of turning the corner and being tripped up by little puppies—tripping up the policeman, do you see, the Keystone Cop who's tripped up by little pets—is the persistent dream of the chap who thinks his younger siblings have enjoyed the affection of his father far more than he has, or that he will trip up authority, etc. Oedipal tensions, over and over again, stalk us. Homosexuality is adopting a female persona, a passivity rather than face the possible castration threats that go along with the Oedipal conflict—so that this is all very Gothic, very imagistic theorizing.

Well, it does turn around that Delphic requirement that we know ourselves: "*Gnothi seauton.*" Now we would actually need a psychoanalyst if we would know ourselves, and the self that we are going to know this way turns out to be a gift of evolutionary theory, and not something suspected by the rationalist and ultra-civilized Arnoldian visions that we have confronted earlier in this course.

Freud was and is a force to be contended with. We can't avoid him in departments of English literature these days. Psychoanalytic theory still has a great, great following. Its manifest lack of success in every arena has had no effect on its popularity. This is one of those things we all are going to learn to live with—and maybe even enjoy from time to time.

The Radical William James

Lecture 46

James preserved the scientific perspective and approach to the nature of mind but required science to come to terms with the facts of mental life.

James quipped that every time the Hegelians refer to the "absolute ego" they sound like they're going up in a balloon. What he urges instead is a philosophy and a science that will come to terms with the world that is known and knowable, that centrally includes every aspect of experience that is reliable.

William James surely is the quintessential Yankee philosopher. He comes along when Hegelian thought and Romanticism are fixtures in the American philosophical world. Transcendentalist and back-to-nature movements—this is the world of Thoreau, Emerson, Channing—are prominent. James will not reject these perspectives but will bring his characteristically Jamesian view to bear on them. James comes along in a world of mystery. As late as 1907, Professor Henry Jones wrote, with a sense of alarm, about how Hegelian thought has overtaken English thought and the English universities. His fear is that the epidemic is spreading almost without challenge.

James's project is to rescue thought from the seductions of the worlds of mystery, while preserving its fluidity, purpose, and variegated nature. James, the eldest of four children and grandson of a multimillionaire, arrived at his project in a rather plodding way. James took longer than usual to complete his studies at Harvard, because of interruptions by bouts of illness. He read voraciously and retained what he learned.

He spent six years (1863–1869) completing required studies for a medical degree. He dropped out once for what proved to be an unsatisfying exploration of the Amazon conducted by Louis Agazzis and a second time for travels in Germany, where lectures by Helmholtz and Wundt aroused James's interests in sensory processes and psychology. After completing his medical training at Harvard, James joined the faculty there in 1872.

Within a few years, we find him giving lectures in physiological psychology and presiding over some experiments. Still, James suffered from various maladies and was beset by interludes of fear and depression. He treated his psychological turmoil by wide and deep reading.

There were questions about whether Wundt or James deserves the title of the first academic experimental psychologist. James was a bit prickly on this subject, insisting that he didn't really get the credit he deserved. His work *The Principles of Psychology*, however, remains perhaps the classic treatise in academic psychology.

After the completion of *The Principles of Psychology*, almost all of James's writing addresses chiefly the grounding of our knowledge, as well as the ethical dimensions of life, for reasons that grow out of what he called his *radical empiricism*. The usual adoption of, or concession to, empiricistic philosophies is hedged—though there are some things we cannot know by way of experience; by and large, we use our senses to gather information about our world in most of the ordinary business of life. This most assuredly is not the position of a radical empiricist. Radical empiricism maintains that no set of experiences has an authority superior to some other set of experiences. It is not the province of science or philosophy to declare, for instance, that religious experiences and visions are more or less valid than other experiences.

What figures in the human imagination in a reliable way must be dealt with on its own terms. This is the core of James's famous critique of associationist thought and philosophy. The associationist theory of mind is based on the notion that corpuscular and elemental mental entities are somehow held together as a result of repetition and, thus assembled, stand as real ideas.

In so many words, he asks, "How did philosophy ever come to a view like that?" It surely could not be on the basis of experience. Nobody has ever had an experience of that kind. Give each of seven men one word of a sentence, none of them knowing words assigned to the other six, and not one of them will have the meaning of the sentence itself.

James refused to make "consciousness" into a palpable entity or a "substance," but he insisted that, as a process, it introduced something new into the ontological realm. Every idea is *someone's*; it is owned. Mental life is not an empty container filled with experiences agglomerating with one another. A thought is not *a* thought; it is *my* thought. The external world is *chosen* for the content that will be experienced and associated. *Selection* is at the core of experience.

Where does this consciousness come from? Evolution offers a kind of progressive, associational sort of theory. On the matter of mental life, James is satisfied that it, too, has followed an evolutionary course in the animal kingdom. But we now have to consider whether this settles or even recognizes the problem of the origin of consciousness. Darwin's is a continuity theory, according to which what we find at the level of human psychology is approximated to some degree further and further down in the phylogenetic series. If we find some creature that has a bit less consciousness and then another with even less, have we explained or settled the problem of consciousness? James knows that we do not explain consciousness by pointing to earlier manifestations that are small consciousnesses. The small consciousness is as difficult to explain as the larger ones.

Every idea is *someone's*; it is owned. ... A thought is not *a* thought; it is *my* thought.

There are two ways we can consider survival of the fittest, or evolutionary pressures conducing to adaptive behavior. It can be seen from the outside, as a natural process working on attributes, selecting the more useful ones and eliminating the lesser. In the realm of experience, it appears very differently: as an intention to survive. James asks us to consider what happens when we consult again the authoritative realm, which is the realm of experience:

> We treat survival as if it were an absolute end, existing as such in the physical world, a sort of actual *should be*... We forget that in the absence of some such superadded commenting intelligence... the reactions cannot be properly talked of as "useful" or "hurtful" at all. ... The moment you bring consciousness into the midst,

survival ceases to be a mere hypothesis. No longer is it "*if* survival is to occur …" It has now become an imperative degree: "Survival *shall* occur …" *Real* ends now appear for the first time upon the world's stage.

James was among the first of the scientific community to accept the criticism that the Hegelian camp had assembled an associationist psychology and atomist science, but James put it to constructive use. James exposed a dangerous and overlooked connection in scientific work between the phenomena to be studied and the method of investigating it. James called "the psychologist's fallacy" the fallacy of assuming that the mental process to be studied operates in the same manner as the experiment works. Methods that study memory by giving subjects repeated exposure to materials, then testing how much is retained after certain frequencies of repetition, *assume* that repetition is what forms memories. What is called for is the adoption of experimental modes of inquiry able to accommodate mental processes as they actually take place. Don't abandon the laboratory; make it sensible!

James took up the "common sense" tradition of Thomas Reid that had been lost during the ascendance of John Stuart Mill. Common sense is how a species meets daily challenges—to be skeptical about its existence is pointless. But the common sense of one species is not that of another, as the challenges to one species are not that of another. James sits and reads a book, his eyes slowly passing over one line at a time; his dog watches this unintelligible behavior. Is one set of experiences authentic, the other not?

James preserved the scientific perspective and approach to the nature of mind but required science to come to terms with the facts of mental life. He rejected all attempts to filter experience such that only those contents compatible with favored theories were preserved. Adopting a common-sense realist position, James was able to fend off the Hegelian criticism of science's one-sidedness and honor that criticism that requires science to be faithful to the complexities of its subject matter. We are fire *and* clay; consciousness is not easily found in the body, but neither science nor philosophy advances by denying it is there. ∎

Suggested Reading

James, W. *Essays in Radical Empiricism* and *A Pluralistic Universe*. Phoenix Books, 1977.

Perry, R. B. *The Thought and Character of William James*. Vanderbilt University Press, 1996.

Questions to Consider

1. Explain whether evolutionary theory honors the Jamesian sense of survivalism as a force in the natural world.

2. Summarize what theory of the "self" is needed in James's conception of mental associations.

The Radical William James
Lecture 46—Transcript

I've titled this lecture on William James, the first of two on William James, "The Radical William James," and William James surely is the quintessential Yankee philosopher. I can't imagine another culture and country producing him.

James does come along in a world of mystery. He comes along when the American philosophical world is featuring the American Hegelian movement, and Hegelian thought and Romanticism are fixtures—not only in the thinking parts of America, but in what at the time was probably the most intensely thinking part of America, namely New England. Transcendentalist movements are there, and back-to-nature movements—this is a world of Thoreau, Emerson, Channing—the list is long. These are not perspectives that James will reject by any means, but James himself is going to bring to bear on them a characteristically, shall we say, Jamesian view.

Now, when I say "a world of mystery," is this just an academic thinking that the world at large concerns itself with, whatever academics are concerned with? Well, let me read a passage from a 1907 magazine article that Oxford's own Professor Henry Jones composed, writing here on how Hegelian thought has overtaken English thought and the English universities. His fear is that the epidemic is spreading almost without surcease, almost without challenge. Here's the passage; there are ellipses throughout, but here's the main point. He says, quoting now Hobhouse:

> The Rhine has flowed into the Thames. Carlyle introduced it, bringing it as far up as Chelsea Then, Jowett and Thomas Hill Green and William Wallace and Lewis Nettleship guided the waters into the Isis. They have passed up the Mersey. They pollute the bay of Saint Andrews, and swell the waters of the Cam. The stream of German idealism has been diffused over the academical world of Great Britain. The disaster is universal.

Hegel's influence, then, on American philosophy was broad and deep in the second half of the 19th century. Centered first in non-academic intellectual circles—chiefly St. Louis—Hegelianism would be embraced by leading academic figures such as John Dewey and Josiah Royce. The latter would become a friend and philosophical adversary of William James during the time both were on the Harvard faculty, Royce there as a result of James's admiration and support.

Here, then, is an American philosophy at home with idealism, discoursing energetically on the "Absolute," splitting hairs over whether absolutism is compatible with free will, etc.

This is a world of deep and only suggestive mystery that William James is entering, and it's a world that he's going to try to set aright through clear, pragmatic, practical, basic—may I say it?—Yankee thought; a confidence in the evidence of sense; a firm belief that for all its faults, common sense is about the best thing we've got going for us; and in thorough Reidian fashion, I would say, the belief that when philosophy and science conflict directly with the central precepts of common sense, it better be science and philosophy that give way. James's project is to rescue thought from the seductions of the worlds of mystery, while preserving its fluidity, its purpose, and its variegated nature.

James didn't arrive at his project all of a sudden; he got there in a rather plodding way. Life began for him as a child of privilege, born in Manhattan in 1842, the eldest of four children and grandson of a multimillionaire. His father, Henry, was a man of academic tastes and religious conviction, a disciple of Swedenborg and an internationalist in perspective. Swedenborg, recall, was the 18th-century genius—philosopher, scientist, mystic—whose theological works were consonant with Christianity but in a different voice, as it were. His "New Jerusalem" won adherents. There is still an active Swedenborgian Society, and Henry James, Sr., was a member of that.

The James children were well traveled, often at the expense of a stable school life. By age 18, William had settled on a career as a painter, but he abandoned it in less than a year for, of all things, the Chemistry program at Harvard. It took James longer than usual to complete his studies at Harvard. They were interrupted by bouts of illness. It is clear that he learned more at home during periods of recovery than in the Harvard classrooms. He read voraciously, and he retained what he learned.

Still casting about for a career—which is what one settles for when there is no calling—he spent six years completing required studies for a medical degree, this between 1863 and 1869. He dropped out once for what proved to be an unsatisfying exploration of the Amazon that was being conducted by Louis Agazzis and a second time for travels in Germany, where, thanks to lectures by Helmholtz and by Wundt, his interests in sensory processes and in psychology were aroused. He wrote to his father from Germany, indicating his intention to take in these lectures. He was clearly impressed by the findings reached through experimentation, and by the ability to decipher scientifically at least one feature of the mind at work. He returned to Harvard forthwith, completed his medical training, and joined the faculty in 1872. Within a few years, we find him giving lectures in physiological psychology, and indeed, actually presiding over some experiments in a laboratory he set up himself.

Still, James suffered from various maladies, and he was beset by interludes of fear and depression. His psychological turmoil was treated best by wide and deep reading. Here was a doctor doctoring himself, chiefly by way of the consolations of philosophy. No career in sight, William James now had a vocation. As for his famous brother, travel brought him to an England that seemed much like a homeland from the first. In time, then, Henry James would obtain British citizenship, and he would have a flat in Chelsea and a house outside of London. His brother, William, felt no such pull at all.

There were questions about whether Wundt or James deserves the title of the first academic experimental psychologist. James was a bit prickly on this subject, insisting that he didn't really get the credit he deserved for that. Of course, the work that every psychologist knows is by William James is *The Principles of Psychology*, which he promised his publisher in two years and that actually took him a dozen years to complete. May I say that it remains the classic treatise in academic psychology. It's a good read to this day. Where it's overtaken by history is not all that important; you can fill in those gaps, but the perspective is wonderful and rich. It is a thoroughly documented work—rich in footnotes. He knows everything going on in the world of psychological thought. He takes out of that world of thought what is most worthy of attention; he treats it fairly and in an utterly winning way. I might say that he may be the only author in that family—and I am a fan of Henry James—and has certainly put together the most interesting of that otherwise arid species, the textbook.

After the completion of *The Principles of Psychology*, almost all of James's writing is addressed chiefly to the grounding of our knowledge—the basis upon which we accept things as true; what the right attitude *should be* toward our experiences of the world; what the right attitude should be toward issues of verification, the vindication of theories, their falsification. He will also address himself to the ethical, and indeed, spiritual dimensions of life, for reasons that grow out of what he called his *radical empiricism*. I am going to pause here to make clear just what it means to be a radical empiricist and to be the radical William James, for it is this that gives power and consistency to the entire range of James's thought.

Now, usual adoption of, or concession to, empiricistic philosophies is a hedged one. The apologist is likely to say something along these lines: "Well, of course, a lot of the things we know, we know as a result of experience. There are some things we can't know by way of experience, these being sort of abstract, Leibnizian, Cartesian sorts of things, and, anyway, the senses really can deceive us from time to time; by and large, I'm certainly going to use my senses in most of the ordinary business of life."

This, I say, is a position that is as boring as it is probably faultless. It most assuredly is not the position of a radical empiricist. John Locke, for example, is not a radical empiricist. When Locke says that the mind is furnished by experience, but then includes certain original acts of the mind, he sounds a bit like Descartes—but not at all like a radical empiricist would say.

How about religious experiences and visions? How about premonitions that are reliably experienced by people? How about out-of-body experiences, near-death experiences? What would James say about all of this? James is consistent. What radical empiricism requires is this: No set of experiences has an authority superior to some other set of experiences. It is not the business or province of science or philosophy to declare which experiences are legitimate.

The business of science and philosophy is to come to terms with experience as it is had, experience as it is reported. No experience is off-limits. Find a set of experiences that don't match up very well with the received wisdom of science and philosophy, and that signals a problem for science and philosophy. Experience is under no obligation to justify itself before some court that would declare itself to be of greater authority.

That is the consistent position. What figures in the human imagination in a reliable way is to be dealt with—not dismissed as too complex, too strange, etc.—and is to be dealt with on its own terms. Hence, we have James's famous critique of associationist thought and philosophy, a form of thought we find in Aristotle, Locke, Hume, and scores of others. The associationist theory of mind is based on the notion that mental entities are corpuscular and elemental—that these are somehow pulled or held together as a result of repetition or some such, that thus assembled, they now stand as real ideas, etc.

Well, one can nearly feel James's impatience and amusement. In so many words, he asks, "How did philosophy ever come to a view like that?" It surely could not be on the basis of experience. No one has ever had an experience of that kind. For example, suppose we line up a half dozen people, and we give each of them a word on a card. Nobody can see anyone else's cards, only his own card. You can't get a sentence out of something like that. No one has a sentence, not one of them has a sentence—and this is what the theory of association calls for. First, we record sensation element or corpuscle "A," then "B," then "C." These are utterly independent according to the associationist theory, but, through some sort of mechanism or process, they become connected, but who possesses the outcome of all this? Is there any authorizing intelligence that's integrating all this?"

James notes that:

> This argument has never been answered. It holds good against any talk about self-compounding amongst feelings, against any blending or complication or mental chemistry, in the absence of a

supernumerary principle of consciousness. The mind-stuff theory, in short, is unintelligible.

The mind-stuff theory is unintelligible, because what it does not include is what James calls a "supernumerary principle of consciousness." You've got to have an intact, alert, sensitive, willful being who draws upon the resources of the world and frames ideas, not as corpuscles. Nobody ever had an experience like that. There is no empty can that becomes filled up with corpuscles held together mindlessly. Rather, there must be a supernumerary, authenticating, integrating intelligence.

Mind, however, is not going to be treated as some sort of Cartesian substance or entity. On James's account, "consciousness" is not an entity, but a process. This is not to depreciate consciousness. Rather, it is a process not only as real as anything else, but the one on which something ever enters reality as known, anything would enter reality as known.

James again on associationism will be a gloss on this point:

> The class of phenomena which the associationist school takes to frame its theory of the Ego are feelings unaware of each other. The class of phenomena the Ego presents are feelings of which the later ones are intensely aware of those that went before. No shuffling of unaware feelings can make them aware.

James's point here is that in the stream of consciousness, the ideas that we have invariably look back on those that preceded them, and ahead to those that are to come. There is a continuity of thought, a continuity of mental life, that is not only not captured by the mind-stuff theory, but associationism and the mind-stuff theory simply can't deal with the continuity of thought, which happens to be its central characteristic, as revealed immediately by what? By our experience.

For example, every thought is *someone's* thought. Every thought is "owned." Associationism makes no provision for the owner. David Hume's parade formation will not work absent someone viewing the parade. There isn't anybody whose parade this is. James here is not trying to restore a substance

243

theory of self or soul. Rather, he is reflecting on the nature of his own experience—experience is the rule here—and he concludes that his thoughts are his own, and any plausible theory of ideation must take account of that fact. There can be no "philosophy of thought," only a philosophy of the thoughts that persons actually have. James is certain that the traditional Anglo-European "mental chemistry" just misses the main point.

The other characteristic of thought is that it inevitably includes the element of *selection*. The world is a world of incessant stimulation. We don't see and hear it all; we couldn't. We pick out things that we're going to look at. We pick out things based on what we judge to be in our interest to pick out. Again, you have to have a psychologically active, dynamic mental life in the first instance for these experiences to take the shape and form that they actually do, and any developed philosophy of mind is going to have to come to grips with this. It's going to have to come to grips with those conscious processes on which we erect notions of will, attention, selectivity.

In Chapter 11 of his *Psychology*, James develops the point this way:

> Four characters in consciousness: How does it go on? We notice immediately four important characters in the process.
>
> One, every "state" tends to be part of a personal consciousness.
>
> Two, within each personal consciousness states are always changing.
>
> Three, each personal consciousness is sensibly continuous.
>
> Four, it is interested in some parts of its object to the exclusion of others, and welcomes or rejects—chooses from among them, in a word—all the while.

Where does this consciousness come from? Suppose you consult evolutionary theory, which itself is a kind of progressive, associational sort of theory.

Now, James is this way and that way about evolutionary theory, for he tends to be uncomfortable with theory as an alternative to experience, but on the matter of mental life, he is satisfied that it, too, has followed an evolutionary course in the animal kingdom and, thus, "animal consciousness" is a warranted assumption, but we now have to consider whether this settles or even recognizes the problem of the origin of consciousness.

Look, let us grant that we are conscious. On the evolutionary account, what would we then say about, for example, other primates? Would we say they are less conscious than dogs and cats, rabbits and sparrows, fish and frogs? Darwin's is a continuity theory, according to which what we find at the level of human psychology is approximated to some degree further and further down in the phylogenetic series. Now, if we do find some creature that has a bit less consciousness, and then another with even less, have we explained or settled the problem of consciousness?

James had a bit of fun with this one. He offers us an amusing example in a play that was making the rounds in James's day, *Midshipman Easy* by Captain Frederick Marryat. In the play, a young servant becomes pregnant out of wedlock. When finally confronted, her defense is that, "Well, sir, it's a very small baby." James knows that we do not explain consciousness by pointing to earlier manifestations of it that somehow are very small consciousnesses. The small consciousness is as difficult to explain as the larger one.

When we turn this back again to evolutionary theory, we see that the notion of survival now takes on a radically different character. That is, there are two ways you can consider survival of the fittest, or evolutionary pressures conducing to adaptive behavior. One way is that there is some sort of process or force going on somewhere in nature, do you see? Natural selection, whatever it is, and it's sort of playing on the attributes of animals, such that some of those attributes are picked out for propagation, and others of those attributes become the basis upon which the species is eliminated. That's one view, but James asks us to consider what happens when you consult again the authoritative realm, which is the realm of experience. He says:

> We treat survival as if it were an absolute end, existing as such in the physical world, a sort of actual *should be*... We forget that in the

absence of some such superadded commenting intelligence...the reactions cannot be properly talked of as "useful" or "hurtful" at all.... The moment you bring consciousness into the midst, survival ceases to be a mere hypothesis. No longer is it "*if* survival is to occur...." It has now become an imperative degree: "Survival *shall* occur...." *Real* ends now appear for the first time upon the world's stage.

You see, then, intentionality, interest, selectivity, consciousness, self-consciousness—this is what experience turns up as real; a philosophy of mind unable to come to terms with that must be defective.

Now, I think here it's worth noting that James's criticism is not unlike the criticism of the Romantic idealists going back to Goethe's criticism of Newton's theory of light. Newton's optical theory tells us everything about light, except what we see. James's argument is that the scientific reductionist approach is a one-sided affair that can only explain the natural world by traducing it into something entirely unnatural.

James is part of that tradition; he's not immune to it. He derives benefit from the Romantic idealist critique of reductionistic science. At the same time, though, he cannot accept the Hegelian philosophy. He resists an agenda that is anti-scientific, even while reserving the right to reveal the defects of a defective science. The Hegelian claims to an understanding of the universe, its "through-and-through" complexity, its accessibility to logical demonstrations—all this strikes James as learned hubris. In Chapter 12 of his *Essays in Radical Empiricism*, he offers this memorable critique of the entire Hegelian enterprise:

> The through-and-through philosophy seems too buttoned-up and white-chokered and clean-shaven a thing to speak for the vast slow-breathing unconscious Kosmos with its dread abysses and its unknown tides.

James quipped that every time the Hegelians refer to the "absolute ego" they sound like they're going up in a balloon. What he urges instead is a philosophy and a science that will come to terms with the world that is known and knowable, that centrally includes every aspect of experience that is reliable; recorded in the daily life of sensate; attending, selecting, conscious human beings—so, the summons is to realism, even a common-sense realism.

When James canvasses the ways in which mental life is examined, he notices a pervasive fallacy, and a dangerous one. Here he was not only ahead of his time, but I think ahead of our time, too. He notes the troubling connection between what is said about a phenomenon and the method chosen to examine it. There is an unblushing tendency to assume that the real nature of the phenomenon just is whatever the chosen method has turned up. He refers to it as "the psychologist's fallacy," and he treats it this way in Chapter 7 of his *Principles of Psychology*:

> The great snare of the psychologist is the confusion of his own standpoint with that of the mental fact about which he is making his report. The psychologist stands outside of the mental state he speaks of. Both itself and its object are objects for him.

"The psychologist's fallacy," generally, is assuming that a mental phenomenon is of a certain kind, because your method of inquiry was able to examine only that feature of it or examine it only in that way—the fallacy of assuming that what goes on in reality is just what mimics what was going on in your experiment, given the method that you were choosing. It is the fallacy of assuming that the experience as experienced, or the thought as thought, has the properties or essential nature of whatever it is the researcher notes, based on a chosen method inevitably limited.

In these several respects, James was picking up a tradition that had largely been lost during the heyday of John Stuart Mill's philosophy. Mill's very influential *An Examination of Sir William Hamilton's Philosophy* claimed Thomas Reid as one of its principal casualties. In that work, Mill identified Reid with Kant and others in what he called the "intuitionist school," treating common sense principles as a kind of intuition. Surely one of the reasons Reid fell out of favor was because of the perceived success of John Stuart Mill's critique of the intuitionist school, and I should say, the wrongful assignment of Reid to that school.

James is picking up the Reidian baton and defending the following precepts, which are largely Reidian: First, the proper method of investigation is a scientific method that takes the facts where it finds them. That is, you don't develop a theory that excludes facts as a condition of the theory working. You develop a theory capable of meeting the facts on the facts' own terms.

Secondly, what constitutes a fact is any reliable representation in experience. That is, facts do not become facts through the authority of scientific or philosophical systems, but through the actual engagement of human beings with the world in which they live.

Now, what about common sense principles? Well, James speaks directly of common sense principles, and he does so in a context that is quite congenial to, let's say, evolutionary theory in the broader—I'm inclined to say, softer—sense. Creatures, human and otherwise, face challenges daily. Common sense is the means by which we come to terms with these challenges. To be skeptical about common sense is to be skeptical about that one resource that is most serviceable as we go about trying to meet the challenges and overcome the obstacles of daily life. It turns out, however, that the challenges to one are not the same as the challenges to all. The kind of creature you are determines what is of greatest interest to you.

James illustrates this in a particularly winning way. He says that when he sits in his chair reading a book, his eyes are moving across its pages; he is engrossed, but sitting in front of him is his dog, looking up, watching the eyes moving across these pages, and lamenting the fact that James doesn't seem to know that, in a matter of moments, a stick could be in the air.

Now, what are we to say about the dog who just can't wait for the stick to be in the air, and William James who just can't wait to get to the next chapter? Do we want to say that one set of those experiences is inauthentic and the other one authentic, or do we want to say that there are different interests that will express themselves in different attentive selections, in different conscious processes devoted to something uniquely important to a given species, a given person, uniquely important to one person, under particular circumstances in life? To try to wash this out with allegedly general laws that become lawful only by ignoring the facts of daily life is not to prosecute the agenda of philosophy or science, but to engage in a species of self-deception.

We're to be empiricists, says James, in the radical sense. We are to accept the contents of our conscious life, not consciousness as something we see when we look inside the head. James is satisfied that at the end of the day, we come to the grips with the fact that we are fire *and* clay—that there is a brain and an embodiment, and that our biology is always and ever with us. There seems to be a set of conscious mental processes that, fire-like, are not easily encapsulated into the husk of the body or found in the biological details. That these—that this twoness in one is an inevitability to be dealt with by philosophy and science is unavoidable, but that neither philosophy nor science can advance by denying the reality of either, as some attempt to celebrate the other or establish its hegemony, is what has to be avoided.

James, then, is a practical, common sense, experience-based, American philosopher, wanting to get on with the show—taking the facts where he finds them, leading him to a pattern of thought that will go in any direction that experience reliably points to. He's not going up in a balloon, and he's summoning some of his American colleagues back to earth as well, their having gone up in a balloon and having very little to show for it, except for a kind of dizziness. Bill James, American radical empiricist. Read him. You'll love it.

William James's Pragmatism
Lecture 47

The pragmatic theory of truth is not based on the proposition that nothing is true in science or elsewhere until it matches up with some concrete experience. What it does assert, however, is that the ultimate court in which competing theories will vie for our allegiance is the court in which are located our highest interests.

We now move from William James's radical empiricism to his pragmatism and pluralism. The practical side of James's philosophy begins with functionalism. His *Principles of Psychology* put in place an essentially functionalist psychology and formed the foundation for American behaviorism. James takes the position that the creatures of nature, via evolution, obviously are fit to deal with the environment they find themselves in.

There's a famous brief treatise by James on the question "Does consciousness exist?" The answer James gives is "yes and no." If we think of consciousness as immaterial, spaceless, massless but nonetheless an ontologically real thing, no, that doesn't exist. But if we think of it as a flow of ideas, the stream of perceptions and thoughts and feelings, the process by which a supernumerary intelligence knits together experiences over a course of time, then consciousness is indubitable. Without invoking Aristotelian "final causes" or attaching himself to every feature of Darwinian biology, James nonetheless ties processes to functions, to larger purposes and possibilities.

What, then, is the function of consciousness? What is it *for*? What does it achieve that could be achieved in no other way? The brain is a fabulously complex organ, consisting of millions of cells constantly at work processing sensory input. Yet the result is not simply a "blooming, buzzing confusion." For survival, we must not only be able to sense our environment with great subtlety but react to stimuli instantly and correctly: This is the "hair-trigger" nature of brain functions. Our conscious processes are declared to be necessary to regulate the flow of mental functioning, through such specifically conscious functions as *attention*, *selection*, and *will*.

It is out of experience that the will itself is constructed. This is James's *ideomotor* theory of the growth and function of the will:

- It is under purely reflexive control at first, as the infant responds to stimuli.
- These reflexive experiences continue, and they persist as a reservoir of behavior the individual can draw on.
- By *attending* to the possibilities around us, we are able, in responding, to *select* one behavior over another from the reservoir we have accumulated.

For James, the will is simply part of our nature, as it must be if the game of living is to get going in the first place.

James's pragmatism is tied to his functionalism. Critics of pragmatism often take pragmatists to be claiming, "If it works, it's true." On this understanding, there would be no way to distinguish between competing scientific worldviews if both of them led to comparable practical success. This shortchanges James's version of pragmatism and that of Charles Sanders Pierce, with whom James was closely and not always happily associated. James held that the pragmatic method is primarily a method of settling metaphysical disputes that otherwise might be interminable by trying to trace each notion to its respective practical consequences. Pierce had earlier framed his own version of pragmatism: "Consider what effects, which might conceivably have practical bearings, we conceive the object of our conception to have. Then the whole of our conception of those effects is the whole of our conception of the object."

The two views are similar but different. Pierce preferred to refer to his position as "pragmatistic," James's as being "pragmatism." What they have in common is the standard to be applied in determining whether a concept or meaning is clearly comprehended. Pragmatism on James's account matches up with James's notion of our interests. What we do, we do on behalf of our highest interests.

What, then, *are* our highest interests? Aren't they different for different people, at different times, in different cultures? James's pluralism will admit of answers, but no *final* answers. For all we know, the universe itself is evolving such that, in its dynamism, even its own laws change. Thus does James reject the *block universe*, a static mass about which there is some last word that will be true of it for all time. As the human race finds itself in different contexts, equipped with new and promising thoughts and possibilities, there is always another broad perspective that replaces an earlier one, a perspective that cannot be expected to be the same everywhere. In their given context, and for the lives actually lived in that context, certain beliefs and attitudes directly fortify and give direction to those lives. No unifying theory will replace this diversity of outlooks, because such a theory presupposes a uniformity (over time and context) of "highest interests."

James countered the reigning positivism of his day with *fallibilism*.

James sees our highest interests as not tied to culture. We cannot enforce our habits and practices on others, but we can discuss what our natures are and what the highest interests of natures such as ours might be. If we have no higher interests in common, is it possible to bring moral claims against what the Nazis, the KKK, or the Mafia name as their highest interests?

James the pluralist is not a relativist of the modern stripe. He countered the reigning positivism of his day with *fallibilism*. There is always *more* to the account than any current version *can* include, because there are always other experiences, other beliefs, and needs. We must conduct ourselves in such a way as to record what we take to be our highest interests, while never knowing if we have them right or have matched our interests by our actions. There is no final word.

William James was, above all, a realist: We must accept what is. Unlike the positivists, however, James took this to mean that we must accept that there is a religious element to life, because credible report points to the existence of one, as well as to a striving to perfect oneself and to needs that go beyond the individual soul or body. There are, however, things that we cannot finally know. The fallibilist doesn't deny that there is some absolute point of focus on which human interests can converge, but we are warned to be suspicious of those who come to us with final answers. ■

Suggested Reading

James, W. *Essays in Radical Empiricism* and *A Pluralistic Universe*. Phoenix, 1977.

———. *The Will to Believe and Other Essays in Popular Philosophy*. Harvard University Press, 1979.

Robinson, D. *Toward a Science of Human Nature*. Columbia University Press, 1982, chapter 5, "William James."

Questions to Consider

1. Conclude whether James's pluralism is simply relativism by another name.

2. Suppose our highest interests are simply features of our merely contingent biology. Summarize whether this implies that our developed knowledge, too, is simply something credible to an organism of a certain kind.

William James's Pragmatism
Lecture 47—Transcript

Let me stay with William James, moving now from his radical empiricism to his *pragmatism* and *pluralism*, and as pluralism is now one of the preferred words in our politically correct civil discourse, I will make some distinctions between what contemporary commentators mean by pluralism and what James meant by it. James's pluralism is essentially an epistemological position, but more on that later.

To begin, the practical side of William James's philosophy begins with his *functionalism*. Functionalist theories of mind abound today, and an essentially functionalist psychology was put in place largely by William James's *Principles of Psychology* and would actually form the foundation for, of all things, American behaviorism. For all of the criticism that John B. Watson would levy against his predecessors, William James's arguments for functionalism are very much in the background of Watson's own thoughts as Watson develops behaviorism—so I want to pick up some of these themes that we find in James's diverse writings.

Now, what do we mean by functionalism? James takes the position—it's at once a "common sense" position and also a quite subtle metaphysical position—in James it's a common sense position—that the creatures of nature, having undergone an evolutionary history over a course of many millennia, obviously are fitted out to deal with the environment as it is generally found, as the particular creatures find it. We know, for example, that the organs of the body serve specific functions: digestive, respiratory, and the like. The question that naturally arises then is: "If we're to develop a philosophy of mind, or a science of mental life, are we not going to have to address what the functions of mind are? That is to say, an explanation of the mental is inextricably bound up with an understanding of what the mental is for.

With James there is little interest, then, in enumerating particular faculties, which was the preoccupation of the school of psychology known as "structuralism," research designed to isolate such structural elements of mind as sensations, images, and feelings; these, on James's account, just court the psychologist's fallacy. The functionalist approach seeks something else. It seeks to establish what mental life achieves, which is to say what could not be achieved in the absence of mental life.

There's a famous brief treatise by James on the question "Does consciousness exist?" And, of course, the answer James serves up is "yes and no." It depends on what you mean by consciousness. If you think of it as a kind of medieval substance—some immaterial, spaceless, massless, but nonetheless ontologically real thing—no, that doesn't exist at all. But, if you think of it as this flow of ideas, this stream of perceptions and thoughts and feelings—the process by which a supernumerary intelligence knits together experiences over a course of time—then consciousness is indubitable.

What, then, is it for? After all, we can imagine an animal kingdom capable of surviving, adapting, achieving certain things, taking in food, engaging in procreative activity, coming in out of the rain, going toward the sunlight—all this being done automatically, without the need for, or benefit of, consciousness. Couldn't such activities be accomplished by robots or by zombies? In a word, just what is gained by having consciousness added on to whatever adaptive behavior is taking place? What is it that consciousness could achieve that could not possibly be achieved without it?

Now, James circles this question; he jumps in and answers it, and then jumps back, I think somewhat fearful that maybe he seems to be giving a *final* answer to it, but there's one approach James takes that I've always found quite interesting. It is the neuropsychological approach. He recognizes that the brain is an incalculably complicated organ. It's made up of billions of cells, and it's on the air constantly. We are sensitive to every little fluctuation in the environment. This is an organ, this brain—this is an organ that has a "hair-trigger" sensitivity; left to its own devices, it would be popping off constantly. Mind, as such—mental processes, as such, consciousness as such—should be understood as having this one function: the regulation of the activity of the brain itself. It's an odd notion, but an interesting one.

I don't know that James ever would have allowed himself the title of a formal, philosophical dualist, dualist interactionist, but there certainly is a dualist functionalism in his philosophy of mind in that mental processes—

mental, as such—seem to be regulating a system that otherwise would get out of line. How does it do this? It does this through the processes of the *will*, of *attention*, of *selection*. If the nervous system were simply turned on automatically, what would stop it from picking up everything and anything? Nothing. On what basis would it ever arrive at some coherent picture of the world? No basis at all; it would be like taking a photographic emulsion, room-sized, hanging it on the wall, and opening up the windows and letting the affairs of the world come in and hit the screen. What you would get is a "blooming, buzzing confusion" of things. Why is it that this doesn't happen?

It doesn't happen because our mental functions include selection, attention, and the will, by which we are able to deploy and organize our resources—thus confining brain functions to the particular business at hand.

In the matter of the will, James accepts that there is an indubitably volitional element in our mental life. We choose to pick out certain things and react to them. James is prepared to take this in good, Reidian, common-sense fashion as something that's just part of the constitution of our nature. It is not subject to reductive modes of explanation. Earlier in his life, melancholy plagued him, and issues of freedom and determinism plagued him. James had read Charles Renouvier's *Defense of Free Will* and was rescued by it. In fact, in his diary of 1870, he summarizes the defense this way: "The sustaining of a thought because I choose to when I might have other thoughts." Do you see? That's what he means by free will. "I can keep a thought that otherwise I can refuse to keep." The clouds lifted as James declared that his first act of free will would be to accept that his will is free.

Now, the freedom in question is necessary just to put the scientific and philosophical ball in play. Science and philosophy simply have to accept that and make the best of it, make the best of this freedom that we have. Now, when James gets to this matter of the will, he sees it as involving choices from all the alternatives available—so the behavioral reservoir of available and possible responses does have to be considered. This is not something that nature can present ready-made. James develops, then, what he calls an *ideomotor* theory of the will, which initially involves only reflexes.

Now, let me try to make this clear if I can. James's ideomotor theory assumes that, initially, the behavior of infant organisms—human and otherwise—is under reflex control. Included here are basic patterns of reflex adaptation to painful stimuli, pleasurable stimuli, an eye-blink when a puff of air is directed at the cornea, removing a limb from a sharp object or a hot object. These adaptations are native endowments. However, these arrangements that exist between experience and the reflex response to it continue to exist as what might be called ideomotor elements of a sort; that is, there is a reflex reservoir of behaviors tied to specific stimulus events. James has to put this kind of reservoir of possibilities in place so that selectivity has something to *select* from.

Now, in the course of a lifetime of experiences, and as we gain ever more purposive control over our behavior, the particular behaviors that are available to us now become the volitional version of what initially was reflexive. We move toward and away, the hand goes up or comes down, we look this way or that, we blink our eyes intentionally or otherwise, but intentionality itself is the characteristic of actions that already are there potentially. What now qualifies them as volitional is that we are choosing these and not those. Initially, he says, this is set down in the reflex repertoire of the organism, but is subsequently becoming part of the volitional repertoire.

The will for William James is, as with consciousness, not a disembodied entity or substance. "Volition" refers to the selection of certain behavioral patterns from the large set of ideomotor options that arise from native endowment and early experience. With maturity comes a ripening and refinement, an ever more successful pattern of adaptations and adjustments, but, says James: "Even with this in place Nature may, I say, indulge in these complications."

He's thus prepared to offer a non-reductive, original, and natural endowment, which itself is not the gift of experience: "Nature may indulge in complications." That is, Nature can put in place rather complex patterns and arrangements.

James's pragmatism is tied to his functionalism, and pragmatism is a philosophy that has been libeled by more than one secondary source. Critics of pragmatism claim—I don't know where in the pragmatist literature they get this—that pragmatism is the vulgar view, according to which, if something "works," it's true. On this understanding, there would be no way to distinguish between competing scientific worldviews if both of them led to comparable practical success. The textbook illustration, of course, of this would be Ptolemy and Copernicus. The Ptolemaic view is geocentric, earth being the center of the cosmos and all else—the sun included, orbiting the earth. The Copernican view is heliocentric—the sun taken to be at the center and the earth going around it. Both accounts, though, lead to successful navigation, finding your way home at sea, knowing where in the sky the sun is going to appear. One can achieve pretty much the same outcomes on either theory and, in fact, until fairly recently in the history of science, there wasn't too much to choose from, practically speaking, between the Ptolemaic and the Copernican views, and so, critics of pragmatism would say: "Well, therefore, on pragmatic grounds you'd have no basis to choose one over the other."

This, I think, very substantially shortchanges both William James's version of pragmatism and that of the complex personality with whom he was closely and not always happily associated, Charles Sanders Pierce.

James's version was developed in a series of eight lectures dedicated to the memory of John Stuart Mill. In published form, the lectures appeared in 1904 under the title *What is Pragmatism?* In the first of the lectures, James amuses his audience with the tale of a human being clinging to a tree trunk, on the opposite side of which a squirrel also clings. Each moves quickly—the man trying to see the squirrel, and the squirrel striving to remain invisible. Who is going around whom? Stating the question this way, James is then able to make clear what pragmatism is. First and chiefly, it is a method:

> The pragmatic method is primarily a method of settling metaphysical disputes that otherwise might be interminable. The pragmatic method in such cases is to try to interpret each notion by tracing its respective practical consequences. What difference would it practically make to any one if this notion rather than that notion were true? If no practical difference whatever can be traced, then the alternatives mean practically the same thing, and all dispute is idle.

Pierce had earlier framed his own version of pragmatism in an essay titled "How to Make Our Ideas Clear," which was published in 1878. Here is Pierce's maxim:

> Consider what effects, which might conceivably have practical bearings, we conceive the object of our conception to have. Then the whole of our conception of those effects is the whole of our conception of the object.

That's a rather truncated way to put it. The two views are similar but different. Pierce preferred to refer to his position as "pragmatistic," James's as being "pragmatism." What the two versions have in common is the standard to be applied in determining whether a concept or meaning is clearly comprehended. James emphasizes the use of the standard when conceptions seem to be in conflict. Pierce ties the meaning of a concept, let's say, the concept of a motor, to the practical effects we expect such an object to have. Quite apart from what the object really is, our concept of it is exhausted by our comprehension of the effects we expect it to have practically. Thus, one whose conception of a motor is limited to something that does work has a less developed conception than one who knows that, in doing work, the motor is governed by the second law of thermodynamics, do you see?

Pragmatism on James's account matches up with James on the notion of our interests. The will expresses itself on behalf of what we take to be our "highest interests." What we do, we do on behalf of our highest interests. We are not simple reflex machines. There is an incessant stream of consciousness, a stream of thought that relates us to the world around us, that exposes certain possibilities for action, and we have to choose from among those possibilities. The grounds of choice sooner or later—and sooner is better—must match up with just what the highest interests of a creature of a certain kind are. For the puppy in front of us, the stick in the air may qualify; given our own nature, it could be the book in our laps, but for the creature whose interests are not served by his actions, survival is in doubt, and the world becomes a perilous place.

Now, does this boil down to "If it works it's true"? No, that's not what the pragmatic theory of truth is. The pragmatic theory of truth asks a different question: "What criterion or standard would you apply to any proposition such that you would be prepared to declare it true?" Put another way, what gives us the warrant to declare a statement to be true?

What options are on offer? Well, we might say it's the conclusion of a valid syllogism, and if the syllogism is valid, and the major and minor premises are true, necessarily the conclusion is true. This is a formal, logical relationship in which the terms might be A, B, and C, but which match up with nothing that ever existed in the world, nothing that ever could exist in the world—so that from the point of view of a striving, surviving, thoughtful, selective, attentive being, the truths of the syllogism are merely abstract, pertaining to nothing in particular. It is only in virtue of the premises being true that the syllogism preserves the truth. It is not the means of discovery. It is a means of preservation.

What of the truths of science? Consider Newton's law of universal gravitation. Why do we accept it? It is accepted because it matches up quite accurately with certain observations we are able to make—why do we accept something as true because it matches up with certain observations? This must be because of a fundamental tie between the evidence of sense and the practical, needful affairs of life. We do not question the aptness of testing a proposition against the evidence of experience, because the evidence of experience just is the ultimate evidence we have. James does not regard this as a source of deception but as a veritable principle of human nature and animal nature as well. Thomas Reid, recall, speaks of the lowly caterpillar that crawls across a thousand leaves until it finds the one that's right for its diet. The warrants of belief here are pragmatic warrants.

Let's rehearse this: Why is it we accept a Newtonian or Einsteinium vision of the world? Here we seem to have a choice that opposes James's pragmatic standard. After all, quantum physics, quantum electrodynamics, is based on propositions and principles that not only are not subject to experience, but that seem to violate everything we take to be true at the level of experience.

What would James say about that? James would have us recall the passage I took from his first lecture. The function of pragmatism is to settle disputes that would otherwise be interminable. It is the method of choice when all other methods have failed. Presumably, the Newtonian world of absolute mass and momentum, with nary a place for uncertainty, is subject to empirical challenges by a competing theory based on quantum theory.

However, to say that one theory is subject to challenge is already to grant that a given standard has proven its worth in settling disputes of a given kind. How did the standards of scientific research and measurement attain pride of place? Well, by successfully putting an end to a given genre of dispute that would otherwise have been interminable.

The pragmatic theory of truth is not based on the proposition that nothing is true in science or elsewhere until it matches up with some concrete experience. What it does assert, however, is that the ultimate court in which competing theories will vie for our allegiance is the court in which are located our highest interests. Our highest interests are to be distinguished from moment-to-moment interests. These, too, are served by pragmatic considerations, but considerations that call for what is best regarded as the standard of common or vulgar pragmatism. I'm referring, now, to what matches up merely with moment-to-moment interests.

The issue of interests is wrapped in a web of complexities and idiosyncrasies. Some are economic; others pertain to health; others pertain to religion and spirituality, and others to interpersonal relationships—still others to careers, to politics, or art. Now, the highest interest can't be the same under all of these descriptions. Moreover, is it always the case that I'm the best judge of what are, indeed, my highest interests? Might my highest interests change? Aren't my highest interests often foisted by the magic wand of the philosopher, who presumes to dictate to humanity? Interests are so various and mutable.

Now, mindful of this, keenly so in light of his own life, James recognizes that as thought merges with what precedes and what follows in the stream of consciousness, so too do interests. There is no final word on such things, and for all the striving and momentary confidence, new experiences nonetheless bring forth new possibilities. There is always more to be said, more to be seen, more to be thought. In a word, there is a plurality of possibilities.

Properly understood, the universe is not a block, neatly bounded such that we know its beginning and end. It is not a solid block known once and for all, each bit of it causally determined by an earlier bit of it. Nor will it surrender to the tidy remedies of mathematics and logic. Rather, says James:

> Changes, in short, occur and ring throughout phenomena, but neither reasons nor activities in the sense of agencies have any place in this world of scientific logic, which compared with the world of common sense is so abstract as to be quite spectral, and merits the appellation, so often quoted from Mr. Bradley, of "an unearthly ballet of bloodless categories."

These lines are from chapter 12 of James's *Some Problems of Philosophy*, which he dedicated to Charles Renouvier about whom he says:

> But for the decisive impression made on me in the 1870s by his masterly advocacy of pluralism, I might never have got free from the monastic superstition under which I had grown up.

The universe must always be "pluralistic" because we're always going to be looking at it from different perspectives, directed by shifting interests. There were times we looked at it with the naked eye; there were other times we looked at it through a telescope, then a radi telescope, then from an Apollo capsule. At times, its vastness will confer on it a spiritual character; at other times, its vastness will find it inviting exploration. Once we come to gauge and take the measure of these possibilities, yet new thoughts begin, yet new possibilities, new ways of regarding things set in, and this is the case as much in physics as in psychology, or philosophy of mind, or governance.

So, James's radical empiricism, which leaves room for the great welter and variety of experiences to dictate the next point in the stream of consciousness, inevitably will give rise to his conception of a pluralistic universe. This is the way James himself defines pluralism:

> For pluralism all that we are required to admit as the constitution of reality is what we ourselves find empirically realized in every minimum of finite life. Briefly it is this, that nothing real is absolutely

simple…that each relation is one aspect, character, or function, way of its being taken, or way of its taking something else.

Let's look at it again: Briefly it is this, that nothing real is absolutely simple, that each relation is one aspect, character, or function, do you see, one way of being taken, or way of its taking something else, so that the *block universe* we see is mythic and paralyzing; nothing real, including and especially the universe, is absolutely simple.

From a moral point of view, does this lead to the view that "anything goes"? This is not an easy question in James scholarship. His most concentrated effort in this area is the essay, "The Moral Philosopher and the Moral Life," in which he distinguishes three basic questions pertaining to moral philosophy. These he dubs the "psychological" question, the "metaphysical" question, and the "casuistic" question. "Casuistry" refers to the application of moral principles to specific problems. James clearly rejects the form of relativism that would allow each of us "a wayward personal standard of our own," and requires of philosophers that their test of competing standards be impartial. Note, then, that the principle to be applied is one that does not give *a priori* weight to one's own strong beliefs and convictions. In a word, then, James the pluralist is not a relativist.

This becomes clear as he fashions a world consisting of two persons only, each of them indifferent to the interests and demands of the other. In such a world, the only values will be those arising from each of them individually and independently—all value as such now ontologized at the level of individual desires. Increasing the number of such persons would then produce a world as conceived by ancient Skeptics, for whom all was relative, for whom each person is the measure of all things. To that possibility, James answers unequivocally:

> This is the kind of world with which the philosopher, so long as he holds to the hope of philosophy, will not put up. Among the various ideals represented, there must be, he thinks, some which have the more truth or authority, and to these the others ought to yield.

James's pluralism is tied to considerations of highest interests, and in that there's all the difference, because the question arises, bringing us back once more to Plato and Aristotle—the question is this: Is it just in the nature of being human that the highest interests are going to be far more similar than they are different? If so, then it would not be for one culture to serve as a referee or to authorize the convictions and practices of another culture, but for one to step outside the context of any given culture to ask what kind of culture is right for beings whose central interests are these.

Now, I do want to pause on this point because it's a vitally important point. It's particularly important in the context of our own social and political life. The Nazi party was prepared to bring about a certain kind of culture—a certain political regime—that, according to the architects of that regime, was to last for a thousand years. There is another more modest culture that we refer to as the Mafia, comprised of families that have joined together for the purpose of gaining profit illicitly. There is yet another culture that has absorbed into its membership any number of people proud to refer to themselves as members of the KKK. They attend rallies wearing white sheets, set fires, and commit acts of violence against innocent others. Now, each of these collectives are also collectives of personal interests and the values tied to these interests. Are we to understand that it is simply not possible, in light of James's pluralism, to bring some kind of moral criticism to bear on these respective cultures? Clearly not—at least not while still holding out some hope that there can be philosophy itself.

James's pluralism is not a relativism of the modern stripe; what it is is a *fallibilism*, and that's something rather different. There's all the difference in the world between claiming that the complexities, the organicity, the evolving nature of reality being what it is, we're never going to have the last word on anything that really counts. We must conduct ourselves in such a way as to record our recognition of what our highest interests are. This is to be distinguished from the question of whether we'll ever perfectly identify them and reconcile our behavior to them. To understand that there is a plurality of perspectives on a given issue is not to say that the final position we take, morally speaking, is relative to the shifting desires and shifting experiences of a busy life.

Wittgenstein and the Discursive Turn
Lecture 48

In his *Philosophical Investigations*, the question is asked: "What is your aim in philosophy?" Wittgenstein's answer is: "To show the fly the way out of the bottle."

One of the most influential 20th-century philosophers, Wittgenstein tended to express himself in homiletic or aphoristic ways, leaving it to others in the philosophical world to plumb them for their deeper meaning and significance. Wittgenstein changed the way we understand the very problems in philosophy. Indeed, if he is right, there are no "problems" as such, only misunderstandings and puzzles arising from errors in using the logic and grammar of language itself.

His only book published in his lifetime bears the daunting title *Tractatus Logico-Philosophicus*, known simply as his *Tractatus*. The problem of knowledge must ultimately be rooted in how we describe the world, then link these descriptions in such a way as to arrive at correct accounts of "the case" at hand. "The case" at hand must be part of the world, because that is the realm in which any and every case occurs. To state the case is to offer a proposition, a picture of reality. To give the essence of a proposition means to give the essence of all description and, thus, the essence of the world. The limits of my language mean the limits of my world.

This sort of approach clearly will not work, because there is little in the propositions that convey any sort of picture at all. The "picture theory" of meaning is one that Wittgenstein could not retain. However, the *Tractatus* sets the stage for a more penetrating examination of the role of language.

Who was Ludwig Wittgenstein? He was born in Vienna in 1889, the youngest of eight children in a wealthy family. Three of his four brothers were suicides, and Ludwig himself had a lifelong problem with depression and anxiety. In 1908, Wittgenstein enrolled in the engineering program at Manchester, England. Exposure to mathematics drove him to question the very foundations of mathematics. Wittgenstein moved on to Cambridge, where Bertrand Russell was engaged in pioneering work in mathematical logic. After serving on the Austrian side in World War I, Wittgenstein returned to Cambridge. His *Tractatus* was the result of his years with Russell. Regarding the book as having solved all of philosophy's "non-problems," Wittgenstein simply dropped all scholarly projects and took a position in Austria teaching children in elementary school.

As long as we subscribe to a "picture theory," we can tap into the knowledge of another only through the other's introspective reports. Likewise, we publicize our knowledge by revealing "our pictures" to others. My knowledge, as regards my own mental life, is private and incorrigible. It can't be corrected by anybody else. The central claim of science, in the patrimony of Bacon and Newton, is that the suitable subject of scientific inquiry is that which is, in principle, accessible to observation. But if the contents of my mental life are something over

Wittgenstein changed the way we understand the very problems in philosophy.

which I have total epistemological authority and if all of my mental life is filled up with the facts of the external world, solipsism seems to be lurking everywhere. Thus, the problem of knowledge is just the problem of my knowledge of the external world.

This is the received view, and Wittgenstein set out to show that it is based on any number of mistakes, largely grammatical. They have to do with the way we play what Wittgenstein famously refers to as the "language game." To illustrate the necessity of such rules, Wittgenstein uses the *beetle in the box* exemplum: Consider a room with a half-dozen persons, each with a small box. No one can see the contents of any box but his own. When questioned as to the contents of his box, each person responds, "Beetle."

Wittgenstein asks: If each person had his own private language, how could anyone know the meaning of the word *beetle* in any language but his own?

To carry the example further, suppose you are alone—the only thinking being in the cosmos—and wanted to identify the contents of the box. How to do it? A name signifies something only to the extent that it is understood to stand for the thing signified. But "to stand for" anything, a sign must be related to that thing by some sort of rule or conventional understanding. But the adoption of conventions is a social act. Conventions are part of the actual practices of people in the world. It is simply impossible to apply a private rule to a private occurrence! You can't even *violate* the rules of the language game unless there are other players.

Wittgenstein concludes that our minds are not black boxes to which we alone have access, whose contents we name for ourselves. How could anyone, seeing only *something* in the box, know it to be a beetle, without prior agreements on what a beetle is? Thomas Reid took the position that if there were not a *natural* language, there could never be an artificial language of cooperative and expressive content. It is a language of sounds and facial expression, of intonation and posture. Wittgenstein takes very much the same position.

The natural language of pain, for instance, is grimacing, crying and cringing. This is not something that's learned; it is in place. Artificial, conventional forms and signs can be grafted onto that natural language. We use the resources of our natural language to build the shared reality represented in our artificial language.

Where there is meaning, there must be social conventions and social practices. There is a discursive history behind every experience by which that experience gains its meaning. It begins as a public phenomenon and might be internalized in some way thereafter. Thus, the language game is a set of *social* practices not reducible to the experiences of any one person, not possibly confined to the arena of a private mind. "Beetle" *refers* to an object that can be dubbed "beetle" only by those with a sufficiently shared form of life for such denominations to come to have settled meaning. Thus, meaning is *socially constructed* through the actual practices of the community.

As philosophy is a search for meanings, a search for truth, a search for rules of conduct, and so on, it is an inevitably *social* undertaking proceeding according to accepted grammatical (rule-governed) forms. Personal identity? Wittgenstein recalls Aristotle: Our names for ourselves—baker, Christian, father, child—do not inhere in us biologically. Gender (though not sex), nationality, morality—the authority and creativity to bring about such identities—is social. Wittgenstein offers that once this is understood, the fly might find the way out of the bottle—or Theseus out of the labyrinth.

The problem of knowledge now becomes part of a language game. It becomes a problem of meaning, and what's called for here is an essentially linguistic analysis, rather than an epistemology or metaphysics. Metaphysics is built up linguistically. Wittgenstein was keen to note that his purpose was not to solve problems but to show the fly the way out of the bottle. This is not to change the nature of the fly. Out of the bottle, it's still a fly. Out of the bottle, it's still an entity that might be attracted to sweet things in the bottom of some other bottle. As Wittgenstein says in the *Philosophical Investigations*:

> Think of the tools in a toolbox; there is a hammer, pliers, a saw, a screw-driver, a ruler, a glue-pot, nails and screw…. The functions of words are as diverse as the functions of these objects… It is easy to imagine a language consisting only of orders and reports in battle…. Or a language consisting only of questions and expressions for answering yes and no. And innumerable others—*and to imagine a language means to imagine a form of life.* ∎

Suggested Reading

Budd, M. *Wittgenstein's Philosophy of Psychology*. London, 1989.

Wittgenstein, L. Philosophical Investigations. Blackwell, 1997.

Questions to Consider

1. If the contents of the mind are not "private," infer just what is the domain reached by introspection.

2. Conclude whether there are no *natural* constraints on what things might mean.

3. Summarize whether philosophy is simply (or not so simply) a kind of word game.

Wittgenstein and the Discursive Turn
Lecture 48—Transcript

In his *Philosophical Investigations*, the question is asked: "What is your aim in philosophy?" Wittgenstein's answer is: "To show the fly the way out of the bottle."

Wittgenstein is surely one of the most influential 20th-century philosophers. A veritable cottage industry exists to interpret Wittgenstein, to make Wittgenstein accessible to non-Wittgensteinians. As a non-Wittgensteinian, I'm ever grateful to those who keep writing books saying that the disciples themselves got it wrong. Wittgenstein is responsible for all this, dear man that he was—a very complex personality, with an often-cryptic mode of instruction.

He had a tendency—a strong tendency—to express himself in homiletic or aphoristic ways, actually numbering his philosophical utterances, and leaving it up to the more agile members of the philosophical world to plumb them for their deeper meaning and significance. Nonetheless, that plumbing has gone on, and we do get to see a Wittgenstein of immense philosophical power and subtlety, a philosopher who has changed the way we understand the very problems in philosophy. Indeed, if he is right, there are no "problems" as such, only misunderstandings and puzzles arising from errors in using the logic and the very grammar of language itself.

His only book published in his lifetime—his only book—bears the daunting title *Tractatus Logico-Philosophicus*, known simply as his *Tractatus*. Wittgenstein oddly refers to it as a treatise in ethics; however, if by "ethics" we mean to address the problem of conduct, one might say that the *Tractatus* is about how philosophy is to be conducted. The work itself is in the form of seven sets of numbered propositions, beginning with:

> The world is all that is the case.

Thus understood, the problem of knowledge—or at least the puzzles that arise within epistemology—must ultimately be rooted in how we describe the world and then link these descriptions in such a way as to arrive at correct accounts of, what? "The case" at hand. "The case" at hand must be part of the world, for that is the realm in which any and every case occurs.

To state the case is to offer a proposition. Wittgenstein is at pains to clarify the nature and functions of propositions. Thus, at 4.01:

> A proposition is a picture of reality.

At 5.4711:

> To give the essence of a proposition means to give the essence of all description and, thus, the essence of the world.

At 5.6:

> The limits of my language mean the limits of my world.

Now, it is clear that this sort of approach will not work, for there is little in the seven sets of propositions that convey any sort of picture at all and, therefore, most would fail as propositions. The "picture theory" of meaning is one that Wittgenstein could not retain, but the *Tractatus* nonetheless does set the stage for a more penetrating examination of the role of language. Indeed, at 4.003 in the *Tractatus* there is a clearer sense—though not a picture—of Wittgenstein as diagnostician:

> Most of the propositions and questions of philosophers arise from our failure to understand the logic of our language, and it is not surprising that the deepest problems are in fact not problems at all.

Who is this intriguing fellow? He was born in Vienna in 1889, a child of wealth. His father headed the Austro-Hungarian iron and steel industry, was a patron of the arts, and a magnet to leaders of Viennese culture. Brahms was a friend of the family. There were eight children in the Wittgenstein family; Ludwig was the youngest. Three of his four brothers were suicide victims; Ludwig himself had a lifelong problem with states of depression and anxiety.

Conflicts of a religious nature were present from the first. His paternal grandparents were Jewish, but were Protestant converts. His mother was Roman Catholic, and she saw to it that Ludwig was baptized as Catholic, but no religious observance seems to have been habitual with him at any time in life beyond childhood.

As a member of one of the wealthiest families in Europe, Wittgenstein surely did not need either a career or a job, but he had a deep interest in mechanical matters, ranging from the aerodynamics of kites to domestic architecture. In 1908, we find him enrolled in the engineering program at Manchester, England. One thing led to another in the restless mind of his. Exposure to mathematics drove him to question the very foundations of mathematics. He expressed his concerns to Gotlob Frege. Wittgenstein was advised then by Frege to move to Cambridge, where Bertrand Russell was engaged in pioneering work in mathematical logic that Wittgenstein's questions related to.

The Cambridge years were interrupted by World War I, Wittgenstein serving with valor on the Austrian side. At war's end, he returned to Cambridge. His *Tractatus* was the result of his years with Russell. Regarding the book as having solved all of philosophy's problems, or "non-problems," the eccentric Wittgenstein simply dropped all scholarly projects and took a position in Austria teaching children in elementary school. Do you see what was going on? He believed that the *Tractatus* was handling everything, nothing more there, so he went off and became an elementary schoolteacher.

By 1929 he was back in Cambridge, nearly all of the rest of his life spent there and at Oxford, until his death in 1951. He was, as it happens, given a Catholic burial. There's much more to all of this, but I must move on. This should be sufficient to qualify Wittgenstein as, shall we say, a square peg moving from one round hole to another.

Now, to appreciate the magnitude of his contribution and influence, let's rehearse where the typical philosophical position would be on the matter of the problem of knowledge, on the matter of philosophy of mind, the nature of mental states, and so forth.

As we have learned from previous lectures, the preferred method of inquiry in addressing such matters is an introspective method. I sit back and consult the contents of my own consciousness. I understand the world to the extent that I am able to represent the facts of the world in my mind. Skeptics may come along and point out that I will never know whether those mental representations are reliable depictions of what's actually in the external world. There may be some grave distortion imposed by the organs of perception themselves, but nonetheless, what we would be arguing about, then, is not whether the organs of perception are the best way. They are the only tools we have. Even in choosing John Stuart Mill's psychological method instead of introspection, we would still be taking for granted the individuated nature of knowledge; knowledge as someone's knowledge.

Now, we can argue about the quality of the representation. That is, to see the world you need the camera. We can now argue about which cameras have good lenses and whether the lens is chromatically defective, etc. This, in turn, leads us on to one or another version of the "picture theory" of knowledge. I know the external world because I have a mental picture, or a mental representation, of it. Indeed, as we see in his *Tractatus*, early Wittgenstein stands behind a depiction of just that sort. That's quite a traditional way of understanding the problem.

As long as we subscribe to a "picture theory," a representational theory, we can only tap into the knowledge of another through the other's introspective reports, and the way we publicize our knowledge is, then, by revealing our pictures to others. With respect to the contents of my mind, they can only be reached introspectively, and I have a unique—even ultimate—authority when it comes to declaring what's in there, because only I can see the contents of my mind. My knowledge, as regards my own mental life, is private and incorrigible. It can't be corrected by anyone else.

We can illustrate my incorrigibility this way: I've got an intense toothache in my lower, right jaw. I enter the room—my cheek red and swollen—and I say something like this: "I have an excruciating pain in my jaw, unless I am mistaken." What an odd thing that would be to say. How can anyone possibly be mistaken about something like that? When someone claims to be in pain, then we understand that; though there may be deception, the person really has the last word on whether there is pain or not. That's the sense, then, of first-person reports of sensation being regarded as incorrigible. The ghost of Descartes seems to be haunting philosophy here, but this is a quite interesting state of affairs. Let's think about it for a minute.

The central claim of science, in the patrimony of Bacon and Newton, is that the suitable subject of scientific inquiry is that which is, in principle, accessible to observation. Empiricism claims that knowledge is exhausted by just such encounters with the external world and the exercise of the senses. But, of course, if the contents of my mental life are something over which I have total epistemological authority and if all of my mental life is filled up with the facts of the external world—well, then, solipsism seems to be lurking everywhere.

Now, I say, that is more or less the common-sense world of epistemology, featuring the credibility of first-person reports, the "picture theory" or representational solution to the problem of knowledge. Thus, the problem of knowledge is just the problem of my knowledge of the external world. I have a certain standing with respect to the contents of my own mind. The external world represents itself in something called my mind, which is, as noted, somewhere inside me and reached only by that tried and true technique called "introspection," and although I can share my experiences with others, no one can know the tree that I see. That is private. It's for me alone. No one has direct access. I can't even invite others in.

This is the received view, and Wittgenstein set out to show that this received view is entirely untenable. It's based on any number of mistakes, and the mistakes are largely grammatical. They have to do with the way we go about using words, the way we—not "grammatical" as in a textbook on grammar, but the real nature of the game that we play when we go about talking about things like this—that is, the way we play what Wittgenstein famously refers to as the "language game."

Now, one way Wittgenstein illustrates the futility of a model of this kind is with the example that he refers to as the *beetle in the box*. Now, let's say that everyone in the room or everyone listening to this lecture is given a very small box. It has a lid on it, and each person can take the lid off the box he or she is holding and can look inside to see what's inside the box, but he or she cannot see the contents of anyone else's. Now, the master of ceremonies goes around the room and asks each person: "What is in your box?" Each person inexplicably says the same thing. As we go around the room—the room might have a million people in it—we hear over and over again, "Beetle," "Beetle," "Beetle," "Beetle." Everybody claims to have a beetle in the box. Now, you've never been able to see inside any other box. You don't know each other. You've not entered into any shared or cooperative form of life. You're not from any known culture.

Now, the question is this: How could you possibly know that when the person next to you says "Beetle" that person is referring to *something* very much like what you're referring to when you say "Beetle"? Suppose that person comes from a place where the utterance "Beetle" equals "empty"? "What do you have in your box?" "Beetle" means "empty." Suppose the person comes from a place where when you put your lips together and force air out and make the sound beetle, it means candy. Or soufflé? Or a beetle, a bug, an arthropod? How could you possibly know what this utterance means?

Matters are actually more complex. Suppose, in fact, you are the only person in the whole cosmos, and you've never met anyone like yourself. You've got some rudimentary resources. You can create sounds. You come across a little bug in the road, and you pick it up, and you've made a box. You've made a little box, and you put this little bug in the road in the little box that you've made. Now, suppose you want to name the bug "beetle." How would you go about doing that? To assign a name to something is to conform to some sort of rule, but, of course, a rule is a convention. It's a convention that is, as it were, adopted, but the adoption of conventions is an ineliminably social act. Conventions are part of the actual practices of people in the world. You wouldn't even know when you were violating the rule if you called the bug something other than a beetle. How could you possible *violate* a rule if you're the only entity in the cosmos? You can't break a convention unless there is a convention, and no one brings about a convention singularly. In fact, then, you can't even know what's in *your* box, except in virtue of having certain resources of a grammatical, linguistic nature available to you.

The first thing that Wittgenstein wants to challenge, then, is the proposition that there is some private domain to which only the experient has access, and that whatever he claims to find there is incorrigibly the case. In his *Philosophical Investigations*, he makes his project clear:

> When philosophers use a word—"knowledge," "being," "object," "I," "proposition," "name"—and try to grasp the essence of the thing, one must always ask oneself, "Is the word ever actually used in this way in the language-game which is its original home?" What we do is to bring words back from their metaphysical to their everyday use.

Now, what about the chap with the toothache? Is Wittgenstein doubting that people couldn't actually have pains in their jaws unless they're engaged in some social or cultural lie? No, Wittgenstein is not doubting that someone can have itches and pains. He is, instead, making clear that statements about being in pain are not descriptions; they are avowals. The words developed in the language game come to serve as substitutes for a national expression that may take the form of crying, sobbing, grimacing, groaning. "I have a toothache" is not, then, a description of some object in my mind or, for that matter, some object in my tooth. It is the socially adopted alternative to cries of anguish. If "the world is everything that is the case," then, there are no private worlds of which *we can meaningfully speak*.

How does the language game actually get played? Well, the game actually gets played this way: There's little Billy, who falls off his chair and hurts his knee. One of the natural consequences of damage to the body is reflex crying; tears are formed, and lacrimation takes place. Billy's lower lip quivers, and his eyes are half-shut; he's cringing. He sees his own blood, and this is an awful thing, and adults come over and reassure him and say: "That's all right, Billy. We'll clean this up, and it'll heal, and everything will be okay, and little boys, you know, you shouldn't cry that much, and when you get older, you won't cry that much." Through acculturation, reports of pain replace the natural expression. The report is simply something that is substituting for the earlier behavioral expression that signals the presence of pain. Little Billy has become William, and he doesn't cry. He says such things as "I bruised myself." "I have a toothache."

Let's do this one more time, so we understand precisely what's going on here. Pain talk is not descriptive; it's substitutive. When one invokes the language of pain, one is not looking on a private screen and describing its features to somebody else. One is engaged in a form of behavior that is intelligible within a given community and, indeed, might be entirely unintelligible outside that community. The pain talk itself is constructed out of the discursive resources of the community. Had those resources been entirely different, had the very grammar of pain statements been different, the entire affair would have been different.

Let me refer again to Thomas Reid for a moment, who challenged the standard view of language as it had been defended by Locke and many others. Now, on the standard account, language is a collection of symbols whose meaning is established by convention. Reid took the position that if there were not some sort of *natural* language, there could not be an artificial language, and for this reason: If all of language is acquired, there could be no conventional meaning, for in order for persons to agree on what certain signs will mean, there would already have to be some system by which to signal agreement. Thus, says Reid, there must be a natural language of cooperative and expressive content. It is a language of sounds and facial expression, of intonation and posture. It is in virtue of this natural language that we are able to establish such patterns of agreement, such covenants as will make artificial language have the meaning that it does. We agree by having a natural means of signaling agreement, and it is on this natural language by which we signal agreement that artificial languages can be grafted, do you see? Reid says, then, in order for there to be an artificial language, there must be a natural language. An artificial language is a set of conventions; for there to be conventions, there has to be some way of signaling agreement and covenants, and therefore, there must be a natural language for there to be an artificial language.

Wittgenstein is taking very much the same position. What, after all, is the natural language of pain? It's grimacing and crying; it's cringing and tearfulness, and this is something that isn't learned. This is something that's in place. Now, what can be grafted onto that are rather artificial forms—conventional, artificial forms and signs—by which we no longer have to emit the natural language, but we now can make ourselves clear in what Reid would call an artificial language.

I say the analysis provided by Reid briefly, and at length by Wittgenstein, is a very similar analysis. Namely, we begin with certain purely natural resources that then become the resources a culture will use in order to create a genuinely discursive community that is able to share and exchange ideas, meanings, experiences, and the like. It's not a matter of making public what is private. The mind is not a screen, and introspection is not a tool of discovery. What we have are public ways of reacting to certain events, and linguistic resources available by way of culture, such that these events can become shared. As he wrote in the *Tractatus*, "The limits of my language mean the limits of my world."

With Wittgenstein, the traditional view of the mental is rejected and is replaced by an essentially discursive model. Meaning is shared. The sole occupant of the cosmos, were there such a being, could have experiences and feelings but could not know the meaning of anything. Such a being can have experiences, flashes, odors, and tones, but how could such a being see a tree? Not an object with certain colorations and forms, which can be seen by all visually competent organisms, but seeing a tree?

Let me make it a little harder than that. Seeing an automobile? Suppose oneself to be the only person in the universe—only one, there had never been any other—and miraculously, a Ford station wagon appears. Now, you recognize immediately that that person could not possibly know what it is. In fact, we could find people in the world today who wouldn't know what it is. There are instances to this day in which members of quite remote tribal communities think of the occasional airplane they see flying overhead as a divinity. They say prayers to it.

To know that something is an airplane, or an automobile, or a sandwich, or a school, then, is to be a participant in a kind of game, in a settled discourse, in which there are rules that govern how things are to be described, how things are today ordered, and just what it is that confers meaning on them. This is all ineliminably social. It is not an individual achievement; it is a cultural achievement.

Where there is meaning there must be *social* conventions and social practices, then. The task, then, is not one of the individual finding some truth within him and trying to figure out a way of making it public—rather, there is a discursive history behind every experience by which that experience gains its meaning. The discursive history is what gives it the meaning. It begins as a public phenomenon, and it might be internalized in some way thereafter.

Consider the venerable problem of personal identity discussed in the lectures on Locke, Hume, and Reid. The Wittgensteinian philosophy is well illustrated by the approach to this problem. What does it mean to be who one is? Butcher, baker, candlestick maker, teacher, student, policeman, nurse, airline pilot, child. Is the concept of a child consistent across cultures and across time? Did Roman law regard one as a child for purposes of law if one was 13 years old? Who was a "child" in the medieval period? What of the notion of a family? Is the family just a breeding pool, or is it some pattern of obligations, duties, and the like, as Aristotle taught? What does it mean when one asks: "What's your nationality?" and you say: "I'm American"? Or your occupation, and you say: "I'm an engineer"? Or your religion, and you say: "I'm a Lutheran"? Where does all this apparatus come from?

Now, it certainly isn't something that inheres in entities in virtue of their biological being—so, these are all culturally produced, and in fact, they're not only culturally produced, but the person himself is culturally produced. If you strip away everything that is conferred by way of discourse, social institutions, and the like, what's left? What's left is a merely biological entity, a physiological specimen or system, with some moving parts, perhaps some experiential aspects or capabilities, but with no identity at all.

Now, how far might one want to go with this? Let's say gender. Is gender— as opposed to one's sex—*socially constructed*? Is morality socially constructed? Understand what I mean by "socially constructed." I mean this: If it is the case that meaning arises from covenants and conventions within a community of shared lives, then that's how you finally decide what a beetle is. We decide what a beetle is as a community that has authorizing privileges with respect to what words *refer* to. If it is the case that each cultural enclave has the creative power to bring about bakers, and candlestick makers, and Lutherans, and if it is further the case that what we mean when we refer to

"Smith" is a person who is a Lutheran baker of Dutch ancestry who owns a Ford, then what is left of the individual when these discursive indexicals and qualifiers are removed may be nothing.

Well, there's much more to be said about this, but, of course, it has to raise questions about the problem of knowledge and the problem of conduct—otherwise not anticipated, or richly anticipated, by those who preceded Wittgenstein.

The problem of knowledge now becomes part of a language game. It becomes a problem of meaning, and what's called for here is an essentially linguistic analysis, rather than an epistemology or metaphysics. Metaphysics gets built up linguistically. Wittgenstein, I say, was quite keen to note that he's not here to solve problems; he's here to show the fly the way out of the bottle. This is not to change the nature of the fly. Out of the bottle, it's still a fly. Out of the bottle, it's still an entity that might very well be attracted to sweet things and attracted to the bottom of some other bottle, but, to show the fly the way out of the bottle is not unlike Ariadne providing the golden string that Theseus used to find his way out of the labyrinth. With Wittgenstein, the string is replaced by a toolbox. As he says in the *Philosophical Investigations*:

> Think of the tools in a toolbox; there is a hammer, pliers, a saw, a screw-driver, a ruler, a glue-pot, nails and screw.... The functions of words are as diverse as the functions of these objects...It is easy to imagine a language consisting only of orders and reports in battle.... Or a language consisting only of questions and expressions for answering yes and no. And innumerable others—*and to imagine a language means to imagine a form of life*.

I've read Wittgenstein with optimism and respect, and I still think at the end of the day there's more to philosophy than is contained in our grammars. I think there is more to philosophy than the collection of puzzles, but then, I'm not entirely out of the bottle yet myself.

Alan Turing in the Forest of Wisdom
Lecture 49

Turing is a fascinating figure, a tragic figure in his own right. He was born in 1912, British, a prodigious intellect evident from the very earliest times, one of those people destined to be a mathematician and to worry about problems that perhaps no one ever worries about except that small class of abstract thinkers who can only find a place and function in life by removing themselves from it.

Alan Turing's writings and theorizing are so ever-present in this world of computer science and computational models of the mind that one gets the impression that he is still writing papers and guiding dissertations on these subjects. Born in 1912, British, Turing was a prodigious intellect, someone destined to be a mathematician and abstract thinker. At age 19, Turing entered King's College, Cambridge, and was elected Fellow of the College in 1935. He proposed his famous *Turing machine* in 1936. He earned a doctorate from Princeton, where he studied logic and number theory.

During World War II, Turing was engaged in cryptographic and cryptological work aimed at breaking enemy codes, specifically Germany's Enigma cipher machine. He was instrumental in breaking what the German high command had declared to be an unbreakable code. Turing was elected as Fellow of the Royal Society in 1951. A year later, he was arrested for homosexual activity and was no longer able to hold a security clearance. He killed himself with cyanide on June 7, 1954.

Breaking a code is a mental activity that requires actually getting into the mind of another. In Turing's most famous accomplishments, we find the question: "How do problems get solved?" In 1936, Turing published a paper titled "On computable numbers, with an application to the *Entscheidungsproblem*." He established that there is no method by which to decide all mathematical questions. The method he developed to make this argument would prove to be the foundation for all of computer science.

A mathematical problem is decidable when a problem-solving algorithm exists for it. The most common algorithm would be arithmetic. We can think of arithmetic as a "machine" for answering all questions about addition, subtraction, and so on—we will always get a right answer. Any number of mathematical problems were and are "undecidable": no algorithm exists by which they can be solved. For example, until 1994, when Professor Wiles produced his own brilliant proof, Fermat's last theorem was undecidable: The equation $x^n + y^n = z^n$ has no solution in integers for any value of n larger than 2.

Turing did not solve the most-general-algorithm problem, but he succeeded in developing an algorithm by which to determine whether a problem is computable. Turing began by considering how he himself computed: In adding a long series, he performed the same small operation over and over as often as necessary. Therefore, a device could theoretically be constructed that could solve problems in the same way: (1) Equip it with an infinitely long strip of tape and a means by which to either print or erase a limited set of symbols, for example, a 0 or *no* symbol, a 1 or *yes* symbol. (2) Reduce a problem of any degree of complexity to a number of 1-0 or *yes-no* steps. (All numbers can be represented in a binary system by only two digits.) (3) Solve the problem through an indefinitely large number of basic operations of an essentially computational sort.

Thus, the *Turing machine*: an algorithm, not a machine as such, that translates any *input* signal into a determinate *output*. A vending machine is a complicated mechanical device working on precisely these terms: Put a quarter in the vending machine and the device yields a cupcake; put in a half-dollar and the device yields ginger ale. The child may imagine that there must be a person in the machine making these decisions, but there need not be. The problem is computable as input-output. The particular "machine" that instantiates these processes is irrelevant. *Function is all!* What determines the type of activity is the algorithm instantiated. It could be a pattern-recognizing device that turns on water or turns off the fire alarm.

Is the human being a Turing machine? Is there anything significant about us as intelligent beings that differs from a sufficiently powerful computational device? It is agreed by all philosophers that what is unique to human beings is the ability to reason. We can solve problems. An intelligent being is one able to perform a set of functions associated with intelligence, for example, solving problems.

Turing addressed this in his *Computing Machinery and Intelligence* (1950) by applying the *Turing test*: Place a person and a device behind curtains and address each with questions: Are all bachelors unmarried? How do you get from Paris to New York? If the productions from behind one curtain match up well enough with those from the other, on what grounds would you deny the non-human entity status as an intelligent being, beyond prejudice? If the proper definition of a rational, intelligent being is one who is able to perform certain computational operations, to achieve certain ends by problem-solving, human beings just happen to be biological instantiations of something that can be instantiated non-biologically.

There's a problem with this Turing-like perspective on things that certainly Wittgenstein would be among the first to notice. The symbols of a Turing machine mean nothing in themselves, because meaning can only be agreed upon in a social context. John Searle developed a comparable criticism, exemplified in what came to be called his *Chinese room test*: A person ignorant of Chinese, alone in a closed room, has cards with Chinese ideograms on them and instructions in his own language to follow as to what shapes to search for and which shapes to put next to which others. The person constructs Chinese

The symbols of a Turing machine mean nothing in themselves, because meaning can only be agreed upon in a social context.

sentences by this means, meaningless to himself, but that Chinese speakers can understand. Does the person therefore "know Chinese"? Or does the *room*, containing speaker, ideograms, and instructions, "know Chinese"?

Searle thinks that the missing ingredient is intentionality, the term here referring to meaning itself.

In the Upanishads, the disciple sitting "next to the teacher" (*upanishad*) in the Forest of Wisdom is asked, "When the sun is down, by what means do you see?" He answers, "by the moon." And when the moon is dark? By a candle's light. And when the candle is out? Then the only remaining light is within, known but unseen, working toward the truth by means never found in the external world of flesh, blood, and dead matter. Alan Turing lived much of his life in the Forest of Wisdom, searching by his own inner light. Like Pythagoras, he sought in a realm of symbols not instantiated by any physical beings but only in *relations*. In part because of his search, our humanity now is understood not in biological terms but in informational terms, as a set of computational operations. ∎

Suggested Reading

Hodges, A. *Alan Turing: The Enigma of Intelligence*. New York, 1983.

Turing, A. "Computing Machinery and Intelligence." *Mind*, 1950, vol. 59, pp. 433–460.

Questions to Consider

1. Conclude whether "intelligent" machines should have rights.

2. Explain whether the only difference between the "intelligent machine" and the person is to be found at the level of feelings.

Alan Turing in the Forest of Wisdom
Lecture 49—Transcript

Alan Turing is a contemporary in more ways than one. He died in 1954, so at least for some of us, he certainly falls within our own lifetime, our own time frame. His writings and theorizing are so ever-present in this world of computer science and computational models of the mind that one gets the impression that he is still writing papers and guiding dissertations on these subjects.

Turing is a fascinating figure, a tragic figure in his own right. He was born in 1912, British, a prodigious intellect evident from the very earliest times, one of those people destined to be a mathematician and to worry about problems that perhaps no one ever worries about except that small class of abstract thinkers who can only find a place and function in life by removing themselves from it.

At 19, Turing entered King's College, Cambridge, and was quickly elected Fellow of the College in 1935. His famous *Turing machine* was proposed in 1936, and about that I will have some more to say. He then earned a doctorate from Princeton, where he studied logic and number theory from 1938 and for a time after that.

With the outbreak of World War II, he was assigned to a secret project at Bletchley Park associated with breaking enemy codes, and specifically Germany's Enigma cipher machine. He was engaged in cryptographic and cryptological work. He had a team working under him, and he was instrumental in breaking what the German high command had declared to be an unbreakable code. The success he and his group achieved came to play a major part in final victory in the Atlantic.

His contributions continued apace after the war, earning him election as Fellow of the Royal Society in 1951. A year later, he was arrested for homosexual activity. He no longer could hold a security clearance; his embarrassment and depression were apparently relentless. He killed himself with cyanide on June 7, 1954, the day following the annual D-Day celebrations.

I want to say that Alan Turing is one of a handful of philosopher-scientists who changed the world in ways from which, I'm inclined to say, there really can't be any turning back.

I think I should say something about breaking a code, and what kind of mental activity this is. It's not like doing a crossword puzzle or a double crostic; you actually have to get into the mind of another to break a code. This is what breaking the code is all about: "I wonder what this person would be doing as a way of signaling this, that, or the other thing, and signaling it in such a way that I won't be able to figure it out."

What is required, then, is an unusual empathic faculty, a great elasticity of thought, being able to think as others think, while preserving the integrity of one's own thought. There is much in the achievements of Turing that reflect just that talent. What we find in his most famous accomplishments is the question: "How do problems get solved; what steps in thought must be taken to reach a solution?" Even before that, to satisfy oneself that there is a solution. Put another way: "How would we go about the task of putting together a code that couldn't be broken?" To break a code is already to have answered that question.

Alan Turing was a homosexual, and he wasn't coy about it. He wasn't flagrant about it; he was about as discreet as a fellow of Alan Turing's innocence could be. It got him into trouble. He did enjoy great celebrity for his achievements during the war. He was always respected, deeply admired by that small fraternity of people in mathematics, but his life soon became unbearable to him. Some of the relationships he entered into were not of a particularly elevating sort, and so Alan Turing in 1954 killing himself, this was a great loss, I'm sure, to his friends and a great loss to the intellectual world at large. There's actually a quite successful and faithful drama based on his life, which I think is titled *Enigma*, named after the code that he helped break.

Now, mathematicians are always giving themselves impossible problems. There's probably a separate psychology that should be done on the mind of the mathematician, and it might be quite a sketch to get 15 or 20 of them in a room and just listen to what it is that they talk about.

There's a search here for a kind of truth that may have absolutely no bearing on anything at all, and a search for great abstract principles that are universally applicable in all circumstances, no matter what. Mathematicians at once relish, and are punished by, problems that can't be settled or decided.

One of the bequests of the world of mathematics available at the time to excite Alan Turing's generation was a problem bequeathed by David Hilbert, the *Entscheidungsproblem*.

Entscheidung is German for "decision," and the problem is that of finding a method for deciding all decidable questions in mathematics. Let me just pause for a moment to say what the *Entscheidungsproblem* is. It is a problem of deciding if something is decidable.

In 1936, Turing published a brilliant paper titled "On Computable Numbers, with an Application to the *Entscheidung*." In that classic essay, Turing established that there is no method by which to decide all mathematical questions, but the method he developed to make this argument would prove to be foundational for what? For all of computer science.

The method he discovered is one that establishes whether a problem is computable; that is, whether a problem finally could be dealt with computationally and, thus, could be decided by some computational procedure.

Now, let me give you an example of this kind just so you can reach for something when you try to think of the domain in which Turing's thoughts operated. A mathematical problem is decidable when, in fact, there is a problem-solving algorithm that you've found for it; you've got a technique or a device that will handle problems of a certain kind. Now, probably, the most common algorithm would be arithmetic. All problems of addition, multiplication, subtraction, and division can be handled by the rules and principles of arithmetic, which together stand as the algorithm or problem-solving device. We can think of arithmetic as a "machine" of sorts for answering all sorts of questions about addition, subtraction, and the rest. Using this algorithm, you will always get the right answer. That's the algorithm for problems of addition.

I want to say that generically. An algorithm is a device, a technique, if you like, a machine, generating right answers to problems of a certain kind.

Now, let's consider a different mathematical problem—not addition. Let's consider the one famously bequeathed by Fermat and often referred to as "Fermat's Last Theorem." In his notes, Fermat claimed to have solved the problem, but—as the successful solution so recently reached by Princeton's Professor Wiles comes to some 200 pages and depends on a mathematics not yet invented in Fermat's era—it is highly doubtful that he actually did solve it. We think that Fermat may have just been playing fast and loose with his marginal notes.

The problem is this: To prove that the expression $X^n + Y^n = Z^n$ has absolutely no solution in integers for any value of n larger than 2, so that when I say that Turing had bequeathed to him one of these core mathematical problems— how do you find a general, universally applicable solution or answer to the question: "Is a mathematical problem decidable?" That's the domain he's working in. Do you see?

Now, to determine whether a problem is computable, Turing asked himself: "Well, how do I compute?" That is, he actually took the domain of the mental as a model for what later will be, famously in his work, the domain of computers and computer operations. Well, suppose you take something like addition. You have a large column of numbers; you go down the column, number by number, adding each to the sum already reached, carrying over the remainder to the next column, and then the next, in step-by-step fashion. You generally add one at a time. There really is no limit to the number of sums you can compute, except of course the limit imposed by our mortality. An arithmetic problem could contain numbers that run from here to the end of the universe, but the same algorithm will give you a correct sum, just in case there finally is a last number and you live long enough to do the arithmetic. So you see, there is no temporal limit on how much adding one can do.

Well, suppose in fact you had an infinitely long tape, a tape without limit, on which you could inscribe certain symbols. In fact, you'd need very few operations. You'd need an operation for putting a symbol down or erasing the symbol, or having put the symbol down, moving the carriage or the armature in such a way as to put a symbol next to it. This is sort of the machinery of the thing. The question now becomes this: "Is there anything in the computable realm that couldn't be represented by an instrument of this kind, assuming that the tape is long enough and that the symbology is, shall we say, appropriately economical?"

For example, suppose I say: "Where there's nothing, the symbol is 0; where there's 1, the symbol will be 0 1. Where there's 2, the symbol will be 1 1. Where there's 3, the symbol will be 1 1 1. Where there's 10, the symbol will be 1 0."

I mean, suppose I just do that; any positive integer could be represented, then, just by stringing out 0s and 1s, and presumably, then, any number of positive integers could be added or subtracted or divided, because division is just serial subtraction, or multiplied, because multiplication is just serial addition. So the entire domain of arithmetic certainly could be handled by so simple a device, with very few characters, very few moving parts, and just a strip of tape long enough—for all theoretical purposes, anyway, infinitely long—to handle a problem of any complexity.

Well, of course, I can code things other than numbers. In fact, we have mechanical devices that do this all the time. You go to a vending machine. If you put in 25 cents, let's say, you get a cupcake. If you put in 50 cents, you get a can of ginger ale. Now, there are probably children who think there is somebody actually inside. "Well, it's a quarter. I'd better throw out a cupcake." Well, there's a sort of childish view that says: "Well, if every time I put a quarter in I get a cupcake, and every time I put 50 cents in, I get a can of ginger ale—there must be some little person in there who catches the quarter and says: "You only get a cupcake for that, and so forth." Of course, though, as we know, there isn't anyone in there, but there is something in there and there's something reading the input solely in terms of the number of circular objects of a certain dimension that will interrupt a light path and the number of times it does interrupt the light path. If it does it twice, the gearing mechanism releases ginger ale, and if it does it once, it releases cupcakes.

The overarching assumption is that any problem that is "decidable" can be expressed in a series of steps, and by a device of this kind. The first thing you have to do, of course, is to determine whether the problem, indeed, is a modelable problem. Is it that kind of a problem? That becomes just a species of the genus "computable." Is it a computable problem?

Now, Turing's technique for doing this was to lay out in tabular form the number and manipulations of symbols that would work, just in case a problem is a computable problem, and wouldn't work if it were not a computable problem. That layout is what is rather misleadingly referred to as a *Turing machine*. Actually, it's not a "machine," but the specification of a set of mechanical procedures for problem-solving, which is just what is meant by an algorithm. Instead, it's a table of sorts, a kind of logic table, or really a kind of mathematical table of commands of the sort: "If you are in state 2, then, when the symbol '1' appears, replace it with '0,' and move to the next position." You get the picture. It's an elaboration of the machine that serves up cupcakes and ginger ale. Know clearly, if the strip of tape is long enough, there really is no practical limit to the instruction-string that can be assembled. Any problem that is in principle reducible to a number of discrete steps is thus solvable.

We've made a lot of headway, because what we discover, then, is not only arithmetic operations, but, indeed, any number of recognition tasks can be modeled by such a procedure, and, therefore, experience itself presumably could be modeled by such a procedure peered—suppose you take experience to be experiences in time and space, experiences of things with extension. If you've got a device that reads quarters, you could have a device that reads dollars, and if you have a device that reads dollars, you might have a device that reads whether it's Uncle Harry or Aunt Jane. You might have some kind of pattern-recognizing device that, indeed, itself will be based on computational operations: "If this, then that," or, "If that, then this," and that's what the moving tape is doing. If I come to a 1, I go down one notch; if I come to a 0, I go up one notch—and depending upon whether I'm going down or going up a notch, or two notches, or five notches, I turn on the water, I turn off the fire alarm, more oil is added to the burner, et cetera. Whole buildings are maintained this way, and they're maintained by essentially computational devices of a Turing nature that are simply taking *input* signals and providing the corrective, or adjustive, or adaptive, *output* signals.

Well, what, then, is an intelligent being then? How should we understand human intelligence? What does it mean to say that man is a rational being as such? Well, doesn't it mean we're problem solvers; isn't that finally what's at the bottom of being intelligent ought to mean—that you give us inputs of a certain kind and through the right kind of coding and computational procedure we serve up outputs? I mean, to those who say that being intelligent is something different, Turing is presenting a challenge. Actually, what we usually mean at the end of the day by a kind of intelligence is a problem-solving ability.

I know without even being reminded that there's more to us than that; as Aristotle says in the *Rhetoric*: "Young men have strong passions which they tend to gratify indiscriminately; they love too much and hate too much." I know all about Aristotle and the *Rhetoric*. When we refer to ourselves as intelligent beings, however, it's not because we love too much or hate too much; it has nothing to do with sentiment or passion; it's problem-solving ability, do you see?

Now, let me pause for a second just to make this clear. Turing is not going to put together a model of our humanity. The question is: "Can we model human intelligence?" That's going to leave out very much. That's going to leave out all sorts of poetic and aesthetic considerations, the passions, and so forth, but, of course, what we pride ourselves on is ourselves as intelligent beings. Is that modelable?

We describe ourselves as rational beings. Now in the history of philosophy, this generally means we've put all the sentiments and emotions on hold. So the question that Turing raises, then, is if to be intelligent is to be a problem-solving sort of entity—and if, in fact, with the right computational resources, well, almost any expressible problem, any decidable problem, any computable problem, is going to be solved—well, then we can examine what we mean by the nature of mind as such, at least in its intelligence dimension.

Turing wrote a famous article in the journal *Mind* in 1950 titled *Computing Machinery and Intelligence*. There he raised the $64,000-dollar question: "Is there anything about us that is significantly different vis-à-vis a properly programmed computational device? Is there anything about us as rational, problem-solving beings that is, in principle, not expressible by a properly programmed, sufficiently powerful, computational device?

This is not to degrade humanity. In fact, regarding high-powered computational devices—to match up with them, you might actually gain a bit of pride by that kind of comparison.

Now, how do you want to set up a test to determine what the right answer to that question is? Well, Turing proposed this test; in fact, it's called the *Turing test*. Let's take a human being and something else. We need not go into what the something else is, but what we're going to do is this: We're going to put both of them behind curtains so that an interrogator doesn't really know what's behind which curtain, and what we're going to do is this: We're going to address questions to each of these entities, questions that require problems to be solved, certain facts to be recognized, certain propositions to be put together in a certain way.

Well, now suppose it's the case that you ask a question like this. Mind you, I'm loath to draw attention to this, but in Turing's actual example, the key question is whether what is behind the curtain is male or female. Well, let's take this question: Are bachelors married? No, no. How do you get from Paris to New York? What do you think the right temperature is for roasting potatoes?

Well, not yet can virtue be taught—but can virtue be taught? I mean, that's a higher-order question and that may not be computable, by the way, and therefore nobody's got the answer to that at all—so look here: If the question is: "Can virtue be taught?" and neither entity behind the curtain can come up with an answer, that will tell equally for or against what's behind the curtain. If you know one of them is a human being, only one is a human being, neither can answer; that is neutral as regards the two of them.

Now, suppose we get into a different set of questions. We've got productions coming from the entity you recognize to be a human being, an intelligent being, an intelligent human being. What are the grounds on which you would deny the other entity that status as an intelligent being, other than mere rank or some kind of prejudice? If the answers are the same from both, do you see, on what basis would you discriminate against one of them being human?

Now, understand what's at issue here; what's at issue is the definition of our humanity as rational and intelligent beings. If the proper definition of a rational, intelligent being is one who—in virtue of certain computational abilities, a certain memory that has been read in, as it were, by the programming functions of experience—is able to perform operations on those inputs such that the outputs bear a coherent relationship to the input and, indeed, function properly, and allow the device itself to achieve certain ends by way of problem-solving—if that's all that's going into your notion of an intelligent human being, you've got it. Human beings just happen to be biological instantiations of something that otherwise could be instantiated non-biologically; it can be instantiated by galenium sulfide crystals, by popping diodes, printed circuits, all sorts of things made in the Silicon Valley and sold by Japanese companies. Do you see what I mean?

One of the questions, then, raised by this entire venture has to do with the fact that when we go back to the problem of knowledge, the problem of knowledge becomes a computational problem. The problem of knowledge boils down to this: There are some things we can know, things that are computably determined or decided, and then there are other simple vexations of life—you know, the *quaestio vexata* of the medieval period, things you're never going to have an answer to. Well, if there are things you're never going to have an answer to, that's true of computational devices as well. If they're not answerable, they're not answerable, and they're answerable by anything. If they are answerable, then presumably they're modelable. The question that will admit of a solution will have some algorithm out there; you may not have it yet, but there'll be some algorithm out there, and once you find it, questions like that get solved, and five will get you ten that the algorithm is finally computational, a computational kind of procedure. Oh, well.

Now, one interesting consequence of this is that it's no longer necessary to reserve the domain of intelligent life to the domain of brainy life, and so one thing I say that comes out of Turing's efforts here is what is sometimes referred to as "machine functionalism within philosophy of mind." That is, the real challenge and philosophy of mind becomes not an understanding of how the brain works as a biological entity, but an understanding of the computational achievements of an organ like this, and the extent to which those achievements can be mimicked or mirrored in many other kinds of devices, many other kinds of machines properly programmed and having sufficient power. So, the task for a developed philosophy of mind, then, doesn't become a task in neurophysiology; it becomes a task in computer science. The brain, then, is just one kind of device that does that sort of thing; it can be achieved by many other ways, and what makes a performance an intelligent performance, then, is not that it's achieved by a brain, but that it solves problems of a certain kind. Thus, anything that also solves problems of that kind is performing intelligently. So, you do get this other sense of a kind of quasi-Jamesian, really non-Jamesian, sense of functionalism, machine functionalism, as a solution to the mind-body problem—the mind now as an essentially computational instrument, which when properly programmed and having sufficient power does it all. James would be, I would say, reluctantly at home with this sort of thing.

Now, I don't want to say that all this is attributable to Alan Turing. Rather, I want to say that he was an extremely influential person in these developments, and he is still widely cited for his contributions. I present him as much as an illustration of 20th-century developments and philosophy of mind, and the linkage between philosophy of mind and computer science, an important development that is likely to be with us for some time, and I say that Alan Turing is very much in the center of that. He was very much at the beginning of that, and he is still in the center of it.

There is a problem with this Turing-like perspective on things that certainly Wittgenstein would be among the first to notice, however, and, of course, the problem is this: In the interstices of this device, inside this instrument with its programming and so forth, it really isn't clear what's going back and forth. You've got these little symbols that are being recorded on a running tape; now, what could they possibly *mean*? Of course, they couldn't mean anything, because on the Wittgensteinian account, meaning is a social construct. For anything to have meaning is for it to be given meaning by a collection of beings who have a sufficiently shared form of life, to have conventional positions on just what linguistic utterances count for. In other words, these are simply movements of a pen, or a carriage, with no meaning as such.

A comparable criticism was developed by John Searle, and it is exemplified in what came to be called his *Chinese room*, which is amusing and instructive. Suppose we have a stack of Chinese ideograms written on cards, and an instruction sheet. The instructions are in English, and they tell us to take the card with such-and-such a pattern and place it next to a card with three dots and an oblique line, or some such. Now, we, as it happens, know no Chinese at all, and we have never before seen Chinese ideograms. As we follow the instructions, we soon have a series of cards placed side-by-side in John Searle's Chinese room.

At this point, a native Chinese speaker enters and finds that the series is a delightful poem. Of course, we hadn't the foggiest idea of what any of this meant; we simply have put these cards in an order based on some instructions—so, how have we functioned? We have functioned in the manner—if you want to use the patois of computer science—of a "compiler program," and the fact that we constructed a meaningful sequence does not suggest for a moment that we have comprehended anything about it. So, meaning is entirely lost on us even as we go through all the procedures capable of presenting something meaningful, which is to say on our part, there isn't any "intelligence" whatsoever, real or artificial.

Now to whom is this meaningful? It's meaningful to those who know the language, who share the culture, who understand what's going on here—those who are capable of playing this particular language game. From the perspective of purely computational operations of moving symbols left and right, nothing follows as regards genuinely mental life. Searle thinks that the missing ingredient here is intentionality, "intentionality" here referring to meaning itself. Searle is quite comfortable with the proposition that all of this that we refer to as our "intelligence" is achieved by the dynamics and functions of the brain—so he's not rejecting an essentially materialist account of mind. This is a subject for a later lecture

As for Alan Turing, he is something like Pythagoras. When I think of Turing, living in this realm of abstraction, a kind of pure realm of symbols, the manipulation of symbols, where the ultimate truths are not instantiated by physical things but rather by relationships, by truth relationships, and propositional relationships—all taking place somewhere in the printed circuits—there is something otherworldly about it.

Recall one of the Upanishads, which is referred to as "The Forest of Wisdom." It features the master and his pupil sitting next to each other (*upanishad*). "Upanishad" actually refers to a seating arrangement of this kind, and the master asks: "How do you see when the sun goes down?" The pupil replies: "Well, in that case, Master, I see by the moonlight." "How do you see when the moon is no longer present?" "Ah, well, Master, when the moon is no longer present, by candlelight." "Then, when you blow out the candle, and there is no sun, then no moon, then no candle, how now do you see?" "Well, then, Master, somehow I see by a light within."

Well, I think Alan Turing lived much of his life in the Forest of Wisdom, and he did see by a light within.

Four Theories of the Good Life
Lecture 50

> One desires not to suffer, and, of course, the surest route to suffering is desire, the unrequited desire. ... So the true hedonist is not out for any and every pleasure, the true hedonist is trying to track that narrow path between pain and pleasure, never wanting a pleasure so much that its deprivation constitutes pain, and never avoiding pain so assiduously as to miss out on every and any conceivable pleasure.

In this final lecture on the "big picture" part of the project, I hope to distill much of what has come before and address that aching question about the examined life and, yes, "the good life." It seems to me that the "theories of the good life" traditionally advanced by the most influential philosophers can be boiled down to four. In choosing four—or, for that matter, 44—one has at least implicitly accepted an essentialist theory of human nature.

The good life, then, is good for a certain form of life, and as the pun would have it, one man's fish is another man's *poisson*. Aristotle, in his conception of the contemplative life, takes a page from the Socratic maxim that the unexamined life is not worth living. The same Aristotle—along with a whole legion of philosophers, some Stoic, some medieval—will offer the active life, which is lived, not just thought about, as the right sort of life.

There is also a fatalistic model of the good life. The good life is something that you're extremely lucky if you end up living any part of your life in. There is a sense of inevitabilities, that somehow the future is already known at some level and the most we can do is give it a good try. A key element of fatalism is that resignation is an essential property in the good life. The good life is just coming to grips with inevitabilities and being realistic about one's chances.

Finally, there is hedonism. The true hedonist is not out for any and every pleasure. The true hedonist is trying to track that narrow path between pain and pleasure, never wanting a pleasure so much that its deprivation constitutes pain and never avoiding pain so assiduously as to miss out on every and any conceivable pleasure. The goal of a hedonistic life is tranquillity.

What sort of life do the saints or heroes choose? We think of saints as persons who have engaged in what ethicists call supererogatory actions, which is to say, actions above and beyond the call of duty. Yet saints and heroes do not usually think of themselves as such. "It gives me joy," says the saint. "It's just my job," says the hero. The lives of saints and heroes do not seem to match up with any of the schemes of the good life enumerated above; they seem rather to be *exemplary*: "Think of how I would have lived my life if I were as good as that person." This has to do with how we think about ourselves and others. How we think about anything depends on brain activity and the programming that we've gone through, life's experiences, the cultures that mold us.

> **Aristotle's notion of *eudaimonia*—doing something for its own sake—can be translated as happiness or flourishing.**

If all we know is just the result of a conditioning history, the best life could be supplied to us by artificial stimulation of our brains, separated from our bodies and nourished in a vat. We could have pleasure *or* be saints and heroes. Presumably, brain centers could be stimulated that would have us doing Fermat's last theorem. Even activities could be simulated; what one can dream of experiencing can also be brought about by stimulating the brain.

If this option were available—to have any life of your choosing played into you—on what grounds would one reject it? All students interested in philosophy should address this question. It raises the possibility that the esteem of others and ourselves, along with our experiences, may not be the core desires of the good life. Aristotle's notion of *eudaimonia*—doing something for its own sake—can be translated as happiness or flourishing. If synthetically generated experiences are not acceptable, there must be something else.

The story of Cleobis and Biton, said by Solon to be "the happiest of men," suggests that the good life may be living a life you don't know is a good life. Cleobis and Biton pulled their mother to the Temple of Hera so that she could implore the goddess Hera to see to it that her sons die the happiest of men. Cleobis and Biton never awaken. If Cleobis and Biton indeed derived *eudaimonia* from their virtuous deed, they were not conscious that they would be so remembered, because they never awakened. They may have been conscious of nothing more than the effort of the struggle to get mother to the temple on time; yet Hera guarantees they died the happiest of men.

One of the lessons that comes from the lives of saints and heroes is that a saintly and heroic life is not lived self-consciously. Rather, it's lived in a way that's conscious of others. Hallucination won't do: We don't want the *sensation* of having done for others; we want to actually do it. First off, one has to determine what is in the best and abiding interest of others. And I don't know how anybody can do that except through what is finally a *contemplative* mode of life. Then, it's a matter of getting out there and doing it. And I don't know how anybody can do that except by way of what finally is an *active* form of life. Because you have no promises in advance as to whether your actions will succeed or fail, or even how they'll be perceived, you must adopt an essentially *fatalistic* position.

A great and exalting pleasure comes from enlarging the possibilities in the lives of others; this has to meet the fundamental objectives of the *hedonistic* individual. Indeed, there must be great joy and pleasure in the life of a Mother Teresa, a deep sense of satisfaction for a hero knowing that he or she has saved a life. ∎

Suggested Reading

Consult *all* readings suggested for Lectures One through Forty-Nine.

Questions to Consider

1. If philosophy doesn't presume to answer the very questions that bring one to philosophy, conclude what the use of it is.

2. If philosophical pluralism is unavoidable and even desirable, infer what the implications are for a sense of community among rational beings.

Four Theories of the Good Life
Lecture 50—Transcript

I've attempted in these 50 lectures to paint with a fairly broad brush, but I hope not at the expense of details that matter. There will be 10 additional lectures added to this series in which a few neglected figures and a number of more specialized subjects will be considered, but in this final lecture on the "big picture," so to speak, on the major part of the project, I hope to distill much of what has come before and address that aching question about the examined life and, yes, indeed, "the good life." Now, I think anyone who has endured 49 lectures on topics in philosophy certainly has a right to hear a few words about the good life, which to some extent might be the life we live when we're not sitting through 49 lectures in philosophy.

I also think that the 50th lecture is either the right time—or, perhaps, 49 lectures too late—for some sort of apologia. Now, in the unlikely event that it has not dawned on my audience, 30 minutes on the issues and persons that we have addressed in the previous 49 lectures could not possibly do justice to the subjects—either to the people themselves, or to the issues they dealt with. The point of the lectures, rather, has been to introduce those who are interested in philosophy, and more generally in the history of ideas, to a collection of ideas and perspectives that have had an animating and vitalizing effect on thought across the board—and over the centuries.

Well, a few words are in order as well on some of the ideas and persons selected for these lectures, though not usually considered in survey courses in philosophy. Think, for example, of the time I devoted to Goethe and to Schiller. I've spoken also, and all too briefly, on the *Federalist Papers*, and about the ideas of James Madison, John Jay, and Alexander Hamilton. These, too, are generally ignored in philosophy courses, philosophy texts, even in treatments of the history of ideas.

Here, and with respect, I think an apologia is due, and if it is due, it should come from the more conventional quarters, perhaps, rather than from this lecture. I believe that any course in political philosophy that will feature Plato and Aristotle and, of course, Machiavelli, but will not include the *Federalist Papers* deserves criticism. I should think that any course in philosophy of science that features the writings of Bacon and Newton, and says almost nothing about what so deeply troubled Goethe and those in the wake of Goethe's criticism, is guilty of a narrow, one-sided rendering of an important chapter in intellectual history—a chapter that, of course, is still writing itself.

Indeed, like most instances, one side of a story is hardly a story at all; it's rather more like propaganda, when you think about it, so if you've been tolerant and patient, this is the time to tell you that your tolerance and patience was not ill served. The issues and people discussed, though to some extent outside mainstream considerations in some places, very much deserved the attention they received, which is just another way of saying that courses of lectures like this suffer, or benefit, from what William James meant by selection. The selections in these lectures were intended to match up with what we would be inclined to take as our higher, if not our highest, interests.

Well, now, four "theories of the good life." What are those theories, and are there only four? Maybe there are 12 or 13. Maybe I won't even get to ones that match up most directly with what listeners and viewers have in mind when they think of the good life. Actually, it does seem to me that the ones traditionally advanced by the most influential philosophers really can be boiled down to four, granting as well that each is subject to refinements and qualifications.

However, in choosing four or, for that matter, 44, one has at least implicitly accepted what might be called an essentialist theory of human nature. After all, to speak of "the good life," or "the right life," is comparable to speaking of—I say, "comparable" as analogous to speaking of "the right diet," or "the right move" in a game of chess. What I mean to say here is that a diet is "right" for a given biochemical and physiological system, supporting a specific kind of life as that life unfolds under expected or even under extreme conditions.

Similarly, a chess move is "right" when it is plausibly related to a winning strategy within the framework of what finally is a specific game, though a game that is essentially a chess game.

The "good life," then, is good for a certain form of life, and, as the tiresome pun would have it, one man's fish is another man's *poisson*. So, with apologies to philosopher colleagues who might resist the notion of "natural kinds" and "essentialism," I say at the outset that I take human nature to be expressed in a set of essential properties—at once rational, moral, and aesthetic—and that in the absence of these properties, the nature in question is incomplete in its development, or simply and alas essentially different from human life.

Let me begin with Aristotle, then, and his conception of the *contemplative* life. Here, Aristotle takes a page from that Socratic maxim according to which the unexamined life is not worth living—so, there surely is that contemplative life, life on the "isle of the blessed." I shall have a few words to say about that. It is clearly a candidate for "the good life."

Well, there's the active life. The same Aristotle will offer that as the right sort of life—Aristotle, not to mention a whole legion of philosophers, some of them Stoic, some of them medieval. Life, after all, is something to be lived, not just thought about—so, the active life.

Let's be fair about these things; there is also a *fatalistic* model of the good life. The good life is something that you're extremely lucky if you end up living any part of your life in. It's highly unlikely *a priori* that you or anybody else will have an uninterrupted good life. You're likely to suffer the slings and arrows of outrageous fortune, and if you do decide to take arms against a sea of troubles, look out, because you're probably almost certainly going to lose. Anyway, keep your nose clean, keep your shoulder to the wheel, and nine times in ten, things won't work—so be happy over the one-tenth of the times where things do work.

I am reminded of the precious scene in the motion picture *Lawrence of Arabia*, when fatalistic pronouncements are made. It is the story of T. E. Lawrence, made famous as British military liaison to the Arab revolt against the Ottoman Turks during World War I. He wrote a wonderful memoir, *The Seven Pillars of Wisdom*, which includes this revealing passage. This is T. E. Lawrence, now:

All men dream, but not equally. Those who dream by night, in the dusty recesses of their minds, wake in the day to find that it was vanity, but the dreamers of the day are dangerous men, for they may act their dream with open eyes, to make it possible.

Here is this Englishman, then, leading an Arab throng through the desert, under conditions making survival itself unlikely. Safely reaching the other side, Lawrence realizes that his aide has been left behind in the desert, and that he must go back into the desert to save him, but he is told by a worried member of the group that he should accept what fate has ordained, for: "It is written that no one shall go into the desert twice and come out," and there's Lawrence sitting up on his horse; he might just as well be Apollo. He has this clear, cold, calculating almost Hellenic confidence as he looks down at this chap and says—not derisively, but with a kind of pained patience: "Nothing is written." In he goes, and he rescues the fellow.

Well, he comes out with him, but then some sort of fracas breaks out in the camp, and the chap he saved is killed, and he is approached again by the same caring aide who reassured him earlier and warned him about all of this—well, now, the fellow comes over and says to him: "It's all right, don't let it trouble yourself. It was written."

Well, there is this sense of inevitabilities when we undertake great and massive projects that somehow the future is already known at some level, and the most we can do is give it a good try, and that's what I mean by a fatalistic perspective being the perspective you need for the good life. That's one of the options, do you see?

I don't want to emphasize the fatalistic element, but I do want to use the fatalistic element to get at resignation as an essential property in the good life, and, of course, we immediately turn to certain of the later Stoics as the model for this. I often repeat that line of Epictetus's in the face of a tragedy experienced by one of his friends, where Epictetus says: "Never say of anything that I have lost it, only that I have given it back."

Do you see? The things we have, we have for the moment. Life itself is a transitory sort of thing; one can be joyous and appreciative and respectful for the very fact of it, while recognizing all the time that it is something that will have to be given back, and it's simply in the cards, and there isn't anything we can do about that. Now, that is the element of resignation. It becomes something that will then guide one through the perilous and vexing seas of life. The good life, then, is just coming to grips with inevitabilities. What I mean when I say: "We mean to live a good life," well, we mean to be realistic about one's chances, and that's that. That's the fatalistic element.

Well, and then, of course, there is hedonism. Now, H. L. Mencken, who was not a philosopher as the textbooks would have it—H. L. Mencken—that famous journalist, the American journalist—insisted that the right definition of Puritanism is "the haunting feeling that someone somewhere may be happy," and indeed, hedonists are constantly being cuffed about as debauchers, people you'd certainly—you would change the sheets after they stayed at your house; you'll surely count the knives and forks when they leave. These are people who are up to no good. The only thing they can think of 24 hours a day is pleasing themselves. Of course, this is not what a *hedonistic* position on the good life is all about. I did mention this in connection with Epicurus's own teachings on this subject. Hedonists, if they're really faithful to the school—*hedone* is desire, do you see? What is it one desires, then?

Well, certainly, one desires—among other things, one desires not to suffer, and, of course, the surest route to suffering is desire, the unrequited desire. Wanting what you can't have, wanting what you shouldn't have, wanting what hurts, what punishes, what deprives or restricts, what constrains, what transforms in the wrong direction—so the true hedonist is not out for any and every pleasure. The true hedonist is trying to track that narrow path between pain and pleasure, never wanting a pleasure so much that its deprivation constitutes pain, and never avoiding pain so assiduously as to miss out on every and any conceivable pleasure.

Nonetheless, the grounding of this form of life is some state of comfort, as it were, some state of security, some reduction in anxiety and confusion. Some peace is what it is all about. The hedonistic life, then, true to the school, is a peaceful life, a life of tranquility, a life in which one has moved oneself as much as possible from threatened harm, from real harm, and within that now protected context, one is able to search out such pleasures. One will not forfeit the sanctuary itself in the process, however.

What form of life do saints choose? Let's consider this for a moment. Very recently, the world has lost Mother Teresa, and I should think by most accounts, if Mother Teresa isn't a saint, then I don't know who would be a saint, at least among contemporary people. Now, sometimes we think of saints as persons who, in the ethical domain, have engaged in what ethicists call "supererogatory actions," which is to say actions above and beyond the call of duty. That is to say, from an ethical point of view, what Mother Teresa has done with her life is almost unbelievable, but, of course, none of us is morally at fault for not having lived Mother Teresa's form of life. That's how the argument would go. What she has done is above and beyond the call of duty.

Now, we certainly have an obligation to provide such help as we can when we come across people desperately in need of help. I mean, someone who's the victim of an automobile accident, lying there in the middle of the street, and there's a phone box right on the wall, and you've got a quarter in your hand, if you can still get a call made for 25 cents. What sort of a blackguard or dastardly person would you be not to go so far as to walk over and dial 911, or ring up a hospital and get an ambulance?

However, you certainly aren't going to quit your job, leave your family, don the robes of poverty, and go and pick dying people up out of trash cans and give them a final hug, and caress, and kiss—and alert them to the dignity that was always theirs in the final moments of lives, let them know that much. I mean that's the sort of things saints do. That, at least, is the way I would go about justifying my otherwise useless existence, simply by saying: "Look, I'm not a saint."

However, if you actually ask someone like Mother Teresa whether she thinks she is engaged in what ethicists call a supererogatory form of activity, well, I suspect she might not know what you're talking about. I don't think anything I've ever heard her say would lead me to conclude that she thinks she's doing something beyond the call of duty. I would guess she thinks she's doing what one is supposed to do. She thinks that what she's doing is quite right, actually, that there isn't anything deeply sacrificial about it. In fact, it's a source in her life—she claimed that it was a source of continuing joy and pleasure, that as she would love the most suffering of God's children, she would love God himself. She was respecting and expressing appreciation for the gift of life, et cetera, so that the one thing I would want to note here is that when it comes to saints and when it comes to heroes, we reflect on saints and heroes as if they were saintly and heroic, and I think we have every reason to do that, but they don't reflect on themselves as saintly and heroic.

It's a rare day, indeed, that when a medal is pinned on someone for valor in battle, and he's asked to say a few words, he begins by saying: "Well, let me tell you how I became a hero." This isn't the way heroes talk. They usually say things—it's entirely disarming, by the way—they usually say things like: "Well, I don't know what the fuss is all about." In the modern patois they would say: "Well, it was my job." You know, "It's my job to go into a burning building with timber falling over, the likelihood of my getting out alive being almost zero, because there's a cat in there. I mean that's my job." Well, of course, that isn't anybody's job. Whatever is compelling that activity, it isn't anybody's employment.

One thing I would say as regards theories of the good life, then—people whose lives very often strike us as emulable are people living lives that don't match up very well either with a life of contemplation, or a hedonistic life, or a fatalistic life, or even a life of activity—well, one is inclined to see as an alternative this life of the hero and the saint. The lives they're living are not essentially political, for example. They're not "civic" in the restricted sense of civics. There's something utterly selfless about these lives that we nonetheless come to regard as *exemplary*. Now, perhaps not exemplary as in: "If I could only get myself to do it, I'd start living that life," but exemplary as in: "Think of how I would have lived my life if I were as good as that person." That's usually what one means by that sort of thing.

Well, this has to do with how we think about ourselves and others, but, of course, on a very famous theory, how we think about anything depends on brain activity and the programming that we've gone through, life's experiences, the cultures of which we—that as members—have been molded by, do you see? We're constructed by essentially linguistic, cultural, and social forces and resources, and there surely would be a world in which Mother Teresa might be regarded as foolish for spending a life doing the sort of things she did—and why would anybody run into a burning building under any circumstances?

Now, if behaviors of this kind are just the result of a conditioning history, if they are just the result of certain grammatical nuances or fallacies and the like, then perhaps the best life of all, depending on the culture you're in, is to specify what sort of life you would wish you were living, and then have the scientists put your brain in a vat and play that sort of life into it. The brain in a vat; there you are. You want to be Mother Teresa; you'll be Mother Teresa. We already have people suffering from various forms of psychosis, forms of paranoid schizophrenia, where they do think they are people other than themselves. They might think they're Jesus, or Napoleon, and the like. Now, presumably, if that can happen as a result of disease, it should be produced by scientific means, somewhere down the road—not next year, but maybe 100 years from now.

The question that arises, then—and it must arise in any time version of either hedonistic, contemplative, active, or fatalistic models of the good life—well, the question that arises is: "Why don't we just bring about the desired state of affairs created by way of brain stimulation. Presumably, you could find centers that, when triggered or activated, have people doing Fermat's Last Theorem. After all, how did Fermat do Fermat's Last Theorem, except by way of Fermat's brain activity? Presumably, again, whatever was going on in Fermat's brain surely can be made to go on in somebody else's brain.

Similarly with activity—everyone in this room, everyone listening to this lecture, or almost everyone anyway, has had a dream in which they've been doing things. Now, they weren't doing things, they were dreaming of doing things. You might be dreaming of riding a bicycle or dreaming of taking an airplane. You aren't actually riding a bicycle or taking an airplane; yet, in the realm of experience, you have knowledge that you are doing precisely these things. Well, if that can be brought about by a dream, it can be brought about by stimulating the brain.

Again, then, the argument goes this way: Suppose you had the option? Suppose, indeed, you could be given any life of your choosing played out into you by way of stimulating the brain? What are the grounds on which you wouldn't do it? By what grounds would you reject or deny this option? I'm not going to answer the question. I'm offering it not as a rhetorical question, but as a question that should be dealt with. What's the basis upon which you would forfeit a life that is frustrating, in which desires remain unrequited, in which you cannot achieve the level of excellence, or goodness, or decency—the basis upon which, nonetheless, you would choose that life over a life in which, by way of the direct activation of your brain, all of these desiderata would be achieved, and all the negative things eliminated?

Suppose you say: "Well, of course, in this latter case, they wouldn't be anything I earned; they wouldn't be anything I was responsible for." Well, suppose I said that there's also a responsibility receptor in the brain, do you see? It hasn't been found yet, but if you stimulate that, then everything else going on in your experiences, you now assume you were responsible for.

I would ask all students interested in philosophy—at least philosophy as a general guide to address the question: Why would you not accept that kind of life? Why would you not be a brain in a vat? Now, I think the reason for rejecting—first of all, I think this is an extremely important question. It raises the possibility that the esteem that others hold us in, the esteem in which we hold ourselves, the experiences of pleasure that we have when we regard ourselves as having accomplished something, may finally not be the core desire of the good life, because if all that could be produced in us, and produced in us reliably and regularly, and yet we would not choose that mode of having the experience, then there must be something missing in just that experience.

Aristotle, when he moves toward the notion of *eudaimonia*, you see—that everything is done for the sake of something else, which is done for the sake of something else, but we don't have an infinite regression here; ultimately, you get to the point where that is done for its own sake and not in order to secure anything else, but because it is desire in itself—do you see? That *terminus ad quem*. This is *eudaimonia*, which—as I noted in an earlier lecture—can be translated as "happiness" or "flourishing."

I'm suggesting that we do the same kind of analysis at this point. If those experiences, if that recording of the esteem in which one is held, that self-recording of the esteem in which one holds oneself in virtue of one's accomplishments, if all that actually could be brought about synthetically by brain stimulation, then the refusal to accept it on those terms means there must be something else desired at a more fundamental level. The question is: What is that something else, and does one find that in the search for happiness? Is one fated never to know it? Does one reach it by contemplation? Is it found in the external world through a life that is active? If brain in vats won't do it, what will?

Recall Cleobis and Biton, those two young worthies pulling their mother to the Temple of Hera as if they were a pair of ox themselves, sweating the whole five miles, probably tearing up the soles of their feet, their sandals having been ripped by the rough roads. There their mother is imploring the goddess Hera to see to it that her sons die "the happiest of men," and Cleobis and Biton never awaken. They die the happiest of men.

Solon thinks they have died the happiest of men. Solon, as reported by Plutarch, recall, having come out of that Hellenic tradition in which the esteem in which you are held by others, your standing within the *polis*, how men and women who are decent, how men of virtue, come to regard you, the pride they take in the fact that you were one of them—that to know all that is finally what it means to be happy, well, Cleobis and Biton, if indeed they derived *eudaimonia* from that, if in dying in that state they left the world having lived the right kind of life, the good life—of course, they're not conscious of how they are remembered. I say if all of that were the case, they had attained *eudaimonia*. They went to sleep, didn't they, so this isn't something that you can play into their brains, because it isn't something they even know about. You see living the good life, then, if the Cleobis-Biton model is the right model, may be living a life that you don't directly recognize as the good life. It may be living life as a certain kind of being, as a certain kind of person, indeed, whether you're particularly happy with it or not. The good life may not be the personally happy, happiness-filled life.

Now, I wasn't there to interview Cleobis and Biton just before they fell asleep. One of them might have said to the other: "My goodness, what an exhausting pull that was. I've got new sympathy for ox," and Biton might have said: "Yeah, we can't even get a lemonade in this town. You know, you think if they could put up a Temple of Hera someplace, there might be some outdoor takeaway stand of one sort or another. Nonetheless, Mom had to get here on time, and the only way she was going to get here on time is if we brought her, and thank goodness, for her sake, that she got to where she wanted to be, to do what she wanted to do," etc. They might have been saying, in effect, that: "We want what is good for Mom, for her sake," and in that they would've been expressing themselves as her true friends, *teleia philia*, a completed friendship, where you want what is good for others for the sake of others, for what is so good for them to warrant that, you see. So, Cleobis and Biton might actually—though I don't mean this in the Freudian sense, goodness knows, and if goodness doesn't know it, no one does—Cleobis and Biton might have been living the good life—ready? Well, unconsciously. I prefer to say "unself-consciously."

I think one of the lessons that comes from the lives of saints and heroes is that when a saintly and heroic life is lived, it's not lived self-consciously in saintly and heroic terms. In fact, it's not lived self-consciously at all. It's lived in a way that's conscious of others—their needs and desires, their deserts. The good life very often turns out to be a life of service, a life of sacrifice, and the problem with having that played into your nervous system, you see, is that you know what the game is already. If the position you've taken is: "My life can't be a good life unless I've actually served the legitimate interests and needs of others," then playing it into the brain is merely an hallucination according to which I'm doing what I'm doing simply defeats the whole project. It isn't going to work at all. It's not that I want to experience the *sensation* of having done it; it's that I want to have done it, and that means that, first off, one has to determine what is in the best and abiding interest of others. I don't know how anybody can do that except through what is finally a contemplative mode of life. Then, of course, it's a matter of getting out there and doing it. I don't know how anybody can do that except by way of what finally is an active life.

You have no promises in advance as to how your actions will succeed or not, or even if they'll be perceived. They may be misperceived. Some very good people have been crucified for doing good things. So, you have to take an essentially fatalistic position that although you do not know what the future will bring, you do know what your duties are and the great and exalting pleasure that comes from enlarging the possibilities in the lives of others. This has to meet the fundamental objective that the hedonistically inclined individual might have.

Indeed, there must be great joy and pleasure in the life of a Mother Teresa. There must be that deep sense of satisfaction that a hero has knowing, not that he is a hero, but that he has saved a life.

Well, of course, this all gets fairly—I mean, one could become nearly sentimental of considerations of this kind if one weren't careful, and I find any time that I have this penchant toward sentimentality—and the answer to the question: "Well, what's wrong with sentimentality?" is that it tends to cheapen sentiment itself, but you do see in all of this that the good life is active, contemplative, somewhat fatalistic, and selfless.

Ontology—What There "Really" Is
Lecture 51

> **Questions of "real being" are complicated by the fact of development and change, of metamorphosis and evolution.**

In his *Metaphysics*, Aristotle states: "There is a science which investigates being as being and attributes which belong to this in virtue of its own nature. This is not the same as any of the so-called special sciences, for none of these treats universally of being as being." What do we mean when we refer to "being" as such?

In his *Critique of Pure Reason*, Kant said that if the question has to do with "existence," it is important to understand that existence is not a predicate because it is logically or conceptually entailed by the subject of which it is supposed to be a predicate. Propositions, on Kant's account, are either analytic or synthetic. In the former, the meaning of the predicate is included in or synonymous with the meaning of the subject ("Bachelors are unmarried men"). Synthetic propositions, on the other hand, are factual but subject to confirmation ("Some bachelors are tall").

The distinction between analytic and synthetic propositions is problematic in itself, as Willard Van Orman Quine pointed out in his 1951 article "Two Dogmas of Empiricism," published in the *Philosophical Review*. Quine notes that if analytic propositions are tautologies, whatever is true of the subject term will be true of the predicate term. With tautologies, there is free replacement and substitution of subject and predicate by each other with no loss of truth. But in "Bachelors are unmarried men," we could insert for *unmarried men* the phrase "*Bachelors* has less than 10 letters." The substitution fails and can be restored only using far more by way of conventional understandings than Kant's scheme allows. In Quine's account, it is folly to seek a boundary between synthetic statements, which hold contingently on experience, and analytic statements, which hold come what may. Any statement can be held true, come what may, if we are prepared to make drastic enough adjustments elsewhere in the "system" of conceptualized reality.

Unless the entire human race has been subject to constant hallucinations and delusions, common sense and daily experience testify to the truth of the claim: "There are things distinct from myself that continue in time and in space independently of my concepts of them." Matters become more daunting, however, once we set out to identify such things, classify them, and claim to have knowledge of their properties.

The inclination to classify is as common in childhood as it is in science and philosophy. One of the most general concepts employed in classifying things is that of *essentiality*. Certain objects are understood to be *essentially* what they are, no matter what merely accidental differences obtain among them (that is, all varieties of apples are still, essentially, apples).

The "essence" of a thing is not limited by its observable features, but arises from a conception of some internal, intrinsic feature that causally brings about these features. Among these features is the concept of *executive causation*, the concept of a central cause that accounts for the observed properties of an object. Ruled out by this are properties that are merely correlated with the object.

Were knowledge confined to empirical facts and empirical modes of knowing, there could be no concept of necessity or impossibility.

Taking an event or object to be what it is "essentially," however, raises the question about the nature of "universals" and the relationship between universals and particulars. Some followers of Socrates thought that a higher-order plane or reality was necessary for particular things to have the properties they have. In other words, the actual particular "types" of things have their defining properties in virtue of the universal of which they are but instances. Aristotle rejected this view, insisting that properties inhere only in particulars. Medieval philosophy showed renewed interest in the so-called *nominalist-realist controversy*. Nominalists insisted that universals were the names given to collectives of particulars. Realists argued that the universal had to be real; otherwise, the particulars would have nothing from which to derive their essential natures.

Peter Abelard (1079–1142) made clear that universals are references to how *we* have conceptualized our experiences. Nonetheless, he granted validity to the realists' position, because universals encompass a limitless number of possible experiences. For instance, the term *mankind* is the conceptualized category into which we would validly place an indefinitely large number of instances; there is no "mankind," as such, just men, women, and children.

Locke distinguished between what he called the "nominal" and the "real" essence of things. The *real essence* of an object is determined by its ultimate microstructure, which we cannot perceive. But on the basis of experience, we come to treat certain reliable ensembles of properties as instances of a certain type of thing, thus giving the object its *nominal essence.*

On this account, ontological issues arise from different levels of reality— as perceived, as conceptualized, and as constructed by discourse. At one level of reality, cyanide gas is a chemical composed of certain elements. At another level, the gas is a poison. And at still another level, it has been used suicidally. Is any one level in some way more "real" than the others? Questions of "real being" also are complicated by change and evolution. Though favoring conditions will cause a large oak tree to arise from an acorn, none of the superficial features of acorns predicts or explains the oak tree.

In his *Being and Time*, Martin Heidegger (1889–1976) made a sharp distinction between existence and essence. There is nothing "essential" about something before its existence. Man acts as though he were the master and shaper of language, but in fact, language remains the master of man.

The American philosopher Richard Rorty suggested that we give our own version of competing accounts priority in order to preserve solidarity. Thus, ontology becomes a branch of sociology. Rorty said, "Truth is simply a compliment paid to sentences seen to be paying their way." We attribute "truth" to sentences that allow us to get on with things, to get things done.

Against this line of thinking appears Roger Penrose, distinguished for his work in mathematics, who argued that the perceived reality is grounded in a mind-independent reality. What really exists, then, are formal relational properties constitutive of the cosmos and subject to mathematical representation.

In his *Personal Knowledge*, the scientist-philosopher, Michael Polyani (1891–1976) opposed the notion of science as value-free, purely rational and empirical, fact-based and systematic. Rather, the history of science is laced with intuitive leaps, leaps of faith, the effort that only passion can supply. His concept of "tacit knowledge" connects discovery to intuition. Polyani's theory resembles Kant's modality category, in which he places three pairs of subcategories: possibility-impossibility, existence-nonexistence, and necessity-contingency.

Were knowledge confined to empirical facts and empirical modes of knowing, there could be no concept of necessity or impossibility. These modal categories raise yet another ontological question: From the fact that an apple now is on the table, it must be the case that at some previous time, this apple was a possibility. The question, of course, has to do with the ontological standing of "possibles."

There is widespread belief that, as difficult as the ontological questions are, we at least possess a method by which to test ontological claims when they are made. The method, of course, is science itself. What really exists, presumably, is what is predicted and explained by and obedient to the laws of science. Even more basic than the ontological question of what really exists is the question of why anything exists, why there is something rather than nothing. ■

Suggested Reading

Aristotle, *Metaphysics*. W. D. Ross, trans. (downloadable).

Loux, Michael. *Metaphysics: A Contemporary Introduction*. Routledge, 2002.

1. Identify in what senses an apple (a) really exists, (b) is a figure of speech, (c) is a "natural kind," and (d) is essentially a fruit.

2. If Rorty's sense of truth is taken seriously, how is the project of philosophy altered?

Ontology—What There "Really" Is
Lecture 51—Transcript

In Book IV of his *Metaphysics*, Aristotle begins Part I with these words:

> There is a science which investigates being as being and attributes which belong to this in virtue of its own nature. This is not the same as any of the so-called special sciences, for none of these treats universally of being as being.

Well, just what do we mean when we refer to "being" as such? We would all agree that the statement "The present King of France is bald" is a false statement, but by that logic, we seem compelled to say that it is true that "The present King of France is not bald." The conundrum arises from the fact that France has not had a king for more than a century, and, therefore, we shouldn't be able to make any factual statement at all about the present King of France. That is, the entity, "the present King of France" has no existential status at all.

In his *Critique of Pure Reason*, Kant considers this very attribute or, as it is called in philosophy, this "predicate," and he judges it to be illicit. Existence is not a predicate, for it is logically or conceptually entailed by the subject of which it is supposed to be a predicate.

To say, then, that Schubert existed is to add nothing whatever to the concept "Schubert." It is informative to say that Schubert was a contemporary of Mozart's, or that the *adagio* movement of his Schubert's *Quintet* in C-major is perfected beauty, but it is utterly uninformative to say that Schubert "existed," or, for that matter, that recordings of his *Quintet* now exist.

Kant states the case this way:

> It is absurd to introduce into the conception of a thing the conception of its existence. I ask, is the proposition analytical or synthetical? If the former, there is no addition made to the subject of your thought by the affirmation of its existence; but then the conception

in your minds is identical with the thing itself, which is but a miserable tautology.

Recall the distinction between analytical and synthetical propositions: The former are such that the meaning of the predicate is included in, or is synonymous with, the meaning of the subject, as in: "All bachelors are unmarried men."

Now, synthetic propositions, on the other hand, are factual. They may be wrong, and when right, they do add to our fund of knowledge, as in: "Some bachelors are tall." On the Kantian scheme, there is no discovery of ontological consequence in assigning "exists" to a subject. Presumably, if the subject-term has ontological standing outside the context of thought, there will be methods by which to establish the fact. What must be abandoned is the ageless habit of confusing logical with real predicates, or regarding as "real," or whatever it is of which we have a concept.

However, you see, the neat division between analytical and synthetic propositions was quite exploded by Willard Van Orman Quine in a famous 1951 article titled "Two Dogmas of Empiricism," which appeared in the *Philosophical Review*.

Let's take the textbook example, "All bachelors are unmarried men." Quine resists the convention according to which this is an analytical proposition, a "miserable tautology," as Kant would have said. Were it a tautology, then we should be able to substitute *unmarried men* for *bachelors* in any proposition without altering the truth value of the proposition; now, a truth-saving substitution, a substitution *salva veritate*, in Leibniz's useful term would be given in this example by Quine "*Bachelors* has less than 10 letters." Well, this shows that such a substitution will not inevitably be successful. We wouldn't say that all unmarried men have less than 10 letters. It would be meaningless to say that unmarried men have less than 10 letters. Quine therefore concludes:

> It becomes folly to seek a boundary between synthetic statements, which hold contingently on experience, and analytic statements which hold come what may. Any statement can be held true come

what may, if we make drastic enough adjustments elsewhere in the system. Even a statement very close to the periphery can be held true in the face of recalcitrant experience by pleading hallucination or by amending certain statements of the kind called logical laws. Conversely, by the same token, no statement is immune to revision. As an empiricist, I continue to think of the conceptual scheme of science as a tool, ultimately, for predicting future experience in the light of past experience. Physical objects are conceptually imported into the situation as convenient intermediaries, not by definition in terms of experience, but simply as irreducible posits comparable, epistemologically, to the gods of Homer.

Well, this is quite a mouthful. Taken together, the arguments of Kant and of Quine create an unsettled and unsettling state of affairs as regards the means by which to establish whether a percept or concept or ours has a real-world "being," whether it is independent of our mental and linguistic constructs and, if so, whether it could be known to be so.

Kant makes clear that the certainties of our analytic propositions are won at the cost of uninformativeness. Quine goes so far as to challenge the very distinction between such alleged tautologies and the world of experience itself as we conventionally describe it. The propositions that seem to us to be most basic are themselves grounded in larger and more general "systems" of thought, which, if radically enough adjusted, would require the abandonment of these very core propositions and the adoption of other propositions that might presently seem preposterous.

Well, unless the entire human race has been in an uninterrupted state of hallucinations and delusions, we have common sense and daily experience testifying to the truth of the claim: "There are things distinct from myself which continue in time and in space independently of my concepts of them." Matters become more daunting, however, once we set out to identify such things, classify them, and claim to have knowledge of their properties.

As for the inclination to classify, it is as common in childhood as it is in science and philosophy. One of the most general concepts employed in classifying things is that of *essentiality*. Certain objects are understood to be *essentially* what they are, no matter what merely accidental differences might obtain among them. Thus, there are Delicious apples, Macintosh apples, and green apples, not to mention rotten apples and apples with worms inside, but all are essentially apples, we are inclined to say.

However, there is now substantial research to show that, whatever the ontological status of "essences" might be, at the psychological level we do, indeed, essentialize. The prevailing view is that such cognitive dispositions are positively adaptive, making the external world more coherent and manipulable. The processes at work are not of the descriptive, empiricist sort: What one regards as the "essence" of a thing is not exhausted by its observable features alone, but arises from a conception of some internal, intrinsic feature that we believe causally brings about these external properties. Among these is the concept of *executive causation*, the concept of a central cause that accounts for the observed properties of an object, something central that makes a thing an apple. Ruled out by this would be properties that are merely correlated with the object, as in "it is in a basket." Whatever it is that makes apples grow on trees is different from what finds some of them housing worms. Yet another feature is what has been called the "rich inductive potential" contained in the concept of something being essentially what it is. That is, knowing that something is an apple permits predictions that go well beyond what has been experienced and broad explanations of events that arise from the apple-ness of apples. It allows us to predict things that we haven't experienced about apples.

However, this very mode of cognizing raises the ancient and, indeed, the current question about the nature of "universals" and the relationship between universals and particulars. There is little debate on the question of whether or not some things found in trees can be used in baking, such as to make something as American as apple pie. The things in question are, ready? Apples.

However, is there some higher-order plane or reality necessary for these particular entities to appear on trees and to have the properties they have? Some of the followers of Socrates were inclined to think this was the case— that the actual particular "types" of things have their defining properties in virtue of a universal of which they are but instances. Thus, if $a^2 + b^2 = c^2$ is the "true" form of all right-angle triangles, there can be such triangles only insofar as the universal right-angle triangle has real existence—and so, also, then, for truth, beauty, and justice. Aristotle rejected most of this, insisting that properties inhere only in particulars.

Throughout the productive period of medieval philosophy, there was renewed interest in the so-called *nominalist-realist controversy*. Nominalists insisted that universals were the names given to collectives of particulars; realists argued that the universal was of necessity real, otherwise the particulars would have nothing from which to derive their, what? Essential natures.

It was Peter Abelard (1079–1142) who began to put the house in order by making clear that our references to "universals," or references to how *we* have conceptualized our experiences, are really summaries of particular experiences. The references are actually to really existing entities based on perception. Nonetheless, says Abelard, there is a validity to the conceptualizing of universals, for universals encompass a limitless number of possible experiences of a certain kind. The universal class-term *mankind* is the conceptualized category into which we would validly place an indefinitely large number of instances. It is, however, a conceptualized category, not a distinct and living entity in its own right. There is no "mankind," as such, just men, women, and children.

For a time, the matter seemed to be settled by Locke's distinction between what he called the "nominal" and the "real" essence of things. Locke was won over, as I mentioned, to Newton's corpuscularian physics, and thus took the ultimate reality of things to be of an invisible, sub-microscopical character, beyond the reach of perception. As a result, then, the "real" essence of things could never be comprehended by the mind, which, on Locke's account, is furnished solely by experience, and we don't experience these subatomic events. However, *real essences* have the power to affect the sensory apparatus, giving rise to experiences that include such properties as color, hardness, shape, duration, pitch, etc. On the basis of experience, we come to treat certain reliable ensembles of properties as instances of a certain type of thing that, once named, gives that thing its *nominal essence*. The roundish, reddish, sweet-tasting object that can be plucked from that tree is an apple.

Now, on this sort of account, ontological issues arise from what are finally different levels of reality—reality as perceived, reality as conceptualized, reality as constructed by discourse, by naming, for example. At one level of reality, cyanide gas is a chemical composed of certain elements. The elements combine in a manner that is derivable from the periodic table, though, in point of fact, the elements themselves are comprised of subatomic particles whose behavior can be described in only statistical terms. At yet another level of reality, the gas is a poison, which is a fact not derivable from the behavior of the subatomic particles of which cyanide gas is nonetheless formed. At still another level of reality, cyanide gas has been used suicidally, yet another fact you couldn't derive either from the periodic table or the behavior of its subatomic constituents. Are all such "levels" of reality real? Is one level in some way more "real" than the others?

Then, too, questions of "real being" are complicated by the fact of development and change, of metamorphosis and evolution. Granting that there is something in the acorn such that, under favoring conditions, a large oak tree will come about, but clearly none of the superficial features of acorns will either predict or explain the oak tree. Similarly, absent the zygotic and embryonic stages, there could have been no Thomas Jefferson or Joe DiMaggio, but nothing in the zygotes would allow anticipations of either the Declaration of Independence or a 56-game hitting streak.

In his *Being and Time*, Martin Heidegger made a sharp distinction between existence and essence. There is nothing "essential" about something before its existence. It begins as just an entity, its essence then derived over a course of development. The "essence" of something nominally human is what comes about through acculturation and historical forces—nothing before that.

I must note that, from 1933 to 1939, Heidegger was faithful to the Nazi party, and he spoke approvingly of its practices and policies. One of his famous aphorisms and a direct guide to his metaphysics was this: "Man acts as though he were the master and shaper of language, while in fact, language remains the master of man." Hear the discursive turn, the linguistic source of reality.

A veritable Heidegger industry seems to have grown out of this insight of his, which I would say is rather less profound than derived. To some extent, it rehearses Locke's distinction between nominal and real essences, and even Quine's examination of the malleability of allegedly basic truths. At bottom, the thesis attributes to culture, history, and discourse the power to produce the only reality we can know. What there is, then, on this account, is what our particular culture—in its current state of development—declares to be the case. To reject this is to be either homeless or judged mad. Other times and places would set store in different accounts. One of Heidegger's admirers, the eminent American philosopher Richard Rorty, has suggested that we have a right, as it were, to give our own version priorty over competing accounts, at least for the purpose of preserving solidarity within our tribe. Thus does ontology become, as it were, a branch of sociology, or the sociology of knowledge. As he said in an interview given to the *New York Times*: "Truth is simply a compliment paid to sentences seen to be paying their way."

Truth, then, is a way of talking about things. Rorty's sense of sentences that are judged to be "paying their way" is the pragmatic sense. We attribute "truth" to sentences that allow us to get on with things, to get things done. A sentence of the sort, $F=ma$, is declared to be "true," just in case it finds us succeeding in a whole range of essentially mechanical tasks and projects. We would be prepared to withhhold the attribution of truth, just in case the sentence for some reason ceased to guarantee success.

Against this line of thinking might be arrayed the philosophical contributions of Roger Penrose, quite distinguished for his work in mathematics. On Penrose's account, there's a good reason why some sentences "pay their way," and the reason is they are true. Penrose argues that the perceived reality—in which we successfully not only cross the street, but also journey to the moon and back—is grounded in a mind-independent reality. This reality is grasped most firmly by our very intuitive resources, which reach possibilities beyond the range of sense-data, and find formal expression in, for example, mathematics.

Penrose's ontology, at the most fundamental level, recovers something of the Pythagorean thesis according to which ultimate reality is in the realm of number. What really exists, then, are formal relational properties constitutive of the actual cosmos and subject to mathematical analysis and representation. That the conscious mind is able to comprehend and represent such relationships is based on non-computational, intuitive resources. The reality in question is not a linguistic invention, nor is it a cultural nuance. It is really real.

This line of thought is reminiscent of a thesis developed by another scientist-philosopher, Michael Polyani, whose dates are 1891–1976. I think his most interesting work is a book he titled *Personal Knowledge*. In that work, Polyani opposed the notion of science as value-free, purely rational, utterly empirical, fact-based and systematic. He knew too much science to believe that. Rather, the history of science is laced with intuitive leaps, leaps of faith, the effort that only passion can supply. His concept of "tacit knowledge" is summed up in the phrase: "We know more than we can say." Polyani wrote down these lines:

> We must conclude that the paradigmatic case of scientific knowledge is the knowledge of approaching discovery. To hold such knowledge is an act deeply committed to the conviction that there is something there to be discovered.

As I say, "really real"? Knowledge that is tacit and only intuitively reached? Evidence for this abounds, of course. Anyone who can ride a bicycle "knows" how to do it, but would be hard pressed to state in propositional form just what the knowledge is by which one successfully rides a bicycle. In just about any area of expertise, there are achievements that cannot be defined in words but only exhibited in the performance itself. From an ontological point of view, then, the question must arise as to whether our conceptions of reality are also shaped by intuitive and tacit modes of knowing, with skepticism arising as a result of the inability to articulate or justify the grounds—but these resources have notoriously led to error and even disaster. Don't tell me that it must be so because you hold intuitively.

Penrose highlights human fallibility, but he seems to offer no non-pragmatic direction as to the right sort of test to be passed by our claimed intuitions. In any case, knowledge that is tacit sooner or later must be incorporated into more explicit metaphysical propositions if there is to be any intelligible "whole" rather than a set of mere intimations and hunches.

There is a family resemblance between tacit knowledge and Kant's "postulates of empirical thought in general," as he put it. As usual, the Kantian version of an idea is a rather more complex and laboriously developed one than the passerbys might wish more. In that categorical framework, he represents exhaustively the very modes of the understanding; one of the categories is that of modality. It is under that heading that Kant places three pairs of modal subcategories. There is the pair of possibility-impossibility, the pair of existence-nonexistence, and the pair of necessity-contingency.

Now, nothing in the realm of empirical fact takes place of necessity. Thus, were knowledge confined to empirical facts and empirical modes of knowing, there could be no concept of necessity. Nor, indeed, would there be the concept of impossibility, for nothing of a purely factual nature is impossible except on an hypothesis, but such an hypothesis requires "impossibility" as a cognitive category. Well, let me not get into the details of this part of Kant's *First Critique*. I point to these modal categories to raise yet another ontological question: From the fact that an apple now is on the table, it must be the case that at some previous time, this apple was a possibility. Indeed, from the fact of any object or event, it follows that at some earlier time it was but a possibility. The question, of course, has to do with the ontological standing of "possibles."

If we answer the question with a dismissive shrug—what is merely possible has no ontological standing whatever—then something must have come from nothing, and this seems to require of a thing that it be its own cause. If we say, instead, that the present object or event was not itself at some previous time, but was made possible by some other sort of object or event, then we have the problem of causality to deal with, now made more cumbersome by having to show how the present object or event was in some way "imminent" in this other sort of object or event. You see, the party is getting awfully rough at this point. No one thinks that very tiny oak trees are present in acorns, thereupon growing taller with time.

This line of thinking generally leads to thoughts about genetic processes as these are understood in the biological domain. Here some sort of template or functional plan becomes realized by way of gene-action at the level of protein synthesis and enzyme, enzyme function and the like, but for a functional plan to be realized—the "that for the sake of which"—all the molecular biological processes that take place must have some sort of being. It would strain credulity to insist that it all takes place by accident. We are, then, left with the question as to how potentialities should be understood ontologically.

These issues duly noted, there is widespread belief that, as difficult as the ontological questions are, we at least possess a method by which to test ontological claims when they are made. The method, of course, is science itself. What really exists, presumably, is what is predicted and explained by, and obedient to, the laws of science. In the next lecture, this assurance will be examined critically. Is science to be the last word on this, and what is the last word on this?

Even more basic than the ontological question of what really exists is the question of why anything exists, why there is something rather than nothing. Theology offers one answer to the question, and I will reserve theology's answer to the final lecture in this series. For now, though, understand that the realm of ontology, the realm of what really is, is alive and well in contemporary philosophical discourse. The problems are vexing and interesting, and the problems are—well, shall I say it? Real.

Philosophy of Science—The Last Word?
Lecture 52

If the thinking parts of what we are pleased to call the 21st century agree on little else, there is the widespread conviction that the last word on the composition of reality and the principles that give it its character is finally drawn from the vocabulary and the methods of science.

The 21st century is marked by the widespread conviction that the last word on the composition of reality and the principles that give it its character is finally drawn from the vocabulary and methods of science. The modern world is radically and qualitatively different from any preceding age, and the differences are largely the bequest of science.

However, *science* is one of those troublesome terms that can seem to convey too little by standing for too much. *Science* encompasses widely varied studies, ranging from physics to economics, both of which are areas for which Nobel prizes are awarded. The word *science* is applied to different disciplines, as well, including political science, social science, and cognitive science, to name a few. The *philosophy of science* must analyze the various senses of the term and find such shared features as might justify the inclusion of otherwise disparate activities under the same general heading.

Carl Hempel advocated that the defining features of science are the logical form of scientific explanations and the restrictions on the class of events to be explained. Differences in subject matter, equipment, or methods of inquiry do not determine the status of a discipline as a science. That status is earned by the special "logic" of scientific explanations and by the class of occurrences for which there is to be such explanations.

Hempel's model of science is actually a model of scientific explanation. To warrant scientific explanation, the event in question must be empirical in principle. There must be a universal law specified that covers events of this sort. All conditions relevant to the particular event must be specified or otherwise controlled. At the end of the exercise, the subject event and all such events are explained scientifically when they are *logically deducible* from a universal law known to be true. Hempel's theory is called the *deductive nomological* (derived from the Greek word for "law," *nomos*) model of explanation. He contrasts this with explanations based on inferences from past occurrences, referring to this mode of explanation as *inductive statistical*, or what might be called the *inductive nomological* model.

The question arises, then, as to the status of those disciplines that lack universal laws and, thus, cannot explain events by deducing them from such laws. This is where the *inductive statistical* model comes in. Hempel acknowledged that the most stringent criterion for full-fledged scientific explanations was missing from many disciplines understood on commonsense grounds to be scientific. These disciplines get their scientific "status" via their discovery of reliable relationships permitting accurate prediction.

For all its neatness and intuitive appeal, the Hempelian scheme is plagued with problems. To some extent, the "statistical" nature of reality itself raises questions as to the adequacy of a model of scientific explanation calling for absolute and universal laws allowing perfect predictions. Also, the logical structure of Hempelian explanation leaves room for nonsensical examples nonetheless qualifying as scientific explanations. A further difficulty with the model is that it seems to permit spurious causal inferences.

> *Science* is one of those troublesome terms that can seem to convey too little by standing for too much.

The attempt to extend this model of explanation to the realm of social phenomena produces yet another wave of compelling criticism. Historical events are nonrecurring. Accordingly, what a "general law" would cover in the realm of history isn't clear. The character and intelligibility of a historical event derive from the specific persons, motives, and contexts involved. What is true in history would be the same wherever actual persons, with their individuated needs, judgments, and aspirations, constitute the events to be explained.

It would strain credulity to believe that the lawful and time-ordered sequences in the natural world come about without the participation of occult forces, hidden powers, and the like. Gravitation, for instance, refers to a physical reality that causes objects to behave in predictable ways toward each other. The behavior is not simply reliable but seemingly *necessitated*. We find in the laws of science the *real* structure of reality, the truth behind the merely cluttered pictures of everyday life.

Realists regard the laws of science as reflecting reality as it really is. The anti-realist perspective takes such laws to be useful generalizations and valid within the contexts in which they were developed but insufficient to account for all that "really is the case." Princeton's Bastian van Fraassen, a defender of the anti-realist school, argues that what counts as a good explanation is not the logical structure of the argument but the extent to which it answers a "why" question arising in a given context. In her book *How the Laws of Physics Lie*, Nancy Cartwright suggested that the idealized world in which the laws are unfailing is a world occupied by no one in the real world, physicists included. Reality is disorderly, contextually fluctuating, resistant to any set of simple and simplifying laws.

The realist invokes the concept of *inference to the best explanation* as a defense of realism. NASA's space program was based on the assumption that the laws of classical physics and the accuracy of available instruments provide an account of reality. Based on this assumption, rockets were built, astronomical calculations were performed, a date was chosen, and a launch took place. Astronauts reached the moon, then returned safely to earth. The "best explanation" of the result is that the laws accepted and implemented capture the fabric of reality as such.

These debates illustrate a far less tidy world of science than the one depicted in textbooks. For all its technical and theoretical achievements, science is a human product and will always bear the mark of its maker. In *The Structure of Scientific Revolutions* (1962), Thomas Kuhn drew attention to the guild-like nature of the scientific community. Kuhn referred to this as "normal science," to distinguish it from those radical departures that constitute truly revolutionary changes. A key feature of this enterprise is that the research guided by such considerations unearths only what was known in advance.

The same set of commitments and method, the same paradigm, dictates that problems are chosen to the extent that they promise fairly ready solutions.

Karl Popper, the eminent philosopher of science and logician, criticized Kuhn's reliance on the concept of ruling paradigms as "the myth of framework." Popper himself had made an important contribution to philosophy of science in his critique of *verificationism* and his alternative methodological standard, *falsificationism*. In the scientific positivism of the 1930s and 1940s, the meaning of statements was nothing more than the method by which they could be verified. Any statements that did not lend themselves to empirical modes of verification were essentially meaningless or merely argumentative. Popper observed that such a standard would render all the laws of science nonsensical. He replaced the concept of verification with falsificationism: Though a law cannot be verified an infinite number of times, it need only be falsified once to lose credibility. ■

Suggested Reading

Hempel, Carl. *Aspects of Scientific Explanation*. Free Press, 1965.

Van Fraassen, Bas. *The Scientific Image*. Oxford University Press, 1980.

Questions to Consider

1. If the laws of science do not reflect reality as it "really" is, how should we account for practical success?

2. How do the laws of physics "lie," and what standard is there for telling the difference between the truth and the lies?

3. Is the culture of science hostile to criticism and novelty of thought?

Philosophy of Science—The Last Word?
Lecture 52—Transcript

If the thinking parts of what we are pleased to call the 21st century agree on little else, there is the widespread conviction that the last word on the composition of reality and the principles that give it its character is finally drawn from the vocabulary and the methods of science. This is not a conviction based on blind faith, but on the real accomplishments that have been made in physics and chemistry, in medicine and biology, in engineering and computer science, etc. The modern world is radically and qualitatively different from any preceding age, and the differences are largely the bequest of science. Science has earned our respect and confidence.

That much said, *science* is one of those troublesome nouns that seem to convey too little by standing for too much. Nobel prizes are awarded in physics and in economics, but it is scarcely clear what those subjects have in common, except that in some sense both are "sciences," so-called. Then, too, there is political science, not to mention social science, not to mention what was in the 19th century called "moral science." Many psychologists refer to themselves as "behavioral scientists" or, more recently, "cognitive scientists." I needn't press on with "Christian Science" or "Scientology" to indicate the very broad reach of this noun and the seemingly arbitrary applications that are made of it.

It is the task of *philosophy of science* to consider a matter of this sort, to analyze the various senses of the term, to find such shared features as might justify the inclusion of otherwise disparate activities under the same general heading. There is, one might guess, little by way of doctrinal agreement between, say, Hinduism and Presbyterianism, but both qualify as religions. There is little by way of shared data between botany and astrophysics, but we say that both qualify as "science." We ask, then, on what understanding does this come about?

It has been cogently advocated, especially by Carl Hempel during the 1950s and 1960s, that the defining features of science are actually in the logical form of scientific explanation and the restrictions on the class of events to be explained. These are the two features that determine whether something is a science, what kinds of events are to be explained, and what the nature of the explanation is. That is, differences in subject matter as such—in equipment, in methods of inquiry—do not determine the status of a discipline as science. Instead, that status is earned by the special "logic" of scientific explanations and by the class of occurrences for which there should be such explanations.

In his classic essay of 1965, "Aspects of Scientific Explanation," Hempel defined an explanation this way. He said it is "an argument to the effect that the phenomenon to be explained was to be expected in virtue of certain explanatory facts."

The mode of explanation then proposed has this general form. First, to qualify as an event that even warrants scientific explanation, the "even" in question must be empirical in principle. This is not to say that science is indifferent, say, to the other side of the moon that can't be seen—let's say, long invisible. Rather, it is to say that the domain of what can be explained scientifically is the domain that includes what is at least in principle subject to observation. A shorthand way of putting the matter is to say that the sciences are empirical disciplines.

Let's take the textbook example of an object released from a height and falling. This is the sort of event that would qualify for scientific explanation. It is an empirical event. We refer to the statement of that which is to be explained as the *explanandum*, and that which provides the explanation as the *explanans*.

In this example, a falling object is the explanandum statement. Now, one way of explaining this is to say that experience teaches us that objects released from a height have always fallen—and so, this instance is a warranted generalization based on past experience.

This, however, is not what would characterize a scientific explanation in Hempel's sense. Rather, we would be inclined to turn to Newton for the right sort of explanation. To wit, all objects attract each other with a force that is proportional to their respective masses and inversely proportional to the distance-squared between them. As both earth and the item we've released are objects, they attract each other. Here, the object must fall just in case Newton's universal law of gravitation is true.

Now in this we have the essential ingredients of Hempel's theory of explanation in science. First, there is an empirical event to be explained—an object falling from a height. Second, there is a universal law specified, which covers events of this sort. In this case, it's the gravitation law. Third, though I didn't mention it, all the conditions relevant to the particular event have been specified or otherwise controlled. For example, the observations are made on earth rather than on the moon; the space within which the object is released is not made turbulent or unstable by other forces, etc. There are these initial commissions, then, that we must specify. With all this in place, we can say that the event and all such events are explained scientifically when they are *logically deducible* from a universal law known to be true. The descent of the object is now understood not merely as something that reliably takes place, but as something that necessarily takes place, just in case the universal law covering it is valid.

The Greek for "law" is *nomos*, and the anglicized adjectival form for lawfulness is *nomological*. Thus, Hempel's theory is called the *deductive nomological* model of explanation. He contrasts this with explanations based on inferences from past occurrences, referring to these as a mode of explanation called *inductive statistical*, or what might be called the *inductive nomological* model, so that you are contrasting the *inductive nomological* with the *deductive nomological*.

Considering this as the very criterion by which to qualify an enterprise as a science, the question naturally arises as to the status of those disciplines that lack universal laws and are, therefore, unable to explain events by deducing them from such laws. Mind you, there are few if any universal laws beyond classical mechanics. In fact, even Newton's laws have undergone challenge as a result of relativity theory. What, then, can be said for much of biology and psychology in the matter of their scientific status, given that neither of those disciplines can explain events by deducing them from universal laws known to be true? Why is that? Because psychology and biology don't have universal laws known to be true.

This is where the *inductive statistical* model comes in. Hempel acknowledged that the most stringent criterion for a full-fledged scientific explanation will be missing from any number of disciplines understood on commonsense grounds to be scientific disciplines. What gives them this "status," even though they are not in possession of universal laws? What gives them that status is their possession of statistically reliable relationships that do permit accurate and reliable prediction. Thus, the very statistical laws are, after all, reliable, and that must indicate that they are grounded in yet-to-be-discovered more fundamental laws. If there weren't more fundamental laws, all you would have would be accidents and chance things.

There is no reason in principle, now, any time you find regularities, to discount the possibility of some ultimate discovery of truly universal laws that would then permit a full-fledged scientific explanation, and, as such regularities are already catalogued in biology, psychology, economics, sociology—well, these disciplines qualify for full scientific membership, joining physics and chemistry where work is also and always in progress. They are less developed than physics, but moving along the same path.

For all its neatness and intuitive appeal, the Hempelian scheme is plagued with problems. To some extent, the very "statistical" nature of reality itself— at least at the quantum level—raises questions as to the adequacy of a model of scientific explanation that calls for absolute and universal laws allowing perfect predictions.

Then, too, the logical structure of Hempelian explanation leaves room for what actually turn out to be nonsensical examples that, nonetheless, would qualify as scientific explanations. Consider this, first suggested by Wesley Salmon:

The explanandum: John is not pregnant.

Initial Conditions: 1. John is male. 2. John takes birth control pills.

Explanans: No man taking birth control pills becomes pregnant.

We see that the event to be explained is, indeed, subsumed under a universal law bounded by these relevant initial conditions. There is nothing in the Hempelian scheme itself that would require us to conclude that John failed to become pregnant because men never become pregnant. Rather, it is the very neutrality of the model that leaves room for the possibility that it was because he took birth control pills, do you see?

A further difficulty with the model is that it seems to permit spurious causal inferences. Consider an example that finds the indicator approaching "empty," and a universal law that declares: "When indicators are on 'empty,' the car stops." The event to be explained is the car stopping. The law in question seems to make this outcome the effect of a meter reading, as if it is the meter that causes the loss of motion. Again, the Hempelian model and its formal features don't rule out things like that.

The attempt to extend this model of explanation to the realm of social phenomena—those attempts produce yet another wave of compelling criticisms. Consider historical phenomena. Hempel is perfectly prepared to apply the model to historical phenomena, but one of Hempel's early critics was the philosopher William Dray, who wrote a very fine work entitled *Explanation in History*, which draws attention to the limitations of Hempelian explanation, at least when it comes to history. First, historical events are non-recurring. They are not like balls rolling down incline planes, or objects dropped from a height. Accordingly, it isn't even clear as to what a "general law" would cover in the realm of history.

Second, what gives an historical event its character and intelligibility are the specific persons, their motives and contexts, etc. There really is no Battle of Waterloo without Napoleon—without Napoleon, actually without events in Europe at that time, without the aims and strategies adopted by particular nameable persons. The Battle of Waterloo cannot be explained except in such terms, and surely not by involving some sort of impersonal law, and what is true in history would be the same where actual persons—with actual, highly individuated needs, judgments, and aspirations—constitute the events to be explained and, indeed, bring about the events to be explained.

What is missing in the Hempelian account of physical events, then, is a place for actual causal powers as being responsible for these events. It isn't because the meter reads empty that stops the car. We need really real, causal powers in any defensible explanatory scheme. What is missing in the Hempelian account of social or psychological events is a place for reasons, motives, and desires, as being responsible for what took place.

It was an objective of the Logical Positivists to rid science of metaphysics, and for some this meant doing away with occult forces, hidden powers, and the like. Nonetheless, it would strain credulity to believe that the lawful, time-ordered sequences in the natural world come about without the participation of just such forces. Gravitation finally refers to some feature of physical reality as a result of which objects behave in predictable ways toward each other. The behavior is not simply reliable, but seemingly necessitated. What is more obvious than the reality of such necessitating powers when we consider space travel, high-speed computers, even the kitchen dishwasher? Such achievements and inventions are based on the laws of science, and it is owing to these very achievements that we are strongly inclined to accept as valid expressions of what "really is the case," just those laws that produce such success. We find in the laws of science the *real* structure of reality, the truth behind the merely cluttered pictures of everyday life. There's a position that we can take in the philosophy of science.

Against that reassuring view, however, several powerful arguments have been directed. The struggle is between groups somewhat ambiguously designated as "realists" and "anti-realists." The former are those who regard the laws of science as reflecting reality as in itself it really is. On this understanding, scientific laws work because they are expressions of how things actually, really are—the laws being the very near of nature. The anti-realist perspective takes such laws to be very useful generalizations, valid within the contexts in which they were developed, but scarcely sufficient as accounts of all that "really is the case."

One of the leading defenders of the anti-realist school is Princeton's Bastian van Fraassen, who made the case for his position most cogently in the 1980 book, *The Scientific Image*. He, too, focuses on the nature of explanation, but he treats it as a highly contextual matter. What counts as a good explanation for van Fraassen is not the logical structure of the argument but the extent to which it answers a "why" question that arises within a given context.

The quality of the explanation, then, is inextricably bound up with the interests and aims of those who have raised the question whether or not the best answer to: "Why is this car stalled?" is rendered in terms of the principles of internal combustion engines or a misunderstanding as to who was supposed to fill the tank is not settled simply by declaring the scientific explanation as "correct." "The car is stalled because Jack was supposed to fill the tank, and he didn't" is a good explanation, and in the circumstances might be far superior to all sorts of statements about internal combustion engines.

In both cases, the usefulness of the concept of "cause" is finally what preserves our commitment to causal explanations. It is a pragmatic criterion that finally will vindicate causal concepts, surely not something seen to be at work in the world. Science does not discover real causes, but it provides accounts in which causal concepts simply make the cognitive part of explaining more useful.

There's another criticism of scientific realism well exemplified in a 1983 book by Nancy Cartwright, with the wonderfully controversial title *How the Laws of Physics Lie*. Her thesis, developed with cogent arguments and highly technical examples and findings, is that the laws of science are really highly idealized accounts of reality. The idealized world in which the laws are unfailing is a world occupied by no one in the real world, physicists included. She puts it this way: "Fundamental laws do not govern objects in reality; they govern only objects in models."

As she notes in her more recent book, a 1999 book called *The Dappled World*, reality in fact is disorderly; it is contextually fluctuating. It's resistant to any set of simple and simplifying laws. Ruled out as not merely impractical and impracticable, but contrary to fact, is the proposal to reduce mental, social, and economic realities to some more basic science. As she says in *The Dappled World*, by way of rejecting such reductive strategies: "Laws hold as a consequence of the repeated successful operation or what, I shall argue, is reasonably thought of as a nomological machine."

The solar system is such a machine, but in this it is an uncommon feature of what is generally a highly "dappled" world. Cartwright rejects all realist conception of laws, but is herself a realist about what she calls "capacities." Given something like a nomological machine, with such stable capacities as are imminent in matter, we are often enough able to record regularities. In her words, the nomological machine contains:

> ...a fixed (enough) arrangement of components, or factors, with stable (enough) capacities that the right sort of stable (enough) environment will, with repeated operation, give rise to the kind of regular behaviour that we represent in our scientific laws.

Cartwright's position is not radically anti-realist—rather, she identifies her target as a scientific "fundamentalism" that leaves insufficient room for reality itself to gain entry. I would take her opposition to fundamentalism as drawn from the same considerations that led William James to reject what he called the *block universe*. The great obstacle to the progress of understanding is complacency. A fundamentalist "scientism" risks developing a hostility, or at least indifference, toward criticism—and, thus, risks depriving itself of its own traditional sources of inspiration.

Now, the realist reply to this line of criticism takes several forms. To begin, few scientists engaged in serious and fundamental work regard their activity as driven by considerations of what might be called "cognitive security." The undertaking is predicated on the assumption that there really is a "reality" out there, and that scientific laws can be derived with which to understand it, predict it, and yes, control it. On yet another plane, the realist presents to the anti-realist not only such achievements as space travel and quantum electrodynamics, but a challenge: What inferences about these achievements lead to the "best explanation" of them?

Now, let me pause for a second and rehearse that. Supposed you wanted to account for the success itself. That is, you have a problem of explanation, here. What is the best explanation for success in attempts to get to the moon? Thus does the realist invoke the concept—an important one—of *inference to the best explanation* as a defense of realism itself. It goes something like this, an all too brief summary: "One, NASA's space program was based on the assumption that the laws of classical physics and the accuracy of available instruments would provide an account of reality."

Second, on this assumption, rockets were built, astronomical calculations were performed, a date was chosen, and a launching took place.

Three, astronauts reached the moon and then returned safely to earth.

Now, what's the best explanation of Three? The best explanation of Three is that the laws accepted in One and implemented in Two capture the fabric of reality as such.

We see in these debates a far less tidy world of science than one that's depicted in schoolroom textbooks. For all its achievements at the technical level, and in India, the theoretical level, science is a human product. It will always bear the mark of the maker on the works. Judgments vary as to the nature of this mark—whether it is indelible, whether it obscures the very reality to be understood and explained. It is to the credit of Thomas Kuhn that these very questions took on something of an urgency after the appearance in 1962 of his book, *The Structure of Scientific Revolutions*. In that work, Kuhn drew attention to the guild-like nature of the scientific community, where membership requires a set of shared beliefs, confidence that one's community has privileged access to the truth. Retaining membership in that community, on Kuhn's understanding, calls for regular rehearsal of what the community has achieved, this in the form of repeated studies of the same sort, often with monotonous repetition. Kuhn referred to this as "normal science," to distinguish it from those radical departures that constitute truly revolutionary changes within science.

As with Nancy Cartwright, Thomas Kuhn expressed concern over the strong impulse to compress and distort reality in such a way as to make it fit into what prevailing modes of inquiry require. He also drew attention to the corporate aversion novel findings—that square peg that refuses to be compressed into the ideological round hole. Kuhn put it this way: "Men whose research is based on shared paradigms are committed to the same rules and standards for scientific practice." His guild-like matter. Commitments of this sort lead most to engage in nothing more elevating than a kind of mop-up activity in which one shows the community that one has mastered the tricks of the trade and can use them to produce conventional copies of the standard fare. The remarkably overlooked feature of the enterprise is that the research guided by such considerations unearths what was really very well known in advance. It is the same set of commitments, the same etiquette, that will dictate which problems are chosen to the extent that they promise fairly ready solutions. You don't take on problems not likely to succeed.

Many have rejected one or another part of Kuhn's critique of science, his attempt to understand science. Karl Popper, the eminent philosopher of science and logician, referred to Kuhn's reliance on the concept of ruling paradigms as "the myth of framework." Popper drew attention to the intuitive, passionate voyages toward discovery characteristic of science, and he rejected the sociological account of what makes problems significant. Of course, Popper himself had made an important contribution to philosophy of science in his critique of *verificationism* and his alternative methodological standard of *falsificationism*. It was something of a maxim in the scientific positivism of the 1930s and 1940s that the meaning of statements was nothing more than the method by which they could be verified, and the further proviso was that those statements that did not lend themselves to empirical modes of verification were literally nonsensical, in that no supporting science-based evidence was available.

On this understanding, statements immune to empirical modes of verification were declared to be meaningless, merely argumentative, but it was Popper who was quick to observe that such a standard would render all the laws of science nonsensical. After all, a scientific law is universal in its reach, meaning that a candidate law would require an infinite number of verifying attempts. As that is impossible, scientific laws would fail the verificationist stricture. He therefore replaced that with falsificationism, making clear that, though a law cannot be verified an infinite number of times, it need only be falsified once or twice to lose its credibility. Falsificationism itself, which is a fixture in science, tells against Kuhn's notion of science as hostile to criticism and challenge.

What is more challenging than a strategy that commits one to find fault at every level, to falsify wherever possible?

At the end of the day, then, a journey to the moon and back looks like something calling for a firmer grasp of reality than can be gained by obedient "normal science," or a science so idealized as to make little contact with what there really is. Getting to the moon and back is largely the work of rockets, once the basic laws and the necessary engineering have been worked out.

The question that survives even so momentous an achievement is whether those laws and that engineering are drawn from a "culture," so to speak, that is to have pride of place in the matter of assessing all of reality. The word itself, *reality*, presupposes a percipient. It is not a Sophist's trick to ask: "Whose reality?" or, "Reality in relation to what?" The aim throughout is to understand the setting of our own lives, that setting being at once physical, social, political, and moral—and it remains to be debated whether ultimate authority in these respects is held by science.

Philosophy of Psychology and Related Confusions
Lecture 53

The very breadth and diversity of phenomena strike many as excuse enough for the unsettled nature of psychology in its attempts at unity and disciplinary coherence.

At least three times in the 20th century, psychology has settled on its subject matter, only to unsettle itself and adopt yet another "reality." The problem should not be attributed to psychology's alleged "youth." Psychological laboratories do not appear that much later than laboratories in other disciplines. Chemistry laboratories appear at universities no earlier than 1830. Non-academic settings for research were numerous, and psychology experiments were performed in them as early as the 18th century.

Psychology is a hybrid science, because its interest ranges over both scientific and humanistic issues. The special subject of philosophical psychology also reflects on the disordered state of the discipline. Attempts to create order and a "system" must be arbitrary but are also necessary, or else there really would be no subject at all.

The starting point presumably is the identification of what psychology is *about*, what its practitioners identify as good reasons for having the discipline, and what other reasonably informed persons would reasonably expect of it. The *Oxford Pocket Dictionary* defines psychology as "the study of the human soul or mind; a treatise on or system of this," a definition that does little to clarify the discipline. A more informing approach would be to examine offered courses and assigned texts in major departments of psychology. These days, the courses and the activities would be highly particularized, focusing on any number of questions that, at best, relate obliquely to what has traditionally been understood to be human mental life.

Aristotle used the term *psyche* in his treatise on the subject to mean the "first principle of living things." What is "psychic" is a complex process, not a thing occupying a place and having some existence outside the creature so animated. Also, this animating principle is expressed in various ways and confers different powers or faculties on different living things.

With the 17th century's scientific achievements, Descartes, then Locke took a more daring approach to these concepts. The two had in common the idea that fundamental questions in philosophy require a systematic treatment of psychological states and processes. Locke and Descartes were virtually *inventing* psychology as an independent field of inquiry, developed via systematic observation. One finds out about mental processes by consulting one's own patterns of thought.

It was not until the 20th century that cogent arguments against the philosophizing of psychology transformed the discipline into what many hoped to be a scientific psychology. The late-19th–century movement toward scientific positivism was influential. In the early 20th century, America's John B. Watson (1878–1958) argued for the abandonment of all who continued to tie psychology to something reachable only by way of introspection. Watson insisted that, for a subject to earn scientific status, its subject matter had to be public, observable, and measurable. For all things psychological, it must be translated into behavioral terms and observations.

The behaviorist movement grew first slowly, then—primarily through the influence of B. F. Skinner—accelerated. By the 1960s, many psychology departments had come to identify themselves as departments of "behavioral science." Behaviorism offered a purely descriptive science of behavior that was to be independent of, and indifferent to, events occurring under the skin. The project of predicting and controlling behavior required no support and accepted no challenge from the biological sciences.

The ultimate question is whether the right approach to understanding psychological processes and phenomena is nomothetic or idiographic.

Given this orientation, it is easy to see just where the resistance and criticism would come from. Psychologists trained in neuropsychology and physiological psychology were aware that behavior depends on the biochemistry and electrophysiology of the nervous system. They were not prepared to abandon the important and long-productive program of research on brain-behavior relationships.

Studies of animal behavior turned up results that were simply uninterpretable in terms of external determinants. In a 1948 article titled "Cognitive Maps in Rats and Men," E. C. Tolman summarized many studies, all pointing to the cognitive nature of problem-solving. These, in conjunction with the long-standing Gestalt theory in psychology, required preservation of the "mental," if only as a way of rendering the results of behavioral studies coherent and intelligible.

The method to which psychology committed itself is loosely described as "experimental," but it carries much more baggage than the word suggests. In most instances, the method of inquiry includes the following main ingredients. First, some response-indicator is identified, drawn from the behavior of the subject and intended to signify the reception of a stimulus or successful performance of a task. The response-indicators are sampled repeatedly, and the resulting dataset subjected to various analyses to determine the validity of the findings. Every effort is made to control stimuli or experimental conditions and to establish the relationship between these and comparably restricted response-indicators.

These methods raise two fundamental questions: To what extent is such an idealized context representative of the actual world and actual life in which the events and processes of interest routinely occur? And do we find in such experiments how persons actually solve problems or comprehend stimuli, or are we merely calling on subjects to respond as if they see the world the way the experimenter would have it seen?

We can highlight the problem of validity by considering a frequently studied phenomenon in psychology—emotion. The emotional aspects of life are profoundly important to behavior and thought. However, attempts to predict and control behavior or model psychological life via examination of the emotions in the context of laboratory research ultimately are useless for real-world, practical purposes.

On top of all this, we must question the aptness of using statistical modes of analysis in the study of complex processes. There are few instances in the developed sciences where the most common psychological experimental model—the *analysis of variance*—is employed. In this model, one would identify the separate influences of several variables on the event or effect of interest. Analysis of variance and comparable statistical analyses may actually describe or identify the effects of these variables on no one in particular within the sample of subjects.

The ultimate question is whether the right approach to understanding psychological processes and phenomena is nomothetic or idiographic. The former—from the Greek *nomos* for "law"—searches for general laws describing trends and regularities in datasets. The latter—from the Greek *idios* for "personal"—is sensitive to the unique and individuated nature of perception, comprehension, and adjustments to the surrounding world. It is often assumed that the nomothetic approach must use large samples to obtain general laws. However, in basic research, a single observation often reveals the general law.

To the extent that the discipline is or aspires to be scientific, another set of questions arises as to the proper model or template, for science itself is not singularly committed in this regard. Being neither a physical science nor a biological science in the strictest sense, psychology has evolved as something of an engineering science. The general approach to problem-solving in engineering is first to reduce the problem to a model, usually including a number of distinct modules. The modules have such properties to encompass both the given function and the means by which that function can be integrated into the performance of the overall system. Following this rationale, psychology attempts to use the laboratory context as a simplified model, with the experimental variables chosen to tap into one or another functional module.

Perhaps the most successful application of this line of thinking can be seen in contemporary cognitive neuroscience. Any cognitive achievement, no matter how complex, is reducible to an ensemble of distinguishable functions. Each function is accomplished by processes and networks in the central nervous system. Manipulation of relevant variables in the controlled conditions of laboratory research is the means by which to put thought and action on a scientific foundation. It does not take too much by way of objective distance to see that the entire undertaking rests on confusions and even mistakes. It is important to understand the difference between an engineering module that actually performs a task and a cognitive event subject to interpretation.

Surprisingly, the leaders of the "cognitive revolution" have been aloof to a fruitful set of possibilities arising from the Wittgensteinian quarter. There is great attention in psychology to language, especially language development, but little to the productive use and constitutive power of language. It is time to step back and re-examine the methods. ∎

Suggested Reading

Flanagan, O. *Consciousness Reconsidered.* Cambridge, MA: MIT Press, 1992.

Fodor, J. *The Modularity of Mind.* Cambridge, MA: MIT Press, 1983.

Foster, J. *The Immaterial Self: A Defence of the Cartesian Dualist Conception of Mind.* London: Routledge, 1996.

Kim, J. *Mind in Physical World.* Cambridge: MIT Press, 1998.

Robinson, D. N. *Philosophy of Psychology.* Columbia University Press, 1982.

Questions to Consider

1. What does a "descriptive science of behavior" leave out?

2. Can any science be "purely" descriptive?

3. Is science the right home for psychology?

Philosophy of Psychology and Related Confusions
Lecture 53—Transcript

Sigmund Koch, the distinguished American psychologist, often complained that psychology was the only scientific discipline that settled on a method before deciding what its subject matter was. Actually, psychology has settled on its subject matter—at least three times in the 20th century—only to unsettle itself and adopt yet another "reality" for its consideration.

The problem should not be attributed to the alleged "youth" of psychology. True, the first academic laboratories devoted to psychological research, at least university laboratories, do not appear until the last quarter of the 19th century, but academic laboratories for research in any science do not appear until the second quarter of the same century—so we can't say that psychology is "young" in that respect.

Of course, much scientific work was accomplished beyond the narrow gates of colleges and universities—much in the ancient world that had no such institutions, but here again, psychology was not neglected. Depending on what one requires of a demonstration for it to qualify as "research," psychological research is at least as venerable as studies conducted by Galen in the second century A.D. and probably by Aristotle in the fourth century B.C. If there is confusion in psychology, then, it is not "youthful" confusion, but rather more a species of habitual confusion made durable by practice.

It has often been observed that psychology is a hybrid science or discipline, this designation attempting to reach the fact that psychology's interests range over both scientific and humanistic issues. The same discipline attempts to provide room for those interested in the pigment chemistry of the human retina, and those who wish to identify just what it is that makes a joke funny.

The very breadth and diversity of phenomena strike many as excuse enough for the unsettled nature of psychology in its attempts at unity and disciplinary coherence. Indeed, but physics has somehow been able to make room for those interested in the red-shift of stars retreating from the Milky Way and those whose subjects of interest come into being and out of existence in less than a billionth of a second. Again, though the range and variety of phenomena offer daunting challenges to those who seek integration and coherence, the challenge is no greater in psychology than in physics, unless, of course, there is something special about the phenomena themselves—not the emerging diversity, but something intrinsic to them.

The special subject of philosophical psychology reflects on the disordered state of this somewhat undisciplined discipline. Attempts to create order and a "system" must always be, to some extent, arbitrary but also necessary, or else there really would be no subject at all. Where, then, to begin?

The starting point presumably is the identification of what psychology is *about*, what its practitioners identify as good reasons for having the discipline, and what other reasonably informed persons would reasonably expect of it.

A dictionary is helpful here, but only in a limited way. How something is defined, after all, is determined not by those who compile dictionaries, but by the uses and meanings of terms in actual practice. Consider the entry in the *Oxford Pocket Dictionary*, which defines psychology this way: "the study of the human soul or mind; treatise on or system of this." In my edition of the *Oxford Pocket Dictionary*, this is followed by the definition of a "ptarmigan" as: "a kind of grouse changing to white in winter." For all the help the little dictionary provides on the matter of psychology, one might just as well have used the definition of a ptarmigan. I don't know that psychology turns white in the winter, but you do get the point.

A more informing approach than the dictionary approach would be to locate the inquirer in major departments of psychology—where things are examined, courses are offered, texts are assigned, research and writing engaging the residents. These days, very few instances would be found of a study of the soul, and nearly as few attempts to develop a treatise or system of the mind. Rather, the courses and the activities would be highly particularized, focusing on any number of questions that, at best, relate only obliquely to what has traditionally been understood to be human mental life. Who's to blame, who is to praise, for this turn of events? A breathless romp through history will put matters in perspective. Well, let's have the breathless romp.

We mustn't fault the dictionary for the word. "Psychology" is rooted in the Greek *psyche*, which was rendered as *anima* in the Latin translators of the Greek, and *anima* is the root not only of the English "animal," but also, and suggestively, of "animated." This also nicely expresses Aristotle's use of *psyche* which, in his treatise on the subject, he defines as the "first principle of living things," the archaezoan.

For Aristotle, then, what is "psychic" is a complex process, not a thing occupying a place and having some existence outside the creature that is thus animated. Additionally, for Aristotle, this animating principle is expressed in various ways and confers different powers or faculties on different kinds of living things. In some, the psychic process is limited chiefly to nutrition and reproduction. In more complex creatures, the power of movement is added. Then, in even more creatures, those that qualify as animals for the first time, the psychic processes include that of the sensation. Aristotle states that this power or faculty virtually defines an entity as "animal." Human life includes all these other processes and one special one in addition—a national power or faculty, permitting deliberation and choices based on deliberation.

In the same ancient Greek world in which Aristotle was composing treatises on psychic functions, the Hippocratic physicians were recording the reliable association between injury to the brain and disturbances to perception, memory, movement, and thought. Here, then, was an early commitment to what might be called a "psychobiological discipline."

The medieval and Scholastic philosophers tended to fall into either Aristotelian or Platonist schools in their own speculations on the nature of what we call "psychological processes." By the 17th century's scientific achievements, a more daring approach to these was taken, first by Descartes and then by Locke. In earlier lectures, I've discussed their approaches and quite different conclusions. Here I would draw attention to what the two held in common: namely, that fundamental questions in philosophy do require a systematic treatment of psychological states and processes. Both Locke and Descartes virtually *invented* psychology as an independent field of inquiry, to be developed by way of systematic observation. Of course, in both of their cases, the observations were introspective. One finds out about mental processes by consulting one's own patterns of thought.

It was not until the 20th century that quite cogent arguments against the philosophizing of psychology succeeded in transforming a philosophical psychology into what many hoped to be a scientific psychology. The late-19th-century movement toward scientific positivism was quite influential here, as was the comparable impatience with all things Hegelian.

In the first quarter of the 20th century, America's John B. Watson (1878–1958) argued for the abandonment even of William James's and John Dewey's renditions, and all who continued to tie psychology to something "mental," or reachable, only by way of introspection. Watson insisted that, for a subject to earn scientific status, its subject matter had to be public, observable, measurable, "out there," and as regards anything that qualifies as psychological, it must be translated into behavioral terms and observations. His opening salvo to this effect appeared as an article in the 1913 *Psychological Review* with the title "Psychology as the Behaviorist Views It." The opening lines leave no doubt as to what is on offer by way of Watson:

> Psychology as the behaviorist views it is a purely objective experimental branch of natural science. Its theoretical goal is the prediction and control of behavior. Introspection forms no essential part of its methods, nor is the scientific value of its data dependent upon the readiness with which they lend themselves to interpretations in terms of consciousness. The behaviorist, in his efforts to get a unitary scheme of animal response, recognizes no dividing line between man and brute.

Thus spoke Watson.

The behaviorist movement grew first slowly, and then—primarily through the influence of B. F. Skinner—in an accelerated way. By the 1960s, many psychology departments had come to identify themselves as departments of "behavioral science." The famous rat lab was now a fixture, most psychologists confident that neither consciousness nor humanity itself presented any barrier to a "purely descriptive" science of behavior.

Three major obstacles continued to support resistance to all this, but we must be clear as to what was included in "all this." A purely descriptive science—as if this adverb could never be correctly used to qualify the adjective—of behavior was to be independent of, and indifferent to, events occurring under the skin. That is to say, the project of predicting and controlling behavior required no support and accepted no challenge from the biological sciences. As Skinner argued, from the perspective of the behavioral scientist, it wouldn't matter if, on examination, the behaving organism were found to have nothing at all inside the body. It could be an "empty organism," but would remain the proper object of study if it continued to behave. Similarly, as this science needed no support and brooked no opposition from physiology, it was under no obligation to address questions arising from allegedly "mental" sources or causes of behavior.

On the behaviorist account, the determinants of behavior were to be found, it was urged, outside the organism, in a reinforcing environment, and not inside, in the form of thoughts and motives.

Given this orientation, it is easy to see just where the resistance and criticism would come from. Psychologists trained in neuropsychology or physiological psychology were all too aware of the utter dependency of behavior on the biochemistry and the electrophysiology of the nervous system. Though supportive of the behaviorist's commitment to an objective science of behavior, then, they were surely not at all prepared to abandon the important and long-productive program of research on brain-behavior relationships. As these were readily observable in the neurology clinic—where introspection has always been a major diagnostic instrument—if you want to know what's bothering the patient, you ask the patient—the theoretical asceticism of the behaviorist seemed as unpromising as it was pretentious.

Then, too, any number of studies of animal behavior turned up results that were simply uninterpretable in terms of external determinants. A most influential and suggestive article by Edward Chance Tolman appeared in the *Psychological Review* in 1948 under the title "Cognitive Maps in Rats and Men." Here, Tolman summarized many of his own studies, all pointing to the cognitive nature of problem-solving. These, in conjunction with long-standing research and theory in Gestalt psychology, required the preservation of the "mental," the cognitive, if only as a way of rendering the results of behavioral studies coherent and intelligible.

Needless to say, as behaviorism strived for hegemony in academic psychology, psychoanalytic theory was still the perspective of choice for the much larger community of psychologists in clinical and counseling psychology.

Offered as a branch of natural science, presumably with family ties to biological and medical sciences, behaviorism just seemed unfaithful to its family members. It provided no significant part or place for the obviously relevant field of genetics. It was stridently anti-theoretical, but with membership in a community of disciplines firmly grounded in theory. It was stridently anti-mental, but then seemed unable either to account for, or to develop, ways of studying behavior that clearly proceeded from some kind of cognitive, internal integration of environmental inputs. Thus did behaviorism give way to the now ruling rubric, cognitive neuroscience, about which I shall have some things to say toward the end of the lecture.

Let me return to Sigmund Koch's witty indictment: Psychology committed itself to a method before it settled on a subject. What is the method? The method is loosely, even disarmingly, described as "experimental," but it carries much more baggage than the word suggests. Rather, in most instances, the method of inquiry includes the following main ingredients.

First, there is the identification of some response-indicator, drawn from the behavioral repertoire of the human or animal "subject," so-called, that is intended to signify the reception of a stimulus or the successful performance of a task. As these response-indicators are sampled repeatedly, the resulting dataset then has to be subjected to various statistical tests and analyses in order to determine whether the main findings stand on firmer ground than mere chance effects. In the usual experimental setting, then, every effort is made to restrict stimuli or experimental conditions to specifiable types, rigorously controlled, in order to establish statistically reliable relationships between these and comparably restricted response indicators. Just picture the rat pressing the bar.

Two fundamental questions arise from the adoption of such methods. First, to what extent is such an idealized context representative of the actual world and actual life in which the events and processes of interest routinely occur?

Second, in so restricting the problem or stimulus sets and the response indicators, is there not a veritable invitation to what William James dubbed the "psychologist's fallacy"? Do we find in such experiments how persons actually solve problems or comprehend stimuli, or are we merely calling on subjects to respond as if they see the world the way the experimenter would have it seen?

To reduce both of these fundamental questions to a word, what is at issue here is the very validity of the experimental method—to the extent that the purpose of the method is to unearth the manner in which the environment is processed, comprehended, and otherwise negotiated by real and different animals, including those who are in the sophomore class.

We can highlight the problem of validity by considering a frequently studied phenomenon in psychology—that of emotion. Surely the emotional aspects of life are profoundly important as sources of behavior and as influences on thought itself. States of love, happiness, contentment, anger, fear, hatred, frustration, affection—the list is long, and the items are often the best predictors of what persons will do, and they provide the best explanations for why they are doing it. Thus, a discipline devoted to the prediction and control of behavior, or to the development of theories and models of psychological life, presumably has every reason to examine the emotions with care and thoroughness.

However, attempts to do this within the context of a laboratory have proven to be unconvincing, hopelessly narrow, and I would have to say, ultimately useless for all real-world, practical purposes. The reasons are obvious, and thus the failure is, to some extent, pardonable.

How does one realistically establish in a laboratory setting intense hatred, undying love, or deep and enduring happiness within a one-hour laboratory session? If mild shock can be used to create anxiety, what intensity would be needed to create a state of dread, or panic, paralyzing fear? Would that be permissible, even if possible?

Moreover, emotionality generally does not come in the form of one emotion at a time. Real-life instances are complex mixtures, shifting in intensity and vividness, subject to sudden alteration, tied in various ways to perceptions and thoughts, often modulated by certain predispositions at once perhaps hereditary and otherwise bequeathed by a life of experiences. Now, if all this militates against laboratory studies of emotion having any broad, valid part to play in our understanding of emotion, then the same reservations must arise when the topic shifts—for instance, thought, motivation, memory, social interaction, etc.

To all this must be added questions as to the aptness of using essentially statistical modes of analysis in the study of complex processes. There are very few instances in the developed sciences, for example, where the most common experimental model in psychology—namely, the *analysis of variance* model—is employed. I refer here to the *analysis of variance* model, which would identify the separate influences of several, or even many, variables on the occurrence of the event or effect of interest. The relative contribution, for example, of age, weight, level of education, and gender on, say, incidence of depression. You do this analysis of variance and comparable statistical modes of analysis; it has been noted, this may actually describe or identify the effects of these variables on no one in particular within the sample of subjects. As there is no family on earth with 2.27 children, so, too, there may be no subject in the experiment to whom the data revealed by this analytical model are applicable or of whom they are in any way descriptive.

To reduce this set of issues to basic terms, the question is whether the right approach to understanding psychological processes and phenomena is—two technical terms coming—nomothetic or ideographic. The former—from the Greek *nomos* for "law"—is an approach that searches for general laws describing trends and regularities in datasets. The latter—from the Greek *idios* for "personal"—is an approach that is sensitive to the unique and individuated nature of perception, comprehension, and adjustments to the surrounding world.

It is important to point out here that there is a common misunderstanding within psychology as to the nature of nomothetic and idiographic approaches. It is often assumed that the nomothetic approach must use large samples in order to obtain general laws, these now applicable to group data, though not always to a given individual within the group.

This, however, is not the case. In basic research in medicine and physiology, as in physics and chemistry, the single observation will often reveal the general law. Consider the Krebs's cycle, which established the manner in which carbohydrates are metabolized. The Krebs's cycle was not discovered by sampling thousands or hundreds of persons as they ate bread. Within psychology itself, the basic laws of visual and auditory information processing, as discovered within the specialty field of psychophysics—these laws are based on experiments in which it would be rare for more than a few subjects to be used. The point worth making here is that the nomothetic approach, and aspiration, are not bound to essentially statistical modes of analysis and may actually be retarded by such modes of analysis. There is all the difference between a method that relies in the mere counting of numerous instances and the actual measurement of any one of them. Counting is not a mode of measurement.

Left aside in all this, however, is whether or not the very search for general laws makes any sense in light of the several aims ordinarily associated with psychology. Presumably, a discipline striving to explain and predict human behavior or human mental life or, more grandly, human life at large, must confront the objections levied against Hempel's model of explanation. As it seems utterly unsuitable in accounting for or explaining historical events, why would there be confidence in its application to any complex psychological phenomenon? Put another way, to the extent that neat and basic "laws" are unearthed in the psychology laboratory, one might ask whether what has been found to be lawful in that case is, in the end, at all relevant to the larger mission of understanding life as lived.

To the extent that the discipline is or aspires to be scientific, yet another set of questions will arise as to the proper model or template, for science itself is not singularly committed in this regard. Modes of measurement, experimentation, theory construction, and theory validation are different in particle physics and classical mechanics, in inorganic chemistry and evolutionary biology. The pairings should be obvious. There would seem to be a more natural tie between psychology and the biological sciences, but the connection here is not an easy one, as will be clearer in the next lecture. Being neither a physical science nor patently a biological science in the strictest sense, then, psychology has evolved, some might say willy-nilly, as something of—I do hesitate to use the term—well, something of a kind of engineering science, but in respects that are surely not faithful to engineering. Let me try to make this important point clear.

The general approach in engineering, when facing the challenge to develop a device or technique to solve a problem, is first to reduce the problem to a model of some sort. The model itself typically includes a number of distinct modules, each having a function necessary to the operation of the system as a whole. Attention is then paid to giving the modules such properties as allow not only the given function, but a means by which that function can be integrated into the performance of the overall system. As a strategy, this approach can point to no less a group of authorities than Newton, Boyle, Galileo, and Descartes in the 17th century, and a whole army of productive and creative disciples ever since.

Following this rationale, psychology in its experimental and theoretical productions attempts to use the laboratory context as a simplified model, with the experimental variables chosen to, as it were, tap into one or another function—one or another functional module necessary for the system to perform as a whole.

Perhaps the most successful, or at least the most obvious, application of this line of thinking is what animates contemporary cognitive neuroscience. The core assumptions are, first, that any cognitive achievement, no matter how complex or context-dependent, is finally reducible to an ensemble of distinguishable functions; second, that each of these functions is accomplished by processes and networks in the central nervous system; and finally, that the manipulation of relevant variables within the controlled conditions of laboratory research will be the means by which to put thought and action on a scientific foundation, and just in case anyone doubts it, we now have functional MRIs indicating not only that there are such modules in the brain, but even which ones are at work.

However, it does not take too much by way of objective distance from such optimism to begin to see that the entire undertaking rests on a set of confusions and even a few mistakes. To begin the critical appraisal, it is important to understand the difference between an engineering model that actually performs, say, a filtering of a class of input signals, and some sort of cognitive event that might be interpreted as if filtering were taking place. When Jack ignores what Jane is saying, we can provide a model of the failure to record the utterance, but it would be hazardous to say that all that is taking place is filtering. To add another box—say one with the label "filter unpleasant inputs"—is a game anyone can play, but surely not one on which the profession of engineering would depend. Jack's filtering is a very active sort of thing.

Apart from this, there is widespread confusion as to what should count as a model of something, and what it is that is finally modeled. Consider the task of getting dirt off the floor. In one instance, Jack sweeps the floor and puts the dirt in a dustbin. In another case, Jack uses a vacuum cleaner. In a third case, a robot is designed that operates the vacuum cleaner, and in another case the robot sweeps the floor. Engineers, analyzing what it takes to get dirt off the floor, may build a number of models before producing the robot. What is modeled here is the process of removing dirt. It would be odd to think that the robot was a model of Jack, and even more odd to think that floor sweeping is a model of vacuum cleaning. As Norbert Wiener, the father of cybernetics, once said decades ago: "The best model of a cat is a cat; preferably, the same cat."

The leaders of the "cognitive revolution" have been aloof to an especially fruitful set of possibilities arising from the Wittgensteinian quarter. There is great attention in psychology to language, especially language development, but very little to the productive use and constitutive power of language. Much of the confusion in psychology, philosophically understood, is based on grammar, a kind of reckless or unattended grammar—one that leads us to believe that we are modeling X, when in fact we are modeling Y, or we may not be modeling anything at all. It is time to step back, re-examine the methods, get clear on just what it is that we are trying to model, and then become clear on whether what we are trying to model can be modeled except through life itself.

Philosophy of Mind, If There Is One
Lecture 54

We claim to be aware of objects in a world external to ourselves, and even to know much about what is in that world. At the most fundamental ontological level, however, the physical objects in the external world are comprised of nothing but matter and energy.

Descartes drew a sharp distinction between himself as a thinking thing—*res cogitans*—and as an extended thing—*res extensa*—drawing criticism from the likes of Thomas Hobbes and Pierre Gassendi. Both would surely have agreed with the broad scientific perspective according to which the physical sciences are "complete." That term refers to the view that nothing in the domain of the "really real" falls outside the realm of the "really physical," of physics. In other words, reality is not composed of two radically different kinds of stuff but of one kind only—the physical.

This position is referred to as *ontological monism* and stands in opposition to *ontological dualism*. For the ontological monist, there is but one kind of furniture in reality. For the ontological dualist, there are two; the dualist adds the mental to the physical. Were the latter position to be correct, it is argued that physics would be "incomplete," because its laws and principles do not account for this other immaterial, non-physical aspect or part of reality.

The ontological monist can retain mentalistic terms and concepts as a form of "folk" psychology. For practical purposes, it may be impossible to conduct normal social and personal lives without this age-old language of mental states and mental events. Donald Davidson dubbed this use of language *anomalous monism*: a recognition both of the validity of ontological monism and the fact that our mentalistic terms and concepts will never be reduced to physical events and processes.

The position one takes on the mind/body problem is likely—either implicitly or explicitly—to inform positions taken on a far wider range of issues within the philosophy of mind. The mere appearance of mentalistic terms and concepts will shape the more general approaches to problems in philosophy of mind.

The problem of *representation* is a central part of the problem of knowledge and an enduring issue in philosophy of mind. At the most fundamental ontological level, our experiences of the external world are complex arrangements of matter and energy. We might ask whether we or a honeybee—whose vision is sensitive to an electromagnetic spectrum to which we are essentially blind—more accurately "represents" the properties of roses and lilies. Thus, the question of representation can be stated: Is our knowledge of objects in the external world direct or mediated?

The problem of *representation* is a central part of the problem of knowledge and an enduring issue in philosophy of mind.

Locke and others emphasized that perceptual properties do not match up with the physical properties that cause them. This account rejects the theory of *direct realism*, which says that we see the actual object, not a "representation" of it. Presumably, any thorough account of the properties of an object will include such causal powers or measures of causal efficacy it possesses. Without attempting to settle the problem, it is sufficient here to ask just how the external world could be "represented." As the concept is generally employed, the real external world is seen or heard or felt *as if* it holds certain properties.

In his 1986 article "What Mary Didn't Know," Frank Jackson suggested that Mary didn't know the experience of color until she saw it, despite a lifetime of learning about the physical properties of light and color perception. Jackson reasoned that if physicalism is true, then to know everything physically the case about something is to know everything. But physicalism is false, because Mary knows everything that is physically the case about light, but she does not know what it is like to see color until she leaves the isolation chamber. One counter-argument is that, in the light of day, Mary does not come to know something about light but about experiences she has when exposed to certain stimuli.

The fact is that vision and sensory experiences in general comprise properties of a distinctly "experiential" quality. Nothing we could know about the physics of roses would translate into a sweet smell, or sensory *qualia*, a term introduced in philosophy by C. I. Lewis in 1929 to refer to such properties as shape, color, or pitch. The qualia of experience capture the "how it appears to us" feature. A common feature of perception is "shape constancy." For instance, a 25-cent coin is round. However, only when it is projected onto the retina in a straight-on plane will it form a circular pattern on the retina. At any other angle, it will be elliptical. But, knowing what the object is, it is invariably seen as round; the roundness thus experienced is a *quale*.

The decisive mark of the mental is consciousness itself, the theater within which qualia are featured. Some regard consciousness as *the* problem in philosophy of mind. We can expect that there is some solution available, at least in principle, possibly from the realm of science. Science is not expected to disprove that we have experiences, thoughts, motives, feelings, and desires. However, it should be able to establish either the causal factors of those mental states or permit the conclusion that these states, long described in mentalistic terms, are actually physical states of the brain.

Epiphenomenalism, a term advanced in the 19th century by Thomas Henry Huxley, offers a solution to the problem of consciousness. Mental states are mere byproducts of the complex operations taking place in the nervous system. Consciousness arises from the operations of the nervous system but has no effect on these operations or on what they lead to. Epiphenomenalism gives renewed vitality to the question of just what consciousness is for or even good for. Though it may seen incredible to think human life could have amassed the same record of achievement without consciousness, it is not *logically* impossible. Credible or not, epiphenomenalism does not do the work required by monistic materialism. To grant that there are bona fide mental states distinguishable from any and all physical states and events is to concede dualism.

A more promising theory is a version of the *identity theory*. The first step in developing such a theory is to acknowledge the wide use of mentalistic terms and seek their reference. Thus, with qualia terms, such as *red* or *melodic*, the question is just what in reality such terms refer to. The answer is this: All such terms refer to states or events in the brain. This does not confer infallibility on the percipient or rule out self-deception. Rather, it puts a dividing line between the epistemic standing of any third-person report and that of any first-person report where qualia are being reported. In its most interesting and most extreme form, this approach gives rise to what is called *eliminative materialism*, which says that science need not worry about explaining the "mental," because there are not minds as such, nor is there anything mental to explain.

To this point, reductionistic strategies by which to get from the mental to the physical have been emphasized. But philosophy of mind offers alternatives to brains and neural events. Any number of animals succeed in negotiating the challenges afforded by the environment with nervous systems radically different from our own. What matters is that a given function is performed in such a manner as to yield adaptive success. For some contemporary philosophers, the soundest approach to problems in philosophy of mind is to translate the mental into a set of functions.

Daniel Dennett recommended that one adopt what he calls the *intentional stance*. Take the position that the actions of any complex system are goal-oriented, based on felt experiences, motives, and feelings. Examine the functional components in virtue of which this sort of evidence is produced. The *functionalist* account may well assume "mentality" or simply put it on "hold."

One version of functionalism that attracts wide attention is found in such specialized fields as artificial intelligence and expert systems. IBM's chess-playing computer defeated Kasparov, one of the greatest chess masters of the age, in 1997. What is philosophically interesting about such outcomes is not that computers can outperform human beings, but that the performance suggests that the best understanding of our own mental operations is computational.

There are sound philosophical and conceptual reasons for caution here. It's scarcely clear that a computer can "play" chess or can "play" any game at all or can, in any sense, have the cultural resources with which to recognize an activity as a game. But imagine if, in some defensible respects, computers were intelligent, had expert judgment, and could see the world even more clearly than their inventors. None of the issues in philosophy of mind would be settled, because now the same issues would arise as we discussed the mental life of computers! ■

Suggested Reading

Robinson, D. N. *Philosophy of Psychology*. Columbia University Press, 1982.

Questions to Consider

1. What is anomalous about anomalous monism?

2. Is epiphenomenalism finally a dualism after all?

3. If all knowledge is mediated and representational, what epistemological standard was employed to establish as much?

Philosophy of Mind, If There Is One
Lecture 54—Transcript

Descartes's famous distinction between himself as a thinking thing—a *res cogitans*—and as an extended thing—a *res extensa*—was controversial in its own day, arousing cogent criticism from both Thomas Hobbes and Pierre Gassendi. Although neither of them would have used the expression, both would surely have agreed with the broad scientific perspective according to which the physical sciences are "complete." As a way into this lecture on philosophy of mind, I should like to stay for a moment with the notion of the completeness of physics.

The "completeness" envisaged by the phrase refers not to confidence that all the problems in physics will be solved or that physics will ever be able to explain everything coming under the heading of the "really real." Rather, it is the view that nothing in the domain of the "really real" falls outside the realm of the "really physical," of physics. Reality is not composed of two radically different kinds of "stuff" but of one kind only—and that is physical stuff. No doubt our conception of physicality will undergo revision; it has in the past. We may always be in error or incomplete in our catalogue of the physical. Nonetheless, the correct catalogue will never contain non-physical entries. Metaphysically speaking, this position is referred to as *ontological monism* and stands in opposition to *ontological dualism*. For the ontological monist, there is but one kind of furniture in reality. For the ontological dualist, there are two. What the dualist adds to the physical is, alas, the mental, understood more or less as the Cartesian *res cogitans*. Were the latter position to be correct, it is argued that physics would be "incomplete," in that the laws and principles of physics, confined as they are to matter and energy, would leave unaccounted for this other immaterial, non-physical aspect or part of the really existent.

It should be noted that the ontological monist need not reject or forbid the use of mentalistic terms and concepts. These may be retained as a convenient form of "folk" psychology. After all, long after we discovered that lightning is actually an electrical discharge, we continued to speak of lightning as we still do. Indeed, many persons who speak of lightning may be unaware of the fact that the event so named just is an electrical discharge. For all practical purposes, it may prove to be simply impossible to get on with the business of social and personal life without the age-old language of mental states and mental events, even as the scientific case against their reality becomes overwhelming.

To use the phrase advanced by Donald Davidson, we may well have to settle for an *anomalous monism*: a recognition of the validity of ontological monism, but also the recognition that our mentalistic terms and concepts will never be reduced to physical events and processes.

Still, that there are or may be discursive or social justifications for using a certain set of terms does not establish an ontological justification for assuming the reality of what such terms refer to. There may be good conversational or folk reasons to refer to "Lady Luck" or "Santa Claus," but this is distinct from the question as to whether either exists.

Although the mind/body problem is but one of a number of interesting issues, the position one takes on that problem, either implicitly or explicitly, is likely to inform positions taken on a far wider range of issues within the philosophy of mind. Moreover, whether the form of dualism at work in addressing these issues is fundamental and ontological or merely by way of figures of speech, the very appearance of mentalistic terms and concepts will shape the more general approaches to problems in the philosophy of mind.

We might best begin with the problem of *representation*, which is at once a central part of the problem of knowledge and an enduring issue within philosophy of mind.

Now, we claim to be aware of objects in a world external to ourselves, and even to know much about what is in that world. At the most fundamental ontological level, however, the physical objects in the external world are comprised of nothing but matter and energy. This is as true of stars and planets as it is of roses and rabbits. The differences among such items are understood to arise from different ways in which the material and physical elements combine. What we experience in the external world are, therefore, complex arrangements of matter and energy, only some of the ingredients directly accessible to perception.

If, for example, we test the chemical pigments in the visual system of the honeybee, we discover that the greatest response is to energy in the ultraviolet region of the electromagnetic spectrum, which is a region in which our own visual systems are essentially blind. We may ask, then, whether we or the bee more accurately or faithfully "represents" the properties of roses and lilies. Even to ask the question is to assume that something in the external world is represented, which is different from its being seen straightaway. Thus, does the problem of representation become the question of representation? Is our knowledge of objects in the external world direct or mediated?

As noted in earlier lectures, Locke and many other philosophers made much of the fact, or seeming fact, that perceptual properties do not match up with the physical properties that cause them. To see a flower as blue is not to see something in the corpuscular or atomic composition of flowers that is itself blue. Rather, whatever it is—let's say electromagnetic radiation in the short wavelength end of the spectrum—whatever gives rise to the experience blue is a physical property that is not itself blue. Instead, "blue" is our mode of representing that property.

Rejected on this account is the theory of *direct realism*, according to which what we see is, for example, a blue flower and not a "representation" of a blue flower. The defender of direct realism I have discussed in these lectures, Thomas Reid, is not persuaded that color as such can't be included in the composite structure of the object seen as blue. Why is that? Presumably, any thorough account of the properties of an object will include such causal powers or measures of causal efficacy that the object possesses. A thorough account of the properties of a billiard ball, then, will include its smoothness and sphericity, though none of the constituent molecules is smooth or spherical. More than this, the account will include the effect the motion of the ball will have on another ball with which it makes contact. By the same token, a complete account of the properties of the flower will include its reliable effect on the visual system of normal trichromats. In a word, one of the properties surely will be "is seen as blue under proper illumination."

Without attempting to settle the problem, it is sufficient here to ask just how the external world could be "represented," just in case it is represented. As the concept is generally employed, we are to understand that the real external world is seen or heard or felt *as if* it were blue or melodic or smooth.

If, however, this is the result of some inventive process by which physical impingements are translated to experiences of different qualities, there would seem to be some version of dualism lurking in the wings. After all, photocells are produced that react differentially to different wavelengths of light. What we see as color—and respond to accordingly—need not be seen as a color at all. Evolution could achieve the same adaptive ends by forging ever more sensitive photocells, which report nothing more than patterns of radiation.

A most suggestive approach to this issue was taken by Frank Jackson in his 1986 article, "What Mary Didn't Know," which appeared in *The Journal of Philosophy*. Although Jackson has retreated from his conclusions in that essay, I would be strongly inclined to support the conclusions. Here's what Mary didn't know: Even as over the course of a lifetime she learned everything about light, color, wavelengths, optics, retinas, photopigments, lenses, optic nerves, brains, painters, and decorators—a lifetime, that is, with books and words, all presented in black and white books read in a black and white world in which she was kept from the time of her birth. There is nothing pertaining to the physics and the physiology of light and vision Mary does not know. Again, what is it that Mary didn't know? Well, until she actually stepped out of the confinement and entered a wide sunlit world, she didn't know what the experience of color was.

Jackson's reasoning in this article was straightforward: If physicalism is true, then to know everything that is physically the case about something is to know everything. Mary does know everything that is physically the case about light, but she does not know what it is like to see red until she leaves the isolation chamber. Therefore, physicalism is false.

Obviously, one counter-argument to this is that what Mary comes to know in the light of day is not something about light, but about experiences she has when exposed to certain stimuli. Suppose one is exposed to a high-intensity picture of a bright yellow lemon. After several minutes of such exposure, the lemon is no longer projected onto the white screen, but the observer is required to continue to look at the screen. The reliable effect of this will be a vivid blue after-image, a blue lemon. Jackson's thesis may be challenged by noting that the experienced after-image is not a fact about lemons, but a fact about vision.

Then, however, what is the fact about vision or about sensory experiences at large? The fact is that such experiences are comprised of properties of a distinctly—shall I say? —"experiential" quality. The rose as rose had no odor at all, but smells sweet to creatures of a certain kind. Nothing we could know about the physics of roses would translate into a sweet smell, into what generally are called *qualia*.

The term itself *qualia* is the plural of the Latin *quale*, and was introduced in philosophy by C. I. Lewis in 1929 to refer to such properties as the roundness of an object, or its color or loudness, or pitch or sound. In general, the qualia of experience captures the "how it appears to us" feature. There may be close correspondence between qualia and the physical objects that are associated with them, but, whereas we are often mistaken in our estimations of the physical properties, we are not mistaken in our estimations of qualia, for these are not estimations at all but experiences as such. Let me illustrate the point with a common feature of perception, what is called "shape constancy."

A 25-cent coin is round. However, only when it is projected onto the retina in a plane that is absolutely normal to the plane of regard will it form a circular pattern on the retina. At any other angle of regard, the actual projection will be elliptical. Nonetheless, knowing what the object is, it is invariably seen as round—not just reported as if it were round, but seen as round. The roundness thus experienced is a *quale*, and while the observer's report of the shape of the object as projected on the eye is subject to error and illusory effects, the observer's report of what is being experienced is not corrigible. It is not correctable. That is, it always makes sense to say: "What you say are the properties of the object is incorrect," but it makes little sense to say: "You are mistaken in what you say you are experiencing." On this and other grounds, it seems that qualia have an ontological standing of their own, independent of the physical objects and events that they are associated with. To this extent, qualia seem to be drawn from a domain different from the domain of purely physical entities.

The decisive mark of the mental, of course, is consciousness itself, which is the theater within which qualia are featured. Some regard consciousness as *the* problem in philosophy of mind, and it is instructive to see why. If we regard philosophical problems of any sort as something other than verbal quibbles, we have the right to expect that there is some solution available, at least in principle, somewhere down the road. In the matter of mental phenomena, many have thought that the solutions would come from that trusted and productive quarter, science. The expectation is not that science will disprove that we have experiences, thoughts, motives, feelings, and desires, for this would be silly. Rather, science would establish either the necessary and sufficient causal factors in virtue of which mental states come about, or it would permit the conclusion that these states, long described in mentalistic terms, are, in fact, physical states of the body, and especially the brain. The first of these expectations labors under the somewhat confusing heading of *epiphenomenalism*. The second is a version of what is called the mind-brain identity thesis. Consciousness is a challenge to both.

Epiphenomenalism, the term advanced in the 19th century by Thomas Henry Huxley, is a solution to the problem of consciousness or, more generally, of mental states predicated on the thesis that such states are mere byproducts of the complex operations taking place within the nervous system. A crude analogy is the squeaking sound made by the wheels of a horse-drawn carriage. The sounds are caused by the friction of wheels against their mounting, but the sounds have no effect whatever on the movement of the wheels or the destination of the carriage. So, too, consciousness arises from the operations of the nervous system but has no effect either on these operations or on what they lead to. It's rather a kind of sideshow, an ontological dangler, of sorts, so to speak, but nothing that can get in the way of the causal laws that science discovers.

Epiphenomenalism gives renewed vitality to the question of just what consciousness is, what it's for, or what it is even good for. Surely any number of imaginable devices could be constructed to solve the problems faced in daily life, to record and report events in the world, to retain in memory a record of past successes and failures, to adjust behavior based on this record, and overall, to accomplish all of this without consciousness. Though it may seem incredible to think human life could have amassed the same record of achievement without consciousness, it is not *logically* impossible. Indeed, each of the achievements could have been brought about by placing stimulating electrodes in an indefinitely large number of sites in the brain and, through the proper sequence of stimulations, had the unconscious body—a humanoid sort of thing—build a house, paint a portrait, and sign a treaty.

We can think of epiphenomenalism in still another way. As a thought-experiment, consider being able to create a clone of oneself—such that one is able to reflect, remember, and comment on all the actions performed by the original, even as the original engages in various activities. The difference between the clone and the original is that only the clone has retained consciousness. As a perfect physical replica of your original self, you not only do what the original is doing, but you are conscious of it. The original is doing the same things, even speaking about the activities just as you do, but is not conscious of any of this. On what basis would it be apt to say that your consciousness was causally necessary for you to engage in such activities in light of the fact that the same actions are proceeding at the same time from a being lacking consciousness?

Whether or not epiphenomenalism is credible as an account of the role of consciousness, or the lack thereof, it surely does not do the work required by monistic materialism. To grant that there are bona fide mental states that are distinguishable from any and all physical states and events is to grant dualism, and that's the end of it. As for the details, one then has every right to ask just how in the din of neurophysiological clutter and clatter something pops out that is, lo and behold, consciousness. This would seem to be more miraculous than a Gothic cathedral being built by a group of zombies. What, after all, would we call an entity that is seemingly purposive in its behavior, like us in so many ways, but stripped of consciousness? Well, we would call such an entity a zombie.

There is something else that is interesting about zombies—at least the zombies featured in philosophy of mind. By stipulation, they can do all that we do, even in the way we do it, though without benefit of consciousness or qualia. To the extent that that is the case, and to the extent that a complete physicalistic account of everything that is the case with zombies is possible, then a complete physicalistic account is possible for everything human beings do come about. As human beings also are conscious and experience qualia, the success of science in the matter of zombies carries no implications as to the success of science in the matter of consciousness.

Let's put it this way. If science can explain everything about zombies, and zombies don't have consciousness, and we do have consciousness, the ability to explain everything about zombies doesn't extend to us, because we have consciousness.

Let me put this less awkwardly: The feasibility of attempts to reduce the mental to the physical is based on the prospect of science accounting in purely physical terms for the various psychological processes and functions at work in creatures engaged in complex, goal-directed behavior. From this behavior, inferences are drawn as to patterns of motivation, states of emotion and need, etc. However, a complete account of all this in the case of zombies shows nothing different from a comparably complete account of all this in those who are conscious of these very aims, states, and experiences. In that case, the scientific account fails in the reductive mission. It has not "reduced" the mental, for it hasn't even found it.

By far, the more promising theory is one or another version of the *identity theory*. The first step in developing such a theory is to acknowledge the widespread use of mentalistic terms and then seek their reference. Thus, with qualia terms, such as *red*, *toothache*, or *melodic*, the question is just what in reality such terms refer to. And the answer is this: All such terms refer to states or events in the brain. It is not that such states or events cause the qualia; it's that the qualia just are these events. Thus, if, when I say I am seeing a yellow tulip in the garden, I am referring to anything at all, then what I'm referring to is a congeries of actions in my sensory apparatus and brain. On this understanding, "pain" statements are ultimately about C-fiber events, not mental events.

Needless to say, we can always be mistaken about statements regarding C-fiber activity, but percipients are not mistaken about—or at least not provably mistaken—when reporting their pains. The epistemic standing of the percipient in this regard is unchallengeable, then, which is not the case with anyone reporting something about events in the nervous system. This does not confer infallibility on the percipient, nor does it rule out self-deception. Rather, it does put a dividing line between the epistemic standing of any third-person report and that of any first-person report where what is being reported are qualia. I can be wrong about what my brain is doing, but not about whether or not I smell something.

In its most interesting and most extreme form, this identity theory approach to the reduction of the mental to the physical gives rise to what is called *eliminative materialism*. Science need not worry about explaining the "mental," for there are not minds as such to be explained, nor is there anything mental as such to explain. The camel's nose may be said to have poked into this tent in 1949 with the appearance of Gilbert Ryle's *The Concept of Mind*, but it was surely not Ryle's intention to lay the foundation for eliminative materialism. Rather, Ryle set out to establish the odd and quirky notions that arise from Cartesian conceptions of a distinct mental world to which only the percipient has access—a world in which events are projected onto a private screen and viewed by something called a mind. It was not Ryle's aim to promote skepticism about the reality of experience, but skepticism about theories that would account for that reality in terms of what he called "the ghost in the machine." Ryle, in a word, set out to expose certain linguistic sources of confusion, not to challenge the ontological status of qualia.

To this point, emphasis has been placed on reductionistic strategies by which to get from the mental to the physical via mind-brain relations or mind-brain identities, but in philosophy of mind, there are alternatives to brains and neural events as such, for it is clear that any number of animals succeed preeminently in negotiating the challenges afforded by the environment—but they do so with nervous systems radically different from our own. What matters is that a given function is performed in such a manner as to yield adaptive success. What matters not at all is the precise physical means by which the function is performed. If the task is arithmetic, then, and only arithmetic, then a simple computer and a grade-school child will achieve success with apparatus having nothing in common; one has a circuit board within which algorithms have been programmed; the other has an evolved brain comprised chiefly of fat, protein, and water.

For some contemporary philosophers, the soundest approach to problems in philosophy of mind is to translate the mental into a set of functions and establish the number and interactions of such functions sufficient to produce the outcomes or outputs that match up with the sort of evidence we do use in assuming others have minds and mental states. Daniel Dennett has recommended that one adopt what he calls the *intentional stance*: Take the position, in examining the behavior of any complex system, that its actions are goal-directed—based on felt experiences, motives, feelings, etc. Examine further the functional components in virtue of which this sort of evidence is produced. So, too, in the human case, and in both cases, the best account is just a *functionalist* account that may well assume "mentality" or simply put it on "hold."

One wonders what the nature is of a constructed device as makes assumptions and puts others on hold, and knows it's doing so. I mean, how is Dennett doing what Dennett is doing?

In any case, one version of functionalism that attracts wide attention is found in such specialized fields as artificial intelligence and expert systems. The chess world gasped audibly in the spring of 1997 when Kasparov, one of the greatest chess masters of the age, was actually defeated by IBM's chess-playing computer, Deep Blue. What is philosophically interesting about such outcomes is not that computers can outperform human beings; adding machines do as much all day long. Rather, the performance itself suggests that the best understanding of our own mental operations is computational.

The debts to Alan Turing here are obvious, and the debts seem to increase in value as computational approaches to problems move from games like chess to such vitally important areas as medical diagnosis, national defense, and economical models and their moment-to-moment predictions. If a properly programmed computer with a broad database offers expert diagnosis with success rates vastly superior to what is accomplished by the general practitioner, might it not be the case that the leading experts are "expert" in just these computational ways?

There are sound philosophical and conceptual reasons for caution here. It's scarcely clear that a computer, as such, can "play" chess or can "play" any game at all or can, in any sense, have the cultural resources with which to recognize an activity as a game. The occasional dose of Wittgensteinian remonstrance is often an effective remedy for metaphorical excess in these domains. But imagine if, in some defensible respects, computers were intelligent, had expert judgment, and could see the world even more clearly than their inventors.

Ah, none of the issues in philosophy of mind would be settled, for now the same issues would arise as we discussed the mental life of computers—so that here's the paradoxical situation. We can make computational devices with such great power and agility that in all of the respects in which we regard ourselves as mental, they seem to be indistinguishable from us. If we happen to succeed in this venture, then, we will sit back, engaged in the philosophy of mind, and have the same sort of questions regarding how it is now that these devices can do all of these mental things.

It looks to me as though the mental is going to be around for quite awhile, when it rises to a level somewhat higher than mere opinion and gets something rather deeper than mere folkways, but this is a book writing itself, and there is more to come.

What Makes a Problem "Moral"
Lecture 55

Insofar as statements of value are significant, they are ordinary "scientific" statements, and insofar as they are not scientific, they are not in the literal sense significant, but are simply expressions of emotion, which are neither true nor false.—A. J. Ayer

In philosophy, as in life, there are moments when one cannot be sure whether the claims on conscience are a matter of custom, a dictate of reason, an expression of sincere feeling, or even a matter of taste. Both philosophy and daily life present problems when we attempt to develop a rigid scheme of classification for infractions. Everyone is prepared to classify a given act as morally permissible or morally wrong, but we have difficulty making clear just what in the act—or in the judgment of the act—provides the distinguishing mark of the "moral." The difficulty lies in the subjective nature of morals. What is ruled out in one culture is fashionable in another. What is a crime under one set of laws is an act of heroism a few miles down the road.

Slavery offers an example. The majority of citizens in Western democracies would declare slavery to be morally wrong. Nonetheless, the institution of slavery was a fixture during all of Western civilization until relatively recently and is still practiced in the non-Western world. In many instances, those who bought and sold slaves declared the practice to be immoral but essential to the attainment of some allegedly higher good. But is an immoral act justified if it leads to a greater good? And if so, is it still immoral, or might it be considered not only permitted but *obligatory*?

Philosophy has hosted diverse perspectives on morality, among whose subtle differences several distinct patterns have emerged. In one, the classification of actions in moral terms is based on rational principles, applicable across the board and independent of cultural values or merely personal inclinations. Moral precepts can be shown to be valid and binding through a process of rational analysis.

David Hume, in the tradition of British sentimentalists, suggested that morality is based on human emotions, that virtue is what brings us pleasure, and that vice is what brings us pain. In this, Hume reaches something found also in rationalist Thomas Aquinas's moral theory, according to which if our nature were different, our duties would be different. Whatever has us judging actions and events in moral terms is universally distributed in the human community. If there is some sort of moral "reality," it must be found empirically, its character determined by our empirical resources.

Moral estimations of "right" and "wrong" are not in the external world but in the sentiments of the observer. For a 20th-century perspective, A. J. Ayer suggests that moral concepts are pseudo-concepts; they cannot be plumbed for meaning as can terms referring to actual objects. In the closing quarter of the 20th century, there have been further refinements and qualifications. For instance, Gilbert Harman states the case economically when he argues that no descriptive statement of fact entails a moral statement. What is common across all these renderings is an opposition to the thesis that there are real moral properties to which we can have either experiential or rational access.

Over and against considerations of desire or sentiment, Kant's moral theory ties good will to a willing and faithful allegiance to, and reverence for, law.

For all the support this tradition has gained in recent decades, it is clearly at variance with still other commonsense notions about morality. More often than not, the dictates of morality require avoidance of actions that are otherwise pleasurable or performance of actions that are, in and of themselves, highly odious. In all, then, there seems to be something about moral imperatives not included in the catalogue of pleasure, pain, or even utility.

Such arguments seem to leave little room for a distinction between what is morally right and what we choose on the basis of taste. If it is just an accident of evolution that we have a nearly universal set of emotions or sentiments, then the morality arising from these is itself an accident of evolution. Our current morality, then, could be replaced by one radically different if our evolutionary emotional makeup were to change in future generations. Evolutionary theory has already been invoked to account for altruism and other seemingly ethical dispositions. The same rationale must lead to moral skepticism. If the entirety of moral discourse and moral judgment is reducible to evolutionary pressures and utility-maximizing behavior, we must reject some standard of morality existing outside a given point in evolution and a given species evolving.

Also problematical within this sentimentalist tradition in moral philosophy is its failure to allow for any kind of moral disagreement. About a century ago, G. E. Moore argued that two individuals, upon consulting their own feelings to judge a course of action, could arrive at different conclusions as to whether course of action X or Y was preferable. Neither person can judge whether the other's sense of "more wrong" and "less wrong" is better. Without the ability to argue the different points of view, the two individuals cannot refer to those sentiments that, according to Hume, are universally distributed in the community of human beings.

We might find it more profitable to avoid notions of internal sentiment and consider the expression of sentiments in judgments of utility. Hume emphasized considerations of utility in marking out moral boundaries. His disciple, John Stuart Mill, developed *utilitarianism* into a full-fledged ethical system. But the very concept of utility leaves the door nearly wide open to all of the traditional moral theories. We must identify for whom, for what, and under what conditions a course of action is "useful." It does not help to suggest that each person answer these questions individually, because no one has the right to impose standards of utility on another.

The frequency with which utilitarian factors match up with ordinary understandings of moral obligation would seem to make the thesis something of a happy accident from a moral point of view. It becomes a serious contender, however, when the concepts of happiness and utility begin to take seriously what is generally regarded as Aristotle's sense of *eudaimonia*.

In his 1788 *Critique of Practical Reason*, Kant presents an entirely different conception of morality. Over and against considerations of desire or sentiment, Kant's moral theory ties good will to a willing and faithful allegiance to, and reverence for, law. The law in question is not statutory or legislative but the moral law within each person. It is applicable in all contexts, not subject to prevailing standards, local conditions, or situational nuances.

Kant suggests that the moral law is a categorical imperative, an imperative that applies *come what may.* Kant expresses the categorical imperative in several ways, one of them forbidding the use of another moral being merely as a tool, but always and only as an end in himself. Kant's moral philosophy bases morality on reason and, thus, reserves the moral domain to creatures who are rational. This still leaves open the problem of moral relativism, in that human rationality routinely leads to different conclusions on matters of moral consequence.

To gain greater clarity, we might consider the realist–anti-realist positions. The realist takes the laws of science as *really* operating in the world, not as shorthand for perceptual regularities or abstractions based on an idealized world that has never been. The anti-realist regards the laws as having great usefulness to aid our predictions and descriptions, but as tools of investigation, not as discoveries about reality itself.

Just as the scientific realist regards the properties of the physical world to be mind-independent, so, too, does the moral realist regard the moral properties of reality to be independent of human reason, passion, or perception. The moral realist—at least a radical one—is prepared to argue that the cosmos itself includes relational features and requirements constitutive of a moral order. Human perception and judgment might pick this up faintly and incompletely, though progressively. If beauty has a comparable independence, a set of properties waiting for the prepared mind to recognize them, then perhaps Socrates was on the right track after all in contending that truth, beauty, and justice were not only real but, finally, the same. ■

Suggested Reading

Hare, R. M. *Moral Thinking.* Oxford, 1981.

Mackie, J. L. *Ethics: Inventing Right and Wrong.* Penguin, 1977.

Robinson, D. N. *Praise and Blame: Moral Realism and Its Application.* Princeton, 2002.

Questions to Consider

1. What is a "moral" sentiment?

2. Is there any fact that could entail a moral "ought"?

3. How does Kant's conception of a "duty to the law" work when the law itself is immoral?

What Makes a Problem "Moral"
Lecture 55—Transcript

In philosophy, as in life, there are those Hamletian moments when one cannot be sure whether the claims on conscience are a matter of custom, a dictate of reason, an expression of sincere feeling, or even a matter of taste.

There seems to be little dispute but that the taking of non-threatening life is wrong, that telling false tales about another is also wrong, as is adding 5 to 3 and getting 11, not to mention letting a door close in someone's face, failing to give aid to persons in distress, painting one's house in colors likely and even intended to offend the entire community, shouting vulgar statements in the middle of a wedding ceremony, and putting a jacket that says "dry clean only" in the washing machine. It seems counterintuitive to say not only that all such actions are wrong, but that they are wrong in the same sense of "wrong." Some seem to reach the level we reserve for moral wrongs, whereas others are better described either as mistakes or as failures of etiquette, or as imprudent.

Yet, when we attempt to develop a rigid scheme of classification so that we know under which headings to place one or another infraction, then again, both philosophy and daily life present problems. Everyone is prepared to classify a given act as either morally permissible or morally wrong, but we soon have difficulty making clear just what in the act—or in the judgment of the act—provides the distinguishing mark of the "moral."

The difficulty seems to be based on the hopelessly subjective nature of morals. What is ruled out in one culture is fashionable in another. What is a crime in one historical era or under one set of laws is an act of heroism a few miles down the road. Confusion abounds owing to the subjectivity of morals, for were moral properties objective, there would be widespread agreement. So it would seem.

Consider the example of slavery. Citizens in all the Western democracies would, by very substantial majorities, declare slavery to be morally wrong. Nonetheless, the institution of slavery was not only a fixture during all of

Western civilization until relatively recently, but is still practiced in the non-Western world.

Surely the ancient Greek world—which developed the philosophical foundations of moral thought itself—did not lack the intelligence or the sentiments that would lead any decent person to regard enslaving others as wrong. Surely Thomas Jefferson and George Washington, both of whom owned slaves, were not deficient in whatever faculties or powers are required to weigh the moral weight of a practice. In many instances, those engaged in the practice of buying and selling slaves declared the practice to be immoral but so essential to the attainment of some other allegedly higher good as to be justified. Is it the case, though, that an immoral act is somehow justified if it leads to a greater good, and if it is justified thereby, are we still permitted to call it "immoral"? Indeed, if actions of a certain kind are reasonably expected to lead to a greater good, are they not for that reason not only permitted but *obligatory*?

Suppose, for example, that you have control over which of two tracks an unstoppable railway car will shift to, one leading to the certain death of three persons, the other to the certain death of 10, and you have no choice but these two alternatives. Regrettably, most will state that the choice costing the fewest lives is the morally right one. Suppose, further, however, that the group of 10 includes one of your closest friends, and that's the reason you chose this alternative.

Does the act become morally tainted in virtue of the fact that it was based on what finally was a personal interest? Is not moral rectitude itself a "personal" interest? Let's stay with this same example but modify the options. Let's say that the runaway train, through no fault of yours, is headed toward the group of 10. You are able to act in such a way as to divert it, but with the certain knowledge that your action will cost the life of an innocent person. Were you to do nothing, your inaction would result in death, but if you do act, there will be a death directly caused by you. How should the moral scales move in cases of this sort?

If the field of moral philosophy remains cluttered, it is not for want of strenuous attempts to bring it to a state of order and reasonableness. In this noble aspiration, philosophy has hosted a diversity of perspectives, but amidst the variety and the subtle differences among them, several distinct patterns have emerged. In one of these, the moral terrain is mapped by our rational resources such that the classification of actions in moral terms is based on rational principles, presumably applicable across the full range of possible events and independent of cultural values or merely personal inclinations. To commit a moral offense, on this understanding, is to violate a moral precept, and the precept itself can be shown to be valid and binding through a process of rational analysis.

Against this is the tradition so eloquently and influentially defended by David Hume, and best summarized by his own words as they appear in his *An Enquiry Concerning the Principles of Morals*:

> The final sentence, it is probable, which pronounces characters and actions amiable or odious, praise-worthy or blame-worthy; that which stamps on them the mark of honour or infamy, approbation or censure; that which renders morality an active principle and constitutes virtue our happiness and vice our misery; it is probable, I say, that this final sentence depends on some internal sense or feeling, which nature has made universal in the whole species.

The tradition behind this statement of Hume's is that of what I discussed in an earlier lecture, the theory of "moral" sentiments whose advocates are grouped under the heading "British sentimentalists." The term does not mean to imply that they were sentimental, as we now would use the word, but committed to the view that our moral judgments originate in a natural sense we have, or sentiment we have, innate and universal. It should be noted that this passage from Hume also reaches something found also in Thomas Aquinas's moral theory, according to which if our nature were different, our duties would be different. For all the significant differences between a moral rationalist such as Thomas Aquinas, then, and a moral sentimentalist such as Hume, there is agreement on this much: that whatever it is that finally has us judging actions and events in moral terms, it is, for all practical purposes, universally distributed in the human community.

What confers this universality—if there is such universality—is what many moral theorists take to be the universality of the very ends or purposes of our actions. Aristotle concluded that the otherwise infinite regress arising from the "why" question regarding our actions is avoided by establishing that it is *eudaimonia* that is the ultimate goal or end toward which all actions proceed. It is the "that for the sake of which" we do all the other things. As I have noted, the common translation of *eudaimonia* is "happiness," so the theory boils down to the claim that the ultimate goal of our actions is the securing of happiness.

Needless to say, on Aristotle's understanding, not everything that is desired is desirable, and there are some counterfeit or degraded forms of pleasure and happiness that are in fact inimical to *eudaimonia*. Thus, the better or truer translation, if Aristotle's sense of the term is to be preserved in translation, is, as I have noticed, *eudaimonia* as "flourishing." Our actions have as their ultimate end the most flourishing form of those powers and faculties we have, in virtue of which we are the kinds of beings we are. The ultimate goal is that of perfecting ourselves as rational beings, and it is this perfectionist ideal then reflected in our political and social lives. Pleasure, as such, then, is a neutral concept, neither "right" nor "wrong." Rather, the key question is what one is disposed to be pleased or repelled by.

To regard any property—moral, biological, genetic—as universally distributed, innate rather than acquired, is, with some exceptions, to regard the possessors of the property as possessing it essentially. Here is essentialism, again. Thus, we can ask: "Are human beings said to be essentially rational creatures but only accidentally blond?" That is to say, specimen A retains human status whatever the color of the hair, but not whatever the state of the specimen's rational resources. Essentialism is, itself, as I've noted, a problematical concept, but it is a useful one here to clarify both Hume's theory of our internal feelings or sentiments, and Aristotle's theory as to what it is that constitutes a flourishing form of life for us. One point needing to be made in this connection is that moral theorists may disagree on just what it is that constitutes the morality of an action, while agreeing that human beings are essentially moral.

The philosophical tradition for which Hume speaks is that empiricistic one that reduces the knowable to what is, in principle, the subject of experience. If there is some sort of moral "reality," it must be found empirically, its character determined by our empirical resources. Let me stay within this tradition for a while, returning now to Hume. He tells us that vice and virtue, these key moral terms, "may be compar'd to sounds, colours, heat and cold, which, according to modern philosophy, are not qualities in objects, but perceptions in the mind."

Note, then, that the moral estimations of vice and virtue on Hume's account are not based on anything observable in the external world. They arise, like the secondary quality of color, from the effect that a feature of external reality has on creatures constituted in a certain way. For Hume, we are so constituted that actions and events of a certain kind will arouse in us feelings of pleasure, or indeed, revulsion. Our moral ascriptions, then, are grounded not in external reality but the internal states, such that the terms "right" and "wrong" are not referring to events in the external world, but in the sentiments of the observer as these are aroused by events in the external world.

Let me jump from Hume's 18th-century statement of the position to a 20th-century elaboration of it. Here are some words from A. J. Ayer, the distinguished Oxford philosopher so influential in the 1960s:

> Insofar as statements of value are significant, they are ordinary "scientific" statements, and insofar as they are not scientific, they are not in the literal sense significant, but are simply expressions of emotion, which are neither true nor false.

For A. J. Ayer, moral concepts are pseudo-concepts, for they cannot be plumbed for meaning in the way that we can unearth the meaning of terms that refer to actual, real objects in the world. They are not even analyzable, for the analysis itself would require some means of verification, some means by which to establish truth and falsehood, but the expression of an emotion is not a factual truth or falsehood. It is simply the declaration of the feeling.

More recently, in the closing quarter of the 20th century, there have been further refinements and qualifications. Within the empiricistic tradition and in the patrimony of David Hume, these all support the famous Humean declaration that "oughts" cannot be derived from statements of fact, the famous "Is 'ought' divine?" That is, there is never a logical or rational warrant by which moral obligations can be derived from what is simply a fact in the real world. Gilbert Harman of Princeton states the case quite economically when he argues that no descriptive statement of fact entails a moral statement.

What is common across all these renderings is an opposition to the thesis that there are real moral properties to which we can have either experiential or rational access. Morality is "real" on such accounts, only in the sense that something is really felt or believed to be so, and this remains the case even if the emotions are universally distributed and aroused by precisely the same facts in the external world. There are, then, no moral facts as such— only "facts," and it is these to which peculiar modes of human sentiment or emotion ascribe moral features.

For all the support this tradition has gained for itself in recent decades, it is clearly at variance with still other commonsense notions about morality. After all, when we actually do find ourselves, Hamletian or otherwise, making moral judgments, these are seldom accompanied by feelings of joy or revulsion. Those who judge the practice of enslaving other human beings as morally wrong may not invariably feel anything beyond what is felt when hearing that the sum of 3 and 5 is 11. That is, moral judgments are often of the form: "Doing X is morally wrong, period." Not that it makes me feel a certain way, but that it is just wrong.

Moreover, it would be widely regarded as some sort of mental illness for someone to claim that what makes an action morally right is that it makes him feel good. More often than not, what the dictates of morality require is the avoidance of actions that are otherwise highly pleasurable—or even the performance of actions that are, in and of themselves, highly odious. Sticking one's fingers down the throat of another to cause vomiting in order to rid the system of an ingested poison is not something one would find pleasurable, and it might be an action that arouses quite marked revulsion. I wouldn't call it immoral. In all, then, there seems to be something about moral imperatives not included in the catalogue of pleasures, pains, or even "utility."

At a certain level, such arguments also seem to leave little room for a distinction between what is morally right and what we choose on the basis of taste. Of course, there is little in the domain of taste that is universally adopted, but this would not spare the Hume-type theory from classification as a form of moral relativism, even moral skepticism. If, for example, it is just an accident of evolution, and one that might undergo significant change in later generations, that we have a nearly universally distributed set of emotions or sentiments, then the morality arising from these is itself an accident of evolution and may well be replaced by one radically at variance with what we now hold to be good and right. Evolutionary theory has already been invoked to account for altruism and other seemingly ethical dispositions. If that theory is the last word on such matters, then "morality," as such, is simply a word used to classify certain stereotypical modes of social interaction in the animal kingdom.

The same rationale must lead to moral skepticism, for if the entirety of moral discourse and moral judgment is reducible to evolutionary pressures and utility-maximizing behavior, we must reject some standard of morality that exists outside a given point in evolution and a given species evolving. "Morality" as a term signifying a class of sentiments, or a process by which emotional states are managed, or just the expression of feelings designed to facilitate social commerce, is a term lacking any real—may I say it?— moral properties.

Also problematical within this sentimentalist or emotivist or expressivist tradition in moral philosophy is what appears to be its inability to make any kind of moral disagreement possible at all. G. E. Moore, about a century ago, illustrated the problem this way. Follow this. This is good.

Suppose that, in judging a course of action, I must consult or be sensitive to certain feelings I have when considering or witnessing such actions. Let's say that, for the course of action X, my feelings are negative or aversive, but for the course of action Y, they are even more negative or aversive, such that

I regard both courses of action as morally unacceptable, but with Y being worse than X.

Now, I meet my good friend, Mr. Smith, who, as it happens, has also been assessing the same courses of actions, X and Y. Smith, however, judges Y to be, let's say, less revolting than X, but as I have no way of knowing just what Smith's actual feelings are, let alone which is the stronger, and, if the stronger, how strong each of them actually is, then I have no way of knowing the extent to which Smith's sense of "wrong," or "less wrong," or "better" is at all similar to the basis on which I make such judgments. Nor is Smith able to gauge my feelings. We are, quite simply, unable to find the nodal points on which we might have an actual disagreement, for all we could be disagreeing about are sentiments to which we have only first-personal access. If Smith and I cannot plausibly argue, being unable to speak for each other's feelings, how on earth can we refer to those sentiments that, according to Hume, are universally distributed in the community of human beings?

We might find it more profitable to avoid notions of internal sentiment and consider instead the expression of those sentiments in judgments of utility. Hume, recall, emphasized considerations of utility in marking out the boundaries of the moral, and his disciple, John Stuart Mill, developed *utilitarianism* into a full-fledged ethical system. However, it is abundantly clear on virtually any formulation of the "ism" that the very concept of utility leaves the door nearly wide open to all of the traditional moral theories. What we are pleased to identify as "useful" invariably raises the questions: Useful for whom? Useful for what? Useful under what conditions? Useful on behalf of what aim or objective? etc. Nor is it helpful to be told that these questions are to be answered by each person individually, for no one has the right to impose standards of utility on another, it might be said, or to be told that no individual person has the right to impose his personal standard or taste on all the rest—or to be told what is "useful" by somebody else, to be told that it is universally the case. Clearly, all this finds us attempting to break a vicious circle by running around it with ever greater speed and seriousness.

Of all those who agitated for the abolition of slavery, I recall none basing the argument on the likelihood that more "net happiness" would result, while granting that the abolition would make some quite unhappy—or that abolition would be good for the economy, or, in the long run, prove to be more useful. In a word, the frequency with which utilitarian factors actually match up with ordinary understandings of moral obligation would seem to make the thesis something of a happy accident from a moral point of view. It becomes a serious contender, however, when the concepts of happiness and utility begin to take seriously what is generally regarded as Aristotle's sense of *eudaimonia,* but then, here, the very concept of utility is already a nearly moral one to begin with.

In his 1788 *Critique of Practical Reason*, Kant presents an entirely different conception of morality. It is in that work that he offers the sublime maxim as to what it is that can give rise to transcendental awe—he says:

> *Der bestirnte Himmel über mir und das moralische Gesetz in mir.*

> The starry sky above me, the moral law within me.

On the matter of just what it is that constitutes the "good" as in "moral good," Kant argues that it must be the "good will." Obviously, one who accidentally or inadvertently brings about a morally desirable state of affairs is not to be regarded as having acted morally. Consequences alone can say little about the moral character of the actions that produce them, but the actual will of the actor says all that needs to be said. For it is on the basis of the principle or the maxim that is generative of the course of action that we are able to determine if the action has been drawn from the domain of morality at all.

Over and against considerations of desire and sentiment, Kant's moral theory ties good will to that fidelity to one's duties, understood as a willing and faithful allegiance to, and reverence for, law. But the law in question is not some statutory or legislative encumbrance framed by others; rather, it is the "moral law within me" "*das moralische Gesetz in mir.*" "The starry sky above me, the moral law within me."

As a law, it is applicable in all contexts. It is not a matter of prevailing standards, or local conditions, or the nuances of the situation. Thus, if slavery is morally wrong, it is always morally wrong—wrong everywhere, wrong under any and every set of social, or political, or economic descriptions.

Just what this law is, apart from its universality, is what Kant develops in his concept of the categorical imperative. As a law, the moral law is an imperative. As universal, it is categorical; it applies *come what may*. It must, then, be a law that one would will to be universal. That is the very logic of the case such that were one able by an act of will to make the universal law of morals a law of nature, one would do so.

Kant expresses the categorical imperative in several ways, one of them forbidding the use of another moral being merely as an instrument or tool, but always and only as an end in himself. Accordingly, slavery could never be justified on grounds of consequences, good on the whole, the lesser of competing evils, etc.

Kant's moral philosophy bases morality on reason and, thus, reserves the moral domain to creatures who are rational as such. This still leaves open the problem of moral relativism, in that human rationality routinely leads to different conclusions on matters of moral consequence. It would be bizarre to conclude that, in any moral dispute, one or both parties are simply irrational, for if both were fully rational, there could be no dispute between them. The history of moral thought as written and argued by philosophers is not a history readily divided into "rational" and "irrational" authors.

It is, however, a history readily divided into debates between moral realists and non-realists, though again these terms have been applied somewhat arbitrarily.

Let's try to gain greater clarity. We might consider the realist–anti-realist positions noted in the lecture on philosophy of science. The realist regarding the laws of science is one who takes those laws as *really* operating in the world, not as shorthand for perceptual regularities or as abstractions based on an idealized world that has never been. The anti-realist regards the laws as having great usefulness, as providing desired economies in our predictions and descriptions, but, again, as tools of investigation, not as discoveries about reality itself.

Now, if we use this distinction, we might say that a moral realist must be prepared to affirm the proposition that any complete account of reality must include irreducibly more properties, and just as the scientific realist regards the properties of the physical world to be independent of us, to be mind-independent, so, too, does the moral realist regard the moral properties of reality to be independent of human reason, human passion, human perception. What would then make a moral state of affairs is not that such is seen to be the case or felt to be the case, but just is the case.

The same G. E. Moore offered a thesis of this sort a century ago, but in the context of aesthetics. Think of it this way. Take the property beauty, and say that, in the end, it is a relational matter, not unlike harmony in music. If that's the case, then presumably such relational features could and do obtain, whether perceived or not. After all, absent all human or animal life, it is still imaginable that purely physical events could occur in such a way as to generate patterns of frequencies in harmonic relationships such that a later record of these events would be called by us "harmonious," though no one was alive at the time the record was formed.

Well, by the same token, we could argue that it is in the relational arrangements of solid objects, of oil on canvass, of sounds, that the property of beauty is instantiated, and that this "beauty" is not the result of, or causally brought about by, or dependent upon, human values, human feelings, or human judgments.

The moral realist—at least the radical moral realist—is prepared to argue in kindred fashion that the cosmos itself includes relational features and requirements constitutive of a moral order. Human perception and judgment might pick this up, maybe only faintly and incompletely, though progressively. If beauty has a comparable independence, a set of properties waiting for the prepared mind to recognize them, then perhaps Socrates was on the right track after all in contending that truth, beauty, and justice were not only real but, finally, the same.

Well, there are very, very few radical realists, but one of them may be nearer to you right now than you think.

Medicine and the Value of Life
Lecture 56

If moral philosophy is vexed by concepts such as rights, it is doubly vexed when occasions call for assigning relative weights to the rights that find themselves in conflict.

One of these, beginning as a theory of the moral sentiments, Hume's moral theory, lays the foundation for utilitarianism based on the goal of optimizing pleasure and minimizing pain. Aristotelian "perfectionist" theories absorb the moral domain into that of character itself, where the decisive factor is the manner in which one's actions accord with the dictates of reason. On Kantian deontological grounds, morality arises from the autonomy of a rational being free to decide, to observe, or to defy the moral law. Kantian moral theory focuses on the intentions of the actor, not the consequences of the action. General theories of this sort are "abstract" in that they do not offer long lists of the actions required or forbidden by the terms of the theory. They do provide a framework within which to weigh significant actions for their moral worth.

All moral theories place a premium on actions capable of causing great harm to the innocent; thus, one of the richest arenas in which to test the applications and implications of competing theories is medicine. Our willingness to favor a given moral theory depends partly on whether, in concrete cases, it calls for actions that appear to be sound and justified, if not obligatory, or whether it seems to allow actions many would reasonably regard as unacceptable.

From a moral point of view, there are a variety of questions surrounding the taking of a life, including how one life may be valued as worth more or less than another, in different situations. With suicide, there is no complication arising from proxy decisions, nor is the judgment of the value of the life in question reserved to any party except the person whose life it is. Kant argues that suicide is a moral wrong because the grounds on which such an act would be chosen—to create or change a state of feeling—entails using a rational being (oneself, in this case) as an instrument to bring about some desired state of affairs. On the other hand, the ancient Roman Stoic Seneca says in his essay *On Fear* that a debilitating disease, for instance, would rob a person of the very dignity Kant accords rational beings. Hume contends that God presumably gave human beings the power of free choice in order to promote their happiness and well-being and that both of these objectives may be best met by ending a life of misery and torment. In his libertarian and utilitarian philosophy, John Stuart Mill places the freedom of the individual as a higher value than the paternalistic concerns of those who would thwart individual efforts and aims. Accordingly, the morality of suicide is to be weighted according to the utilities associated with continuing or ending a life of pain and misery.

Great controversy has surrounded the question of physician-assisted suicide. Proponents have argued that so momentous a decision is likely to be made by patients with degraded capacities under extremely difficult conditions. Thus, the decision to end one's life made, the humane course of action would seem to be implementation by a qualified medical doctor. If one judges outcome X to be morally and legally permissible and further judges that it is best brought about via medical procedure, then it would seem to follow that competent physicians should be prepared to assist as needed. To absolve physicians from such a duty—in case they regard suicide as immoral—would call for a reassessment of the patient's own claim to have some sort of moral right to take his own life.

Another controversial issue in medical ethics is the basis on which resources are committed to preserve life. Technology has now reached a level where a person can be kept alive indefinitely—at least as a continuing and living physiological "preparation." This might require such life-support measures as intravenous feeding and a respirator, or more, in addition to staff, hospital facilities, and so on. A chronically vegetative patient, such as Karen Quinlan, whose case came to the fore in 1975, is an example of what technically *can* be achieved in this arena. She survived in this state for a decade.

Why should a hospital bed, a respirator and feeding tube, nursing and medical specialists, and costly physical facilities be committed to preserving a life such as this? On cost/benefit terms, the decision is simply unwarranted. On Kantian terms, the patient is no longer a "moral" entity at all. In such cases, the fear, of course, is the fear of the "slippery slope"; if Karen Quinlan has no right to be kept alive, owing to the loss of all cognitive and social capacities, what then of profoundly retarded persons? What of those not profoundly retarded but significantly sub-normal?

Even more controversial still is the ending of fetal life through elective abortions, as the entities destroyed in this way are not severely disabled or in states of pain and suffering. Some moralists, granting that fetuses have a right to their lives, have denied that that right imposes a duty on anyone else to sustain and nurture it. Other moralists have denied that fetuses have rights at all, on the grounds that rights properly understood are possessed only by those able to claim and use them. On the other side, it is observed that the fetuses in question are fully human in the genetically identifiable sense, are alive, and are on one point along an unbroken continuum leading to full humanity. Taking their lives is a homicidal act.

From a moral point of view, there are a variety of questions surrounding the taking of a life, including how one life may be valued as worth more or less than another, in different situations.

None of the developed schools of moral philosophy has the resources to settle this matter decisively. The basis on which one demands an abortion is that one has a "right" to this course of action. But moral philosophy and ethics have a notoriously difficult problem with the very concept of a right. Moral philosophy is doubly vexed when occasions call for assigning relative weights to rights in conflict—in this case, the right of a woman to prevent others from requiring her to bring a pregnancy to term versus the fetus's assumed right to its own life.

A final set of issues arises from developments in modern genetics. There are now more than a thousand disorders and diseases that can be matched up with genetic markers, even early in fetal life. Parents might learn that a pregnancy brought to term would yield medical expenses that will impoverish them within a matter of a few years.

In addition to the obvious moral choices entailed by such cases, consider these questions: (1) At work here is the possibility of encouraging a decision to end a life by presenting information regarding risks. How should such possibilities and probabilities be dealt with? (2) Should insurance companies have access to such genetic profiles and be permitted to set premiums on the basis of risks?

Moral philosophy, as such, is not a problem-solver or even a means by which to find the better of equally unwelcome choices. Moral philosophy can, however, make clear to those who must decide such matters the principle that appears to be guiding the decision and the implications arising from such a principle.

Contemporary medical ethics recognizes the *principle of nonmaleficence*, which is different from beneficence. Beneficence is the disposition to bring about good effects. Nonmaleficence comes into play when the options are all likely to harm the patient in some way. "Do no harm" is modified to "Do the least harm where harm itself is unavoidable."

But complications stalk the application of every principle. In many instances, a course of action may have both positive and negative effects. The textbook example features a pregnant woman suffering from a treatable cancer, but where the course of radiation therapy almost certainly will kill the fetus. Here we have the *double-effect*, one intended, the other foreseen but not desired. As far back as Thomas Aquinas we can find moral guidelines to help those facing such dilemmas. First, the action itself must not be one that is intrinsically wrong. Second, the sincere intention must be to save a life, not to take one. Third, the bad effect is not produced as the means by which to bring about the good one. Finally, the good achieved must be greater than the evil unavoidably associated with it.

The moral of this moral tale is that there was moral life before there was moral philosophy, and there were good and worthy citizens before there were treatises on ethics. The subject matter of philosophy is drawn from the actual practices and problems faced by real persons confronting the realities of life. It is not philosophy's mission to limit reality to problems it deals with adroitly. What is faced in the medical clinic and the surgery are issues of such novelty and seriousness that the least helpful instrument in the circumstance may well be the learned essay in ethics. It is a strength and a virtue, not a weakness or a vice, to know and acknowledge one's limits. Ethics as a philosophical subject is no stranger to limits. ■

Suggested Reading

Brock, Dan. *Life and Death:* Cambridge University Press, 1993.

Cassell, E. *The Nature of Suffering and the Goals of Medicine.* Oxford University Press, 1991.

Questions to Consider

1. How does one evaluate evils in order to determine which is the lesser?

2. Is Kant's categorical imperative even practicable within the real world of medical treatments and research?

3. Under what conditions, if any, would you sacrifice an innocent life to save two?

Medicine and the Value of Life
Lecture 56—Transcript

In the previous lecture, I sketched three dominant schools of moral philosophy. One of these, beginning as a theory of the moral sentiments, Hume's moral theory, lays the foundation for utilitarianism based on the goal of optimizing pleasure and minimizing pain. The robustness of the concepts of pleasure and pain determines whether the utilitarian theory is an elevated one or vulgar one. If one were to regard a substantial increase in the number of persons titillated by off-color jokes as a justification for causing a handful of persons great suffering, the charge would be that this is a parody of utilitarianism, which supposes the pleasures and pains at issue really be truly significant.

Aristotelian "perfectionist" theories absorb the moral domain into that of character itself, where the decisive factor is the manner in which one's actions accord with the dictates of reason. On this account, the cultivation of virtue just is the moral life, and the morality of actions is judged accordingly.

On Kant's deontological grounds, morality arises from the autonomy of a rational being free to will, free to observe, or free to defy the moral law. Kantian moral theory focuses on the intentions of the actor and the principle on which the action is based, not the consequences of the action. Where the intention is fidelity to the moral law, the action is moral, and otherwise it's non-moral or immoral.

General theories of this nature are, of course, "abstract" in that they do not offer long lists of the actions required or forbidden by the terms of the theory. They do, however, provide a highly articulated framework within which to weigh significant actions for their moral worth, and, as all moral theories place a premium on actions capable of causing great harm to the innocent, one of the richest arenas in which to test the applications and implications of competing moral theories is in medicine. Our willingness to accept, or adopt, or favor a given moral theory depends at least in part on whether, in concrete cases, it calls for actions that appear to be sound and justified, if not obligatory, or whether, in concrete cases, it seems to allow actions many of us would regard, and reasonably regard, as unacceptable.

Well, what after all is the value of life, and does the question pivot on the identity of the life in question? Is the life of Einstein, say, of greater value than that of a convicted rapist? Are two lives of greater value than one, maybe even twice as great? Is the value of life constant across the lifespan? If only one of two patients can be saved, one of them a healthy five-year-old now entering a life of promise and joy, and the other an aged and sickly person of 94, should both be regarded as of equal value?

From a moral point of view, does it make any difference whether the action taken is designed to end a life, or the non-action is designed to permit a death that could be averted? That is, is there a moral difference between killing and letting die? In this same connection, if there is genetic evidence to the effect that a developing fetus is likely to be seriously disabled, what has moral philosophy to offer by way of guidance here? Similarly, if the value of one's life to one enduring chronic pain and suffering is judged to be negligible, is euthanasia or even suicide the morally right course of action, and in what measures or by what calculus are we to specify the units of value? Dollars? Pleasure? Utility? Intrinsic value? Who is to decide on, and assign, these values? The doctors? The courts? Moral theorists? Patients? Next of kin?

These form a daunting set of questions, and none of them ripe for easy answers. Let me begin with suicide, for, in this instance, there is no complication arising from proxy decisions, nor is the judgment of the value of the life in question reserved to any party except the person whose life it is.

In his *Fundamental Principles of the Metaphysics of Morals*, Kant offers the rationale according to which suicide is a moral wrong:

> He who contemplates suicide should ask himself whether his action can be consistent with the idea of humanity as an end in itself. If he destroys himself in order to escape from painful circumstances, he uses a person merely as a means to maintain a tolerable condition up to the end of life, but a man is not a thing which can be used merely as a means, but must in all his actions be always considered as an end in himself.

Given the categorical imperative and in light of the grounds on which the suicidal act would be chosen—namely to create or to change some state of feeling—the act is morally impermissible. It entails using a rational being (in this case, oneself) as an instrument with which to bring about some desired state of affairs. It is, then, to act on a hypothetical imperative at the expense of the categorical imperative. Kantian moral philosophy judges the very rationale of suicide as degrading the dignity of a rational being by using such a being for some desirable state of affairs. He could only find one exception to this analysis, and that was the suicide of Kato, who killed himself rather than submit to the tyrannical excess of an emperor, because if Kato submitted he felt that his fellow citizens would be inclined to do so as well. We have the so-called "noble suicide," but Kant thinks that that is the only instance he can find of a permissible suicide.

Consider what the ancient Roman Stoic Seneca says in his essay *On Fear*, though, as he contemplates the loss of his intellectual and moral powers to old age and disease. Seneca says that if he feels this state coming then he will take his life, "not through fear of the pain itself, but because it prevents all for which I should live." On Seneca's reasoning, a debilitating disease is precisely what would rob him of the very dignity that Kant wants to accord rational beings.

Hume composed a controversial essay *Of Suicide*, prepared for a collection of his published essays to appear in 1757, but he withdrew it before publication. I should say that it is not an especially discerning essay—surely not up to Hume's standards—but it does offer a novel reply to those who condemn suicide on the grounds that it is an act of ingratitude toward God, or inconsistent with the very natural purposes of life itself.

Both of these factors appear in Thomas Aquinas's argument against the permissibility of suicide. Hume contents that God presumably gave human beings the power of free choice in order to promote their happiness and well-being and that both of these objectives may be best met by ending a life of misery and torment.

In his libertarian and utilitarian philosophy, John Stuart Mill places the freedom of the individual as a higher value than the paternalistic concerns of those who would thwart individual efforts and aims. Where these pose no harm to others—namely, a suicidal act—the individual should be free to ask as he sees fit. Accordingly, the morality of suicide is to be weighted according to the utilities associated with continuing or ending a life of pain and misery.

Staying with suicide a moment longer, great controversy has surrounded the question of physician-assisted suicide. Proponents have argued that so momentous a decision is likely to be made under extremely difficult conditions, often by patients with greatly degraded capacities. Their choice of life-ending measures will be crude and uncertain when compared with what modern medicine might be able to provide. Thus, the decision to end one's life having been made, the humane course of action is for this decision to be implemented by a qualified medical doctor.

It is not clear, however, that proponents would go so far as to require physicians to assist, though it would seem to be inconsistent not to require them to assist. After all, if one judges outcome X to be morally and legally permissible and further judges that it is best brought about by a medical procedure, then it would seem to follow that competent physicians should be prepared to assist as needed. To absolve physicians from such a duty—just in case they regard suicide as immoral—would then call for a reassessment of the patient's own claim to have some sort of moral right to take his own life. Surely, then, there is more to morals than the judgment of one or another person.

Accordingly, from the fact that the potential victim regards suicide as morally permissible, I'm sorry to say that nothing follows. One presumably has as much right to demand an argument in defense of suicide as one would expect if taking the life of someone else were under consideration. St. Augustine, on this very subject, noted that taking an innocent and non-threatening life was the crime of murder, and that it really makes no moral difference just in case the victim of such an assault happens to be oneself.

If the motive for suicide is fear or depression arising from trauma, or lifelong disappointments, or grave medical conditions, what guidance might be received from moral philosophy—just in case a medical, or surgical, or pharmacological modality is available that is likely to alter that motive significantly? Is it permissible to drug a person away from suicidal tendencies? Is it obligatory? How does Kant's categorical imperative work—just in case the manipulation of another human being medically or surgically is for the express purpose of restoring that person to rationality, or rendering a rational being ever more rational?

Let me turn now to another issue in medical ethics: the basis on which resources are committed to preserve life. Technology has now reached a level of development such that—at least as a continuing and living physiological "preparation"—a human being can be kept alive, I want to say, indefinitely. In some instances, the life-support measures may be as basic and inexpensive as intravenous feeding and a respirator. In extreme cases, much more might be required, in addition to staff, hospital facilities, etc. Let's take what would seem to be close to the limiting case of a life having moral claims on others. Let's take the case of Karen Quinlan, which came to the fore in 1975. Here's a sketch of the relevant conditions:

Karen Ann Quinlan consumed alcohol at a party at a time she was taking barbiturates for a mild anxiety. Her reaction to the combination was catastrophic, placing her in what was described as a "chronic vegetative state." Her life was supported by a respirator and feeding tubes. Her EEG was surprisingly normal, or nearly so, such that she did not qualify as an instance of "brain death." Though she occasionally uttered shrill reflex-like cries, she was—or seemed to be—in a deep coma, utterly and always unresponsive to events in the environment.

Initial attempts to secure permission of the court to terminate the life-support measures failed. Against the family's plea that, in light of her condition, what was being done did not constitute an attempted "cure," the court reasoned that insulin for diabetes also does not qualify as a cure. Against the claim that Karen Quinlan's days were numbered, the court found in this no justification for accelerating the process, and in light of the fact that it was the patient's own loving parents who wished to put an end to all this, the court took the position that it is the best interest of the patient, not the desires of the parents, that must be decisive in matters of this kind. As it happens, Karen Quinlan remained in this state for a decade—her parents, by the way, soon coming to be grateful for her continued existence even in this reduced form.

Now, why should a hospital bed, a respirator and feeding tube, nursing and medical specialists, and costly physical facilities be committed to preserving a life such as this? On cost/benefit terms, the decision is simply unwarranted. On Kantian terms, the patient is no longer a "moral" entity at all. In such cases, the fear, of course, is the fear of the "slippery slope." If Karen Quinlan has no right to be kept alive, owing to the loss of all cognitive and social capacities, what then of a profoundly retarded person? What, then, of those not profoundly retarded but significantly sub-normal in other respects? If cases like this raise no significant moral issue—if letting such beings die is the morally permissible course of action—why might not these same "specimens" be used for research, or as sources of vital organs that might be used by others?

Even more controversial than instances of intractable coma is the now-routine ending of fetal life through elective abortions. The entities destroyed in this way are not severely disabled or in states of pain and suffering. They are not profoundly retarded. Medically assisted live births would not result in prohibitive costs, nor does the decision to abort require much by way of justification. Since the Supreme Court decision in 1973, there have been some 40 million legal abortions performed in the United States.

The practice has divided the nation and has revived any number of moral controversies associated with questions of rights and duties. Some moralists, granting that fetuses have a right to their lives, have denied that that right imposes a duty on anyone else to sustain and nurture it. As the argument goes, one may have a right to live, but not necessarily a right to live where "here" refers to a place within the body of another human being. Other moralists have denied that fetuses have rights at all, on the grounds that rights properly understood are possessed only by those able to claim and use them. On this view, even children do not have the full range of rights but may, nonetheless, expect not to be abused or neglected by parents. The child's right to protection and to be spared avoidable pain and suffering is not unlike what is claimed for any sensate animal.

On the other side, it is observed that the fetuses in question are fully human in the genetically identifiable sense; they are alive, and they are on one point along an unbroken continuum leading to full humanity as we take it to be. Taking their lives is a homicidal act certainly in the strict linguistic sense— and, yes, a homicide that counts as a murder in light of premeditation and willful intent. I say that this is a line of argument.

It should be evident—in light of all this and the intense debates on the subject of abortion—that none of the developed schools of moral philosophy has the resources to settle this matter decisively. The reasons are several and subtle.

To begin, the basis on which one demands an abortion, apart from the legal basis now in place, is that one has a "right" to this course of action. But moral philosophy and ethics have a notoriously difficult problem with the very concept of a right. To the extent the term refers to something other than a legally permitted course of action, it is not clear what it refers to at all. The American and British Bills of Rights provide for a range of protections available to citizens against encroachments by the state, but these are just that—bills—which is to say, legal safeguards. These same safeguards permitted the owners of Dred Scott, the runaway slave, to reclaim him as property. From the fact that the U.S. Constitution was understood as permitting this action, it surely does not settle or even address the question of whether slavery is morally permissible. It is just that legally it was permissible.

If moral philosophy is vexed by concepts such as rights, it is doubly vexed when occasions call for assigning relative weights to the rights that find themselves in conflict. Assuming that a woman has something we call a right of such a nature as to prevent others from requiring her to bring a pregnancy to term—and assuming also that the fetus at risk possesses something we call a right of such a nature as to confer some value on the life of the fetus—how are these classes of rights to be quantified? Are they even commensurable?

The final set of issues I'll put forward here arises from developments in modern genetics. There are now more than a thousand disorders and diseases that can be matched up with genetic markers. It should soon be possible to assess disease risk factors early in fetal life. Assessments of this sort will carry an implicit, even an expressed, price tag. In cold terms, parents might learn that if the pregnancy comes to term, they are likely to face medical expenses that will impoverish them within a matter of a few years.

In addition to the obvious moral choices entailed by such cases, consider these questions: At work here is the possibility of encouraging a decision to end a life by presenting information regarding risks. As there is no certainty in such matters, it is possible that providing such information will cause a definite harm to the aborted fetus, but without a compensating avoidance of a greater harm that may well not have taken place at all. How should such possibilities and probabilities be dealt with?

Should insurance companies have access to such genetic profiles? Should they be permitted to set premiums on the basis of risks? After all, insurance companies charge young men more than they charge young women for the same automobile insurance. The differences in the rates just reflect the basic actuarial fact that young men are more prone to auto accidents. That is, being male is a risk factor with respect to auto accidents.

My intention in this lecture has been to provide a small sample of the moral issues arising from life-and-death decisions in medicine, chiefly to make clear that moral philosophy, as such, is not a problem-solver; it is not a foolproof practical guide; it is not even a means by which to find the better of equally unwelcome choices.

What moral philosophy can do, however, is make clear to those who must decide such matters the principle that appears to be guiding the decision, and then, the implications arising from a principle of that sort. The medical research scientist who lies to a patient in order to test the efficacy of a placebo is, of course, using another human being as a means to an end, and not as an end unto himself. The doctor here is violating the categorical imperative. If, however, that imperative is to be regarded as categorical, then, whole fields of medical research would be stifled.

There is a general principle in contemporary medical ethics known as the *principle of nonmaleficence*, which is different from beneficence. Beneficence is the disposition to bring about good effects. Nonmaleficence is the principle where the options are all likely to harm the patient in some way. "Do no harm" is modified to "Do the least harm where harm itself is unavoidable."

However, complications stalk the application of every principle. In many instances, a given course of action may well have both positive and negative effects. The textbook example features a pregnant woman suffering from a treatable cancer, but where the course of radiation therapy almost certainly will kill the fetus. Here we have the standard example of the so-called *double-effect* problem, one effect intended, the other foreseen but not desired.

As far back as Thomas Aquinas we can find moral guidelines to help those facing such dilemmas. The first of these guidelines is that the action itself must not be one that is intrinsically wrong. Second, the sincere intention must be to save a life, not to take one. The third and especially demanding requirement is that the bad effect is not produced as the means by which to bring about the good one. If, for example, the mother's life could be saved only by killing one of her children, the latter act could not be justified by the good resulting from it, and, finally, the good achieved must be greater than the evil unavoidably associated with it. A life for a life fails this test, though perhaps two lives for one might in some circumstances pass the test.

The medical research scientist who lies to a patient in order to test the efficacy of a placebo knows that the categorical imperative forbids this, but he adopts the utilitarian criterion that calls for actions that create the greatest good on the whole. However, the greatest good on the whole might be attained by transplanting organs from retarded persons into the bodies of exceptional persons who will otherwise not live long enough to make their otherwise inevitable and significant contributions to society.

Strapping down and medicating a potential suicide victim abridges that person's autonomy, "deny a right and save a life" being the controlling maxim. Why, then, not take measures to eliminate any number of life-limiting and life-threatening activities—from smoking and drinking, to modes of sexual activity likely to result in the transmission of fatal diseases?

Dr. Johnson reminds us that consistency is the hobgoblin of small minds. Well, it is surely a hobgoblin in medical ethics where the assiduous attachment to but one moral precept soon finds the practitioner perhaps at odds with reason.

What is the moral of this moral tale? It is this: There was moral life before there was moral philosophy, and there were good and worthy citizens before there were treatises on ethics. The subject matter of philosophy is drawn from the actual practices and problems faced by real persons confronting the realities of life. I should say that is not philosophy's mission to limit reality to those problems that, remarkably, philosophy is able to deal with adroitly. What is faced in the medical clinic and the surgery are issues of such novelty and seriousness—so laced through with contingent facts never before witnessed in that degree or arrangement—that the least helpful instrument in the circumstance may well be the learned essay in ethics. It is a strength and a virtue, not a weakness or a vice, to know and acknowledge one's limits.

Ethics as a philosophical subject is no stranger to limits. I recur to the case of Karen Quinlan. The family loved their daughter, a point often made in cases of this kind. In an argument before the Supreme Court, in *Cruzan*, the counsel for the plaintiffs was making clear how much the parents who were seeking the termination of this life loved the potential victim. One of the Supreme Court justices interjected and asked counsel what the position of the family would be just in case they didn't love the potential victim—the point, of course, being that a life, the continuation of a life, should not depend on the degree to which others find it attractive, appealing, or desirable.

In the matter of Karen Quinlan, the family consulted clergymen, and they were assured that the religion their daughter practiced did not require extreme measures to keep in existence a life that already seemed to have been spoken for. The lower court in New Jersey attended to this aspect of the case, responding respectfully, but pointed out respectfully that what they were appearing before was a secular court in New Jersey and not an ecclesiastical court, and that what would be determined in matters of this kind were the statutory requirements of the state of New Jersey.

I want to make a point that I think is at once controversial and commonsensical. Those two can go hand-in-hand. The resources of the law, in matters of this kind, very often seem far more developed, far more supple, more protean, more capable of finding controlling maxims on the basis of the thick record of juridical reason than does the book of moral philosophy itself. I say, it may sound controversial to say that something moral thought can't handle, the court might well handle, but understand what the courts are concerned with, which is the functioning of life as actually lived in a tolerable way—disputes settled by something more benign and humane than pistols and swords.

The courts have a millennial experience with matters of this kind, and I, for one, would be quite disinclined to replace the apparatus, procedures, database, and rationale of justice with the often murky and very often confused, quite conflicting though thick, book of official academic moral philosophy, let alone that truncated field we call bioethics.

On the Nature of Law
Lecture 57

From the time of ancient reflections on the nature of law and until
the first half of the 19th century, the dominant perspective was that of
natural law theory. Though expressed in various ways, the perspective
itself invariably included—and includes—assumptions about human
nature and about the nature of that social and physical reality in which
human nature itself must find a place of security and nurturance.

P hilosophy of law, or jurisprudence, has long been of interest to
philosophers. In his treatise on *Politics*, Aristotle defined law as
"reason without passion." Cicero speaks of law as akin to "the mind
of God" and distinguishes the natural law from both the law of nations and
the civic law.

To keep an already complex historical record and conceptual terrain
manageable, I would stipulate that philosophy of law begins when we can
identify a position taken on the origins and sources of law and its resulting
authority. On this understanding, the oldest tradition in philosophy of law is
theological. Times or settings in which this minimal theoretical framework
is missing are best understood as pre-legal. We see that the defining mark
of philosophy is a mode of *criticism* designed to test the validity or truth
of propositions.

The standard legal "textbook" of the early medieval period—the *Institutes*
of the emperor Justinian (A.D. 533)—divides law into the classification that
Cicero had developed: *natural*, *common*, and *civic*. He preserves the sense of
law as an expression of natural reason, tied to the happiness and security of
the community. Seven centuries later, Thomas Aquinas will put his seal on
natural law theory, declaring law to be "an ordinance of reason, promulgated
by one who is responsible for the good of the community."

The Enlightenment, however, drew attention to the confusion between what
many deemed the natural state of affairs and states of affairs that had simply
gone on too long, with formidable powers seeking to preserve the status

quo. One leader of the Reform movement was Jeremy Bentham, a profound influence on John Stuart Mill's early education. Bentham's student John Austin, during his time in the Chair of Jurisprudence, prepared a volume that would profoundly affect how law itself is understood—*The Province of Jurisprudence Determined.* It would be too much to say that Austin or any single book established the field of analytical jurisprudence. Nonetheless, one searches without success for works before Austin's that so clearly distinguish moral and legal concepts and reserve independent status to each. At the root, law is a command, perhaps in the form of a wish, covering a range of actions and declared by a sovereign. Law is not a moral maxim, a religious belief, the voice of conscience, an ordinance of reason, or the mind of God.

Here, then, is a succinct and early statement of *legal positivism.* Law is what is enacted or authoritatively promulgated and enforced. The focus is on the legal concepts themselves, not on their allegedly moral dependencies or sources.

Legal positivism, however, leaves the fundamental issues in philosophy of law more or less untouched. On neither Austin's account nor those advanced by his successors in legal positivism is it clear just what enters into the concept of *sovereign.* Austin's *command theory* of law, which ties the command-function to little more than the power of enforcement, seems to confer the standing of legislator on unwanted types. The gun-toting thief who commands us to hand over our wallets seems to qualify as a lawgiver.

Hart's attempt to eliminate such counterintuitive possibilities is in the form of something he called the *rule of recognition*—to say that a given rule is valid is to recognize it as passing all the tests provided by the rule of recognition. We "recognize" the Motor Vehicle Bureau as the place that prints valid drivers' licenses; we recognize Congress as the body that passes valid laws. In this way, the rule of recognition corrects one of the basic flaws in the command theory and enables all to determine when a law is valid.

Lon Fuller provided a natural law critique of this entire line of reasoning. The moral and rational powers presupposed by the rule of law are also at work in distinguishing between *law* as something to be faithfully obeyed and *law* as but a word seeking to conceal arbitrary, immoral, and tyrannical modes of control. Fuller is prepared to insulate the rule of law from specific, substantive moral mandates but insists that the very concept of law requires a *procedural* morality ensuring the law's fairness, consistency, and clarity.

Natural law theory and legal positivism do not exhaust the options in philosophy of law. Ronald Dworkin's criticism of legal positivism begins with the observation that courts must often decide cases for which there are no precedents and nothing in the record of "social facts" sufficient to settle the matter. One instance he cited is *Riggs v. Palmer*, which had to decide whether a murderer was entitled to enjoy what his victim had bequeathed him in his will. Dworkin concluded that the authority and validity of law result from its embodiment of moral aims widely shared in the community and of a nature to justify the values and practices of the community. Judges, thus, should decide hard cases by interpreting the political structure of their communities.

Legal positivism, however, leaves the fundamental issues in philosophy of law more or less untouched.

However, much of the South—understood surely as a "community"—accepted slavery as a property right and, more important, the right to make that judgment as a state's right. To some extent, Dworkin's theory descends from that *legal realism* that flourished in American jurisprudence under such defenders as Oliver Wendell Holmes, Rosco Pound, and Jerome Frank.

Kant composed an analytical exposition on the nature of law, understood as part of the metaphysics of morals. Kant says "the science of right" has the principle of law as its object, which can be promulgated by external legislation. The principle states that every action is *right* in itself or in the maxim on which it proceeds if it can coexist with freedom of the will in all circumstances.

Law, then, is derived from a principle that seeks to preserve and honor the moral liberty of rational beings. That freedom, too, comes under the direction of a universal law, which, as we have seen in an earlier lecture, is a moral law.

Of rights, Kant asserts that only one is a natural and inborn right; all others derived from positive law and tradition. Freedom is independence of the compulsory will of another. So far as it can coexist with the freedom of all according to a universal law, it is the one sole original inborn right belonging to all people.

These lines provide a foundation for one of the most influential works in contemporary philosophy of law, John Rawls's *A Theory of Justice*. As with Kant, Rawls's goal is the preservation of freedom from the compulsory will of another. Kant's categorical imperative supports what Rawls calls the *difference principle*: Social and economic inequalities should be arranged so that they are to the greatest benefit of the least advantaged before they improve the condition of the more advantaged. However, Rawls's *A Theory of Justice* is incomplete. It is surely not a Kantian maxim that the claim one has on the general resources is proportioned to the degree of disadvantage.

There is a small step, actually, from the position that law is no more than a social instrument to the use of law to secure social conditions dictated by theories that are presented as if they were protected from criticism, rather than outcomes of criticism.

Philosophy of law is extremely useful at the level of criticism. It makes no promises, however, at the level of great abiding and true discoveries. ∎

Suggested Reading

Dworkin, R. *Taking Rights Seriously*. Harvard, 1977.

Finnis, J. *Natural Law and Natural Rights*. Oxford, 1980.

Hart, H. L. A. *The Concept of Law*. Oxford, 1961.

1. How is natural law theory reconciled to the utter diversity of legal precepts in different cultures at different times?

2. Is Kant's philosophy of law in any sense a practical jurisprudence?

3. If law is sensitive to such factors as what a judge has for breakfast, what claim does it have on our fidelity?

On the Nature of Law
Lecture 57—Transcript

In his treatise on *Politics*, Aristotle raises the question, "What is law?" and as is his matter, proceeds to rehearse what others have said. Some, he tells us, regard it as a gift from the gods. His own definition is characteristically economical and academic. Law, he says, is "reason without passion," "*Dio perinor exios nus namos est.*" Reason without passion.

Philosophy of law, or jurisprudence, has long been of interest to philosophers. Cicero composed a treatise on the subject, and in Book II of the work offered this definition:

> The law was neither a thing to be contrived by the genius of man, nor established by any decree of the people, but a certain eternal principle, which governs the entire universe, wisely commanding what is right and prohibiting what is wrong. Therefore, they called that aboriginal and supreme law "the mind of God."

In the dialogue Cicero stages between Marcus and Quintus, it is Marcus who develops the thesis that, as the divine mind rationally passes on what is virtuous and what is vicious, so, too, does law stand as "right reason." Now contrast this with the remark by the American legal realist, Jerome Frank, to the effect that the outcome of adjudication may well depend on what the judge had for breakfast! Between the mind of God and the dietary preferences of judges, then, will be arrayed a number of theories on the nature of law, and therefore on what our dispositions and expectations should be regarding law itself. Something from "the mind of God," or something determined chiefly by ham and eggs.

Just to keep an already complex historical record and conceptual terrain manageable, I would just stipulate that philosophy of law begins when we can identify a position taken on the origin and sources of law and its resulting authority. On this understanding, the oldest tradition within philosophy of law is theological. Human laws, or at least the principles by which punishment is exacted and disputes settled, are found either in prophetic revelations or in the authority of temple priests, or in the presumably inspired wisdom of the sage or tribal chief. Cicero's reference to "the mind of God" hearkens to this most distant origin of legal concepts. As for times or settings in which this minimal theoretical framework is missing, they are best understood as pre-legal. In this sense, I would classify as pre-legal the merely customary habits of social groups, no matter how large the group, no matter how venerable the customs, if the customs themselves have not been subjected to critical appraisal. Again, we see that the defining mark of philosophy is a mode of *criticism* designed to test the validity or truth of propositions.

From the time of ancient reflections on the nature of law and until the first half of the 19th century, the dominant perspective was that of *natural law theory*. Though expressed in various ways, the perspective itself invariably included—and includes—assumptions about human nature and about the nature of that social and physical reality in which human nature itself must find a place of security and nurturance.

We've heard Cicero on the subject. Consider now the standard legal "textbook" of the early medieval period—the *Institutes* of the Emperor Justinian, promulgated in A.D. 533. The work begins with a definition of justice as, "the constant and perpetual wish to render everyone his due," proceeding then to divide law into the classification that Cicero himself had developed: the *natural*, the *common* and the *civic*. Of natural law, and the difference between it and civic law, Justinian's *Institutes* declares that:

> The law of nature is that law which nature teaches to all animals, for this law does not belong exclusively to the human race, but belongs to all animals, whether of the earth, the air, or the water. The law which a people makes for its own government belongs exclusively to that state and is called the "civil law," but the law which natural reason appoints for all mankind obtains equally among all nations.

Here, then, in the sixth century A.D., the authoritative treatise on law speaks of universally binding precepts recognized by "natural reason."

Seven centuries later, and in this same tradition, Thomas Aquinas will define law as "an ordinance of reason, promulgated by one who is responsible for the good of the community." An ordinance of reason.

Moving ahead to the 17th century, we find John Locke and his *Two Treatises of Civil Government*, leaving no doubt as to the ultimate source of law. Asking how human affairs would be managed in that "state of nature" existing before the advent of all civil society, Locke argues that we would not have an anarchy. Rather, by our very nature, there would be attempts to establish order and justice. John Locke puts it this way:

> And that all men may be restrained from invading others' rights, and from doing hurt to one another, and the law of Nature be observed, which willeth the peace and preservation of all mankind, the execution of the law of Nature is in that state put into every man's hands...For the law of Nature would, as all other laws that concern men in this world, be in vain if there were nobody that in the state of Nature had a power to execute that law.

We see, then, that from the fourth century B.C. to late in the 17th century—that is to say, for more than two millennia—a common thread of jurisprudential reasoning runs through philosophical attempts to comprehend the sources and nature of law.

Knowledge of other peoples with radically different forms of social life did not disturb this conception of law. Aristotle was well aware of cultural diversity, and it led him to conclude that it was entirely fitting that: "Hellenes shall rule barbarians." This was not a defense of imperialism, but of the sound proposition that a people is best ruled by the rule of law itself than by tyrannizing war lords. So, too, with Captain Cook's voyages, and other sources of information about so-called primitive peoples. The standard and often smug view was not that they were a challenge to natural law theory, but that they were "savages," awaiting the civilizing nurturance of a more developed people.

The Enlightenment, however, insistently drew attention to the confusion between what many took to be the natural state of affairs, and states of affairs that had simply gone on too long, with formidable powers seeking to preserve the status quo. Revolutionary upheavals begin with dissatisfaction, but they gain momentum through the force of ideas. Early in the 19th century, England was the setting for major reforms, with specific Parliamentary acts passed in the 1830s. One of the chief aims of the reformers was to break down barriers that had long denied whole segments of society access to the political process. It was also understood that these very segments of society had been denied access to the very education that would prepare them for responsible citizenship and alert them to the historical and social conditions responsible for prevailing conditions.

One of the leaders of the Reform movement was Jeremy Bentham, a friend to James Mill and a profound influence on John Stuart Mill's early education. Born in 1748, a lawyer's son, Bentham was precocious and intellectually inquisitive, learning Latin at the age of four and finding the Oxford curriculum too easy by half. He turned away from the study of law in part as a result, of all things, of William Blackstone's lectures on the subject. Now studying first-hand the sheer complexity of law, the restless Bentham dubbed it "Demon and Chicane" and set off instead to change the world.

In a subsequent lifetime of reformist activity, he could claim as one of his greatest achievements the successful lobbying for a college that would eliminate the traditional obstacles faced by the working classes as well as Catholics, Jews, and dissenting Christians. Though the resulting University College, London—which opened its doors in 1828—was not founded by Bentham, it realized fully his plans for a reformed academic climate. Bentham's preserved body still sits near the entrance to the dining room at University College. I've seen it in recent years. He seems to be doing fine.

Bentham died in 1832, but he lived long enough to have had a hand in the appointment in 1829 of one his own students, John Austin, to the Chair of Jurisprudence at this new University College. Austin by that date had already terminated his law practice. He had an extremely influential circle of friends—including Bentham, James and John Stuart Mill, and Thomas Carlyle. It is remarkable that, in the few years he occupied the Chair of Jurisprudence, he would prepare but a single volume for publication, and that that volume, in time, would profoundly affect how law itself would come to be understood. The book was essentially his lectures, and it was published under the title *The Province of Jurisprudence Determined*. Even this work might have been left on the shelf of forgotten tomes had it not been for his faithful and resourceful wife, Sarah, who saw to it that a revised edition of the work was published as late as 1873.

It would be too much to say that Austin's book, or any single book, established the field of analytical jurisprudence. Nonetheless, one searches without success for works before Austin's that so clearly distinguish moral and legal concepts, and reserve independent status to each. He states the argument this way, in his fifth lecture:

> The existence of law is one thing; its merit or demerit is another. Whether it be or be not is one enquiry; whether it be or be not conformable to an assumed standard, is a different enquiry. A law, which actually exists, is a law, though we happen to dislike it, or though it vary from the text, by which we regulate our approbation and disapprobation.

A law is a law. In German, "*Gesetz ist Gesetz*," an established principle in German law at the time Austin studied at Bonn. At the root, law is a command, perhaps in the form of a wish, covering a range of actions, and declared by a sovereign. The sovereign may be one person; it might be a parliamentary or congressional body, or a group of chieftains. What establishes "sovereignty" is the habitual obedience secured through the power of punishment or the means by which to visit an "evil" in those who disobey.

Note what law—in its essential purity—is, and what it is not: It is not a moral maxim, not a religious belief, not the voice of conscience, not an ordinance of reason, not the mind of God. That a given law may agree with what one takes to be the will of God is, of course, possible; it might even be desirable. That the law does not require what conscience forbids is a distinct benefit to one whose conscience is thus supported, but what makes the law law is neither its agreement with religion and morals nor its compatibility with individual consciences. What makes it law is that it is expressed by those possessing sovereign power.

Here, then, is a succinct and early statement of what came to be called *legal positivism*. Law is what is enacted or authoritatively promulgated and enforced. The study of law is the study of actual enactments or commands. It is a branch of neither moral nor political philosophy, but a subject unto itself, calling for rigorous analysis of such key notions as law, duty, obligation, rights. The focus is on the legal concepts themselves, not on their allegedly moral dependencies or sources.

Austin was fully prepared to accept both moral laws and divine laws, understanding each of these to be different from each other, and both to be different from the positive laws brought into being and enforced by sovereign power. Analytical jurisprudence is the subject of the last of these; moralists and theologians can claim the rest of the terrain, on Austin's account.

This is all neat and quite stimulating, but it does tend to leave the fundamental issues in philosophy of law, more or less untouched. On neither Austin's account nor those advanced by his successors in legal positivism is it clear just what enters into the concept of *sovereign*. Austin's most famous successor was Oxford's H. L. A. Hart, whose *The Concept of Law* appeared in 1961.

One objective of that work was to repair features of the legal positivism that had attracted serious criticism. Austin's concept of sovereign was notoriously fluid, leaving the issue of valid authority intractable, and his *command theory* of law, which ties the command-function to little more than the power of enforcement, seems to confer the standing of legislator on unwanted types. After all, the gun-toting thief who commands us to hand over our wallets would seem to qualify as a lawgiver.

Hart's attempt to eliminate such counterintuitive possibilities is in the form of something he called the *rule of recognition*. What the thief or highwayman lacks, but Congress possesses, is the recognized status of the source of positive laws. Thus, says Hart, to say that a given rule is valid is to recognize it as passing all the tests provided by the rule of recognition.

Understood this way, law is a collection of laws, and each of these stands as a social fact, a social artifact one might say, not unlike other useful items that societies create for their own purposes. We make clay pots, we make teaspoons, we make tractors, and we make laws. As we "recognize" the Motor Vehicle Bureau as the place that prints valid drivers' licenses, we recognize Congress as the body that passes valid laws. Let's say the pizza parlor were to advertise: "Valid drivers' licenses given with every order"; we would be suspicious enough perhaps to call the police, not because the offer is "immoral," or even because the pizza shop would require high standards of visual and motor skills. Rather, it is simply the wrong place to be granting licenses to drive.

Thus, the rule of recognition corrects one of the basic flaws in command theory. It enables all of us to determine whether or not a law is valid by determining whether it satisfies the rule of recognition.

Well, of course, the Nazi party in Germany was a duly elected party, by an overwhelming majority. It appointed judges in the traditional manner that judges got appointed, and otherwise satisfied whatever goes into the rule of recognition in the matter of how law comes about. Do we want to say that this is sufficient to establish that what was ever thereby enacted would stand as valid law?

Now, the natural law critique of this entire line of reasoning has been provided by a number of writers rather early on, and by a contemporary of H. L. A. Hart, Lon Fuller, in what remains a classic treatise titled *Positivism and Fidelity to Law: A Reply to Professor Hart*. Attempts to distinguish between law and morality, as if the former could have any sort of real function in the absence of moral precepts, fail at both the practical and the conceptual levels of analysis, according to Fuller. The moral and rational powers actually presupposed by the rule of law are also at work in distinguishing between *law* as something to be faithfully obeyed and *law* as but a word seeking to conceal arbitrary, immoral, and tyrannical modes of control.

Fuller is prepared to insulate the rule of law from specific, substantive moral mandates, but he insists, nonetheless, that the very concept of law requires a *procedural* morality ensuring the law's fairness, and ensuring its consistency in application, its clarity, etc. In his 1964 book *The Morality of Law*, he puts the matter this way:

> What I have called the "internal morality of law" is…a procedural version of natural law…concerned not with the substantive aims

of legal rules, but with the ways in which a system of rules for governing human conduct must be constructed and administered if it is to be efficacious and at the same time remain what it purports to be.

Natural law theory and legal positivism, however, do not exhaust the options in philosophy of law. An influential writer in this field in recent years has been Ronald Dworkin. His criticism of legal positivism begins with the observation that courts must often decide cases for which there are no precedents and nothing in the record of "social facts," so called, sufficient to settle the matter.

One instance cited by Dworkin is *Riggs v. Palmer*, which had to decide whether a murderer nonetheless was still to enjoy what his victim had bequeathed to him in a will. The maxim according to which "no one is to benefit from the commission of a crime" was not in the settled law of the jurisdiction and, in any case, is a patently moral precept in character, but it was just this reasoning that led to the decision in *Riggs*.

To summarize the conclusions reached by Dworkin in his analysis of law, the authority and validity of law result from its embodiment of moral aims that are widely shared within the community and of a nature to justify the values and practices of the community. In *Riggs*, the court achieved the best outcome, defined as the one that matched most closely the moral principles operative within the community at large, and at that time. On this understanding, says Dworkin:

> Judges should decide hard cases by interpreting the political structure of their community, trying to find the best justification they can find in principles of political morality, for the structure as a whole.

Some will see in this little more than advocacy—indeed, of judicial activism, or even an apologia for the status quo. I want to say that Professor Dworkin has never concealed his support of legal activism, but I should think that, in the Lincoln-Douglas debates, for example, Douglas would have made very good use of Dworkin's understanding of the nature of law. Much of the South—understood surely as a "community"—accepted slavery as a property right and, more important, the right to make that judgment as a state's right. That was therefore endemic to the culture, widely shared values.

To some extent, Dworkin's theory is a descendent—if not an acknowledged one—of that *legal realism* that flourished in American jurisprudence under such defenders as Oliver Wendell Holmes, Rosco Pound, and Jerome Frank. Holmes famously reduced the concept of law to that which would allow him to predict what judges and juries would decide in given cases.

The best understanding of law, on this account, is an instrumental one: Law is just a tool designed to achieve certain desired outcomes. It functions in such a way as to make easier or more efficient the attainment of social goals. Its authority is not found in moral precepts, or even in tradition and custom. Its authority just is the act of deciding cases. Jerome Frank was himself a federal judge. In one of his lectures on legal realism, he discusses a Supreme Court case settled by a 6–3 decision and asked, from the petitioners' point of view, just what was "the law." As Frank observed, until the court ruled, there was no answer whatever to the question. This is Frank:

> Law, then, as to any given situation is either (a) actual law, i.e., a specific past decision as to that situation, or (b) probable law; that is, a guess, as to a specific future decision.

Kant, as might have been guessed, composed a most analytical exposition on the nature of law, understood as part of the metaphysics of morals itself. The heading under which we find his philosophy of law is "the science of right," which, he says, has for its object "the Principles of all the Laws which it is possible to promulgate by external legislation... It is from this Science that the immutable Principles of all positive Legislation must be derived by practical Jurists and Lawgivers," and what is that principle?

Well, as Kant puts it:

> Every action is *right* which in itself, or in the maxim on which it proceeds, is such that it can co-exist along with freedom of the will of each and all in action, according to a universal law.

420

Law, then, is derived from a principle, and the principle is one that seeks to preserve and honor the moral liberty of rational beings, consistent with the freedom of all such beings. That freedom, too, comes under the direction of a universal law, which, as we have seen in the lecture on Kant, is a moral law. With Kant, we are returned to the law's moral purposes, derived from the idea of freedom and the dignity of beings who are rational as such. Of rights, Kant asserts that only one is a natural and inborn right; all others are derived from positive law and tradition.

What is the core right, and the inborn one?

> Freedom is independence of the compulsory will of another; and in so far as it can co-exist with the freedom of all according to a universal law, it is the one sole original inborn right belonging to every man in virtue of his humanity. There is, indeed, an innate equality belonging to every man which consists in his right to be independent of being bound by others to anything more than that to which he may also reciprocally bind them.

These lines provide a foundation for one of the most influential works in contemporary philosophy of law, John Rawls's *A Theory of Justice*. As with Kant, Rawls's goal is the preservation of freedom from the compulsory will of another. The reciprocation discussed by Kant appears in Rawls as a "fairness" criterion": Justice as fairness, grounded in that principle of equal liberty that gives no one more extensive freedom than that possessed by others, and Kant's categorical imperative, in a somewhat quirky way, supports or is intended to support what Rawls calls the *difference principle*: Social and economic inequalities should be arranged so that they are to the greatest benefit of the least advantaged before they improve the condition of the more advantaged.

Well, I should say, for all its celebrity, Rawls's *A Theory of Justice* is disappointing and incomplete. It is surely not a Kantian maxim that the claim one has on the general resources is proportioned to the degree of disadvantage. There are just deserts and cons, after all, such that one might well have *earned* one's disadvantages, and what can be said of "equal liberty," if its exercise leads to the very differences in social and economic conditions that are then to be cancelled or reduced via the difference principle? All due respect to Rawls and his work, but you see that there are more questions raised than answers given.

There is a small step, actually, from the position according to which law is no more than a social instrument to the very use of law to secure social conditions dictated by theories that, rather than outcomes of rigorous criticism, are presented as if they were protected from criticism. In the end, just in case we are vigilant and lucky, law is an ordinance of reason, and it is promulgated by one who is responsible for the common good. What question does this leave wide open? The question it leaves wide open is: Just what is the common good? It is not within the province of philosophy of law to determine what, given the nature of human nature, would be the common good of all.

In order to address that question, one is led inescapably back to fundamentally moral considerations, such that even if one were to accept a positivistic distinction between morals and jurisprudence, moral philosophy and philosophy of law, and were simply to accept that the function of law is to secure ends compatible with the good of the community, with the values of the community, etc., we would still be driven back to a critical assessment, a critical identification, of just what constitutes a benefit to all, what constitutes the good of the community, what would be the means by which to measure and assess the extent to which the freedom of one has been honored in a proportional way to the freedom of all.

Philosophy of law, like philosophy itself, is extremely useful at the level of criticism. It makes no promises—and should not make promises—at the level of great, abiding, and true discoveries. Philosophy of law is alive and well, and by the way, in case listeners are interested, natural law theory, around for so long and then replaced, seems to be sneaking back in, very often under disguise, sometimes under the darkness of night. Stay tuned.

Justice and Just Wars
Lecture 58

The subject of justice is ordinarily thought of as an issue of rights, but this, as it happens, is a relatively late addition to questions of justice.

Neither the ancient Greek nor ancient Roman world devoted much time to the matter of individual rights. To the extent that Socrates, for example, may have had justice as a central concern, the concept applied to the criteria by which we judge a person's character, rather than to the question of whether the state has been the source of justice. In Plato's *Republic*, justice in the state is what leads to harmony and peace, but in the individual, it takes the form of a selfless and rational commitment to do the morally right thing. For Aristotle and Cicero, justice is simply the "virtue of the magistrate" and, more or less, a matter of convention and of law.

There are discussions of certain principles of justice, such as equity and fair distributions of goods. The emphasis is on reasonableness and moderation. Justice is what we are each obliged to strive for in our association with others and our dealings in the world.

The ancient concept of justice is established in an intellectual framework that holds that there is a cosmic rational order and that a comparable rational order is the natural state of affairs for human societies. Rational beings are to be ruled by law rather than by force, and actions by and toward them carry the burden of justification. This line of thought, though foundational for all developed ideas of justice, does not conclude in clear statements of universal human rights.

Once we remove this conception of justice as a virtue and turn to conceptions of social justice or the rights of man, the ancient world has much less to say. Aristotle insists that it is right that Hellenes shall rule barbarians. Plato's republic is anti-democratic, committed to eugenic forms of human breeding, and class-structured on meritocratic grounds. Slavery is commonplace in all of recorded history and often predicated on the belief that some persons or tribes or religious groups or races are simply inferior to their enslaving masters.

The closest we come to a discussion of universal individual rights is in some of the precepts of the ancient Cynics. Diogenes (412–323 B.C.) was a leader of this radically "democratic" school of philosophy, opposed to class hierarchies and even slavery. Here, too, however, notions of universal brotherhood did not capture the sense of "rights" as such, but something more akin to a naturalism that requires social and political life to be stripped of what is merely artificial and self-serving.

Perhaps the most significant development in conceptions of justice was that introduced by the early church fathers, especially by St. Augustine in his discussion of conscience and freedom of the will. *Justice* on this account is obedience to God's law, which may place a person in adversarial relationships with others and with the state. Augustine is also important for his comments on slavery. He sees in slavery only the lust for domination, which condemns the master, but Augustine does not offer any political argument for abolition.

John Locke, regarded as the prophet of American liberty, in the preamble to the Constitution for Carolina in 1669, made express provision for the keeping of "leet-men," holdover serfs of medieval Europe, or slaves. I know of no anti-slavery treatise based on the universal principle of human rights before the 17th century, when the Quakers protested the importation of slaves from Africa.

There are earlier treatises on "human rights" apart from the issue of slavery and its abolition. The Magna Carta of 1215, signed by King John at Runnymede, affirms the rights of the Church against the Crown and grants individuals free exercise of their religious convictions. The document neither affirms universal rights nor focuses on the individual as the bearer of such rights. It lays the foundation for principles that will become more sharply defined in the Reformation and thereafter, as to the limits on royal prerogatives and clerical authority. By the 18th century, the secular version of this conception of justice requires rule by right reason over and against any rule based on no more than revelation or tradition.

Out of the religious wars between Christians and Muslims would come a most significant teaching on the rights of man—Francisco de Vittoria's (1480–1546) *De Indis* and his *De Jure Belli Relectiones*. Vittoria insists that God's laws apply to the children of God and would preserve them from torture and torment. The religious ignorance or waywardness of a people cannot justify inhumane acts toward them, even during war. Vittoria also proposes the idea of a "just war," beyond the ancient concept of "might makes right." Christian theological virtues also must be adhered to, including the stipulation that "mercy is the perfection of justice." Justice now is measured against motives, and the motives must be faithful to Christian values.

In the context of Christian teaching, the two most significant writers on the subject of the just war were St. Augustine and St. Thomas Aquinas. Augustine made clear that, at the personal level, only self-defense can justify the use of lethal force. At the level of nation-states, however, there is a larger purpose served: the preservation of peace. This view specifically rules out as permissible motives or justifications for war "the passion for inflicting harm, the cruel thirst for vengeance... the lust of power."

With Thomas Aquinas, we see the full development of a theory of just war in an attempt to remove the inconsistency that results in what he offers as the sole justifications for war. For a war to be just, three things are necessary. The authority of a sovereign by whose command the war is to be waged. A just cause, namely, that those who are attacked should be attacked because they deserve it on account of some fault. The belligerents should intend the advancement of good or the avoidance of evil.

Once a war has begun, there are comparable principles determining what is justly done in the prosecution of the war. The main criterion is proportionality, recognized immunity of non-combatants. Refinements were added over the centuries by such theorists as Francisco Suarez (1548–1617), Francisco de Vittoria, and Hugo Grotius (1583–1645). The warring party, seeking no more than the advancement of good or the avoidance of evil, must itself avoid evil. The war must be waged with restraint, applying no greater force than is needed to secure the desired good. Its motivation must not be corrupted by considerations of wealth or power.

If these are principles that at least plausibly classify warfare as just, are they *mutatis mutandis*, applicable to relationships between the individual and the state? If a nation may justly make war to secure peace and resist evil, might it not also impose coercively on citizens forms of conduct and life also consistent with peace and decency? In the liberal tradition, the state's justifiable use of force has been limited to the prevention of harm. John Stuart Mill made the harm principle the prime justification for the constraint of liberty.

> **Perhaps the most significant development in conceptions of justice was that introduced by the early church fathers, especially by St. Augustine in his discussion of conscience and freedom of the will.**

But this is unhelpful until and unless the category of "harms" is worked out with some precision. To the harm principle some have argued for the addition of "offense" and "nuisance." Citizens should also be protected against actions that are so patently offensive as to diminish the dignity of civic life. Coercive constraints in such cases must be applied in a measured and proportionate fashion, the motive again not corrupted by self-serving factors.

The problem with this reasonable paradigm is that it leaves plenty of room for excessive forms of state paternalism, as well as excessive forms of state paralysis. What standards are to be applied to notions of offense and nuisance or, for that matter, harm?

Paternalism is nearly unavoidable, except in total anarchies. The compulsory education of children is one expression of it, as are laws requiring seat belts, denying the right to smoke in public places, forbidding the sale of alcohol to minors, and so on. Provable harm is not invariably at issue in these contexts. Nor are those opposed to state paternalism comparably opposed to state welfarism. John Rawls, for example, requires a hands-off policy in the matter of individual liberty but a hands-on policy in compensating for marked inequality in wealth and opportunity.

Virtue, of which justice is an instance, cannot be reduced to a formula nor manifested in the form of trappings and slogans. Justice in the state comes from just citizens, just magistrates, and just legislators. To the extent that, at least metaphorically, we can speak of the state as "virtuous," we can mean only that its institutions and practices are designed to promote virtue and oppose evil. "Do good and avoid evil" is a command accessible to those with common sense and sufficient civic breeding to understand how their actions contribute to the tone of life, their own included. Nothing serves them better than a political world in which the rule is the rule of law, understood to be an ordinance of reason. ■

Suggested Reading

Augustine. *The City of God* (downloadable).

Paine, Thomas. *The Rights of Man* (downloadable).

Walzer, Michael. *Just and Unjust Wars*. New York: Basic Books, 2000.

Questions to Consider

1. What is the right answer to the Athenian claim in the Melian dialogue?

2. Suppose the native population in the Americas were judged to be doomed to hell unless converted. What argument would still require tolerance and a respect for the autonomy of their beliefs?

3. Does the just-war theorist have an answer to the pacifist, and if so, what is it?

Justice and Just Wars
Lecture 58—Transcript

The subject of justice is ordinarily thought of as an issue of rights—of giving one what is due, of respecting one's individual dignity, and so forth—but this, as it happens, is a relatively late addition to questions of justice, for neither the ancient Greek nor the ancient Roman world devoted much time or papyrus to the matter of individual rights as such, and as for one's dignity, in the ancient world this was a property hard won and easily lost, often in a moment.

To the extent that Socrates, for example, may be said to have had justice as a central concern, the concept applied rather more to the criteria by which we judge a person's character, rather than to the question of whether the state has been the source of justice. In Plato's *Republic*, justice in the state is what leads to harmony and peace, but in the individual, it takes the form of a selfless and rational commitment to do the right thing in the moral sense of "right."

For Aristotle, justice in the sense of the actions of the state is simply the "virtue of the magistrate" and, in any case, is more or less a matter of convention and of law. So, too, with Cicero.

The point is not that justice is not of crucial importance in ancient philosophy; rather, it is too important to be reduced to institutional functions or merely personal expectations. Justice is a virtue. Virtues inhere in persons. There cannot be a "just state" populated by felons. So, if we are interested in theories of justice advanced by leading ancient philosophers, we will find texts rich in character analysis and in examples of how the just and the unjust person behave, and behaves toward others. There will be far less on the rights individuals have in relation to others and to the entire community.

This much noted, there are, of course, discussions of certain principles of justice, such as equity and the fair distributions of goods. The emphasis is on reasonableness and moderation, as might be expected of Plato, Aristotle, Cicero, and the rest. As with all the virtues, justice is of intrinsic value, such that it would be odd to ask about its instrumental or cash value. What we would take to be a principle of justice is, in ancient Greek philosophy, a dictate of reason, a reflection of the character of the actor—less attention is paid to what another is "due," so to speak, than what is revealed by those who fail to pay what is due.

When Socrates claims that he would far prefer to be the victim of injustice than its cause, he gives voice to this understanding. Justice is what we are each obliged to strive for in our association with others, and our dealings with the world.

Lest there be confusion on this point, let me repeat that there is an ancient background or intellectual framework for all conceptions of "justice" as we would understand the term today. It is established by the ancient Greek conception of a cosmic rational order, which makes clear that a comparable rational order is the natural state of affairs for human societies. Plato and Aristotle both emphasize this, and the Stoic philosophers make it the linchpin of their moral philosophy. "Justice," on this basis, is but another face of rationality itself, now turned to the manner in which persons are governed and must govern themselves. As rational beings, they are to be ruled by law rather than by force, and actions by and toward them then, now carry the burden of justification. One can always ask, when one is being constrained in one's actions: "By what right do you that?" or, "What is the reason you're doing that?"

This line of thought, though foundational for all developed ideas of justice, does not conclude in any clear statements of universal human rights. Once we remove this conception of justice as a virtue and turn to conceptions of social justice or the rights of man, so to speak, the ancient world actually has much less to say. The same Aristotle who defines "man" generically as a rational animal, thus conferring the power of rationality on humanity at large, will insist that it is right nonetheless that Hellenes shall rule barbarians. Plato's republic is famously anti-democratic, committed to eugenic forms of human breeding, and class-structured on meritocratic grounds. Slavery, of course, is commonplace in all of recorded history of the ancient world and, though routinely justified as one of the wages of defeat in war, is often predicated on the belief that some persons or tribes or religious groups or races are simply inferior to their enslaving masters.

When Aristotle, in his *Politics*, begins his discussion of those he refers to as "natural slaves," the *"dou los physikos,"* he does note that some regard slavery to be wrong in all instances, but he is unable to produce the names of those who are opposed to slavery in all cases.

The Stoic philosophers, as I've noted, do impose rigorous standards of reasonableness on laws and social behavior, locating our "right," as it were, to such treatment in our unique possession of language, but, again, we do not find in their works arguments for the abolition of slavery. Perhaps the closest we come to the universalizing and the individuating of rights is in some of the precepts of the ancient Cynics. Diogenes comes to mind; Diogenes lived from 412 to 323 B.C. He was a leader of this school of philosophy, this Cynics' school. It was a radically "democratic" philosophical school, radically democratic in its political philosophy, opposed to all forms of pretense, to class hierarchies and, yes, opposed to slavery as well. Here, too, however, notions of universal brotherhood did not capture the sense of "rights" as such, but something more akin to a naturalism that requires social and political life to be stripped of what is merely artificial and self-serving.

Perhaps the most significant development in conceptions of justice was that introduced by the early church fathers, and especially by St. Augustine in his discussion of conscience and freedom of the will. This interiorization of morals was intended to liberate conscience from mere convention. *Justice* on this account is obedience to God's law, which may place a person in adversarial relationships with others and with the state. That this idea is "neo-Platonist" is irrelevant to the progress in the world of politics and law in the centuries in which Christianity was the dominating perspective.

Augustine is also important for his comments on slavery in Book 19 of *The City of God*. He says:

> Now, as our Lord above says, "Everyone who commits sin is sin's slave," and this is why, though many devout men are slaves to unrighteous masters, yet the masters they serve are not themselves free. It is a happier lot to be a slave to a human being than to a lust, and, in fact, the most pitiless domination that devastates the hearts of men, is that exercised by this very lust for domination.

Ah, well, trenchant as was this teaching, it did little to extend justice to those regarded as of low standing. If John Locke is to be regarded as the prophet of American liberty—and I have serious reservations about that—it is useful to recall his participation in drafting the Constitution for Carolina in 1669. In the very preamble to the document, Locke wrote that the Constitution was to prevent "a numerous democracy," and made express provision in Article XIX for the lord of the manor to "alienate, sell, or dispose to any other person and his heirs forever, his manor, all entirely together, with all the privileges and leet-men there unto belonging."

The "leet-men," of course, were the holdover serfs of medieval Europe. To put the point briefly, let me say that I know of no anti-slavery treatise based on the universal principle of human rights before the 17th century, when the Quakers protested the importation of slaves from Africa. This idea of human rights is a gradually developing idea itself, then.

There are earlier treatises on "human rights" apart from the issue of slavery and its abolition. These, interestingly enough, are composed in the two radically different contexts of war and of religion. The first is the venerable Magna Carta of 1215, signed by King John at Runnymede. Its provisions include the following:

> That the English Church shall be free, and shall have its rights undiminished, and its liberties unimpaired. This freedom we shall observe ourselves, and desire to be observed in good faith by our heirs in perpetuity. We have also granted to all free men of our realm, for us and our heirs forever, all the liberties written out below, to have and to keep for them and their heirs, of us and our heirs.

Note that the liberties and freedoms pertain to Church elections, and they are reserved only to the "free men" of the realm. This is not a document affirming universal rights, nor does it focus on the individual as the bearer of such rights, but it does lay the foundation for principles that will become more sharply defined in the Reformation and thereafter, as to the limits on royal prerogatives in the matter of religion and, indeed, the limits on clerical authority in the matter of individual conscience. Simply stated, the individuation of rights, and the application of principles of justice to the individual person as the bearer of rights—all this grows out of claims of religious liberty. By the 18th century, the secular version of this conception of justice requires rule by right reason over and against any rule based on no more than revelation or tradition.

In a different context, now the context of warfare and the duties of victors toward the vanquished, there is another path toward the idea of justice as a universal obligation owed to persons as such. This is a complex chapter in political and intellectual history, and one must be wary of generalizations.

The religious wars between Christians and Muslims featured the execution of "infidels" on both sides of the lines of battle, and it was this same mentality that Spanish conquistadors brought with them to the New World. Their brutality toward the native population was relentless. There seems to be little that some won't do to a body in order to save a soul.

Out of that experience, however, would come a most significant teaching on what we may properly refer to as "the rights of man." I refer hereto Francisco de Vittoria's *De Indis*; this was a man who lived from 1480 to 1546. His *De Indis* and his *De Jure Belli Relectiones*—the first including his consideration of the Indians of the New World, and the second his lectures on what? On "just war." The published version of his lectures—he was a professor of theology at the University of Salamanca—would not appear in print until the end of the 17th century, but he had such great intellectual standing, it was such that the ideas themselves were influential before they appeared in print, influential as a result of his teaching.

There is much of interest and importance in Vittoria's lectures, not the least of which is the requirement that, in war, as little harm is produced as is consistent with the need for victory. I will return to this later in the lecture, but here I draw attention to his insistence that God's laws apply to the children of God and would preserve them from torture and torment. The religious ignorance or waywardness of a people cannot justify inhumane acts toward them.

The "just war." Well, what is a "just war"? In Chapter XVII of Thucydides account of the Peloponnesian War, written in 431 B.C., there is a dialogue between the Athenian military and the citizens of the island state of Melos, the famous *Melian Dialogue*. In the complex politics of the ancient Greek world, the main competitors for power were Athens and Sparta, each with a set of client states. Melos, notwithstanding to the contrary their denials in the dialogue, was clearly on the Spartan side, at least in this dispute.

The Athenian expeditionary force numbered nearly 48 ships and thousands of infantry and archers, clearly sufficient to reduce Melos to rubble. When asked to justify their occupation, the Athenians first speak of the Melian allegiance to Sparta, but they clearly do not intend the discussion to go very far. Indeed, they soon reply to further questions with this statement of brute fact:

> For ourselves, we shall not trouble you with specious pretenses, either of how we have a right to our empire, or are now attacking you because of a wrong that you have done us. Since you know as well—you certainly know as well as we do that right, as the world goes, is only a question between those equal in power, while the strong do what they can, and the weak suffer what they must.

What could be clearer? It is "might that makes right," except where powers are so equal as to require each side to look for some other basis on which to gain an advantage; the other basis being perhaps "precious pretences," or what we are pleased to call moral arguments.

The Melians remind these Athenians that the position being advocated here violates their own developed principles of justice and equity—but, of course, this gets them nowhere. Rather, their surrender, they are told, will be the best for everyone, for it will spare them the consequence of total destruction, and it will spare the Athenians the cost of accomplishing their total destruction. This is obviously not Aristotle or Plato speaking.

That the ancient world had a conception of the "just war" there is no doubt, for the terms of such a war are developed in the Homeric epics themselves. Consider Athena's final counsel to Odysseus in behalf of peace, and consider as well the price that all must pay for what is disproportionate or irrational in battle. Again, this is "justice and reason," rather than "justice as rights," but it is a developed conception of justice nonetheless. The same is obvious from the details of ancient Greek and Roman law—replete with trial procedures, rules of evidence, the attempt to fit punishments to the nature of the offense, the allegiance of leaders to the rule of law and the condemnation of tyrants. I repeat: The ancient understandings inform all later understandings of justice—inform, but do not determine them.

Rather, to the ancient understandings must be added a rich and various contribution from, yes, Christian theology. The addition to the classical virtues of the theological virtues that include charity—that is an addition that is a profound addition. The stipulation that "mercy is the perfection of justice" now adds to justice a decent respect for human dignity, for the standing of the person as a child of God. Justice now is measured against motives, and the motives must be faithful to what? Well, faithful to the faith. That all this is routinely violated in the actual affairs of state is lamentable, but the standards of justice are nevertheless clearly developed.

Within the context of Christian teaching, the two most significant writers on the subject of the just war were St. Augustine and St. Thomas Aquinas. Augustine may well be credited with inaugurating the tradition itself in his treatise *The City of God*. Having made clear that, at the personal level, only self-defense can justify the use of lethal force—well, at the level of nation-states there is a larger purpose served: namely, the preservation of peace. Thus, says Augustine:

> We do not seek peace in order to be at war, but we go to war that we may have peace. Be peaceful, therefore, in warring, so that you may vanquish those whom you war against, and bring them to the prosperity of peace.

Aristotle had made the same observation in the *Nichomachean Ethics*: We make war so that we may live in peace, but as the aim of peace is won at the very heavy price of war, it must be the aim of peace alone that is envisaged. As Augustine says, specifically ruled out as permissible motives or justifications for war are "the passion for inflicting harm, the cruel thirst for vengeance...the lust of power."

With Thomas Aquinas, there is the full development of a theory of just war. The Christian duty to seek peace seems inconsistent with war in any form, and it is Aquinas's attempt to remove that inconsistency that results in what he offers as the sole justifications for war. Here's Thomas Aquinas:

> In order for a war to be just, three things are necessary. First, the authority of the sovereign by whose command the war is to be waged, for it is not the business of a private individual to declare war, because he can seek for redress of his rights from the tribunal of his superior. Secondly, a just cause is required, namely that those who are attacked should be attacked because they deserve it on account of some fault. Thirdly, it is necessary that the belligerents should have a rightful intention, so that they intend the advancement of good, or the avoidance of evil.

There are different considerations applicable to the justification for going to war—the *Jus ad Bellum*, and the justified actions that take place in war, the *Jus in Bello*.

Aquinas's actually stand as the first criterion for addressing the question of legitimate authority for waging war. As his natural law theory regards law itself as an ordinance of reason to be promulgated by one who has responsibility for the good of the community, it is then only by way of the sovereign power of princes and states that war could be justly waged. In modern terms, we would say that whatever it is they are doing, terrorists are not waging war. Do you see? Not just sovereigns attempting to secure good.

In light of the costs of war and the inevitable loss of innocent life, then, the cause must be just, the war itself must be the last in a series of measures designed to achieve peace, and there must be a reasonable chance of success. War, in other words, is never to be a futile gesture. Finally, the measures must satisfy the requirement of proportionality, such that the war inflicts no greater harm than is necessary to achieve the just aims of peace.

Once the war has begun, the *Jus in Bello*, there are comparable principles determining what is justly done in the prosecution of a war. Again, the main criterion is proportionality, along with the recognized immunity of non-combatants. Refinements of this sort were added over the centuries by such theorists as Francisco Suarez (1548–1617); and Francisco de Vittoria, whom I've mentioned within the context of Roman Catholic theory; and Hugo Grotius (1583–1645), a Protestant natural law theorist.

These refinements require that the warring party seek no more than the advancement of what is good or the avoidance of evil. There must be the avoidance of evil. Thus, the war must be waged with restraint, applying no greater force than what is needed to secure the desired good. Its motivation must not be corrupted by considerations of merely personal gain in the form of wealth or power. For a war to be just, the cause must be just, and that requires that the enemy be justly regarded as a source of evil.

Now, if these are principles that at least plausibly are classifiable for what makes a war just, warfare as serving the interests of justice, then we might ask whether they are *mutatis mutandis*, applicable to relationships between the individual and the state. That is, if a nation may justly make war to secure peace and resist evil, might it not also impose coercively on citizens forms of conduct and of life also consistent with peace and decency?

Within the liberal tradition, the state's justifiable use of force has been limited to the prevention of harm. John Stuart Mill made the harm principle the prime justification for the constraint of liberty. But this is unhelpful until and unless the category of "harms" is worked out with some precision. To the harm principle some have argued for the addition of "offense" and even "nuisance." That is, harm is not the sole effect from which others should be spared by the police power of the state. Citizens should also be protected against actions so patently offensive as to diminish the dignity of civic life itself—and protected, as well, from actions whose nuisance value is such as to frustrate the legitimate activities of fellow citizens. Coercive constraints in such cases must be applied in a measured and proportionate fashion, the motive again not corrupted by self-serving factors.

Of course, the problem with this reasonable paradigm is that it leaves about as much room as any theorist requires to support excessive forms of state paternalism, as well as excessive forms of state paralysis. What standards are to be applied to notions of offense and nuisance or, for that matter, harm? Many students of human development believe there is convincing evidence to the effect that pornography has a deleterious effect on children, even on adult relationships—that it is harmful in addition to being grossly offensive and, when sold or featured in local establishments, constitutes a public nuisance as well.

To say that it is "protected" by the First Amendment—as if that disposed of the matter—is to fail to acknowledge all varieties of speech and publication not protected by the First Amendment: libelous utterances, statements likely to provoke violence and civil unrest, statements advocating the violent overthrow of the government. What seems to be at issue is not the limitations imposed by the First Amendment, but the more general limitations that the liberal state imposes on the application of state power.

Paternalism is nearly unavoidable, of course, except in total anarchies. The compulsory education of children is one expression of it, as are laws requiring seat belts, or denying the right to smoke in public places, or forbidding the sale of alcohol to minors. Provable harm is not invariably at issue in these contexts. Nor are those opposed to state paternalism comparably opposed to state welfarism. John Rawls, for example, requires a hands-off policy in the matter of individual liberty but a hands-on policy in compensating for marked inequality in wealth and opportunity.

Virtue, of which justice is an instance, cannot be reduced to a formula nor manifested in the form of trappings and slogans. Justice in the state is brought about by just citizens, just magistrates, and just legislators. To the extent that, at least metaphorically, we can speak of the state as "virtuous," we can mean only that its institutions and practices are designed to promote virtue and oppose evil—designed to make war on evil in ways that are proportionate, non-arbitrary, and respectful of the potentialities, if not the current standing, of one or another individual.

The virtuous state, as with the virtuous person, is not controlled by the passing enthusiasms of majorities, or the sophistical and skeptical challenges of the pedant. "Do good and avoid evil" is a command accessible to those with common sense and sufficient civic breeding to understand how their actions contribute to the very tone of life, their own included. Nothing will serve them better than a political world in which the rule is the rule of law, understood to be an ordinance of reason—and ideally, promulgated by one who has the good of the community as his or her responsibility, be she or he in Parliament, in Congress, a president, or a king. To do these things, and to do them virtually, is to presuppose a community accessible to a virtuous form of life. That form of paternalism is the royal rule that Aristotle speaks of—not the command of the tyrant, but the guidance of the good prince.

Aesthetics—Beauty Without Observers
Lecture 59

The status of music was highest among these forms of art, owing to its mathematical structure, thus grounding it in that very eternal, immutable domain that Platonism reserves to the "true form" of things.

In Plato's *Symposium*, Socrates recounts the lessons learned from Diotima, the mysterious woman from Mantineia, wise beyond measure. This is among the first philosophical inquiries into the nature of beauty. It speaks of the essence of beauty as distinct from the particular objects, sounds, and events that might be "beautiful" in the narrower sense. The beauty thus imagined does not depend on us or on any percipient for its reality. It is independent of mental representation or personal preferences. In addressing both the characteristics that constitute beauty in an object and the faculties an observer needs to experience the object's beauty, Plato establishes the *philosophy of aesthetics*. The observer, on this account, is to cultivate a native sensuous and reflective power, which when properly developed, expresses itself in the form of sound aesthetic judgment.

Aesthetics has not been understood in quite the same way in different historical epochs. Medieval conceptions were largely a merging of Greek and Hebrew sources, with Plato and the Old Testament enjoying special authority. The art form that dominated medieval aesthetics was music, one of the featured subjects of the medieval university curriculum. The *quadrivium* comprised arithmetic, geometry, astronomy, and music, the common feature, of course, being the rational structure of all four.

It is not until the Italian Renaissance that aesthetic theory turns away from the formalism of the object to the sensibilities of the observer and to the concept of *taste*. Early in the 18th century, essays begin to discuss the measure of "good taste." To possess good taste is, as the term will be applied later, to be an *aesthete*; to lack it is to be a *philistine*.

An issue regarded as pivotal during the Enlightenment especially pertains to the place of rationality itself in aesthetics. Is the aesthetic "judgment" actually the report of the aesthetic experience, or is it a rational reflection on that experience? Diderot regarded it as a faculty shaped by experience and instruction. D'Alembert, treats it as a form of reasoning. Montesquieu and others regard it as a distinct faculty. Shaftesbury adds the aesthetic sense to the moral sense as a native feature of the human sentiments.

David Hume's philosophy challenges the proposition that taste somehow finds something in an object that is the source of its beauty. *Beauty* itself refers to the manner in which the senses respond to an object. Mental operations then fashion aesthetic judgments of it. However, as in his moral theory, Hume discovers universal aesthetic tendencies, dispositions, and sentiments in the human race at large. There are standards of taste and degrees of competence that qualify some as *connoisseurs*.

Beauty itself refers to the manner in which the senses respond to an object.

An account of this kind seems to be challenged, however, by the radically different aesthetic styles that somehow all render experience highly agreeable or "right." It is doubtful that the best explanation of such developments can be rendered in terms of sentiment, let alone utility. Consider the *Baroque* style of art and architecture that flourished in the 17th century. This style became dominant in certain parts of Europe and rare or even condemned in other parts. Generally, it was featured in Roman Catholic countries, where the Counter-Reformation included a rejection of the spare, ascetic, and puritanical aesthetics of the Protestant reformers.

Giovanni Bernini (1598–1660) led the movement in sculpture and architecture, declaring that the various modes of art should be merged, not divided. Concrete expressions of the thesis are the three magnificent chapels he created in Rome: the Fonseca Chapel, the Albertoni, and the domed Church of Sant' Andrea al Quirinale. He is best known for the Basilica and the colonnades of St. Peter's at the Vatican. In sculpture, perhaps his two most popular works are the *Fountain of the Four Rivers* in the Piazza Navona and *The Ecstasy of St. Theresa* in the Church of Santa Maria della Vittoria in Rome.

The Baroque movement underscores the diffuse influences of the wider culture on how aesthetic forms are received. This is not Hume's sentiment-based theory but a more complex, perspectival theory in which moral, political, and religious thought establish the framework within which art is "seen" and "heard."

The Baroque, for all its influence, was more or less stopped in its tracks by the revolutionary change in perspective in the Enlightenment of the 18th century. The dominant aesthetic form now reverts to classicism and interest in the history of art and architecture, as well as history at large.

Of the many distinct characteristics of the Enlightenment, its identity as the "age of history" is especially revealing. Joachim Winckelmann's (1717–1768) *History of Ancient Art* did much to shape attitudes and impart knowledge about the classical worlds of Greece and Rome. His depictions of ancient Athens were actually rearrangements by Winckelmann himself, intended to give what he took to be greater coherence and "effect" than would be conveyed by the actual record. His characterization of the ancient Greek aesthetic ideal may still be the most informing and surely the briefest word on the subject: "noble simplicity and quiet grandeur." But if not for the contemporary movement of thought toward a secular culture, away from centuries of religious turmoil and its political effects, it is unlikely that a "classic" revival would have been received at the aesthetic level of experience.

Edmund Burke's *Philosophical Enquiry into the Origin of Our Ideas of the Sublime and Beautiful* (1757) gives us an anticipation of the irrationalism and "Gothic" mystery that will pervade the Romantic rebellion. Burke seeks to identify the causes and sources of the experience of sublimity as it is aroused by poetry, art, architecture, painting, and even religion and other spheres of thought and feeling that seem to overcome the senses and the intellect. His thesis is that two dominating ideas stand at the bottom of sublimity: danger and power.

The most influential work in the philosophy of aesthetics in the 18th century was Kant's *Third Critique* (1790). With respect to aesthetic judgments, Kant identifies four characteristics that must be present for the estimation to be at once a judgment and a judgment at the level of aesthetics:

- The judgment must be disinterested, in that considerations of utility are absent.

- It must be offered as universal, not merely personal.

- The judgment presupposes that there is a necessary connection between the relevant properties of the object and the aesthetic pleasure resulting from it.

- The objects of aesthetic judgment are understood as having a purpose, though not intended to serve a purpose—they are "purposive without purpose." The beauty of a natural landscape matches and exceeds the beauty of a painting of the same, but both are conceived as "intended."

This leaves Kant with the question of just how aesthetic judgments are made, because they are neither elementary sensations nor compounds of these but decisively cognitive, even "epistemic" from the point of view of the beholder. Aesthetic judgments, on this account, are drawn from a framework or categorical scheme of possible judgments, a scheme that grounds all judgment and that is neither empirical nor logical but foundational. No friend to the Romanticism of *Sturm und Drang,* Kant nevertheless presents artistic genius as instantiated in beings that nature speaks not so much "to" as "through."

The combined influence of Hume and Kant has shaped the philosophy of aesthetics in such a way as to divorce it from the moral, religious and political worlds in which art originally found its place. On the Humean account, aesthetics is that part of empirical psychology that identifies the features of the external world generally productive of agreeable feelings. How this works is really a matter of scientific research, all attempts to answer the question by examining the actual objects being futile. On the Kantian account, the very disinterested nature of aesthetic judgment divorces it directly from such non-aesthetic judgments as are made in moral and political philosophy—"Art for the sake of art," as it were.

G. E. Moore, in his *Principia Ethica* (1903), offered a different and radical conception of beauty. He posits two worlds: one of exquisite and uninterrupted beauty and one of rank and unrelieved ugliness. He argues that the former is preferable and that this very preference defeats the claim that the concept of beauty is exhausted by the resources of experience and feeling or even those of human judgment. He concludes:

> We shall have to include in our ultimate end something beyond the limits of human existence. I admit, of course, that our beautiful world would be better still, if there were human beings in it to contemplate and enjoy its beauty. But that admission makes nothing against my points. If it be once admitted that the beautiful world in itself is better than the ugly, then it follows, that however many beings may enjoy it, and however much better their enjoyment may be than it is itself, yet its mere existence adds something to the goodness of the whole: it is not only a means to our end, but also itself a part thereof. ■

Suggested Reading

Burke, Edmund. *Philosophical Enquiry into the Origin of Our Ideas of the Sublime and Beautiful and Other Pre-Revolutionary Writings*. Columbia University Press, 1958.

Hume, David. *On the Standard of Taste*. Liberty Fund, 1985.

Moore, G. E. *Principia Ethica* (1903). New York: Prometheus Books, 1988.

Questions to Consider

1. Is beauty in the eye of the beholder, and if so, what must be assumed about that "eye"?

2. Can art ever be totally disinterested in Kant's sense?

3. If genius is innate, why do we praise the genius?

Aesthetics—Beauty Without Observers
Lecture 59—Transcript

In Plato's *Symposium*, Socrates recounts the lessons learned from Diotima, the mysterious woman from Mantineia, wise beyond measure. She speaks to him about the nature of love and of beauty, drawing attention to the limits of ordinary perception and the confusions that arise from quick and passionate responses to things. If these limitations are to be overcome, she says, one must be instructed and shaped from the earliest years, with habitual exposure to what is beautiful, encouraged to love them. Under these favoring conditions, she says:

> Soon he will of himself perceive that the beauty of one form is akin to the beauty of another; and then if beauty of form in general is his pursuit, how foolish would he be not to recognize that the beauty in every form is one and the same, and when he perceives this he will abate his violent love of the one, which he will despise and deem a small thing, and will become a lover of all beautiful forms; in the next stage, he will consider that the beauty of the mind is the more honourable than the beauty of the outward form...until he is compelled to contemplate and see the beauty of institutions and laws, and to understand that the beauty of them all is of one family, and that personal beauty is a trifle; and after laws and institutions, he will go on to the sciences, that he may see their beauty... He who has been instructed thus far in the things of love, and who has learned to see the beautiful in due order and succession. When he comes toward the end will suddenly perceive a nature of wondrous beauty, until from fair notions he arrives at the notion of absolute beauty, and at last knows what the essence of beauty is. This, my dear Socrates, is that life above all others which man should live, in the contemplation of beauty absolute.

Oh, well. Has anything better on the subject ever been written?

This is among the first philosophical inquiries into the nature of beauty. It speaks of the essence of beauty as distinct from the particular objects, sounds, and events that might be "beautiful" in the narrower sense. The beauty

444

thus imagined does not depend on us or on any percipient for its reality. It is beauty independent of mental representation or personal preferences and tastes.

Diotima also emphasizes the conditions under which our access to this is even possible. The importance of early development in the formation of aesthetic sensibilities is clear, as is the need to be saved from regular exposure to what is trite or vulgar. In addressing both—what in the object must be present for there to be beauty, and what in the observer is necessary if this is to be experienced—Plato's dialogue virtually establishes the *philosophy of aesthetics*.

The observer, on this account, is to cultivate a native sensuous and reflective power, which when properly developed, expresses itself in the form of sound aesthetic judgment.

It should be noted that aesthetics has not been understood in quite the same way in different historical epochs. Medieval conceptions were largely a merging of Greek and Hebrew sources, with Plato and the Old Testament enjoying special authority. The art form that dominated medieval aesthetics was music, which was one of the featured subjects of the medieval university curriculum. The *quadrivium* consisted of arithmetic, geometry, astronomy, and music, the common feature here, of course, being the rational structure of all four. It is Plato's "nature of wondrous beauty" that is comprehended in the eternal, immutable laws of mathematics, music and, of course, celestial dynamics.

The status of music was highest among these forms of art, owing to its mathematical structure, thus grounding it in that very eternal, immutable domain that Platonism reserves to the "true form" of things. The same reasoning stands behind the medieval conception of beauty as a moral property and of morals as having an aesthetic quality, and this does help us understand why deviations from strict principles of harmony were regarded as, yes, moral offenses.

Of comparable importance in understanding the aesthetic philosophy of the medieval period is the different attitude toward nature itself. Whereas the classical world idealized nature, the medieval Christian world regarded what was earthly, physical, and accessible to the senses as transitory and misleading. Sensual forms of realism were replaced with symbolic and iconic intimations of what was taken to be the ultimate reality behind a world of mere appearances.

It is not until the Italian Renaissance that aesthetic theory turns away from such formalism, the formalism of the object, to the sensibilities of the observer and, alas, to the concept of *taste*, which, in the Italian, is, revealingly, *gusto*.

The term enters into aesthetic discourse as early as the middle of the 15th century. Rinuccini declares gusto to be the same as "right judgment." He is saying what taste is; it is right judgment.

In the 16th century, such great figures in art as Michelangelo and Cellini invoke the concept of gusto, of taste, to account for the recognition of beauty in all of its manifestations.

Early in the 18th century, essays begin to discuss the measure of "good taste" and, by 1718, we find nothing less than an *Accademia del buon gusto* in Palermo. This was a college, now, for good taste. Whether the Italian "*buon gusto*" or the French "*bon gout*," the possession in question is the possession of good taste. It is regarded as instinctive, discerning, judgmental. To possess it is, as the term will be applied later, to be, what? It is to be an *aesthete*. What are you if you lack it? Alas, that is to be a *philistine*.

An issue regarded as pivotal during the Enlightenment, especially during the Enlightenment, pertains to the place of rationality itself in aesthetics. Is the aesthetic "judgment" actually the report of the aesthetic experience, or is it a rational reflection on that experience? Diderot, as might be guessed, regarded it as a faculty shaped by experience and instruction. His fellow Encyclopaedist, D'Alembert, treats it as a form of reasoning, but others, such as Montesquieu, regard it as a distinct faculty such that individual works are comprehended within a framework that is aesthetic as such. You know, on this account, you could have sound aesthetic judgment, and not particularly good judgment in many, many other areas.

446

In England, a comparable theory would be defended by Shaftesbury, who adds the aesthetic sense to the moral sense as a native feature of the human sentiments. This is something you come into the world with. You might come into the world without it, but when you've got it, you have got it by nature.

Well, as now should be expected, David Hume's philosophy would challenge the proposition that taste somehow finds something in the object that is the source of its beauty. Rather, for Hume, *beauty* itself refers to the manner in which the senses respond to the objects and how the mental operations will then fashion aesthetic judgments of them. He develops this thesis in a 1757 essay "On the Standard of Taste," where he contrasts matters of fact and matters of opinion. Here's Hume, a characteristic Humean passage:

> A thousand different sentiments, excited by the same object, are all right, because no sentiment represents what is really in the object. It only marks a certain conformity, or relation, between the object and the organs or faculties of the mind. Beauty is not a quality in things themselves. It exists merely in the mind which contemplates them, and each mind perceives a different beauty.

With Hume, however, this observation does not lead to aesthetic anarchy or the reduction of taste to what is merely uncritical opinion. As in his moral theory, so, too, in his theory of taste, Hume discovers universal tendencies, universal dispositions and sentiments in the human race at large. It is thus no embarrassment to his theory that there is widespread agreement among persons living thousands of years apart and drawn from radically different climates and cultures that they are equally moved by Homer or Sophocles. As he says:

> Amidst all the variety and caprice of taste, there are certain general principles of approbation or blame, whose influence a careful eye may trace in all operations of the mind. Some particular forms or qualities, from the original structure of the internal fabric, are calculated to please, and others to displease, and if they fail of their effect in any particular instance, it is from some apparent defect or imperfection in the organ. A man in a fever would not insist on his palate as able to decide concerning flavours; nor would one, affected with the jaundice, pretend to give a verdict with regard to

447

colours. In each creature, there is a sound and a defective state; and the former alone can be supposed to afford us a true standard of a taste and sentiment.

If, then, "beauty is in the eye of the beholder," Hume requires that the eye be a healthy one, that the mind be cautious and disciplined in observing the features, that the education of the senses be such as to develop requisite powers of discernment. Even in Hume, then—and I say "even in Hume"— there are standards of taste and degrees of competence that qualify some as *connoisseurs*. An account of this kind seems to be challenged, however, by the radically different aesthetic styles that somehow all render experience highly agreeable or "right," at least with many whose tastes have neither been neglected or refined. It is doubtful that the best explanation of such developments can be rendered in terms of sentiment, let alone utility.

Here, I want to consider the movement in art and architecture from the Italian "High Renaissance" of the 16th century, to the *Baroque* style that flourished in the 17th century.

If I can pause for a moment to say that the purpose of the comparison is not to make a judgment of better or worse, but here we have Hume saying that there are certain universally distributed dot, dot, dot. Now, we are going to see architectural aesthetic styles that are so radically different that there really doesn't seem to be that kind of incorporation of universal elements, but let me proceed.

The Italian word *barocco* actually means "bizarre," a fantasy or phantasmagoria, and consider further that this very style became dominant in certain parts of Europe, and rare or even condemned in other parts. Guesses are invited as to the best predictor of where one will find the Baroque featured. You have three seconds to guess where it will be featured. Yes, chiefly in Roman Catholic countries, where the Counter-Reformation included a rejection of the spare, ascetic, and puritanical aesthetics of the Protestant reformers.

In sculpture and architecture, it was Giovanni Bernini, whose dates are 1598– 1660, who led the movement, declaring that the various modes of art should be merged and not divided. The principles that render a statue beautiful are the same as those that will guide painting and architecture. Thus is a building itself, in Bernini's view, a painted sculpture of sorts.

Concrete expressions of the thesis are the three magnificent chapels he created in Rome: the Fonseca Chapel, the Albertoni, and the domed Church of Sant' Andrea al Quirinale. Bernini, of course, is best known for the Basilica and the colonnades of St. Peter's at the Vatican. In sculpture, perhaps his two most popular works are the *Fountain of the Four Rivers* in the Piazza Navona and *The Ecstasy of St. Theresa* in the Church of Santa Maria della Vittoria in Rome.

I find myself dilating on the Baroque to underscore the diffuse influences of the wider culture on how aesthetic forms are received. In mind here is not Hume's sentiment-based theory but a far more complex and perspectival theory in which moral, political, and religious thought somehow establish the framework within which art is "seen" and music is "heard." The Baroque, for all its influence, was more or less stopped in its tracks by the revolutionary change in perspective in the Enlightenment of the 18th century. You see this radical change, now, from the Baroque to the classic revival. The dominant aesthetic form now does revert to classicism and a nearly sudden interest in the history of art and architecture, not to mention history at large.

Of the many distinct characteristics of the Enlightenment, its identity as "the age of history" is especially revealing. In this connection, I think first of Winckelmann, whose dates are 1717–1768. His *History of Ancient Art*, which appeared in 1764, did much to shape attitudes and to impart knowledge about the classical worlds of Greece and Rome.

His depictions of ancient Athens—I do want to pause for a second here; this is a fine book. It is still a very enlightening and entertaining book, but what is Winckelmann doing in giving this treatise to us on ancient Athens? Well, when you examine the book, in light of what we now know about ancient Athens, what you see is this: Winckelmann actually has rearranged the architecture of the ancient Athenian world. The arrangements in this work are by Winckelmann himself, and he intended to give what he took to be greater coherence and greater "effect" than would be conveyed by the actual record.

Winckelmann actually became Vatican Librarian. He became President of Antiquities of the Papal States. In his *Reflections on the Painting and Sculpture of the Greeks*, which appeared in 1765, he declared straight out that, "The only way for us to become great, or even inimitable, if possible, is to imitate the Greeks."

No one before Winckelmann had captured the spirit of ancient Greek art and architecture, and few had ever attempted a systematic analysis of it as a means by which to understand the ancient world in its fullness. Look at the buildings of a world, and you will know something about its mind, do you see? His characterization of the ancient Greek aesthetic ideal may still be the most informing and surely the briefest word on the subject: "noble simplicity and quiet grandeur."

However, if it were not for the contemporary movement of thought toward a secular culture and away from centuries of religious turmoil and its political effects, is it clear that a "classic" revival would have been received at the aesthetic level of experience? No, I think not. For Winckelmann, this very movement toward secularism and naturalism, and away from the transcendentalist character of Christianity, might have seemed a bad bargain.

Winckelmann was a Catholic convert and a man of deep religious conviction. I should say something about the end of his life. His end came at the hands of a murderer, who attempted to steal some ancient coins that Winckelmann had with him while staying at an inn. What were Winckelmann's dying words? He included in his dying words the forgiveness of his assailant: "Forgive the assailant."

Here's an example of noble simplicity and quiet grandeur.

In the same year that Hume's essay on taste was published, Edmund Burke had published his *Philosophical Enquiry into the Origin of Our Ideas of the Sublime and Beautiful*, again appearing in 1757, in which we discover an anticipation—an almost full anticipation—of that irrationalism and "Gothic" mystery that will pervade the Romantic rebellion. Burke seeks to identify the causes and the sources of the experience of sublimity as it is aroused by poetry, art, architecture, painting, and, indeed, how it is aroused by religion itself and other spheres of thought and feeling that seem to overcome the senses and overcome the intellect. His thesis is that two dominating ideas stand at the bottom of sublimity: the idea of danger and the idea of power. He writes about it this way:

> Sublimity includes, besides the idea of danger, the idea of power also appeared. Strength, violence, pain and terror are ideas which occupy the mind together. The sublimity of wild animals is due to their power; and the power of princes is not unmixed with terror, so that we address them as "dread majesty." It has even been said that fear originated the idea of deity, and true it is that, before Christianity, there was very little said of the love of God.

The most influential work in the philosophy of aesthetics in the 18th century was Kant's *Third Critique*, his *Critique of Judgment*, published in 1790. Though concerned throughout with the grounding of aesthetic judgments, the work is actually a theoretical inquiry into judgment itself, aesthetics being an attempt to illustrate and to test the more fundamental thesis about the nature and validity of judgments.

With respect to aesthetic judgments, Kant identifies four characteristics that must be present for the estimation to be at once a judgment and a judgment at the level of aesthetics: The judgment must be disinterested, in that considerations of utility are absent. Well, that is not surprising in Kant. It is the property of the object itself, not its functions or extrinsic value that is the cause of the pleasure excited in the percipient.

Next, aesthetic judgments are offered as universal, not merely personal. When an experience leads to the estimation of its source as "beautiful," the judgment is assumed to be one that would be shared by all comparably positioned and competent persons. Were it not for this feature of aesthetic judgment, there could be no intelligible basis for disagreements and arguments.

Third, the judgment presupposes that there is a necessary connection between the relevant properties of the object and the aesthetic pleasure arising from it. That is to say, the connection between the object and the experience is judged to be not contingent, but implicit.

Finally, the objects of aesthetic judgment are understood as having a purpose, though not intended to serve a purpose—such objects are "purposive without purpose," so to speak. The beauty of a natural landscape matches and exceeds the beauty of a painting of the same, but both are conceived as "intended," as it were.

In accounting for these criteria of judgment, Kant is actually of the same mind as Hume. The properties thus judged are not "out there," but within the cognitive and affective states of the judge. This leaves Kant with the question of just how such judgments are made, since they are neither elementary sensations nor compounds of these but are decisively cognitive, even "epistemic" from the point of view of the beholder. Kant's answer to the question: "How do we judge X to be beautiful?" is developed in the form of what he calls the four "moments" of aesthetic judgment. I must be terribly brief in summarizing these.

First, as the aesthetic judgment is disinterested, the object need not result in any agreeable feelings or estimations of moral goodness. This is the difference between aesthetic and moral judgments and, to this extent, Kant liberates aesthetics from ethical assessments, from political correctness, from hedonistic calculations. The object is not beautiful because it pleases; it pleases because it is beautiful. Emphasis, then, is on the formal structure of the object rather than such sensuous properties as colors and tones.

The second moment is that of universality. If Hume were right, there really would be nothing to dispute in judgments of beauty, but there are disputes, often tied to very close analysis of formal properties. To make an aesthetic judgment, then, is not to report a preference to, but to declare a truth of sorts, which is entirely different from having a sensation.

The third moment is that of the seeming purposivity in the object. The pleasure aroused by aesthetically worthy objects is not unlike the pleasure of "the job well done." That is, there is the sense of finality, completion, achievement. PS: Modern architecture need not apply.

Again, the irrelevant question is whether this is all really in the object of experience. Kant is laying out the grounds of judgment itself, not the ontological terrain on which we might find real properties.

However, perhaps the heaviest burden of his theory must be borne by what is attributed to the fourth moment, wherein the aesthetic judgment carries with it the concept of necessity. For anything to be necessarily what it is requires that it come about as a result of a non-contingent principle. Rather oddly, Kant at this point invokes an intuitionist notion similar to Reid's conception of a principle of common sense. His treatment of the matter here is laborious, but it matches up—to some extent—with the role of the pure categories of the understanding in establishing the forms of knowledge and, indeed, the pure intuitions of time and space, which establish the forms of experience. Aesthetic judgments, on this account, are drawn from a framework, a categorical scheme of possible judgments—a scheme that grounds all judgment, all judgment, and that is neither empirical nor logical, but foundational.

As a final comment on Kant's aesthetic theory, let me insert his pithy definition of genius:

> Genius is the natural endowment that gives the rule to art. Since talent is an innate productive ability of the artist and as such belongs itself to nature, we could also put it this way: Genius is the innate mental predisposition through which nature gives the rule to art.

No friend to the Romanticism of *Sturm und Drang*, Kant nevertheless presents artistic genius as instantiated in beings that nature speaks not so much "to" as "through."

The combined influence of Hume and Kant, that "odd couple" in which each is best understood through the challenges posed by the other, that pairing has shaped the philosophy of aesthetics in such a way as to divorce it from the moral, religious, and political worlds in which art originally found its place.

On the Humean account, aesthetics is that part of empirical psychology that identifies the features of the external world generally productive of agreeable feelings. How this works is really a matter of scientific research; all attempts to answer the question by examining the actual objects would be futile. On the Kantian account, the very disinterested nature of aesthetic judgment divorces it directly from such non-aesthetic judgments as are made in moral and political philosophy—"Art for the sake of art," as it were.

Early in the 20th century, G. E. Moore, in his *Principia Ethica*, published in 1903, offered a rather different and radical conception of beauty. He posits two worlds: one of exquisite and uninterrupted beauty and one of rank and unrelieved ugliness. He then asks if the former is not preferable, even if no one were left to experience it. He argues that such a world is preferable and that this very preference defeats the claim that the concept of beauty is exhausted by the resources of experience and feeling or even those of human judgment. He concludes that, on this basis:

> We shall have to include in our ultimate end something beyond the limits of human existence. I admit, of course, that our beautiful world would be better still, if there were human beings in it to contemplate and enjoy its beauty. But that admission makes nothing against my points. If it be once admitted that the beautiful world in itself is better than the ugly, then it follows, that however many beings may enjoy it, and however much better their enjoyment may be than it is itself, yet its mere existence adds something to the goodness of the whole: it is not only a means to our end, but also itself a part thereof.

Well, G. E. Moore is giving us the possibility of beauty without a percipient to perceive it. There's something wonderfully Pythagorean about that. The Pythagorean theorem is true; it is the true form of the right-angle triangle, and would remain so whether there ever were actual triangles, or actual beings who learned the Pythagorean theorem.

With G. E. Moore, we get an aesthetic theory according to which the formal properties realized in objects of art, and constitutive of beauty, would be constitutive of beauty whether we were there to see and hear this, or not. Our task, then, is to find beauty, and not to merely attempt to mint it in the busy and cluttered world of our own preferences and penchants. Interesting to think about that. I wonder if today's artists are thinking about that.

God—Really?
Lecture 60

If two people were having a dispute in ancient Athens, we would have expressed the point of the dispute as its *logos*. Thus, the biblical phrase might not have been translated as "In the beginning was the word," but as, "In the beginning was the point of it all." There are good arguments for assuming that the whole thing has a point, and that that point points ultimately to a divine and providential source.

In his *Metaphysics*, Aristotle distinguishes between natural science, or physics, which is theoretical and deals with what is inseparable from matter, and theology, what he calls that "first philosophy," which is prior to all the rest, is not confined to matter, and embraces what is universal. Philosophy of religion is a thriving specialty within philosophy, as much for the richness of religious concepts requiring philosophical analysis as for the substantive claims of religion, the implications of which are judged to be the most momentous. As the claims of religion either transcend the level of experience or include possibilities not given directly in experience, their acceptance requires faith, which has much in common with ordinary belief.

According to Reid, for a child to learn, at least two core principles must be at work; otherwise the child is uneducable. The *principle of veracity* holds that there must be a native and universal inclination to speak the truth. According to the *principle of credulity*, there must be an equally native and universal inclination to accept what others say as truthful. Without the former, there could be no possibility of cooperative behavior, no efficacy to contracts and agreements, no social life. Absent the principle of credulity, we would all begin life as skeptics. If skepticism of this sort were to be habitual, the resulting distrust would deprive us of the greatest benefits of society.

Such basic principles are "intuitive" and foundational for other principles. The specific principle of credulity, for example, is clearly not the gift of philosophical reflection, because this presupposes an inclination to believe the implications and conclusions arising from such reflection. It is what makes the practice and the prospects of such reflection intelligible. Only insofar as one is strongly inclined to believe the evidence of sense, the canons of logic, the potential efficacy of one's actions is any initiative plausible or even conceivable.

William James associates his concept of the "will to believe" with a passage found in Alexander Bain's treatise on *The Emotions and the Will*: "The leading fact in Belief, according to my view of it, is our Primitive Credulity. We begin by believing everything." Though life soon alerts the child to the painful fact that not everyone is trustworthy, credulity is a natural, not an acquired, disposition. It is strongest in childhood and diminished in strength by experience and greater independence of mind.

As credulity gives way to caution and critical appraisals, a standard is developed so that judgment is not arbitrary and counterproductive. In the ordinary course of events, that standard is a pragmatic one. To seek a "warrant" for a given belief is to seek a justification that would distinguish the belief from a merely preferred fantasy. James looked to life on the whole as the source of any such warrant. The objects of the knowable world are made more or less vivid by the process of *selection*, a reflection of one's interests and aims. Actions are then recruited in the service of these interests.

The pragmatic warrant defended by James is expressed this way: A pragmatist turns away from abstraction and insufficiency, from verbal solutions, from bad a priori reasons, from fixed principles, closed systems, and pretended absolutes and origins. He turns toward concreteness and adequacy, facts, action, and power.

The fixed principles, closed systems, and pretended absolutes of philosophy are rejected because they come to stand in the way of success in negotiating the challenges and facts of the world. Hume's famous problem of induction says that we have no rational or logical warrant for assuming that the future is obliged or necessitated to mimic the past. Thus, the faith we have in the continuing operation of the laws of science cannot be rationally justified. Though there is much to be said for the anti-realist philosophy of science, achievements such as visiting the moon and returning home safely have been predicated on the belief we have that the lawfulness of reality is neither chimerical nor episodic. We must find a position between infantile credulity and paralyzing skepticism, and the instrument we are likely to use in locating that position is a pragmatic one, broadly conceived.

Among are our most compelling interests are some reasonable understanding of our nature, of the nature of the world in which we find ourselves, and of the very point of life itself. It would matter to know if it were, in fact, the case that the world is constituted as it is so that we could forge decent and productive lives. It would matter to know if it were, in fact, the case that the laws of physical nature are reliable because the reality was constituted in such a way as to render it knowable and supportive of our form of life.

Philosophy of science asserts the *inference to the best explanation* criterion: Consider an event, then ask which, of all imaginable explanations that might account for it, is the *best* explanation. Two questions arise: (1) What is the standard by which to grade explanations as good, better, and best? And (2) What counts as an explanation?

One explanation is in the form of probabilities. If there is an indefinite number of possible realities, including one law-governed as ours seems to be, the explanation may at some time be replaced by a less lawful one, the increase in entropy eliminating the structured predictability of a world of objects. The explanation may have been preceded by many abortive attempts to constitute a knowable cosmos, until one pattern just popped up and proved to be relatively stable.

This, however, would not defeat the theory of a providential God; it would simply suggest some degree of trial and error as an aspect of the creation. But it would be a weak warrant, because the proposition itself matches up with nothing else in our encounters with highly rule-governed, predictable, and complex systems. We would, then, have a more defensible warrant for believing that the design features of reality suggest a designer.

Thus do we turn to Thomas Aquinas and his famous "five ways" to prove the existence of God, as developed in the *Summa Theologiae*. The first and plainest is the method that proceeds from the point of view of motion.

- Thomas's first proof is based on the concept of a prime mover, now understood as the result of an inference to the best explanation for celestial dynamics.

- The second proof is from the nature of the efficient cause. From the fact that we can now see directly the effects of causal chains originating in times remote from human experience, we are called upon to make plausible inferences as to how the first efficient cause got the game started, and this, says Thomas, is that "which all call God."

- The third proof is taken from the natures of the merely possible and necessary. Given that "nothing can come from nothing" and that there are many things, there must have been something that was the source of the first thing.

- The fourth proof arises from degrees—of goodness, truth, nobility, and the like—that are found in things. There exists therefore something that is the truest, best, and noblest—the greatest being.

- Thomas gives as the fifth proof the natural order itself: "There is something intelligent by which all natural things are arranged in accordance with a plan—and this we call God."

Each of these and all of them together have invited powerful criticism over a course of centuries. Some theologians paradoxically reject the argument on the grounds that if the existence of God can be proved, there is no need for faith! Still others, taking a page from Hume, question the reality of causal powers and, in any case, relegate them to our modes of perception and cognition.

It may also be said that Thomas has not given sufficient attention to the possibility of the "infinite regress," meaning that there may be no "first cause" at all, only a limitless chain of effects back to and through still other effects. Though this is a metaphysical possibility, it does not match any experience we have of causality. Thus, we would have a weaker warrant for assuming an infinite regress than for supposing an initial causal agent.

Still another forceful argument is that the "intelligibility" requirement Thomas asserts is a mere stipulation. One reply to the proposition that, absent an ordering intelligence, the cosmos would be unintelligible is that the cosmos *is* unintelligible! But this calls us back to the Apollo program: How do we successfully shuttle about in an unintelligible cosmos or even in the little sphere of it that is close to home?

There are other arguments against the existence of God apart from the alleged problems of the Thomistic "five ways." Two in particular arise from moral considerations—the "problem of evil" and the presumed threat posed by human freedom to the alleged omniscience of God. How could a God, at once omnipotent and beneficent, create a world so rife with evil? How could a just God permit evil to go unpunished? In *Providence and the Problem of Evil* (1998), Richard Swinburne reasons that the choices made possible by the very existence of evil are the basis on which God's final judgments are made. One of the most authoritative replies to the problem-of-evil argument is that of Alvin Plantinga, in the form of the "free will" defense. As with the law—which does all that it must when it does all that it can—God, too, has awsome power but is constrained by logical and even conceptual strictures.

> **How could a just God permit evil to go unpunished?**

Such rebuttals are carefully crafted but, in the end, not entirely convincing. It certainly seems to be in the realm of possibility that an omnipotent and benficent loving God could create a reality in which there is no evil, no pain and suffering, no crime. A painless world of ceaseless joy and virtue strikes me as a gift beyond the imaginable; a prize without equal. I should think that, unless God is bound by John Rawls's "difference principle," this is a state of affairs that requires more to deserve it than the simple fact that one lacks it.

As for freedom of the will defeating God's claim to omniscience, I am again on shaky ground, not knowing much about omniscience and but a bit more about free will. If God is omniscient, then God knows everything that will ever occur, and this includes everything we will do. If I grasp the sense of omniscience as it is acribed to God, I would expect it to include everything that is actual and possible. Among the items that are actual and possible are all the actions that will ever have been freely taken. Thus, there is no incompatibility between our freedom and God's omniscience.

In the previous lecture, I summarized G. E. Moore's conception of beauty as a state of affairs we would wish to see established even if we knew we would not have access to it; the notion being that, were the choice between a world of beauty and one of ugliness, we would choose the former, despite the fact that it would never be part of our experience. One might ask, in this vein, what one would choose: a dead cosmos of meaningless statistical possibilities or one alive with promise and nurturing of hope. I would regard it as simply curmudgeonly to choose the former. I choose the latter. ∎

Suggested Reading

Plantinga, A. *God, Freedom and Evil.* New York: Eardmann, 1974.

Swinburne, R. *Providence and the Problem of Evil.* Oxford, 1998.

Questions to Consider

1. What is the status of faith if God's existence is provable?

2. How do the "five ways" stand in light of modern physics?

3. What limits are there on omnipotence?

God—Really?
Lecture 60—Transcript

In Book VI of his *Metaphysics*, Aristotle distinguishes between natural science, or physics, which is theoretical and deals with what is inseparable from matter, and that "first philosophy," as he calls it, which is prior to all the rest, is not confined to matter, and embraces what is universal. This science he says, of all things, is theology, which pertains to "so much of the divine as appears to us."

If the previous lectures have been guided by the problem of knowledge, the problem of conduct, and the problem of governance, then surely many will argue that it must be that "first philosophy," prior to all the rest, that most fully illuminates these problems and offers guidance toward the right—and even ultimate—solutions, so enter philosophy of religion.

Now, philosophy of religion is a thriving specialty within philosophy at large, as much for the richness of religious concepts requiring philosophical analysis as for the substantive claims of religion, the implications of which are judged to be the most momentous. In this final lecture, then, I will attempt to do justice—we might see swift justice—to both of these features and to indicate where the two are independent, and where the dependencies are significant.

As the claims of religion either transcend the level of experience or include possibilities that are not given directly in experience, their acceptance requires what is called "faith," which has much in common with ordinary belief. I might begin, then, with a brief consideration of the grounds or what are often called the "warrants" of belief. To clarify what are often extremely difficult concepts, I will rely on two of my old standbys, Thomas Reid and William James.

Consider the dispositions a child must bring to the classroom of life if anything at all is to be learned. Reid was satisfied that there must be at least two core principles at work, absent which the child would be uneducable. He dubbed these the *principle of veracity* and the *principle of credulity*. There must be a native inclination to speak the truth, and a native and universal inclination to accept what others say as truthful. Were the first of these absent, there could be no possibility of cooperative behavior, no efficacy to contracts and agreements, no social life, no shared form of life. Absent the principle of credulity, we would all begin life as skeptics, with the inevitable consequences.

Reid said that even the greatest liars speak a hundred truths for every deception. Moreover, it would be idle to assume that the principle of credulity is routinely suspended until authorized by the arts of reason. Indeed, if skepticism of this sort were to be habitual, Reid says: "Most men would be unable to find reasons for believing the thousandth part of what is told to them. Such distrust and incredulity would deprive us of the greatest benefits of society, and place us in a worse condition than that of savages."

Such basic principles are basic. They are underived, "intuitive" in a special sense of the term, and foundational for still other principles. That the experiences one has are one's own is illustrative. On the specific principle of credulity, for example, it is clearly not the gift of philosophical reflection, for this presupposes an inclination to believe, for example, the implications and conclusions arising from such reflection. It is what makes the practice and the prospects of such reflection, then, intelligible in the first place. Only insofar as one is strongly inclined to believe the evidence of sense, the canons of logic, the potential efficacy of one's actions is any initiative plausible in the first instance, or even conceivable in the first instance.

Now, let me move from Reid's principle of credulity to William James's "will to believe," which James himself associates with a passage found in Alexander Bain's treatise on *The Emotions and the Will*: In his *Principles of Psychology*, James writes of "the primitive impulse to affirm immediately the reality of all that is conceived," and then quotes Alexander Bain. This is from Bain, now: "The leading fact in Belief, according to my view of it, is our Primitive Credulity. We begin by believing everything."

The principle of credulity does not confer incorrigibility, however, and life in the world soon alerts the child to the painful fact that not everyone is trustworthy. Nonetheless, as Reid says, it is a natural and not an acquired disposition, which is why, unlike reason and understanding, it is strongest in childhood and only later diminished in strength by experience and the greater independence of mind.

As credulity gives way to caution and to critical appraisals, some sort of standard is developed, lest the filtering and judging be arbitrary and counterproductive. In the ordinary course of events, that standard is a pragmatic one. To seek, then, a "warrant" for a given belief is to seek some justification for holding it that would distinguish the belief from a merely preferred fantasy.

William James looked to life on the whole as the source of any such warrant. Life on the whole, of course, is an organic, evolving pattern of interests. The objects that make up the knowable world are made more or less vivid by the active process of *selection*, which itself is a reflection of one's interests and aims. Actions are then recruited in the service of these interests, in response to those selected properties of the sensible world that make contact with our significant interests.

The pragmatic warrant defended by James is expressed this way. He says:

> A pragmatist turns his back resolutely and once and for all upon a lot of inveterate habits dear to professional philosophers. He turns away from abstraction and insufficiency, from verbal solutions, from bad a priori reasons, from fixed principles, closed systems, and pretended absolutes and origins. He turns towards concreteness and adequacy, towards facts, towards action, and towards power.

Ah, the fixed principles, and closed systems, and pretended absolutes of philosophy are rejected for the soundest reason: Adopting them comes to stand in the way of actual success in negotiating the challenges and facts of the world.

Consider Hume's famous problem of induction: According to Hume, we have no rational or logical warrant for assuming that the future is obliged or necessitated to mimic the past. Thus, the faith we have in the continuing operation of the laws of science—or just the operation of a can opener—

cannot be rationally justified. So disturbed am I by this that I quickly grab a can opener, open a tin of coffee, and make a strong cup for myself!

As it happens, though there is much to be said for the anti-realist philosophy of science, which we have reviewed in an earlier lecture, we have succeeded in visiting the moon and returning home safely, and all such achievements are predicated on the belief—may I say it?—the faith we have that the lawfulness of reality is neither chimerical nor episodic. When the car fails to start in the morning, we do not become skeptical about the laws governing the internal combustion engine; we assume the car is not functioning properly.

Understood in these terms, the test that a belief would have to pass for it to be warranted is one that relates not to that closed system or block universe according to which physics is complete, but to the facts, actions, and powers at work in our efforts to satisfy our most compelling interests. We must find a position between infantile credulity and paralyzing skepticism, and the instrument we are likely to use in locating that position is a pragmatic one, broadly conceived.

Now, what of our most compelling interests? I would not presume to theorize, let alone legislate, them into existence. I would say only that included among them is some reasonable understanding of our nature, of the nature of the world in which we find ourselves, and of the very point of life itself, as lived with others, and invariably too short by half. To understand the nature of the world is at least to work out what seem to be the rules or laws governing its physical operations, but then also ourselves in relation to these laws, and the possibilities they afford for significant achievements.

Surely it matters to know if it were, in fact, the case that the world is constituted as it is so that we would be able to forge decent and productive lives, and surely it would matter to know if it were, in fact, the case that the laws of physical nature are reliable because the reality was constituted in such a way as to render it knowable and supportive of our form of life. There is little doubt, then, but that it matters, just in case the providential God of the world's major religions is behind the reality in which we find ourselves, and the reality of that God is surely not under challenge, just in case the closest we can get to it is by way of inferences and beliefs, including those *inferences to the best explanation* so common now as noted earlier, in philosophy of science.

Let me repeat this in another way. What the *inference to the best explanation* criterion asserts in philosophy of science is this: Consider an event, then ask which, of all imaginable explanations that might be framed to account for it, just what is the *best* explanation?

Now, two questions jump right out of this criterion: What is the standard by which to grade explanations as good, better, and best? What counts as an explanation in the first place? If the event in question is the successful return trip to the moon, many would agree that the best explanation for this successful venture is that the scientific laws on which the entire project was based are true. That is, they truly capture reality as it really is.

Suppose, however, that we grant this as the best explanation of getting to the moon and back, but then take as the event calling for an explanation the very lawfulness of the cosmos itself. The question now is not what the best explanation is of the success of the NASA mission, but what is the best explanation of the nomic character of physical reality? Why is there a lawful rather than a lawless reality?

One explanation is in the form of probabilities. Let's say there is an indefinitely large number of possible realities, of which one is law-governed in just the way ours seems to be, and, as it happens, this is the one that came about. It may at some time in the future be replaced by a less lawful one, the increase in entropy eliminating the structured predictability of a world of objects. It may have been preceded by all sorts of abortive attempts to constitute a knowable cosmos, until one particular pattern just popped up and proved to be relatively stable. Maybe God does throw dice, so to speak.

What evidence might be adduced to support this explanation? Perhaps we might find in the flotsam of dead stars and disintegrating galaxies evidence of earlier and failed realities, but surely this would not defeat the theory of a providential God; it would simply suggest some degree of—if I might say it—trial and error as an aspect of the creation. On that account, we would be permitted to believe the probabilistic explanation, in that there is always some warrant for believing a proposition that is not logically contradictory, but it would be a weak warrant, for the proposition itself matches up with nothing else in our encounters with highly rule-governed, predictable, and complex systems—like toasters, for example, or the vote-counting machines in Florida. In all such instances, the best explanations we have are in terms of design, designers, and the realization of actual plans and purposes. We would, then, have a more defensible warrant for believing that the design features of reality do, indeed, suggest a designer.

Thus do we return to Thomas Aquinas and his by now famous "five ways" to prove the existence of God, as developed in the *Summa Theologiae*. For all the ink spilled on this set of proofs, they retain their common sense appeal. What are the "five ways"? Let's let the saint speak for himself:

> The first and plainest is the method that proceeds from the point of view of motion. It is certain and in accord with experience, that things on earth undergo change. Now, everything that is moved is moved by something; nothing, indeed, is changed, except it is changed to something which it is in potentiality. Moreover, anything moves in accordance with something actually existing. Change itself is nothing else than to bring forth something from potentiality into actuality. Now, nothing can be brought from potentiality to actual existence except through something actually existing, but this process cannot go on to infinity, because there would not be any first mover. Therefore, it is necessary to go back to some first mover, which is itself moved by nothing, and this all men know as God.

So, Thomas's first proof is based on the concept of a prime mover, now understood as the result of an inference to the best explanation for, what? Celestial dynamics. "Why is all of that stuff moving?" What's next?

> The second proof is from the nature of the efficient cause. We find in our experience that there is a chain of causes; nor is it found possible for anything to be the efficient cause of itself, since it would have to exist before itself, which is impossible, but if the

chain were to go back infinitely, there would be no first cause, and thus no ultimate effect, nor middle causes, which is admittedly false. Hence we must presuppose some first efficient cause, which all call God.

Aha. Again, from the fact that we can now see directly the effects of causal chains originating in times remote from human experience, we are called upon to make plausible inferences as to how the first efficient cause got the game started, and this, says Thomas, is that "which all call God." He continues:

> The third proof is taken from the natures of the merely possible and necessary. If nothing existed, it would be impossible for anything to begin, and there would now be nothing existing, which is admittedly false. Hence not all things are mere accidents, but there must be one necessarily existing being, which all call God.

The "third way," then, is quite straightforward and commonsensical: As "nothing can come from nothing," and as there are many things, there must have been something that was the source of the first thing. Thomas continues:

> The fourth proof arises from the degrees that are found in things, for there is found a greater and a less degree of goodness, truth, nobility, and the like, but more or less are terms spoken of various things as they approach in diverse ways toward something that is the greatest, just as in the case of hotter, more hot, which approaches nearer the greatest heat. There exists therefore something that is the truest, and best, and most noble, and in consequence, the greatest being—and this we call God.

Finally, Thomas gives as the fifth proof the natural order itself:

> We see that some things which lack reason, such as natural bodies, are operated in accordance with a plan. It appears from this that they are operated always or the more frequently in this same way the closer they follow what is the highest, whence it is clear that they do not arrive at the result by chance but because of a purpose.

Therefore, there is something intelligent by which all natural things are arranged in accordance with a plan—and this we call God.

Now, each of these and all of them together have invited powerful criticism over a course of centuries. Some theologians paradoxically reject the argument on the grounds that if the existence of God could be proved, there would be no need for faith!

Still others, taking a page from Hume, question the very reality of causal powers and, in any case, relegate them to our modes of perception and cognition. Then, too, it may be said that Thomas has not given sufficient attention to the possibility of the "infinite regress," such that there may be no "first cause" at all, only a limitless chain of effects back to and through still other effects ad infinitum. Though this is a metaphysical possibility, it is not one that matches any experience we have of causality, and thus we would have a weaker warrant for assuming an infinite regress than for supposing an initial causal agent.

Still another forceful argument is to the effect that the so-called "intelligibility" requirement of Thomas—what he asserts—is actually merely stipulation. One reply to the proposition that, absent an ordering intelligence, the cosmos would be unintelligible is that the cosmos *is* unintelligible! But we impose a certain order on it, and this calls us back to the Apollo program: How do we successfully shuttle about in an unintelligible cosmos or even in the little sphere of it that is quite close to home?

However, there are other arguments against the existence of God apart from the alleged problems of the Thomistic "five ways." Two in particular arise from moral considerations—the so-called "problem of evil" and the presumed threat posed by human freedom to the alleged omniscience of God.

Ah, the problem of evil. How could a God, at once omnipotent and beneficent, create a world so rife with evil—not just the evil perpetrated by felons, but the evil of innocent children wracked by fatal disease, and others born with disabling and even hideous deformities? How could a just God permit the Holocaust? How could a just God permit evil to go unpunished?

In *Providence and the Problem of Evil*, the distinguished religious philosopher Richard Swinburne reasons that a providential God would wish for us to learn and perfect ourselves through realistic encounters calling for choices and inevitably coupled with regret, loss, and sadness. The choices made possible by the very existence of evil are the basis on which God's final judgments will be based.

One of the most authoritative replies to the problem-of-evil argument is that of Alvin Plantinga, in the form of the so-called "free will" defense. As with the law—which does all that it must when it does all that it can—God, too, has awsome power but is constrained by logical and even conceptual strictures. God cannot suspend the law of contradiction, for example. Plantinga takes this as grounding what he calls certain "counterfactuals of freedom." Once free will is deployed in such a way as to commit Smith to do X, and Smith then freely does it, God cannot create a possible world in which Smith does not do it. Thus, if Smith's action is evil, it just isn't in God's power to have it that Smith does not do it.

Such rebuttals are carefully crafted, however, in the end, not entirely convincing. It certainly seems to be in the realm of possibility, anyway, that an omnipotent and beneficent, loving God could create a reality in which there is no evil, no pain and suffering, no crime. All the children have perfect teeth. God could have limited the creation to angels or beagles, comparably delightful.

God, presumably, might even have included versions of us in such a world, but happily shorn of those tendencies we have toward the venal, and even worse than venal. Why not, that, then?

If, after 59 lectures addressed to the ideas of others, I might be permitted some thoughts of my own—not very richly developed, but on a matter on which my authority is, of course, reed-thin—I would say this much: Let's consider a painless world, a world of ceaseless joy, a world of virtue.

Well, that kind of world strikes me as a gift beyond the imaginable; it's a prize without equal, isn't it? I should think that, unless God is bound by John Rawls's "difference principle," this is a state of affairs that requires more to deserve it than the simple fact that one lacks it. It would seem to be a desert and, as such, not a state of affairs simply created for the undiminished happiness of everyone and anyone. Frankly, I should regard it as unjust for such bounty to be spread around willy-nilly. I can even imagine a saint or two who would refuse it.

Now, what about freedom of the will that defeats God's claim to omniscience? I am again on shaky ground here, not knowing much about omniscience, and really only a bit more about free will. I will assume that what the challenge is goes something like this: If God is omniscient, then God knows everything that will ever occur, and this includes everything we will do. As this knowledge is perfect, nothing can occur such that God is mistaken, and that means that nothing can occur "feely" in the sense of unpredictably or as a surprise. God can't be surprised and be omniscient at the same time. The theory seems to be that, of all of God's powers, he lacks the distinct pleasure of being surprised or, for that matter, the pain of disappointment.

I am not omniscient. I do know, however, that if I ask all of my students who happen to have red hair to raise their hands—if I just say to all of you with red hair: "Please raise your hands"—I can predict, I'm inclined to say with perfect accuracy, which hands are going to go up, all the while granting that those who play the game do so freely. Now, I have comparable knowledge that given a choice between a night on the town, and a close study of Kant's *Critique of Judgment*, most of my friends are likely to choose the former. I think I can even predict which ones will so use their freedom while acknowledging that the choices they make are free.

If I grasp the sense of omniscience as it is ascribed to God, then, I would expect it to include everything that is actual and possible. Among the items that are actual and possible are all the actions that will ever have been freely taken. Thus, there is no incompatibility between our freedom and God's omniscience. That is, God's omniscience includes the knowledge of what we will do with our freedom.

I don't want to make light of the problem. I simply don't want to make—if I can use the expression—"heavy" of the problem. I just want to state it as a problem.

470

Now, in the previous lecture, I summarized G. E. Moore's conception of beauty as a state of affairs we would wish to see established even if we knew we would not have access to it; the notion being that, were the choice between a world of beauty and one of ugliness, we would choose the former, despite the fact that it would never be part of our own personal experience. One might ask, in this same vein, what one would choose between a dead cosmos of meaningless statistical possibilities or one alive with promise and nurturing of hope. Now, I would regard it as simply curmudgeonly to choose the former.

Let me say it again. We have these two choices, what William James regarded as momentous choices. We can choose to believe that the universe is a place of dead matter, describable in purely statistical terms, and having no point. There are arguments to that effect. However, there are also many other warrants by way of Thomas Aquinas, and many other arguments, for believing that the design feature, the nomic necessity—all of those things that allow one to negotiate space and time—the machinery, the bottle opener, the whole nine yards so to speak—offer ample evidence of design, intention, plan, intelligence.

Remember that the Greek word *logos* can be translated as "reason." It can be translated as a legal case. If two people were having a dispute in ancient Athens, we would have expressed the point of the dispute as its *logos*. Thus, the biblical phrase might not have been translated as "In the beginning was the word," but as, "In the beginning was the point of it all." There are good arguments for assuming that the whole thing has a point, and that that point points ultimately to a divine and providential source.

That is another conceivable scheme that we might entertain, as to what the universe is all about. I choose that one, and so, "God—really?" Well, yes, really, but I say, the debate goes on, and all candidate good arguments are welcome.

Timeline

800–600 B.C.E. .... Morality tales, such as the Hindu Upanishads, appear in many settled communities.

~750 B.C.E. .... Homer composes the *Iliad* and the *Odyssey*.

700 B.C.E. .... Colonization of Sicily, the east coast of Italy, and islands off the coast of Asia Minor begins, primarily to grow produce that can be sent back to mainland Greece.

6th century B.C.E. .... Schools of critical inquiry emerge in ancient Greece. Parmenides and other pre-Socratic philosophers emerge. *Empirkoi*, or empirical practitioners who followed Hippocrates's philosophy, make up the dominant school of Greek medicine.

570 B.C.E. .... Birth of Pythagoras.

551 B.C.E. .... Birth of Confucius.

4th century B.C.E. .... Isocrates composes the *Panegyricus*, a work that raises the question of whether philosophy is something that just the Greeks do.

479 B.C.E. .... Death of Confucius.

469 B.C.E. .... Birth of Hippocrates.

469 B.C.E. .... Birth of Socrates.

446 B.C.E. .... Birth of Isocrates.

427 B.C.E. .... Birth of Plato.

399 B.C.E. .... Death of Hippocrates.

399 B.C.E. .... Death of Socrates.

384 B.C.E. .... Birth of Aristotle.

360 B.C.E. .... Plato writes his dialogue *The Republic*, generally considered to be the foundational work in political science. It addresses the question of how a man's virtue may be measured.

347 B.C.E. .... Death of Plato.

338 B.C.E. .... Death of Isocrates.

322 B.C.E. .... Death of Aristotle.

300 B.C.E. .... Stoic philosophy develops.

106 B.C.E. .... Birth of Marcus Tullius Cicero.

43 B.C.E. .... Death of Marcus Tullius Cicero.

1st century C.E. .... "Hellenized" Jews build Christianity.

354 C.E. .... Birth of St. Augustine.

397 C.E. .... St. Augustine publishes *The Confessions*, a personal, introspective work of psychology.

430 C.E... Death of St. Augustine.

476 C.E... Fall of Rome.

632 C.E... According to the teachings of Islam, the Prophet Muhammad had revealed to him a divine message that would be faithfully recorded in the Koran.

650–850 C.E..................................... The Dark Ages.

1150–1300....................................... Medieval period.

13th century..................................... Advent of a "renaissance" of scholarly thought, with Roger Bacon and others recovering the spirit of experimental modes of inquiry.

1214... Birth of Roger Bacon.

1225... Birth of Thomas Aquinas.

1274... Death of Thomas Aquinas.

1294... Death of Roger Bacon.

1304... Birth of Francesco Petrarch.

1374... Death of Francesco Petrarch.

15th century..................................... The Italian Renaissance.

1452... Birth of Leonardo da Vinci.

1483... Birth of Martin Luther.

1497... Savonarola burns the vanities.

1517.. Martin Luther protests aspects of the
                                                      Catholic Church.

1519.. Death of Leonardo da Vinci.

1546.. Death of Martin Luther.

1546–1648... The Protestant Reformation, launched
                                                      by Martin Luther's 1517 protest against
                                                      aspects of the Catholic Church.

1561.. Birth of Francis Bacon.

1588.. Birth of Thomas Hobbes.

1596.. Birth of René Descartes.

1626.. Death of Francis Bacon.

1632.. Birth of John Locke.

1633.. Galileo is called before the Inquisition.

1642 .... Birth of Isaac Newton.

1646.. Birth of Gottfried Wilhelm von Leibniz.

1650.. Death of René Descartes.

1660.. The Royal Society becomes the center
                                                      of a growing culture of science.

1660.. Thomas Hobbes publishes *Leviathan*.

1679.. Death of Thomas Hobbes.

1685.. Birth of George Berkeley.

1694...Birth of François Marie Arouet, who wrote under the name Voltaire.

1699...Lord Shaftesbury publishes *An Inquiry Concerning Virtue or Merit*, offering an explanation of moral conduct based on the notion of natural dispositions and affections.

1704...Death of John Locke.

1705...Gottfried Wilhelm von Leibniz offers a significant critique of the Lockean view in *New Essays on Human Understanding*.

1709...Birth of Julien Offray de La Mettrie.

1710...George Berkeley publishes his critique of the Lockean view, *A Theory Concerning the Principles of Human Knowledge*.

1710...Birth of Thomas Reid.

1711...Birth of David Hume.

1712...Birth of Jean-Jacques Rousseau.

1715...Birth of the French philosopher Claude Adrien Helvetius.

1715...Birth of Etienne Condillac, John Locke's translator in France.

1716...Death of Gottfried Wilhelm von Leibniz.

1724... Birth of Immanuel Kant.

1729... Birth of Edmund Burke.

1734... Voltaire writes his *Letters
on the English*.

1739... David Hume publishes *An Enquiry
Concerning Human Understanding*,
which aimed to defeat Skepticism by
putting philosophy on a firmer footing,
grounding morality, science, and
politics in the realm of experience.

1743... Birth of Condorcet.

1748... La Mettrie publishes the banned book
Man—A Machine, which extends
the materialistic drift of
Descartes's psychology.

Mid-18th century .... The "Scottish Enlightenment."

1751... Death of La Mettrie.

1757... Birth of Pierre Cabanis.

1758... Birth of Franz Joseph Gall.

1764... Thomas Reid publishes *An Inquiry into
the Human Mind*.

1770... Birth of Georg Wilhelm Friedrich
Hegel.

1771... Death of Claude Adrien Helvetius.

1772.. Helvetius's *A Treatise on Man*, which maintains that human essence does not precede our existence and experiences in the world, published posthumously.

1773.. John Locke's *Two Treatises* is published in colonial America.

1776.. Death of David Hume.

1778.. Death of Jean-Jacques Rousseau.

1778.. Death of François Marie Arouet (Voltaire).

1780.. Death of Etienne Condillac.

1781.. Immanuel Kant publishes his *Critique of Pure Reason*, which credits David Hume with awakening Kant from his "dogmatic slumber."

1783.. Death of George Berkeley.

1787.. The U.S. Constitution is forged in Philadelphia. During the subsequent ratification period, Alexander Hamilton, James Madison, and John Jay write essays in the New York newspapers addressing and countering the various arguments that had been advanced against the Constitution and the federal model of governance. These essays became known as *The Federalist Papers*.

1794.. Death of Condorcet.

1794.. Death of Pierre Flourens.

1795.. Condorcet's *Sketch for a Historical Picture of the Progress of the Human Mind* published posthumously.

1796.. Death of Thomas Reid.

1797.. Death of Edmund Burke.

1804.. Death of Immanuel Kant.

1806.. Birth of John Stuart Mill.

1808.. Death of Pierre Cabanis.

1809.. Birth of Charles Darwin.

1818.. Birth of Karl Marx.

1822.. Birth of Francis Galton.

1828.. Death of Franz Joseph Gall.

1830.. Auguste Comte publishes his *Course of Positive Philosophy,* which reflected on the achievements of the Enlightenment and concluded that human thought passes through distinct stages.

1830s.. The British Reform Act ends British participation in the slave trade and extends political rights to those long denied the franchise, including those not members of the Church of England.

1831... Death of Georg Wilhelm
Friedrich Hegel.

1833... Charles Lyell publishes his *Principles of Geology*, which provided a time frame compatible with the requirements of Charles Darwin's theory of evolution by natural selection.

1842... Birth of William James.

1844... Birth of Friedrich Nietzsche.

Mid–late 19th century .... The Aesthetic movement.

1856... Birth of Sigmund Freud.

1859... John Stuart Mill publishes *On Liberty*.

1862... In November of this year, Hermann von Helmholtz gives a lecture on conservation of energy at Heidelberg, where he addresses, among other issues, the relatively new division between leading scientists and philosophers.

1867... Death of Pierre Flourens.

1869... Francis Galton, cousin of Charles Darwin, publishes his studies of hereditary genius, which conclude that natural selection yields a very few exceptional human types, but general human flourishing disproportionately depends on their merits.

1871... Charles Darwin publishes *Descent of Man*, which puts forth his theory of natural selection.

1872... Friedrich Nietzsche publishes his first notable work, *The Birth of Tragedy and the Spirit of Music*.

1873... Death of John Stuart Mill.

1875... Birth of Carl Gustav Jung.

1882... Death of Charles Darwin.

1883... Death of Karl Marx.

1889... Birth of Ludwig Wittgenstein.

1890... William James publishes *The Principles of Psychology*.

1896... Sigmund Freud and Josef Breuer publish *Studies of Hysteria*, in which the theory is advanced that hysterical symptoms are the outcome of repression.

1900... Death of Friedrich Nietzsche.

1910... Death of William James.

1911... Death of Francis Galton.

1912... Birth of Alan Turing.

1938... Death of Sigmund Freud.

Timeline

Glossary

apatheia: Freedom from pathos and suffering.

atman: The soul, or core reality of the human individual. Hindu.

Brahma: The "creator" within the Hindu divine triad—Brahma, Vishnu, Shiva.

categorical imperative: Driver for one alternative action over another made on principles whose moral authority takes precedence over any merely hypothetical imperative. Categorical imperatives derive from the intelligible realm governed by "the laws of freedom," rather than the natural realm of physical determination. Unlike hypothetical imperatives, they must be universally applicable. That is, they do not depend on a calculation of utility or on any calculation of possible consequences in particular circumstances.

Chthonic religion: Earth-centered religion, in which women or female deities are central figures because of their procreative power. Common in matriarchal societies.

Common sense: Scottish school of thought from the 18th and early 19th centuries, holding that in the perception of the average, unsophisticated person, sensations are not mere ideas or subjective impressions but carry with them the belief in corresponding qualities as belonging to external objects.

contiguity: Similarity in time or place.

ecstasis: Greek; "ecstasy." Stepping outside oneself or being removed from oneself.

ego: According to Sigmund Freud's theory of psychoanalysis, one of the three parts that make up the self. The ego is purported to stand between the id and the superego to balance our primitive needs and our moral/ ethical beliefs.

eidola: "Phantoms," or atomic emanations from material objects that have some access to the organs of sense. Concept proposed by ancient atomists to explain hallucinations, dreams, religious visions, and so on.

empiricism: The philosophical view that all human knowledge is derived from experience and that which cannot be confirmed via experience is not naturally known.

Enlightenment: Eighteenth-century European intellectual movement that rejected the presumptive authority of the past in favor of a reliance on experience and reason/science.

enthousiasmos: Greek; "enthusiasm." Presenting oneself in such a way that the gods can enter the self.

ephistemonikon: Abstract and universal statements.

episteme: Scientific knowledge.

epistemology: The study of how we know what we know and whether the way we go about knowing is defensible, one of the central questions in the study of metaphysics. Examines the question of knowledge and attempts to characterize the nature of truth and science.

Eudaimonia: The doing of something for its own sake, as the gods do. "Happiness."

experimenta fructifera: One of two types of experiments described in Francis Bacon's *Novum Organum*; these consequential experiments are designed to allow the observer to choose between competing accounts of facts on hand.

experimenta lucifera: One of two types of experiments described in Francis Bacon's *Novum Organum*; these "light-shedding" experiments alert the observer to factors operative in the causal matrix that brings things about. Such studies are essentially exercises in fact gathering.

fallibilism: View that there is always *more* to the account than any current version *can* include, because other experiences, beliefs, and needs are always in existence.

fatalism: The belief that every event is bound to happen as it does no matter what we do about it. Fatalism is the most extreme form of causal determinism, because it denies that human actions have any causal efficacy.

functionalism: The view that consciousness is not a material entity attached to the brain, but a process, a stream of experiences knitted together as they flow by a supernumerary intelligence.

hedonism: Doctrine holding that pleasure is the highest good.

hypothetical imperative: Driver for one alternative action over another made to attain a specific end. Hypothetical imperatives are contingent; they are tied to a particular context and to the needs and desires of natural creatures under the press of the needs to survive, to avoid pain, and to gain pleasure. Decisions thus grounded are non-moral, because they arise from our natures as merely human beings, not as rational beings; that is, they are essentially reactions.

id: According to Sigmund Freud's theory of psychoanalysis, one of the three parts that make up the self. The id is purported to represent primary process thinking—our most primitive need-gratification thoughts.

intuition: An instinctive knowing, or impression that something might be the case, without the use of rational processes.

ius civile: Expression of local values and interests, which differs from place to place and people to people.

ius gentium: Universally adopted precepts of those who live under any rule of law, such as the idea that harm done to another without cause is wrong, as is the taking of what clearly belongs to another.

Jainism: Ethical school based on the Pythagorean teachings, which emphasizes the celebration of all that lives.

labor theory of value: The concept that property is worth only as much as the labor invested in it; the surplus is profit, which accumulates as capital.

logos: The aims and goals generated by the rational intelligence behind the order of the cosmos.

Lyssa: "Wolf's rage"; extreme anger in the heat of battle.

Malleus maleficarum: A coherent theory of witchcraft, a set of tests to determine witchcraft, and a list of appropriate punishments used during the witch hunts from 1400 to 1700 and beyond.

Marxism: A form of communism based on the writings of Karl Marx, who theorized that actions and human institutions are economically determined, that the class struggle is the basic agency of historical change, and that capitalism will ultimately be superseded by communism.

metaphysics: Concept referring to two distinguishable but interconnected sets of questions: first, the question of what really exists and, second, the question of how we know such things and whether the way we go about knowing is defensible or defective. The term is derived from the writings of Aristotle.

mimesis: The imitative representation of nature or human behavior.

mythos: The complex of beliefs, values, and attitudes characteristic of a specific group or society.

naturalism: The meta-ethical thesis that moral properties are reducible to natural ones or that ethical judgments may be derived from non-ethical ones. Also, a scientific account of the world in terms of causes and natural forces that rejects all spiritual, supernatural, or teleological explanations.

natural law: An ethical belief or system of beliefs supposed to be inherent in human nature and discoverable by reason rather than revelation. Also, the philosophical doctrine that the authority of the legal system or of certain laws derives from their justifiability by reason and, indeed, that a legal system that cannot be so justified has no authority.

natural rights: Rights inherent in a being because of its nature as a being of a certain sort.

nomological: The mode of causation employed by God, according to the Stoics; immutable laws control the affairs of the cosmos.

nomos: Prevailing social expectations and requirements, or "the law of the land."

noumena/phenomena: According to Immanuel Kant, knowledge arises from experience; therefore, it must be knowledge of *phenomena*, that is, of things and events as these are delivered by the senses. From the evidence at the phenomenal level, we can reason to the fact that there is a *noumenal* realm of being. Thus, we can know *that* it is but cannot know *what* it is. Ultimately, our knowledge claims must be utterly bounded by the pure intuitions of time and space and the pure categories of the understanding.

ontology: The study of what really exists, one of the key questions central to the concept of metaphysics.

philosophy: The rational pursuit of truths deemed to be answers to perennial questions, as well as a historical study of intractable problems; literally, the love of wisdom.

phrenology: A Victorian-era science of character divination, faculty psychology, and brain theory derived from the Viennese physician Franz Joseph Gall's system, which held that the surface of the skull could be read as an accurate index of an individual's psychological aptitudes and tendencies.

phronesis: Greek term for practical wisdom or prudence; the application of good judgment to human conduct, in contrast with the more theoretical inquiry leading to *sophia*, or wisdom generally.

phusis: Greek, "nature."

physiognomy: The study of the shape and configuration of a person's face to determine his or her character and intelligence.

pluralism: The philosophical doctrine that reality consists of several basic substances or elements.

polis: Life within a settled community, in which one participates and from which one draws lessons for life.

positivism: A form of empiricism that bases all knowledge on perceptual experience, rather than on intuition or revelation.

pragmatism: The doctrine that practical consequences are the criteria of knowledge, meaning, and value.

Providential: The mode of causation employed by God, according to Hellenistic philosophy. The cosmos is created and ordered by a perfect rational entity, whose knowledge is also perfect. The creative entity takes an interest in its creation.

pyrrhonism: An early Greek form of skepticism.

Pythagorean theorem: One of the earliest theorems known to ancient civilizations; named for the Greek mathematician and philosopher Pythagoras. The Pythagorean theorem states: "The area of the square built upon the hypotenuse of a right triangle is equal to the sum of the areas of the squares upon the remaining sides."

res cogitans/res extensa: The metaphysical dualism on which the Cartesian philosophical system rests. *Res cogitans* is God and the human soul; *res extensa* is the corporeal world.

revelation: An enlightening or astonishing disclosure. Also, communication of knowledge to man by a divine or supernatural agency.

Romanticism: A movement in literature, art, and intellectual thought during the late 18th and early 19th centuries that celebrated nature rather than civilization and valued imagination and emotion over rationality.

Sophia: Greek, "wisdom."

Sophists: Greek philosophers who showed complete indifference to the problems of the world of matter and centered their efforts on man. But man can be an object of study in his sense knowledge, as well as in the more profound world of reason. The Sophists stopped at the data of experience—at empirical, not rational, knowledge—and from this point of view, they wished to judge the world of reality.

Stoics: Greek philosophers whose worldview was one of a rationally governed universe of material entities, each answering to its controlling principle and, thus, participating in the overall cosmic *logos*. In its most developed form, Stoicism takes the lawfulness of the cosmos as the model on which human life is to proceed. The rule of law is the defining mark of our humanity, according to this philosophy.

Sturm und Drang: German; "storm and stress." Romanticism perceived this evolutionary struggle that produces new and better things not predictable in a mechanistic view.

superego: According to Sigmund Freud's theory of psychoanalysis, one of the three parts that make up the self. The superego is purported to represent our conscience and counteract the id with moral and ethical thoughts.

tabula rasa: A blank slate. In the Lockean view, the condition of the human mind at birth.

teleia philia: Perfected or completed friendship, the aims of which do not go outside the friendship itself.

teleology: The philosophical study of purpose; a doctrine that assumes the phenomena of organic life, particularly those of evolution, are explicable only by purposive causes and that they in no way admit of a mechanical explanation or one based entirely on biological science.

tetraktys: In Pythagorean philosophy, the sacred integers: 1, 2, 3, and 4.

Thomistic theory of law: Philosophical approach predicated on what is taken to be good for man, given the character of human nature. As "an ordinance of reason," law gives and honors good reasons for certain actions and good reasons for forbearing to act in certain ways. An action is good when it is in accord with the basic goods. A desire is bad when its fulfillment is in defiance of good reasons for action.

Turing machine: An algorithm—not a machine as such—that translates any input signal into a determinate output.

Ubermensch: Friedrich Nietzsche's concept of the "superman," an exemplar of self-creation who is free from the influence of the general populace.

unconscious motivation: Concept central to Sigmund Freud's theories of human behavior; the idea that the subconscious portion of the mind plays a larger role in determining behavior than does the conscious portion.

Upanishads: Pre-philosophical Hindu morality tales that address questions of knowledge, conduct, and governance.

Biographical Notes

Aeschylus (525–456 B.C.): Earliest of the three greatest Greek tragedians, the others being Sophocles and Euripides; known for his masterpiece, *The Oresteia* trilogy. Aeschylus's greatest contribution to the theater was the addition of a second actor to his scenes. Previously, the action took place between a single actor and the Greek chorus.

Anaximenes (585–525 B.C.): Pre-Socratic Greek philosopher who held that the air, with its variety of contents, its universal presence, and its vague associations in popular fancy with the phenomena of life and growth, is the source of all that exists.

Thomas Aquinas (1225–1274): Dominican priest and scholastic philosopher whose "natural law" theory defined law as an ordinance of reason, promulgated by one who is responsible for the good of the community. His treatises on law would form the foundation of critical inquiry in jurisprudence for centuries, integrating classical and Christian thought.

Aristotle (384–322 B.C.): Greek philosopher who, along with Plato, is often considered to be one of the two most influential philosophers in Western thought. Aristotle most valued knowledge gained from the senses and would correspondingly be classed among modern empiricists. Thus, Aristotle set the stage for what would eventually develop into the scientific method centuries later.

St. Augustine (354–430 C.E.): Roman Catholic bishop and Christian Neo-Platonist who was a leader in the widespread merging of the Greek philosophical tradition and Judeo-Christian religious and scriptural traditions.

Avicenna (980–1037): Inspired by Aristotle's *Metaphysics*, articulated a mode of philosophical reasoning that would virtually define medieval thought and scholasticism. Put Arab scholarship and Islamic thought at the center of naturalistic and scientific thinking.

Francis Bacon (1561–1626): Generally considered the "prophet" of Newton and the father once removed of the authority of experimental science. Known for his groundbreaking *Novum Organum* ("*New Method*"), which established the authority of observation in discovering the nature of the external world and the authority of the experimental method as the way to select the correct from competing theories of causation.

Roger Bacon (1214–1294): Thirteenth-century English scholar who stated the basic program of experimental science. Known for his *Opus Maius*, considered one of the foundational works in the modern scientific movement.

George Berkeley (1685–1783): Bishop of Cloyne in Ireland and a scientist. Offered a critique of the Lockean view in his *A Theory Concerning the Principles of Human Knowledge*, which attempts to defeat materialism and the skepticism it spawns by establishing the essentially mental preconditions for a material world to exist at all.

Josef Breuer (1842–1925): Viennese neurologist who worked with Sigmund Freud on the theory of repression.

Ernst Brucke (1819–1892): One of Sigmund Freud's teachers, along with Hermann von Helmholtz, Karl Ludwig, and DuBois-Reymond.

Edmund Burke (1729–1797): British political writer and statesman. Burke's essay on the sublime, written in the period of the Enlightenment, prefigures the Hegelian worldview, defining the *sublime* as that which strikes awe and terror in the heart.

Pierre Cabanis (1757–1808): One of the leaders of thought in the French materialist tradition, known for his series of essays on the relationship between the psychological and physical dimensions of human life.

Marcus Tullius Cicero (106–43 B.C.): Roman orator, lawyer, politician, and philosopher who considered philosophical study most valuable as the means to more effective political action.

Auguste Comte (1798–1857): French writer whose works—a series of essays published collectively under the title *A Course of Positive Philosophy*—influenced John Stuart Mill. One of the fathers of a version of positivism.

Etienne Condillac (1715–1780): Locke's translator in France, who offers the model of the "sentient statue" whose character, knowledge, and conduct are carved into it by a ceaselessly impinging environment.

Condorcet (1743–1794): French philosopher whose *Sketch for a Historical Picture of the Progress of the Human Mind*, written while he was hiding from France's new "liberators" during the Reign of Terror, delivers the idea of progress in one of its most summoning forms. The mind has progressed from murky superstition and timidity toward the light of reason in stages, each stage requiring the abandonment of ancestral ignorance. The advent of the scientific worldview now abets this progress.

Confucius (551–479 B.C.): Chinese philosopher who maintained that adherence to traditional values of virtue is necessary to achieve a state of orderliness and peace.

Charles Darwin (1809–1882): British naturalist who developed the theory of evolutionary selection, which holds that variation within species occurs randomly and that the survival or extinction of each organism is determined by that organism's ability to adapt to its environment.

Democritus (460–370 B.C.): Pre-Socratic Greek philosopher who taught an atomic theory of reality, that all things are made of atoms and void.

René Descartes (1596–1650): Discovered analytical geometry, was an important contributor to the physical sciences, and was, perhaps, the most important figure in that branch of philosophy called *philosophy of mind*. Known for his proof of existence: "I think, therefore I am."

Denis Diderot (1713–1784): Most prominent of the French Encyclopedists. In the circle of the leaders of the Enlightenment, Diderot's name became known especially by his *Lettre sur les aveugles* (London, 1749), which supported Locke's theory of knowledge.

Diogenes (4th century B.C.): Leading philosopher of the pre-Socratic school of Cynicism. Diogenes practiced self-control and a rigid abstinence, exposing himself to extremes of heat and cold and living on the simplest diet.

Erasmus (1469–1536): Fifteenth-century humanist. His best known work is *Praise of Folly*, a pamphlet mainly directed against the behavior of ruling classes and church dignitaries while exposing the irony of mankind's vanities.

Euripides (480–406 B.C.): Greek playwright best known for the tragedy *Medea*.

Pierre Flourens (1794–1867): French physiologist who—along with François Magendie and Xavier Bichat—surgically destroyed selective regions of animals' brains and observed the behavior of the survivors. Through this technique, Flourens discovered that the areas of the brain that Franz Joseph Gall had identified with certain specific functions were not connected with those specific functions.

Sigmund Freud (1856–1938): The father of psychoanalysis. Freud, in collaboration with Joseph Breuer, articulated and refined the concepts of the unconscious, infantile sexuality, and repression and proposed a tripartite account of the mind's structure, all as part of a then–radically new conceptual and therapeutic frame of reference for the understanding of human psychological development and the treatment of abnormal mental conditions.

Franz Joseph Gall (1758–1828): Leading neuroanatomist of his time; propounded the "science" of phrenology, a theory that brain structures are related to brain functions, which became dominant in the scientific thinking of the 19th century and thereafter.

Francis Galton (1822–1911): Cousin of Charles Darwin. Published his studies of hereditary genius in 1869, stating that natural selection yields a very few exceptional human types, but general human flourishing disproportionately depends on their merits.

Johann Wolfgang von Goethe (1749–1832): Eighteenth-century writer best known for *Faust*.

Georg Wilhelm Friedrich Hegel (1770–1831): German philosopher who merged and synthesized many of the strongest tendencies in Romantic thought. First is the idea of progressive and evolving reality—not the staid mechanical repetitiousness of mere causality, but an active principle at work in the natural world. Second, there is the criticism of science as not being up to the task of comprehending this world, tied as it is to reductive schemes.

Hermann von Helmholtz (1821–1894): Nineteenth-century physicist and physiologist; one of Sigmund Freud's teachers. In a November 1862 lecture at Heidelberg, Helmholtz tried to clarify why leading scientists visibly shunned philosophers, when previously, the natural philosopher was the natural scientist.

Claude Adrien Helvetius (1715–1771): French philosopher who, in his *A Treatise on Man*, puts forth a radical environmentalism, which holds that our essence does not precede our existence and experiences in the world; rather, it is a record of those experiences.

Herodotus (5th century B.C.): Greek scholar said to be the first historian in the modern accepted sense of the term; the "father of historical scholarship." Known for his treatise *The Persian Wars*.

Hippocrates (469–399 B.C.): Greek physician considered to be the father of modern medicine.

Thomas Hobbes (1588–1679): British philosopher who rejected Cartesian dualism and believed in the mortality of the soul; rejected free will in favor of a determinism that treats freedom as being able to do what one desires; and rejected Aristotelian and scholastic philosophy in favor of the "new" philosophy of Galileo and Gassendi, which largely treats the world as matter in motion. Hobbes is perhaps most famous for his political philosophy, which maintained that men in a state of nature, without civil government, are in a war of all against all in which life is hardly worth living. The way out of this desperate state is to make a social contract and establish the state to keep peace and order.

Homer (~ 750/800 B.C.): Blind Greek poet who wrote about the Trojan War, considered a defining moment in Greek history and presumed to have concluded a half-millennium earlier. Best known for his two epic poems *The Iliad* and *The Odyssey*.

David Hume (1711–1776): One of the most influential philosophers to have written in the English language, Hume offered an experiential theory of knowledge, morality, and religion. He made more credible the notion that a bona fide *science of the mind* was within reach.

T. H. Huxley (1825–1895): British physician and surgeon who was one of the first adherents to Charles Darwin's theory of evolution by natural selection; Huxley did more than anyone else to advance the theory's acceptance among scientists and the public alike.

Isocrates (446–338 B.C.): Greek philosopher who lived and wrote in the same cultural situation as Plato. Isocrates held that reality is immediate human experience and metaphysical speculation is a waste of time and energy. He also said that all knowledge is tentative and values are relative. Composed the *Panegyricus*, a work that raises the question of whether philosophy is something that just the Greeks do.

William James (1842–1910): American psychologist and philosopher who maintained that every idea belongs to someone, that mental life is not an empty container filled with experiences agglomerating with one another. Thus, the external world is chosen for the content that will be experienced and associated.

Carl Gustav Jung (1875–1961): A younger colleague of Sigmund Freud, Jung divided the psyche into three parts: the ego, or conscious mind; the personal unconscious, which includes anything that is not currently conscious but can be; and finally, the collective unconscious, or reservoir of our experiences as a species, a kind of knowledge with which we are all born but are never directly conscious of. The contents of the collective unconscious are called *archetypes*, unlearned tendencies to experience things in a certain way. The archetype has no form of its own, but it acts as an "organizing principle" on the things we see or do.

Immanuel Kant (1724–1804): Kant's most original contribution to philosophy is his Copernican Revolution that the representation makes the object possible, rather than the object making the representation possible. This introduced the human mind as an active originator of experience, rather than a passive recipient of perception.

Julien Offray de La Mettrie (1709–1751): French philosopher whose naturalism tends toward materialism. His *Man—A Machine* extends to its logical conclusion the materialistic drift of Descartes's own psychology.

Gottfried Wilhelm von Leibniz (1646–1716): Offered a significant critique of the Lockean view in his *New Essays on Human Understanding*, which concluded that an organizing and rationally functioning mind must be present for there to be coherent experience and that nothing in the operation of the biological senses can constitute a thought or an idea.

Leonardo da Vinci (1452–1519): Italian painter, architect, engineer, mathematician, and philosopher who is widely considered to represent the Renaissance ideal.

John Locke (1632–1704): Physician and one of the "fathers" of British empiricism. Locke set out in *An Essay Concerning Human Understanding* (1690) to defend a naturalistic account of mental life and a reductionistic strategy for studying and explaining that life. Accordingly, both knowledge and self-knowledge are derived from experiences and the memory of them. One's very personal identity is but that collection of entities in consciousness entering by way of experience.

Martin Luther (1483–1546): Began the Protestant Reformation with his protests against aspects of the Catholic Church.

Ernst Mach (1838–1916): German physicist who formulated a positivist creed in science that John Stuart Mill would develop. Mach said that we recognize our work as science to the extent that it is *not* metaphysics and that physical laws are only systematic descriptions of sense data that need no metaphysical description or underpinning.

Karl Marx (1818–1883): Philosopher, social scientist, historian, and revolutionary who developed a socialist system that came to be used as the basis for many regimes around the world.

John Stuart Mill (1806–1873): Known for his *System of Logic*, published in 1843, which analyzed inductive proof. Mill provided the empirical sciences with a set of formulas and criteria to serve the same purpose for them as the timeworn formula of the syllogism had served for arguments that proceeded from general principles. Mill's work is not merely a logic in the limited sense of that term, but also a theory of knowledge such as Locke and Hume provide.

Friedrich Nietzsche (1844–1900): German philosopher who sharply criticized traditional philosophy and religion as both erroneous and harmful for human life, arguing that they enervate and degrade our native capacity for achievement. Best known for developing the concept of the *Ubermensch*, or "superman," a rare, superior individual that can rise above all moral distinctions to achieve a heroic life of truly human worth.

Francesco Petrarch (1304–1374): Father of humanism. An Italian scholar and poet who is credited with having given the Renaissance its name.

Plato (427–347 B.C.): Greek philosopher and student of Socrates whose writings convey the spirit of his master's teachings on the theory of forms, the problem of knowledge, cosmological speculations, and the treatment of government.

Protagoras (490–420 B.C.): Pre-Socratic Greek philosopher. A leading figure in Sophist thought, he proposed that "Man is the measure of all things."

Pyrrhon of Elis (360–272 B.C.): Greek philosopher known as one of the great fathers of Skeptical thought.

Pythagoras (c. 580-500 B.C.): Greek philosopher who maintained that the ultimate reality was abstract and relational, depending on numbers. His harmonic view of the universe provided one of the foundations for Platonic philosophy. The first person to demonstrate the theorem that with any right triangle, the sum of the squares of each of the two sides is equal to the square of the hypotenuse.

Thomas Reid (1710–1796): Father of the Scottish Common Sense School. Scottish philosopher who laid the foundations for a "common sense" psychology based on the natural endowments by which we (and the animals) understand the world and act in it. His influence was broad and deep, reaching the leaders of thought at the American founding. Reid was the leading figure in a group of scholars and scientists at Aberdeen committed to the larger Newtonian perspective. He also was David Hume's most successful critic.

Jean-Jacques Rousseau (1712–1778): Swiss-French philosopher, author, and political theorist whose work largely decried the harmful effects of modern civilization.

Girolamo Savonarola (1452–1498): Italian religious reformer best known for his attempt to reform Renaissance Florence society and the Catholic Church from the vices of modern life as he knew them.

Friedrich von Schiller (1759–1805): German historian, philosopher, and dramatist; his *Letters on the Aesthetic Education of Man* maintained that it is freedom that creates, determinism that limits and kills. Friend of Johann Wolfgang von Goethe.

Socrates (c. 469–399 B.C.): Greek philosopher committed to objectifying the self and holding it up to scrutiny in order to examine human nature. Developed the Socratic method, which tests every assumption for its grounding and implications.

Sophocles (496–406 B.C.): One of the great playwrights of the Greek golden age; known for his tragedy *Antigone*.

Herbert Spencer (1820–1903): British philosopher and sociologist who supplied the phrase "survival of the fittest" and gave Darwinism its most portentous set of social implications.

Alan Turing (1912–1954): Mathematician and cryptographer who developed the concept of the computable algorithm.

Voltaire (1694 –1778): French Enlightenment writer and philosopher who maintained that our experience is the key to understanding human nature and the nature of the world around us. His real name was François Marie Arouet.

Alfred Russel Wallace (1823–1913): Worked with Charles Darwin to develop the theory of evolution by natural selection. Wallace concluded that he could not see natural selection at work in three domains: (1) abstract thought, which seems to serve no evolutionary purpose; (2) art, in which resources are willingly squandered in the service of the merely beautiful; and (3) moral thought and ethics, where we sacrifice our own most cherished interests in the service of others.

Ludwig Wittgenstein (1889–1951): Austrian philosopher whose *The Tractatus* stated that the world consists entirely of independent, simple facts out of which complex ones are constructed. Language has as its purpose the stating of facts by picturing these facts.

Bibliography

Essential Reading:

Barnes, Jonathan. *Early Greek Philosophy*. New York: Penguin Books, 1987. A concise and authoritative introduction to the pre-Socratic world of Greek philosophy.

Berkeley, George. *A Treatise Concerning the Principles of Human Knowledge*. New York: Oxford University Press, 1997. Berkeley's systematic critique of materialistic theories and his alternative "immaterialist" thesis.

Brock, Dan. *Life and Death*. New York: Cambridge University Press, 1993. A thoughtful review of the ethical aspects of those "life-and-death" issues arising from modern medicine.

Darwin, Charles. *The Expression of the Emotions in Man and Animals*. New York: Oxford University Press, 1998. Evidence and argument according to which the emotional dimension of human life is on the same continuum as that which includes non-human emotional expression. The utter "naturalization" of human sentiments and their origins in natural selection.

Descartes, René. *Selected Philosophical Writings*. New York: Cambridge University Press, 1988. Excellent selections from the *Discourse on Method* and related works.

Hume, David. *An Enquiry Concerning Human Understanding*. New York: Oxford University Press, 1999. One of the most influential philosophical works in the English language, and one of the most consistent defenses of empiricism.

James, William. *The Will to Believe*. Cambridge: Harvard University Press, 1979. In this work, James analyzes the psychological and philosophical grounds of belief and answers challenges coming from scientific critics.

Kant, Immanuel. *Critique of Practical Reason*. Cambridge: Cambridge University Press, 1997. A difficult work but Kant's fullest development of his moral theory.

Locke, John. *An Essay Concerning Human Understanding*. Amherst, NY: Prometheus Books, 1995. Perhaps the classic statement of the empiricist theory of mind and mental life.

Mackie, J.L. *Ethics: Inventing Right and Wrong*. New York: Penguin, 1977. Among the best of the modern "skeptical" critiques of moral realism.

Plato. *The Dialogues of Plato*. New York: Random House, 1937. The works to which, on Whitehead's account, all subsequent philosophy is but a footnote.

Reid, Thomas. *An Inquiry into the Human Mind*. University Park, PA: Penn State University Press, 1997. The most incisive criticism of Hume's philosophy written in Hume's lifetime; a trenchant analysis of the proper methods of philosophizing.

Robinson, D. N. *Praise and Blame: Moral Realism and Its Application*. Princeton, NJ: Princeton University Press, 2002. A defense of moral realism and appraisal of anti-realist critiques of realism.

Van Fraassen, Bas. *The Scientific Image*. New York: Oxford University Press, 1980. One of the more influential "anti-realist" works in contemporary philosophy of science.

Supplementary Reading:

Annas, Julia. "Classical Greek Philosophy." In *The Oxford History of Greece and the Hellenistic World*. J. Boardman et al, eds. Oxford: Oxford University Press, 1991.

———. *Platonic Ethics, Old and New*. Ithaca: Cornell University Press, 1999.

Aristotle. *The Complete Works of Aristotle: The Revised Oxford Translation.* J. Barnes, ed. Princeton, NJ: Princeton University Press, 1984. Now the standard source of Aristotle's extant works.

―――. *Metaphysics.* W. D. Ross, trans. (downloadable). A useful Internet version of Aristotle's pioneering work in metaphysics.

Arnold, Matthew. *Culture and Anarchy.* New Haven, CT: Yale University Press, 1994. The "classic" defense of the humanistic perspective and the basis on which civilized life depends.

Augustine. *The City of God* (downloadable). An Internet source of Augustine's moral and political philosophy.

―――. *Confessions.* New York: Oxford University Press, 1992. A groundbreaking work in introspective and "depth" psychology and an early analysis of various psychological processes associated with cognition and memory, emotion and motivation.

―――. *On Free choice of Will.* T. Williams, trans. Cambridge: Cambridge University Press, 1993. Augustine was among the first to examine in detail the theory of moral freedom against the claims of determinism. His locating the issue within the Christian canon deprives his analysis of none of its philosophical power.

Bacon, Francis. *Novum Organum.* P.Urbach and J. Gibson, eds. Chicago: Open Court, 1994. Here is the "Baconian" revolution, designed to create an empirical science of discovery as a counter to traditional authority in science.

Barker, S. and T. Beauchamp, eds. *Thomas Reid: Critical Interpretations (Philosophical Monographs).* Vol. 3. Philadelphia: University of Science Center, 1976.

Barnes, J. ed. *The Complete Works of Aristotle: The Revised Oxford Translation*. Princeton, NJ: Princeton University Press, 1984. Now the standard source of Aristotle's extant works.

Bate, W. *From Classic to Romantic.* Cambridge: Harvard University Press, 1946.

Bede. *A History of the English Church and People.* London: Penguin, 1968. Here the "Venerable Bede" presents a record of the early Church in the English speaking world, rich in detail and often astonishing in its claims.

Birks, Peter, ed. *Justinian's Institutes*. Ithaca, NY: Cornell University Press, 1987. The laws codified and promulgated by the Emperor Justinian.

Boardman, John et al., eds. *The Oxford History of Greece and the Hellenistic World*. Oxford: Oxford University Press, 1991. A fine source text edited by distinguished scholars.

Borst, C.V., ed. *Mind/Brain Identity Theory*. New York: St. Martin's Press, 1970. Old but not "dated," the essays in this collection more or less exhaust the candidate "solutions" to this most vexing of issues.

Brown, P. *The Body and Society*. New York: Columbia University Press, 1988. Peter Brown's study of the patristic and early medieval cultures of faith are illuminating at every level of detail. The special significance of man's corporeal nature is examined closely.

Budd, Malcolm. *Wittgenstein's Philosophy of Psychology*. London: Routledge, 1989. The Wittgensteinian "discursive turn" is featured, as the grammatical confusions in psychology are noted.

Burke, Edmund. *Philosophical Enquiry into the Origin of Our Ideas of the Sublime and Beautiful*. New York: Columbia University Press, 1958. Here is one of the earliest contributions to aesthetics and its psychological grounding, presented by a young Burke, already a master of English prose.

Careri, Giovanni Bernini. *Flights of Love: The Art of Devotion*. Linda Lappin, trans. Chicago: University of Chicago Press, 1994. Bernini's philosophy of aesthetics and defense of the Baroque.

Cassell, E. *The Nature of Suffering and the Goals of Medicine*. New York: Oxford University Press, 1991. A balanced and thoughtful treatise in medical ethics.

Cassirer, Ernst. *The Renaissance Philosophy of Man*. Chicago: University of Chicago Press, 1967. An informed summary of major philosophical perspectives in the Renaissance.

Churchland, Patricia Smith. *Neurophilosophy: Toward a Unified Science of Mind-Brain.* Cambridge, MA: MIT Press, 1986. Philosophy of mind can get no more "materialistic" than this.

Clark, Kenneth. *The Romantic Rebellion: Romantic versus Classic Art.* London: J. Murray, 1973. The claims of genius against those of science, the claims of the imagination against those of measurement.

Cohen, J.B. *Revolution in Science*. Cambridge: Harvard University Press, 1994. The author offers a sensible evaluation of the idea of scientific "revolutions" and their relation to the larger intellectual context.

Collingwood, R. G. *The Idea of History*. New York: Oxford University Press, 1994. Essays on the nature of historical scholarship and explanation.

Condorcet. *Selected Writings*. K. Baker, ed. Indianapolis: Bobbs Merrill Publishing Co., 1976. Condorcet was the most scientifically acute of the "philosophes." The subtle and appealing character of his thought comes across vividly in this collection.

Cottingham, J., et al., eds. *The Philosophical Writings of Descartes*. 2 vols. Cambridge: Cambridge University Press, 1988. This is the most accessible collection of Descartes's major philosophical works.

Dane, N., and J. Ambrose, eds. *Greek Attitudes*. New York: Charles Scribners Sons, 1974. The editors select wisely from the literary, political, philosophical and aesthetic offerings of the Classical age of Greece.

de Bruyne, Edgar. *The Esthetics of the Middle Ages*. trans. Eileen B. Hennesey. New York: F. Unger Publishing Co., 1969. A close and informing study of the conceptual and religious grounding of medieval art.

Dworkin, R. *Taking Rights Seriously*. Cambridge: Harvard University Press, 1977. An argument for the liberal state and a defense of "judge-made" law.

Epictetus. *The Discourses*. C. Hill, ed. London: Everyman, 1995. The classic Stoic position on the widest range of social, political, and individual issues.

Erasmus, Desiderius. *Ten Colloquies*. New York: Liberal Arts Press, 1957. More an "op ed" set of essays on the state of the world at the close of the 15th century; a quintessential "humanistic" work.

Fairfield, Roy, ed. *The Federalist Papers*. Garden City, NY: Anchor Books, 1966. All 85, with their analysis of the essential nature and aims of politics and a realistic perspective on the odds for success; the most incisive set of political essays struck at a single time, ever.

Ferruolo, S. *The Origins of the University*. California: Stanford University Press, 1985. The modern university is indebted to the Scholastic age of scholarship and analysis, its commitment to a broadly based curriculum and its major modes of instruction and examination.

Fideler, D. ed. *The Pythagorean Sourcebook and Library*. York Beach, Maine: Phanes Press, 1987. Pythagoras and his disciples did not record their beliefs and discoveries, but here we have a set of maxims and fragments with which to construct a fuller picture of the teachings of the sect.

Findlay, J. *Hegel: A Reexamination*. London: Allen & Unwin, 1958. The ever elusive Hegel comes to life in this treatise, as attention is drawn to the background and to the influences of Hegelian thought.

507

Finnis, J. *Natural Law and Natural Rights.* New York: Oxford University Press, 1980. A modern and authoritative defense of natural law theory.

Flanagan, O. *Consciousness Reconsidered.* Cambridge, MA: MIT Press, 1992. Useful as a critical review of current thinking on the nature of consciousness; a respect for the complexity of the issues associated with the phenomenon of consciousness.

Fodor, J. *The Modularity of Mind.* Cambridge, MA: MIT Press, 1983. A standard defense of the view that mental phenomena as such are composites of functions performed in modular fashion.

Foster, J. *The Immaterial Self: A Defence of the Cartesian Dualist Conception of Mind.* London: Routledge, 1996. One of the most thoughtful of current attempts to defend dualism against the usual lines of criticism.

Freud, Sigmund. *The Interpretation of Dreams.* New York: Penguin, 2003. Here is the essential work in "depth psychology," a treatise that Freud regarded as pointing to the "royal road" to the unconscious.

Galton, Francis. *Hereditary Genius: An Inquiry into Its Laws and Consequences.* New York: St. Martin's Press, 1978. Nativism, unadulterated!

Garland, Robert. *The Greek Way of Life: From Conception to Old Age.* Ithaca, NY: Cornell University Press, 1990. A fine introduction to the social, political, and daily life that was "the Greek way."

George, Robert, ed. *Natural Law Theory: Contemporary Essays.* New York: Oxford University Press, 1992. Arguments for and against versions of natural law theory and on philosophy of law in general.

Guthrie, Kenneth. *The Pythagorean Sourcebook and Library: An Anthology of Ancient Writings.* Grand Rapids, MI: Phanes Press, 1987. The elusive thought of the Pythagoreans captured here in "snapshots."

Hamilton, Alexander, James Madison and John Jay. *The Federalist Papers*. London: Penguin Books, 1987. Perhaps the most detailed and thoughtful set of disquisitions on the nature of politics to appear in one volume.

Hare, R. M. *Moral Thinking*. New York: Oxford University Press, 1981. A classic statement of the universalist and prescriptivist criteria of morals.

Hart, H. L. A. *The Concept of Law*. New York: Oxford University Press, 1961. The most influential defense of legal positivism.

Haskins, C. *The Renaissance of the Twelfth Century*. Cambridge: Harvard University Press, 1927. This is a "classic," drawing attention to the centuries preceding that famous Italian Renaissance, and alerting the reader to the truly original scholarship and science developed in this "Middle" Age.

Hempel, Carl *Aspects of Scientific Explanation*. New York: Free Press, 1965. Hempel's deductive-nomological model defended and defined; one influential approach to the entire nature of science written in the past century.

Herodotus. *The Persian Wars*. G. Rawlinson, trans. New York: Random House, 1942. HISTORY 101, as its inventor intended it.

Hippocrates. Works of various authors, all presumably in the "Hippocratic" tradition, revealing the essentials of Hippocratic medicine.

————. "On the Wounds of the Head," in *Hippocrates*, W. Jones, trans. New York: Putnam, 1923. The Hippocratic understanding of brain-based disorders is a remarkable achievement given its date and the method then available.

Hobbes, Thomas. *Leviathan*. New York: Cambridge University Press, 1996. Here is the "mechanistic" and scientific approach to statecraft by one of the architects of modern thought on the nature of law and society.

Hodges, Andrew. *Alan Turing: The Enigma*. New York: Simon and Schuster, 1983. An interesting account of Turing's background, his approach to the problem of decidability, and his achievements in code-breaking.

Hollingdale, R. J. *Nietzsche: The Man and His Philosophy*. Baton Rouge: Louisiana State University Press, 1965. An accessible account of an elusive and, indeed, troubled mind, as revealed in selections from his major works.

Homer. *The Iliad*. Chicago: University of Chicago Press, 1951. The "Genesis" of Hellenism.

Honore, A. *Emperors and Lawyers*. New York: Oxford University Press, 1994. An authoritative and non-technical introduction to Roman law and to the part taken in its development by a number of emperors.

Hume, David. "Of the Standard of Taste." In *Essays Moral, Political and Literary*. Eugene Miller, ed. Indianapolis: Liberty Fund, 1985. Eugene Miller has collected the most important of Hume's briefer works, including essays that Hume withdrew from publication.

Hume, Robert, trans. *The Thirteen Principal Upanishads*. New York: Oxford University Press, 1971. Snippets that convey the elusive but elevating abstractions of Hindu thought.

Hussey, E. *The Presocratic Philosophers*. Cambridge: Cambridge University Press, 1983. This is a fine collection of the sparse record that remains of this fertile philosophical tradition.

Irwin, T.H. *Plato's Ethics*. Oxford: Oxford University Press, 1995.

Isocrates. *Panegyricus*. George Norlen, trans. Cambridge: Harvard University Press, Loeb Classical Library, 2000. In this work one hears the rhetoric of Isocrates as he attempts to persuade Hellenes to locate their true enemy (Persia) and to cease fighting with each other. In this same place, he identifies the "Hellene" as one committed to a conception of culture.

James, William. *Essays in Radical Empiricism and a Pluralistic Universe*. Chicago: Phoenix Books, 1977. Empiricism with the courage of its convictions, liberated from all forms of the "block universe."

Kant, I. *Critique of Pure Reason*. N.K. Smith, trans. New York: St. Martin's Press, 1965. One of the more difficult treatises in all of philosophy; the most systematic of epistemologies and of attempts to determine the nature and limits of rational comprehension.

―――――. *Groundwork of the Metaphysics of Morals*. Cambridge: Cambridge University Press, 1998. In this work, Kant labors to make clearer what is rather ponderously developed in his *Critique of Practical Reason*. It is, of course, one of the classic works in moral philosophy.

―――――. *The Moral Law*. New York: Hutchinson's University Library, 1948. An abbreviated version of the second critique and rather more accessible.

Kaufmann, W. *The Portable Nietzsche*. New York: Viking Press, 1961. Carefully chosen by a leading scholar, this handy volume samples the full range of Nietzsche's critical perspective on life and thought.

Keen, M. *Chivalry*. New Haven: Yale University Press, 1984. This is the best study of an often misunderstood social institution; the one that conveyed to European civilization much that is "civilizing" in human conduct.

Kim, J. *Mind in a Physical World.* Cambridge: MIT Press, 1998. Another approach to the mind/body problem.

Larner, Christina. *Witchcraft and Religion: The Politics of Popular Belief.* New York: Blackwell, 1984. A most interesting analysis of the "witch" theory and the "science" surrounding it.

Leibniz, Gottfried Wilhelm. *The Monadology and Other Philosophical Essays*. Robert Latta, trans. Oxford: Oxford University Press, 1981. These short and numbered passages convey significant features of Leibniz's philosophy of mind.

Lerner, R., and Mahdi, M., eds. *Medieval Political Philosophy*. Ithaca: Cornell University Press, 1963. The selections leave no doubt but that the medieval age was rich and subtle in its political theories and its recognition of the challenges to ordered liberty.

Levack, Brian. *The Witch-Hunt in Early Modern Europe*. New York: Longman, 1995. Data, trials, theories and informing commentary on a woeful chapter in political history.

Lichtheim, G. *Marxism: An Historical and Critical Study*. New York: Praeger, 1961. This is a readable overview of Marxism and its philosophical underpinnings.

Long, A. A. *Hellenistic Philosophy: Stoics, Epicureans, Skeptics*. Berkeley: University of California Press, 1986. A standard work, featuring informing essays on the major figures in these schools of philosophy.

Loux, Michael. *Metaphysics: A Contemporary Introduction*. London: Routledge, 2002. The book to read before reading Aristotle on the same subject.

Lloyd, G. ed. *Hippocratic Writings*. London: Penguin Books, 1978. Works of various authors, all presumably in the "Hippocratic" tradition, revealing the essentials of Hippocratic medicine.

Luce, A. A. *Berkeley's Immaterialism*. New York: Russell and Russell, 1968. Berkeley explained!

Marx, Karl. *Selected Writings*. Indianapolis: Hackett, 1994. Useful selections for those attempting to extract a philosophical position from Marx's critiques of society.

McDonald, Forrest. *Novus Ordo Seclorum: The Intellectual Origins of the Constitution*. Lawrence: University Press of Kansas, 1985. Surely one of the best works on the American founding, its constitutional jurisprudence, and background philosophies on which major proposals were based.

Mill, John Stuart. *Autobiography*. London: Penguin Books, 1989. Very informative, showing the progress of Mill's thought to and then past Comte and Bentham.

———. *On Liberty*. Upper Saddle River, NJ: Prentice Hall, 1996. The "classic" statement of political liberalism.

Moore, G. E. *Principia Ethica (1903)*. New York: Prometheus Books, 1988. A common sense and intuitionist theory of morals.

Nietzsche, Friedrich. *The Portable Nietzsche*. Walter Kaufmann, ed. New York: Penguin Books, 1976. Choice nuggets from the deeply thinking critique of modernity.

Oates, W., ed. *The Stoic and Epicurean Philosophers*. New York: Random House, 1940. Here is a good sample of the works and wisdom of philosophical schools arising after the period in which Plato and Aristotle were most influential.

O'Daly, Gerard. *Augustine's Philosophy of Mind*. Berkeley: University of California Press, 1987. The book to read before reading Augustine's *Confessions*.

Paine, Thomas. *The Rights of Man* (downloadable). The reader today will probably be moved as irresistibly as were those reading the work in the 18th century.

Perry, Ralph Barton. *The Thought and Character of William James*. Nashville, TN: Vanderbilt University Press, 1996. Still the standard biography.

Plantinga, A. *God, Freedom and Evil.* New York: Eardmann, 1974. One attempt to reconcile the traditional conception of God and the problem of evil.

Quinton, A. *Francis Bacon*. London: Hill and Wang, 1980. A most readable general account of Bacon's life and scientific project.

Robinson, D. *An Intellectual History of Psychology* (3rd ed.). Madison: University of Wisconsin Press, 1995. Brief review of major intellectual and scientific developments associated with the emergence of psychology as an independent discipline.

―――. *Aristotle's Psychology*. New York: Columbia University Press, 1983, chapter 1. This chapter outlines the "Socratic context" of Aristotle's philosophical development, pointing to differences between the two approaches in method and perspective.

Robinson, D. N. *The Enlightened Machine*. New York: Columbia University Press, 1980. A general review of the history and major concepts of the brain sciences, intended for the non-specialist.

―――. *Philosophy of Psychology*. New York: Columbia University Press, 1982. Review of standard problems of explanation, models of mind, the mind/body problem.

―――. *Toward a Science of Human Nature: Essays on the Psychologies of Mill, Hegel, Wundt, and James*. New York: Columbia University Press, 1982. Summaries and appraisals of four who dominated 19th-century thought on the nature of mind and mental life.

―――. *Wild Beasts and Idle Humours*. Cambridge, MA: Harvard University Press, 1996. Historical review of the legal conception of mental competence from remote antiquity to modern times, with emphasis on the insanity defense.

Rorty, A., ed. *Essays in Aristotle's Ethics*. Berkeley: University of California Press, 1980. Fine interpretive essays are offered, illuminating the often subtle aspects of Aristotle's ethical theory.

Rossiter, C. *The Federalist Papers*. Garden City, NY: Anchor, 1963.

Rousseau, Jean-Jacques. *The Social Contract and Discourses*. London: Dent, 1993. The history of the law's conception of mind in health and disease.

Ruskin, J. *The Stones of Venice*. Vol. 1. London: Smith, Eldeer & Co., 1853. This work did much to restore interest in and admiration for the "Gothic"; a work by the leading aesthete of Victorian England and one of the greatest of prose writers.

Stace, Walter Terence. *The Philosophy of Hegel: A Systematic Exposition*. New York: Dover, 1955. This is not a Hegel for beginners, but it is a good introduction to Hegel's phenomenology.

Sulloway, F. *Freud: Biologist of the Mind*. New York: Basic Books, 1979. By far the best study of Freud as scientist, as aspiring scientific theorist.

Swinburne, R. *Providence and the Problem of Evil*. New York: Oxford University Press, 1998. How is the problem of evil to be understood? The author sees "evil" as permitted on the grounds that it improves all who must contend with it.

Turing, A. "Computing Machinery and Intelligence." In *Mind*, 1950. Vol. 59.

Vernant, Jean Pierre, ed. *The Greeks*. Chicago: University of Chicago Press, 1995. Scholars specializing in different aspects of ancient Greek thought offer rich interpretive essays on the major aspects of that culture.

Voltaire. *Philosophical Letters* (downloadable at www.classicsnetwork. com). Voltaire's comparisons of English and French culture, custom, and science were powerfully influential.

Walzer, Michael. *Just and Unjust Wars*. New York: Basic Books, 2000. Major theories of "just war" are considered and appraised.

Walzer, Richard. *Greek into Arabic: Essays on Islamic Philosophy.* Columbia: University of South Carolina Press, 1970. Islamic philosophy, replete with its Greek inspirations.

Westfall, Richard. *Never at Rest: A Biography of Isaac Newton.* New York: Cambridge University Press, 1994. The authoritative biography of a universal genius.

Wittgenstein, Ludwig. *Philosophical Investigations.* Cambridge, MA: Blackwell, 1997. For all "flies" seeking an exit from the bottle!

Xenophon. *Memorabilia.* Ithaca, NY: Cornell University Press, 1994. Socrates as known by a friend and neighbor.

Yates, Frances. *Giordano Bruno and the Hermetic Tradition.* Chicago: University of Chicago Press, 1964. Renaissance science and its shifting movements away from and back toward mysticism.

Yolton, John. *Thinking Matter: Materialism in Eighteenth-Century Britain.* Minneapolis: University of Minnesota Press, 1983. The arguments of Locke, Priestley, Hartley et al. toward a materialist theory of mind.

Young, R. *Mind, Brain and Adaptation in the Nineteenth Century.* Oxford: Oxford University Press, 1970. The author locates the brain sciences within the larger Darwinian context of the second half of the nineteenth century, but with close attention to anticipations.

Internet Resources:

www.epistemelinks.com. Best source for basic materials in philosophy.

http://plato.stanford.edu/contents

Notes

Notes

Notes

Notes

Notes

Notes